*Books on Early American History
and Culture, 2001–2005*

Books on Early American History and Culture, 2001–2005

An Annotated Bibliography

Raymond D. Irwin

Bibliographies and Indexes
in American History

 **PRAEGER**

AN IMPRINT OF ABC-CLIO, LLC
Santa Barbara, California • Denver, Colorado • Oxford, England

Library of Congress Cataloging-in-Publication Data

Irwin, Raymond D., 1966–
    Books on early American history and culture, 2001–2005 : an annotated bibliography /
Raymond D. Irwin.
        p. cm. — (Bibliographies and indexes in American history)
    Includes index.
    ISBN 978-0-313-31427-8 (hardcopy : acid-free paper) —
ISBN 978-1-4408-2922-2 (ebook)   1. United States—History—Colonial period,
ca. 1600–1775—Bibliography.   2. United States—Civilization—To 1783—
Bibliography.   3. North America—History—Colonial period,
ca. 1600–1775—Bibliography.   4. Caribbean Area—History—
To 1810—Bibliography.   I. Title.
    Z1237.I795   2013
    [E188]
    016.973—dc23   2012031278

ISBN: 978-0-313-31427-8
EISBN: 978-1-4408-2922-2

17   16   15   14   13   1   2   3   4   5

Praeger
An Imprint of ABC-CLIO, LLC

ABC-CLIO, LLC
130 Cremona Drive, P.O. Box 1911
Santa Barbara, California 93116-1911

This book is printed on acid-free paper ∞

Manufactured in the United States of America

To my parents, Glenn and Celia

Contents

Preface

This volume is part of a series of annotated bibliographies in early American history—that is, North America and the Caribbean, from 1492 to 1815. It includes monographs, reference works, exhibition catalogues, and essay collections published between 2001 and 2005 and reviewed in at least one of fifty-six general periodicals and historical journals. Each entry gives the name of the book, its author(s) or editor(s), publisher, date of publication, ISBN and/or OCLC number(s), the Library of Congress call number and/or Dewey number, and the number of times the work has been cited in the journal literature covered by the Thomson ISI Arts and Humanities and Social Science citation indexes. Following each detailed citation is a brief summary of the book and a list of journals in which the book has been reviewed.

This book is composed of thirty-three thematic chapters, an organizational scheme that presents both significant advantages for the user and predictable difficulties for the bibliographer. Few books fit neatly and completely into a single category. As a result, I have made decisions about the placement of entries based on what I perceived to be the primary subject matter of each book. An author index is provided, as is an appendix that lists frequently cited works. It should be noted that this list is based upon approximations of scholarly impact; citation counts are limited to journal articles published between 2001 and early 2012 and included in the ISI databases. Therefore, the number of times a book has been cited in another book is excluded. Moreover, every reasonable effort has been made to locate all citations under variations of book title and author name, though some might have been overlooked.

I have tried to make this bibliography as complete and as useful as possible. It is intended to help students, researchers, and teachers of history get a little better grasp on the explosion of scholarly literature that has marked the past several decades. Space limitations, however, make it impossible to give any book its due; rather, this volume should be considered a starting point for further investigation.

Abbreviations

16c J	Sixteenth Century Journal
18c Stds	Eighteenth-Century Studies
Ag Hist	Agricultural History
AHR	American Historical Review
AJLH	American Journal of Legal History
Am Lit	American Literature
Am Stds	American Studies
AQ	American Quarterly
BHM	Bulletin of the History of Medicine
BHR	Business History Review
Booklist	Booklist
CH	Church History
CHR	Canadian Historical Review
CJH	Canadian Journal of History
EAL	Early American Literature
Econ Hist Rev	Economic History Review
EHR	English Historical Review
Ethnohistory	Ethnohistory
FHQ	Florida Historical Quarterly
Geog Rev	Geographical Review
GHQ	Georgia Historical Quarterly
GJ	Geographical Journal
HAHR	Hispanic American Historical Review
Hist Teach	The History Teacher

HRNB	History: Reviews of New Books
IMH	Indiana Magazine of History
J Brit Stds	Journal of British Studies
J Econ Hist	Journal of Economic History
J Interdis Hist	Journal of Interdisciplinary History
J Mil Hist	Journal of Military History
J Mod Hist	Journal of Modern History
J Relig Hist	Journal of Religious History
J Religion	Journal of Religion
J Soc Hist	Journal of Social History
JAAR	Journal of the American Academy of Religion
JAEH	Journal of American Ethnic History
JAH	Journal of American History
JAS	Journal of American Studies
JER	Journal of the Early Republic
JHG	Journal of Historical Geography
JNH	Journal of Negro History
JSH	Journal of Southern History
LJ	Library Journal
NCHR	North Carolina Historical Review
NEQ	New England Quarterly
Penn Hist	Pennsylvania History
PHR	Pacific Historical Review
PSQ	Political Science Quarterly
RAH	Reviews in American History
SHQ	Southwestern Historical Quarterly
Soc Hist	Social History
VMHB	Virginia Magazine of History and Biography
VQR	The Virginia Quarterly Review
WHQ	Western Historical Quarterly
Wilson Q	Wilson Quarterly
WMQ	William and Mary Quarterly

1 General

1 Appelbaum, Robert and John Wood Sweet, eds. *Envisioning an English Empire: Jamestown and the Making of the North Atlantic World.* Philadelphia: University of Pennsylvania Press, 2005. xv, 368 p. ISBN 0812238532 (hbk.); ISBN 9780812238532 (hbk.); ISBN 0812219031 (pbk.); ISBN 9780812219036 (pbk.); OCLC 56481403; LC Call Number F234.J3 J3255; Dewey 973.2/1 22. Citations: 18.

Presents articles on early Virginia's relationship to the wider world. Includes pieces on land possession, Virginia Indians in England, John Smith's maps of Virginia, Richard Frethorne's letters, the image of Spain and Turkey in John Smith's writings, England and Morocco in global geopolitics, Irish colonies, hunger in early Virginia, land use in the colony, slavery in the Atlantic world, and the influence of Aphra Behn's *The Widdow Ranter.*

AHR 111: 789-90; *JAH* 92: 1408-09; *J Brit Stds* 45: 171-73; *GHQ* 90: 123-25; *JAH* 92: 1408-1409; *JSH* 73: 672-74; *RAH* 34: 150-55; *Soc Hist* 31: 245-47; *WMQ* 63: 380-84.

2 Archer, Richard. *Fissures in the Rock: New England in the Seventeenth Century.* Hanover, N. H.: University Press of New England, 2001. xii, 230 p. ISBN 1584650842 (hbk.); ISBN 9781584650843 (hbk.); ISBN 1584650850 (pbk.); ISBN 9781584650850 (pbk.); OCLC 45137424; LC Call Number F7 .A74; Dewey 974/.02 21. Citations: 6.

Examines relations between New England colonists and Native Americans, the relationships among religion, power, and order, social stratification, gender and family roles, the life cycle, economics, and town structure and life. Seeks to put the standard image of "Puritan New England to rest" by synthesizing three decades of historiography to argue that the region during the seventeenth century was remarkably diverse and that "demographics, climate, and soil rather

than virtue made the difference." Contends that the main unifier of New England was Englishness, not Puritanism and that "Acquisitive aspirations" and the struggle "simply to survive" represented significant and engrained impulses. Concludes that "To argue for cultures is not to deny either broad humanity or genuine differences but rather to recognize that a middle world exists as well" and that "Seventeenth-century New England as a coherent whole was in that middle place."
AHR 107: 185; *JAH* 89: 195-96; *NEQ* 76: 151-53; *WMQ* 60: 434-36.

3 Armitage, David and Michael J. Braddick, eds. *The British Atlantic World, 1500–1800*. New York: Palgrave Macmillan, 2002. xx, 324 p. ISBN 0333963407 (hbk.); ISBN 9780333963401 (hbk.); ISBN 0333963415 (pbk.); ISBN 9780333963418 (pbk.); OCLC 49977198; LC Call Number E18.82 .B75; Dewey 970 21. Citations: 137.
Presents papers from Harvard's 1997 International Seminar on the History of the Atlantic World. Includes essays on the early modern British Atlantic, covering migration, economy, religion, civility and authority, gender, class, race, empire, revolution, slavery, and circumnavigation.
Econ Hist Rev 56: 389-90; *EHR* 118: 795-97; *WMQ* 63: 380-84.

4 Bond, Bradley G., ed. *French Colonial Louisiana and the Atlantic World*. Baton Rouge: Louisiana State University Press, 2005. xxi, 322 p. ISBN 0807130354; ISBN 9780807130353; OCLC 56617318; LC Call Number F372 .F853; Dewey 976.3/02 22. Citations: 13.
Presents essays from a 1999 University of Southern Mississippi conference on Louisiana and the Atlantic world. Includes pieces on the historiography of colonial Louisiana, interactions among the French and the Indians in the region, including the roles of gift exchanges and Native cosmology, the impact of French colonial religious policy on the settlement of Louisiana, the Ursuline community of New Orleans and material culture, Antoine Bienvenu and commerce between Lower and Upper Louisiana, geography of the American west and the Louisiana Cession (1762), the population of French America in the late seventeenth and early eighteenth centuries, free and slave populations in colonial Louisiana, refugees from the West Indies to the Lower Mississippi region, and the relationship between St. Louis of Senegal and colonial Louisiana. Seeks to "broadly contextualize early Louisiana as a part of the Atlantic World."
AHR 112: 497-98; *JAH* 93: 180-81; *JSH* 72: 644-46; *SHQ* 110: 130-31; *WMQ* 64: 430-33.

5 Bremer, Francis J. and L.A. Botelho, eds. *The World of John Winthrop: Essays on England and New England, 1588–1649*. Boston: Massachusetts Historical Society, distributed by University of Virginia Press, 2005. viii, 408 p. ISBN 0934909881; ISBN 9780934909884; OCLC 62493127; LC Call Number F7 .W87; Dewey 974/.02. Citations: 5.
Presents essays that emphasize the transatlantic nature of the Puritan movement, including the "practice of piety," the influence of Old World government and legal culture on Massachusetts, views on economics and capital, ethnocentrism

and the idea of the "other" on both sides of the Atlantic, gender and hierarchy in England and New England, and literacy and communication among Protestants of the Atlantic world.
AHR 112: 1135-37; *CH* 76: 441-42; *JAH* 93: 1207-1208.

6   Cayton, Andrew R.L. and Stuart D. Hobbs, eds. *The Center of a Great Empire: The Ohio Country in the Early American Republic*. Athens: Ohio University Press, 2005. viii, 225 p. ISBN 0821416200 (hbk.); ISBN 9780821416204 (hbk.); ISBN 0821416480 (pbk.); ISBN 9780821416488 (pbk.); OCLC 57507047; LC Call Number F495 .C37; Dewey 977.1/03 22. Citations: 1.
Includes articles on the importance of Ohio to the early republic, the Big Bottom massacre and the ideological underpinnings of Indian removal, the politics of Thomas Worthington, Methodism in the region, racial politics in Ohio, early colleges and their influence on public culture, family and kinship in early Ohio, and opportunities for further research.
AHR 111: 285; *IMH* 103: 201-203; *JAH* 93: 204-205.

7   Ekberg, Carl J. *François Vallé and His World: Upper Louisiana before Lewis and Clark*. Columbia: University of Missouri Press, 2002. xx, 316 p. ISBN 0826214185; ISBN 9780826214188; OCLC 50155792; LC Call Number F474.S135; Dewey 977.8/692. Citations: 7.
Traces Vallé's rise to wealth and power in tandem with the growth of the colonial outpost of Ste. Genevieve on the western bank of the Mississippi. Discusses Vallé's vast slaveholdings, his family and business relationships, and his views of marriage, particularly among slaves. Contends that Vallé played many roles in the agricultural community of Ste. Genevieve, including those of banker, foodstuff supplier, militia captain, and judge. Finds that Vallé successfully managed the transition from French to Spanish colonial administrations in the early 1760s and notes that, as a leader in "a vital outpost of empire," Vallé "exhibited remarkable energy, intelligence, honesty, and civility" and thus became indispensable to imperial authorities.
JAH 90: 993; *JSH* 70: 416-17; *WHQ* 35: 382-83.

8   Geiter, Mary K. and W.A. Speck. *Colonial America: From Jamestown to Yorktown*. New York: Palgrave Macmillan, 2002. xi, 228 p. ISBN 0333790553 (hbk.); ISBN 9780333790557 (hbk.); ISBN 0333790561 (pbk.); ISBN 9780333790564 (pbk.); OCLC 50198433; LC Call Number E188 .G375; Dewey 973.2 21. Citations: 1.
Explores American identity during the colonial era, arguing that colonists saw themselves as British subjects until the political realities of the Revolutionary period resulted in the notion of "the American." Describes the five colonial regions, how their societies compared with those in Britain, and how British imperial policy affected Native Americans. Traces the evolution of the colonies from the Glorious Revolution of 1688 to the Declaration of Independence in 1776. Finds that regional development and contemporary differences in identity as British subjects makes determining an American national identity complex.
EHR 118: 1062-64; *HRNB* 31: 147-48.

9 Gray, Edward G. *Colonial America: A History in Documents*. New York: Oxford University Press, 2003. 191 p. ISBN 0195137477; ISBN 9780195137477; OCLC 49565939; LC Call Number E187 .G73; Dewey 973.2 21. Citations: 0.

Presents excerpts from printed and pictorial primary sources on colonial America, from the late 15th century through 1763. Provides thematic chapters covering English and European expansion, the process of settlement, Native Americans and the colonists, indenture and slavery, family life, religion, the genteel classes, and common material goods and luxuries. Includes a timeline and suggestions for further reading subdivided by topic.

Booklist 99: 1062; *Hist Teach* 39: 532-33.

10 Hatfield, April Lee. *Atlantic Virginia: Intercolonial Relations in the Seventeenth Century*. Philadelphia: University of Pennsylvania Press, 2004. 312 p. ISBN 0812237579; ISBN 9780812237573; OCLC 52902674; LC Call Number F229 .H274; Dewey 975.5/02 22. Citations: 17.

Argues that "Seventeenth-century Virginians lived in an Atlantic world held together by a web of connections linking the Chesapeake to England and Africa, to Dutch and other English colonies, and . . . to French and Spanish colonies." Explains that the Indians' overland trails and travel patterns influenced the ways in which Europeans viewed land and the movement of people, goods, and information. Contends that different regions of Virginia were connected to different parts of Europe, the Caribbean, and other North American colonies. Points out that until the 1670s the majority of Virginia's slaves "came not directly from Africa but from other colonies, [so] the ways in which the institution had developed in other places informed the decisions of almost all participants." Finds that Barbadian slaves, slave owners, slave laws, and institutions, were particularly important, as were Spanish models for enslavement. Stresses "the impact of boundary permeability on the spread of ideas and information," highlighting the people and goods "that affected Virginia's political, social, cultural and economic development."

AHR 110: 1159-60; *JAH* 91: 1425-26; *J Brit Stds* 44: 838-39; *J Econ Hist* 65: 278-79; *JSH* 71: 865-66; *Soc Hist* 31: 243-45; *WMQ* 61: 756-59.

11 Hoffman, Ronald, Sally D. Mason, and Eleanor S. Darcy, eds. *Dear Papa, Dear Charley: The Peregrinations of a Revolutionary Aristocrat, as Told by Charles Carroll of Carrollton and His Father, Charles Carroll of Annapolis, with Sundry Observations on Bastardy, Child-Rearing, Romance, Matrimony, Commerce, Tobacco, Slavery, and the Politics of Revolutionary America*. Chapel Hill: University of North Carolina Press, published for the Omohundro Institute of Early American History and Culture, the Maryland Historical Society, and the Maryland State Archives, 2001. 1,768 p. ISBN 0807826499; ISBN 9780807826492; OCLC 45618299; LC Call Number E302.6.C3; Dewey 973.3/092. Citations: 7.

Collects, edits, and annotates letters among members of the Carroll family, comments from public figures, newspaper articles and other material related to the Carroll family. Includes letters between Charles Carroll of Annapolis and his son Charley, who was being educated in France. Arranges letters

chronologically, starting with Charley's time in France from 1748 to 1759 and continuing through his subsequent five years in London to study law. Traces Charley's growth from childhood through adolescence under his father's control to his return to Annapolis in 1765, four years after the death of his mother. Includes correspondence with his English friends on the problems of adjustment to provincial life and later letters that illustrate the younger Carroll's movement from ultraconservative economic and political views to his life as a revolutionary. Follows the family until the death of Charles Carroll of Annapolis in 1782. Identifies persons, places, and incidents mentioned in the various documents and provides full bibliographic information on the sources used and the locations of the original documents. Includes as appendices genealogical charts of the various branches of the Carroll family in Ireland and Maryland, an annotated list of books read by the Carroll men or known to be in their possession by 1782, and all the surviving censuses of the slaves in seven inventories taken of the Carrolls' various estates between 1773 and 1782.
JSH 69: 875-77; *WMQ* 63: 392-403.

12   Hornsby, Stephen and Michael Harmann. *British Atlantic, American Frontier: Spaces of Power in Early Modern British America.* Hanover, N.H.: University Press of New England, 2005. xv, 307 p. ISBN 1584654260 (hbk.); ISBN 9781584654261 (hbk.); ISBN 1584654279 (pbk.); ISBN 9781584654278 (pbk.); OCLC 55960807; LC Call Number E40.5 .H67; Dewey 970/.0971241. Citations: 0.
Surveys the British colonial world from Hudson Bay and Newfoundland across all of continental North America to Barbados and all of the British West Indies. Describes settlement, economic development, material culture, and spatial expressions of imperial power in each region from the end of the sixteenth century to the beginning of the nineteenth century. Interprets the American Revolution as the fragmentation of British imperial geography that developed over the course of two centuries. Defines the "Atlantic staple region" as emerging in the late sixteenth century when England exerted power over portions of the Atlantic at the expense of Spain. Notes that staple production in various regions depended upon trade with metropolitan centers of commerce in England and on the power of the British navy and resulted in the emergence of class distinctions and labor systems. Explains that, over time, the system of staple production, domestic consumption, population growth, social stratification, and increasing political autonomy gradually depended less and less on merchant capital and imperial naval power. Argues that the geographical development of this system formed the basis of the American Revolution and explains why it included only the British mainland colonies from Massachusetts to Georgia. Concludes that where an abundance of land attracted large populations of free people, generally egalitarian societies emerged and that spatial patterns were critical to American independence.
AHR 111: 790-91; *CHR* 87: 697-99; *CJH* 41: 433-35; *Geog Rev* 99: 448-50; *JAH* 92: 952-53; *J Brit Stds* 45: 166-68; *JER* 25: 681-84; *JHG* 32: 684-85; *J Brit Stds* 45: 166-68; *J Interdis Hist* 37: 295-96; *NEQ* 79: 123-33.

13 Jacobs, Jaap. *New Netherland: A Dutch Colony in Seventeenth-Century America*. Boston, Mass.: Brill, 2005. xix, 559 p. ISBN 9004129065; ISBN 9789004129061; OCLC 57477158; LC Call Number F122.1 .J3313; Dewey 974.7/02. Citations: 14.
Focuses on the "cultural forms" on which the Dutch experience in New Netherland was based. Discusses early voyaging and settlement, patterns of emigration, systems of justice and government, trade and the economy, religious life, social structures, and material culture and daily life. Considers whether "the colonists [were] really better off by going to New Netherlands." Concludes that the New Netherland colony did not significantly differ politically, socioeconomically, culturally, or religiously from the United Provinces.
JAH 92: 1408; *16c J* 37: 1100-1101.

14 Kennedy, Michael V. and William G. Shade, eds. *The World Turned Upside Down: The State of Eighteenth-Century American Studies at the Beginning of the Twenty-First Century*. Bethlehem, Penn.: Lehigh University Press, 2001. 336 p. ISBN 0934223629; ISBN 9780934223621; OCLC 45618342; LC Call Number E188.5 .W67; Dewey 973.2/07/2. Citations: 19.
Presents articles that assess the state of early American historical scholarship, eighteenth-century American agricultural history, the history of early American technology, the urban history of the colonial Chesapeake, African cultures in America, popular religion in eighteenth-century British North America, prospects for writing literary history of eighteenth-century America, literacy and education in eighteenth-century North America, the civic humanism debate, early American women and their histories, perspectives on eighteenth-century Native American history, the Spanish mission system in eastern North America, and the impact of Eric Williams on early American history.
WMQ 59: 720-24.

15 Kessell, John L. *Spain in the Southwest: A Narrative History of Colonial New Mexico, Arizona, Texas, and California*. Norman: University of Oklahoma Press, 2002. xvii, 462 p. ISBN 0806134070; ISBN 9780806134079; OCLC 47785659; LC Call Number F799 .K38; Dewey 979/.02. Citations: 22.
Examines the Spanish colonial southwestern borderlands, recounting the reconquest of New Mexico and the settlement of Texas between 1690 and 1731 and the development of the region through the early nineteenth century. Contends that, "even though Europeans and Native Americans were from worlds far apart geographically" they "understood each other very well."
Hist Teach 37: 260-61; *SHQ* 107: 475-76; *WHQ* 34: 501-502.

16 Larson, John Lauritz and Michael A. Morrison, eds. *Whither the Early Republic: A Forum on the Future of the Field*. Philadelphia: University of Pennsylvania Press, 2005. vii, 199 p. ISBN 9780812219326 (pbk.); ISBN 0812219325 (pbk.); OCLC 58728641; LC Call Number E164 .W57; Dewey 973/.072/073. Citations: 2.
Includes papers from the 2004 Society for Historians of the Early American Republic (SHEAR) meeting, a collection of essays intended to examine the "measure of the state of the field." Covers broadly struggles for North America,

economic culture and political economy, environmental history, slavery, market change, labor, and cultural history. Presents essays on continental possessions and crossings, liberal and Christian America, rural life in the early republic, early American entrepreneurship, environmental stewardship in old New England, the southern environment, the state of environmental history, Benjamin Franklin, Venture Smith, human commodification, free will and commodity relations, the limits of anti-slavery ideology in the early republic, the capitalism-slavery question, sex, sexuality and the public, private, and spiritual worlds, space in the early American city, and religious history.
JSH 73: 165-66; *NCHR* 83: 488-89; *WMQ* 64: 884-86.

17 Looney, J. Jefferson, ed. *The Papers of Thomas Jefferson*. Retirement Series. *Volume 1: 4 March to 15 November 1809*. Princeton, N.J.: Princeton University Press, 2004. 778 p. ISBN 0691121214; ISBN 9780691121215; OCLC 55055418; LC Call Number E302 .J442; Dewey 973.4/6/092. Citations: 7.
Begins with Jefferson's preparations to leave Washington for the last time in March 1809 and ends in November of the same year. Includes documents on Jefferson's domestic housekeeping and culinary interests, involvement in an international community of scholars, commercial and maritime activities, and commentary on law, politics, and diplomacy.
JER 26: 682-701; *JSH* 72: 455-56; *RAH* 38: 54-60; *WMQ* 64: 444-48.

18 Mancke, Elizabeth and Carole Shammas, eds. *The Creation of the British Atlantic World*. Baltimore, Md.: Johns Hopkins University Press, 2005. vi, 400 p. ISBN 0801880394 (hbk.); ISBN 9780801880391 (hbk.); ISBN 0801880408 (pbk.); ISBN 9780801880407 (pbk.); OCLC 55955317; LC Call Number E188 .C89; Dewey 973.2. Citations: 35.
Presents articles on European and African migrations to early modern British America, the enslavement of Indians in early America, authority and national identity in the seventeenth-century English Atlantic, captivity and repatriation in the Atlantic slave trade (Antigua, 1724), Catholic and Moravian pietism in the world of Marotta/Magdalena, mariners, merchants, and colonists in seventeenth-century English America, legalism in colonial British America, Jonathan Edwards, the Enlightenment, and the formation of Protestant tradition in America, German Lutheran missionaries in eighteenth-century Pennsylvania, chartered enterprises and the evolution of the British Atlantic world, Florida, Kew, and the British imperial meridian in the 1760s, the British Atlantic world from a global British perspective, and Quakerism and transatlantic genealogies in colonial British America.
AHR 111: 603-608; *BHR* 80: 173-76; *JAH* 93: 181-82; *J Brit Stds* 45: 414-16; *HRNB* 34: 17-18; *16c J* 38: 218-19; *VMHB* 113: 416-18; *WMQ* 64: 203-20.

19 McDougall, Walter A. *Freedom Just Around the Corner: A New American History, 1585–1828*. New York: HarperCollins Publishers, 2004. xvi, 638 p. ISBN 0060197897; ISBN 9780060197896; OCLC 52821381; LC Call Number E178 .M47; Dewey 973.2 22. Citations: 9.
Views America over time as a marketplace of goods and ideas and contends that five major factors shaped the nation's development: geography, technology,

demography, the federative impulse, and mythologies (e.g., civic religion, respect for public virtue, and toleration of diverse faiths). Claims that a primary character trait of Americans is "hustling," which encompasses resourcefulness, deception, reinvention, opportunism, and promotion. Concludes that "The creation of the United States of America is the central event of the past four hundred years" as North America "today hosts the mightiest, richest, most dynamic civilization in history."
LJ 129n4: 91-92.

20 Moore, Bob and Henk F.K. van Nierop, eds. *Colonial Empires Compared: Britain and the Netherlands, 1750–1850: Papers Delivered to the Fourteenth Anglo-Dutch Historical Conference, 2000.* Burlington, Vt.: Ashgate, 2003. ix, 204 p. ISBN 0754604926; ISBN 9780754604921; OCLC 49640568; LC Call Number DA47.3 .A64; Dewey 325.34109033. Citations: 6.
Includes papers on the Anglo-Dutch relationship between the mid-eighteenth and mid-nineteenth centuries, Sir Joseph Yorke and the decline of the Anglo-Dutch alliance at the end of the eighteenth century, the logic of nautical neutrality, perceptions of the overseas world, national identity in the mid-eighteenth-century Anglo-American empire, Dutch debates on colonization between 1770 and 1820, the role of the navy in Anglo-Dutch imperial relations, the Dutch navy overseas between the mid-eighteenth and mid-nineteenth centuries, financing imperial trade, including patterns of investment in the British East India Company between 1750 and 1820, colonial exploitation as a source of growth in the Netherlands from 1815 to 1870, the British state overseas between 1750 and 1850, and the Dutch position in Asia between 1750 and 1850.
EHR 120: 845-46.

21 Mulford, Carla, Angela Vietto, and Amy E. Winans, eds. *Early American Writings.* New York: Oxford University Press, 2002. xxii, 1129 p. ISBN 0195118405 (hbk.); ISBN 9780195118407 (hbk.); ISBN 0195118413 (pbk.); ISBN 9780195118414 (pbk.); OCLC 45791348; LC Call Number E173 .E28; Dewey 973. Citations: 12.
Presents excerpts from Native American creation stories, European experiences in the Americas, Indian accounts of whites, British, French, and Spanish settlement in North America and the Caribbean, British colonial development, the Dutch, Swedish, and Germans in North America, Anglo-American colonial literature and letters, the American Revolution and republican government, and the Native peoples of eastern North America through the late eighteenth century.
EAL 38: 305-17; *WMQ* 60: 207-13.

22 Mulford, Carla and David S. Shields, eds. *Finding Colonial Americas: Essays Honoring J. A. Leo Lemay.* Newark: University of Delaware Press, 2001. 481 p. ISBN 0874137225; ISBN 9780874137224; OCLC 45387509; LC Call Number E162 .F46; Dewey 973.2. Citations: 15.
Provides articles on J.A. Leo Lemay, the missionary utopias of Franciscan New Spain and Puritan New England, captivity torture, martyrdom, and gender in New France and New England, Ebenezer Cook's "The Sot-Weed Factor," new

science and the question of identity in eighteenth-century British America, Caribbean degeneracy and the problem of masculinity in Charles Brockden Brown's *Ormond*, English identities in colonial American writing, Richard Lewis's poetics of anti-mercantilism, reading class structure in Dr. Alexander Hamilton's *Itinerarium*, the reception of Dr. Alexander Hamilton's *History of the Tuesday Club*, early American Methodism, Joseph Dumbleton's "The Paper-Mill," Augustan American poetics and the culture of print in colonial Williamsburg, the topography of Sarah Wister's commonplace book, Franklin's houses, Washington Allston and the Romantic artist as poet and cultivated intellectual, scientific publishing and scientific society in eighteenth-century America, Benjamin Franklin, David Hume, autobiography, and the jealousy of empire, humor and sex in Franklin's writings, the education of Polly Hewson, Benjamin Franklin's "Observations on the Means of Extinguishing a Fire," Benjamin Franklin's library, a selective guide to printed materials relating to the iconography and artifacts of Benjamin Franklin, the ways in which Thomas Prince read Captain John Smith, Thomas Jefferson and the protection of privacy, and Thoreau's subversion of Puritan wilderness discourse.
EAL 39: 129-36; *WMQ* 59: 720-24.

23 Pencak, William, Matthew Dennis, and Simon P. Newman, eds. *Riot and Revelry in Early America*. University Park: Pennsylvania State University Press, 2002. viii, 316 p. ISBN 0271021411; (hbk.); ISBN 9780271021416 (hbk.); ISBN 0271022191 (pbk.); ISBN 9780271022192 (pbk.); ISBN 027102142X (pbk.); OCLC 47651198; LC Call Number GT4803 .R56; Dewey 394.26973. Citations: 19.
Includes essays on mid-eighteenth-century New Jersey crowds punishing violent and adulterous husbands, crowds during the American Revolution, "rough music" as a popular form of discipline, early national adoption of Christopher Columbus as a symbol of republicanism and territorial expansion, African elements in black celebrations, women's participation in pro- and anti-French demonstrations, Palmetto Day celebrations in South Carolina, and southern nationalism.
HRNB 31: 14; *JAH* 90: 620-21; *JAS* 37: 353; *JER* 23: 265-67; *NCHR* 80: 93-94; *PMHB* 127: 434-36; *WMQ* 60: 459-62.

24 Pestana, Carla Gardina. *The English Atlantic in an Age of Revolution, 1640–1661*. Cambridge, Mass.: Harvard University Press, 2004. xi, 342 p. ISBN 0674015029; ISBN 9780674015029; OCLC 55682550; LC Call Number E18.82 .P47; LC Call Number DA425; Dewey 973.2. Citations: 27.
Examines the development of British colonies during the age of the English Civil War and Restoration, arguing that in this period the first British empire took shape. Suggests that the colonies were interlinked as a result of revolutionary experience and that colonial leaders acted in a way to preserve neutrality during the period of uncertainty prior to the execution of Charles I. Describes the actions of the Commonwealth government toward the colonies, including its suppression of royalism, its implementation of trade policies, its notion of religious toleration, and the evolution of the colonial labor force. Finds that the Restoration government in Britain presided over an empire that was

remarkably different from that of two decades earlier, that it was "commercial, diverse, inegalitarian, and prickly about its rights" and had been "born in the crucible of revolution."
AHR 111: 791-92; *BHR* 79: 417-19; *JAH* 92: 951-52; *J Brit Stds* 44: 835-36; *J Mod Hist* 78: 944-46; *J Soc Hist* 39: 1189-91; *NEQ* 79: 123-33; *RAH* 33: 153-61; *VMHB* 113: 84-85; *WMQ* 62: 785-87.

25 Pritchard, James S. *In Search of Empire: The French in the Americas, 1670–1730*. Cambridge: Cambridge University Press, 2004. xxvii, 484 p. ISBN 0521827426; ISBN 9780521827423; OCLC 51810478; LC Call Number E29.F8; Dewey 970/.0971244. Citations: 34.
Presents an overview of France's fifteen overseas colonies that were established in the late seventeenth- and early-eighteenth centuries and reviews demographic, social, economic, political, and military factors and events that shaped their development. Argues that French foreign policy focused on the European continent and that colonies existed to provide the regime with prestige. Finds that "settlers and slaves rather than the metropolitan or even colonial governments largely made their own societies," that the French were outnumbered virtually everywhere in North America and the Caribbean, and that Native Americans exerted extraordinary influence over their French neighbors. Concludes that prior to 1730, "What came to be called the first French or Bourbon empire proved to be little more than the remnants of dreams, the fragmentary pieces of statesmen's ambitions, and the lonely pleas of colonial authorities for succor against their foreign and domestic enemies."
AHR 110: 441-42; *EHR* 120: 531-32; *HAHR* 86: 577-79; *JAH* 92: 187-88; *J Mil Hist* 70: 495-96; *J Mod Hist* 78: 210-13; *NEQ* 79: 123-33.

26 Racine, Karen. *Francisco de Miranda: A Transatlantic Life in the Age of Revolution*. Wilmington, Del.: Scholarly Resources, 2003. xix, 336 p. ISBN 0842029095 (hbk.); ISBN 9780842029094 (hbk.); ISBN 0842029109 (pbk.); ISBN 9780842029100 (pbk.); OCLC 49952577; LC Call Number F2323.M6; Dewey 987/.04/092. Citations: 15.
Describes Miranda as one who "lived and fought on four continents, schemed with the Atlantic world's most powerful leaders, and romanced women of all social ranks." Discusses his activities in Venezuela, France, England, Spain, and the United States, as well as his travels throughout Europe. Argues that Miranda played a critical role in preparing Europe, North America, and Spain's American colonies for revolution. Characterizes Miranda as a devoted husband and father, dilettante, anglophile, and a well-connected and influential thinker. Contends that Miranda's diplomatic skills exceeded his military capabilities.
Ethnohistory 51: 220-22; *HAHR* 83: 778-79; *WMQ* 62: 113-17.

27 Raphael, Ray. *Founding Myths: Stories that Hide Our Patriotic Past*. New York: New Press, 2004. x, 354 p. ISBN 1565849213 (hbk.); ISBN 9781565849211 (hbk.); ISBN 9781595580733 (pbk.); ISBN 1595580735 (pbk.); OCLC 54960633; LC Call Number E296 .R35; Dewey 973.3. Citations: 2.
Examines thirteen well-known stories related to the founding of the United States, including Patrick Henry's "Give Me Liberty" speech, Paul Revere's ride,

the roles of Molly Pitcher and Sam Adams, the "shot heard 'round the world," the Valley Forge winter, the Founding Fathers, and the significance of the battle of Yorktown. Explains how these and other stories developed and were amplified over the course of two centuries.
Booklist 101: 43; *LJ* 129n16: 95.

28 Siminoff, Faren Rhea. *Crossing the Sound: The Rise of Atlantic American Communities in Seventeenth-Century Eastern Long Island.* New York: New York University Press, 2004. x, 211 p. ISBN 0814798322; ISBN 9780814798324; OCLC 54817113; LC Call Number F127 .L8; Dewey 974.7/2101. Citations: 2.
Traces the seventeenth-century development of communities on eastern Long Island. Studies the interactions among English settlers and Pequots and draws distinctions between the Dutch, who established small settlements geared toward trade, and the English, who created farming towns. Explains that the earliest English settlements were aligned with Connecticut and contends that the various "communities of interest" were in fluid states of negotiation and re-negotiation. Characterizes the English as highly adaptable to the environment and stresses the importance of "boundary crossers," persons who played key roles in smoothing relations among various groups.
AHR 110: 1524-25; *JAH* 92: 581-82.

29 Skeen, C. Edward. *1816: America Rising.* Lexington: University Press of Kentucky, 2003. xvi, 299 p. ISBN 0813122716; ISBN 9780813122717; OCLC 52057656; LC Call Number E341 .S57; Dewey 973.5/1. Citations: 8.
Reviews the year of 1816, which was marked by extreme cold and drought, social reform initiatives, extensive westward migration, expanded internal improvement projects, increasingly heated debates over slavery, the maturation of political parties, and optimism about the economic development of the United States. Concludes that the nation was on the "cusp of political, economic, and social change."
AHR 109: 903-904; *IMH* 101: 186-88; *JAH* 91: 614-15; *JER* 24: 491-94; *JSH* 70: 912-13; *LJ* 128n14: 187; *PMHB* 129: 115-16; *WMQ* 62: 117-20.

30 Smolenski, John and Thomas J. Humphrey, eds. *New World Orders: Violence, Sanction, and Authority in the Colonial Americas.* Philadelphia: University of Pennsylvania Press, 2005. vi, 362 p. ISBN 9780812238952; ISBN 0812238958; OCLC 60188955; LC Call Number E18.82 .N485; Dewey 973.2. Citations: 3.
Presents papers from the 2001 McNeil Center for Early American Studies conference, including pieces on English colonization discourse, dialogical encounters in a space of death, marital discord and social order in colonial Quito, private and state violence against African slaves in lower Louisiana during the French occupation in the late seventeenth and eighteenth centuries, rape and race in early America, Dutch colonial authority in the borderlands of northeastern Brazil, cultures of resistance on the northwestern Mexican and eastern Bolivian frontiers, the contest for power on the frontiers of the early American republic, Spanish citizenship in the old and new worlds, beatings,

duels, and "play" in Saint Domingue, and informal and official whiteness in colonial Spanish America.
AHR 111: 1134-35; *18c Stds* 41: 110-13; *HAHR* 87: 180-81; *JER* 27: 196-98.

31 Taylor, Alan. *American Colonies*. New York: Viking, 2001. xviii, 526 p. ISBN 0670872822; ISBN 9780670872824; OCLC 45804613; LC Call Number E188 .T35; Dewey 973.2. Citations: 37.
Surveys colonial North American and Caribbean history, taking note of the various roles played by Native Americans, African Americans, British, Spanish, French, Dutch, and Russians. Considers economic and ecological imperialism, race, cultures, the Atlantic world, religion, and gender.
JAH 89: 1019-20; *LJ* 126n17: 94; *NEQ* 75: 477-87; *PMHB* 127: 106-109; *SCHM* 105: 244-45; *SHQ* 106: 493; *VMHB* 109: 418-19.

32 Taylor, Alan, ed. *Writing Early American History*. Philadelphia: University of Pennsylvania, 2005. xiv, 261 p. ISBN 0812238834 (hbk.); ISBN 9780812238839 (hbk.); ISBN 0812219104 (pbk.); ISBN 9780812219104 (pbk.); OCLC 57429326; LC Call Number E188 .T357; Dewey 973.2/072. Citations: 3.
Presents review essays previously published in *The New Republic* since 1996, grouped by theme and covering colonization, religion, science, war, politics, disease, communication, gender, the nation's founding, American exceptionalism, the Atlantic world, expansionism, and the historian's craft.
HRNB 33: 142; *JAS* 41: 503-504.

33 Thompson, Roger. *Divided We Stand: Watertown, Massachusetts, 1630–1680*. Amherst: University of Massachusetts Press, 2001. xviii, 269 p. ISBN 1558493042; ISBN 9781558493049; OCLC 45873598; LC Call Number F74.W33; Dewey 974.4/4. Citations: 6.
Examines the development of Watertown, noting its economic, social, and religious foundations on English ways. Explains that the American experiences of settlers, however, led to changes in landholding patterns, faith, politics, and labor and that Watertown settlers separated themselves from Boston in much the same way as Bostonians separated themselves from England. Finds that conflict was nearly constant in Watertown, but that the town did not divide in the same way as neighboring settlements because Native Americans provided "a unifying force" for residents and because mistrust of other English men seeking land forced townspeople "to compromise, to conciliate, to arbitrate and show restraint, to recognize a communal 'general will.'"
JAH 89: 1500-1501; *JAS* 37: 363; *WMQ* 60: 216-19.

34 Trudel, Marcel. *La Nouvelle-France par les Textes: Les Cadres de Vie*. Montreal: Hurtubise HMH, 2003. 432 p. ISBN 2894286333; ISBN 9782894286333; OCLC 51243045; LC Call Number F1030 .N68; Dewey 971.01. Citations: 2.
Presents excerpts from 115 documents related to New France, with particular focus on politics, society, and religion. Modernizes language and spelling and provides the documentary source and suggestions for further reading. Reviews

the history of New France from Verrazano through the early eighteenth century and discusses the changing historiography of the region.
CHR 85: 786-89.

35 Vickers, Anita. *The New Nation*. Westport, Conn.: Greenwood Press, 2002. xxii, 296 p. ISBN 0313312648; ISBN 9780313312649; OCLC 48397309; LC Call Number E164.V53; Dewey 973. Citations: 0.
Investigates American popular culture from the end of the American Revolution until 1816. Considers the world of youth, everyday life, advertising, architecture, fashion, food, leisure activities, literature, music, performing arts, travel, visual arts, and the costs of goods.
Booklist 99: 445.

36 Wagner, Gillian. *Thomas Coram, Gent., 1668-1751*. Rochester, N.Y.: Boydell Press, 2004. 218 p. ISBN 1843830574; ISBN 9781843830573; OCLC 53361054; LC Call Number DA483.C69; Dewey 362.73/2/092. Citations: 3.
Examines the life of Coram, the founder of the Foundling Hospital in London, who also built ships and worked to expand the influence of Anglicanism in Massachusetts, encouraged the exploitation of American natural resources, and became known for his advocacy of radical causes, notably women's rights.
EHR 121: 314-15.

37 Warkentin, Germaine and Carolyn Podruchny, eds. *Decentring the Renaissance: Canada and Europe in Multidisciplinary Perspective, 1500 – 1700*. Buffalo, N.Y.: University of Toronto Press, 2001. xii, 387 p. ISBN 0802043275 (hbk.); ISBN 9780802043276 (hbk.); ISBN 0802081495 (pbk.); ISBN 9780802081490 (pbk.); OCLC 46769697; LC Call Number F1030 .D43; Dewey 971.01. Citations: 23.
Includes articles on differences between European and native concepts of time, history, change, and views of early contact, the sixteenth-century French vision of empire, the persons behind sixteenth-century Spanish voyages to Terranova, William Vaughn's Newfoundland, images of English origins in Newfoundland and Roanoke, Native Americans in accounts of those traveling to America, the Roman Catholic clergy in French and British North America in the early seventeenth century, Canada in seventeenth-century Jesuit thought, Pierre-Joseph-Marie Chaumonot and the Holy House of Loreto, the seventeenth-century Canadian view of the environment, French exploration of the St. Lawrence valley, European encounters with Iroquoian languages, the archaeology of the Frobisher voyages and early European-Induit contact, Sir William Phips and the decentring of empire in northeastern North America in the early 1690s, and Native Americans and the horizon of modernity.
CHR 85: 360-62; *16c J* 35: 312-14.

38 Wood, Bradford J. *This Remote Part of the World: Regional Formation in Lower Cape Fear, North Carolina, 1725–1775*. Columbia: University of South Carolina Press, 2004. xviii, 344 p. ISBN 1570035407; ISBN 9781570035401; OCLC 54082155; LC Call Number F262.B9; Dewey 975.6/29. Citations: 4.

Traces the development of the Cape Fear region from settlement to its rise to become the most prosperous area of the colony by the Revolution. Studies early families, slaves, laborers, urban areas, and the economy. Explains that the region's wealth was based on tar, lumber, and turpentine, which distinguished it from most areas of North Carolina, which focused on rice and tobacco. Finds that the Cape Fear region, in terms of slave owners as a percentage in the total population, was very similar to other parts of the South. Stresses the importance of social, political, and economic ties to the region's development and concludes that "Inevitably newly settled areas often become distinct and separate regions." *Ag Hist* 81: 261-63; *AHR* 111: 822-23; *GHQ* 90: 125-28; *JAH* 92: 586-87; *JSH* 71: 665-66; *NCHR* 82: 90-91; *SCHM* 108: 175-77; *WMQ* 62: 129-32.

39 Zuppan, Josephine Little, ed. *The Letterbook of John Custis IV of Williamsburg, 1717-1742*. Lanham, Md.: Rowman and Littlefield, 2005. xxiii, 271 p. ISBN 094561280X; ISBN 9780945612803; OCLC 56214063; LC Call Number F234.W7; Dewey 975.5/425202/092. Citations: 0.
Publishes letters Custis, planter, businessman, burgess, member of the Council of State, and father-in-law of the future Martha Washington. Focuses on English correspondence, including his views on Parliamentary legislation, commentary on his unhappy marriage, social issues, and religion, discussion of difficulties the raising and consignment of tobacco, and desires to remain debt-free. *VMHB* 113: 85-86.

2 Historiography and Public History

40   Bailyn, Bernard. *Atlantic History: Concept and Contours*. Cambridge, Mass.: Harvard University Press, 2005. 149 p. ISBN 0674016882; ISBN 9780674016880; OCLC 56733119; LC Call Number D13.5.A75; Dewey 909/.09821/0072. Citations: 82.
Explores the historiographical origins and development of Atlantic history and its impact on globalization, industrialization, and historical inquiry. Discusses migration, trade and commercial networks, and settlement patterns. Argues that the trend toward Atlantic history emerged from the events of the mid-twentieth century, which led to a "broadening vision" among historians, who responded to "the social situation" and "the interior impulses of historical scholarship." Rejects "defining any specific set of characteristics" in the early modern Atlantic world, noting that its characters, networks, and power relationships constantly changed.
AHR 111: 434-35; *BHR* 80: 171-73; *CJH* 41: 622-23; *JAS* 40: 415-17; *JHG* 32: 655-57; *NEQ* 79: 123-33.

41   Burstein, Andrew. *America's Jubilee: How in 1826 a Generation Remembered Fifty Years of Independence*. New York: Alfred A. Knopf, 2001. xiv, 361 p. ISBN 0375410333; OCLC 43333487; LC Call Number E285 .B88; Dewey 973.3/6 21. Citations: 13.
Sets out to "uncover the soul" of the American generation following the Revolution and to "provide a palpable sense of emotional as well as political currents." Discusses Lafayette's 1824 return to America, the work and recollections of William Wirt, Elizabeth Foster, Ruth Bascom, Ethan Allen Brown, John Quincy Adams, George McDuffie, John C. Calhoun, John Randolph, Lord Byron, Henry Clay, and Andrew Jackson, the jubilee

celebrations of Independence, and the coincidental deaths of Adams and Jefferson. Observes that "In the jubilee year, there was no greater pursuit of purity, no greater gift of perfection, than the Revolution as it was being revived in the collective imagination."
JER 21: 721-24; *PMHB* 126: 506-508; *WMQ* 58: 1048-52.

42 Cañizares-Esguerra, Jorge. *How to Write the History of the New World: Histories, Epistemologies, and Identities in the Eighteenth-Century Atlantic World.* Stanford, Calif.: Stanford University Press, 2001. xx, 450 p. ISBN 0804740844; ISBN 9780804740845; ISBN 0804746931; ISBN 9780804746939; OCLC 45137647; LC Call Number F1412 .C25; Dewey 980. Citations: 14.
Claims that Latin American historiography emphasizes "inordinate social conflict and collective failure" and argues that more attention should be paid to the intellectual achievements of the region and of the Iberian peninsula. Focuses on the work of eighteenth-century northern European historians and of sixteenth-century Spanish scholars and describes the Hispanic historiographical reaction to the likes of the abbé Raynal, William Robertson, and the comte de Buffon. Emphasizes "the density and originality of intellectual debates" in which Hispanic scholars engaged and argues that in the early seventeenth century Spanish scholarship "far surpassed anything then available in English." Points out that "Creole" scholars in the New World, in their critiques of travel literature, "foreshadowed many of our contemporary postcolonial insights."
AHR 108: 149-50; *EAL* 38: 319-24; *Ethnohistory* 51: 848-52; *HAHR* 84: 515-16; *J Interdis Hist* 33: 612-13; *J Mod Hist* 75: 929-31; *Soc Hist* 28: 394; *WMQ* 59: 975-81.

43 Ernest, John. *Liberation Historiography: African American Writers and the Challenge of History, 1794-1861.* Chapel Hill: University of North Carolina Press, 2004. xiv, 426 p. ISBN 080782853X (hbk.); ISBN 9780807828533 (hbk.); ISBN 0807855219 (pbk.); ISBN 9780807855218 (pbk.); OCLC 52901120; LC Call Number E184.65 .E76; Dewey 973/.0496073 22. Citations: 26.
Suggests that historical writing about African Americans both corrected the record that had been distorted by white supremacy and helped to gather a "newly envisioned community of faith and moral duty." Views early nineteenth-century writing as the emergence of "white history," which forwarded nationalist stories and specific ideas about historical truth and objectivity, things that African American writers disputed. Finds that African American historical writing was characterized by systematic analysis, "self-consciously fragmented narrative," and emphasis on the connection between historical reflection and contemporary action. Claims that early African American historians joined together sacred and secular history in order to encourage a reading of the past that would liberate African Americans by asking them to recognize a sacred plan of history. Emphasizes the role of African American oration and periodical presses in creating a "performative" black collective memory. Notices a shift from the writing of slave narratives using the conventions of white abolitionism

that viewed slaves as subjects of a degraded "American" history to one that saw them as "spiritual citizens" who were witnesses to a providential history.
AHR 110: 436; *Am Lit* 78: 880-82; *AQ* 58: 245-53; *JAH* 92: 214-15; *JER* 25: 320-23; *JSH* 71: 881-83.

44 Greenspan, Anders. *Creating Colonial Williamsburg*. Washington, D.C.: Smithsonian Institution Press, 2002. x, 212 p. ISBN 1588340260 (hbk.); ISBN 9781588340269 (hbk.); ISBN 1588340015 (pbk.); ISBN 9781588340016 (pbk.); OCLC 47054695; LC Call Number F234.W7; Dewey: 945.5/4252. Citations: 5.
Surveys the establishment and development of Colonial Williamsburg as a public history site. Contends that Williamsburg illustrates the twentieth-century social history of the United States and the birth and maturation of the public history field. Outlines the contributions of the Rockefellers and asserts that a single wealthy family has been able to influence the historical knowledge of entire generations of Americans. Notes that John D. Rockefeller III reviewed the restoration of Colonial Williamsburg as a way to "indoctrinate visitors in the importance of American ideals" and to draw comparisons from the present to the past. Explains that inculcating values and ideas was particularly important during World War II, when soldiers from nearby military installations visited to learn about why they were fighting. Concludes that, after World War II, Williamsburg stood as a Cold War monument to another tumultuous time in the nation's history that ended successfully for the United States.
JAH 91: 283-84.

45 Knott, Stephen F. *Alexander ·Hamilton and the Persistence of Myth*. Lawrence: University Press of Kansas, 2002. xii, 336 p. ISBN 0700611576; ISBN 9780700611577; OCLC 47767164; LC Call Number E302.6.H2; Dewey 973.4/092. Citations: 9.
Reviews Hamilton's status over time, noting that generally it has been conversely related to that of Thomas Jefferson. Explains that Jefferson's portrayal of his political opponent as a monarchist stuck with Hamilton until the Civil War, when federal supremacy was stringently defended, and when Lincoln acted like a Hamiltonian while frequently quoting Jefferson in speeches. Finds that Hamilton's reputation suffered at the hands of Henry Adams, Franklin D. Roosevelt, Claude Bowers, Dumas Malone, and Julian Boyd, while late in the twentieth century it was revived by the likes of Forrest McDonald and Jacob Cooke. Praises Hamilton for his refusal to pander and for his pragmatism and contends that Hamilton's plans and vision were responsible for the United States' ultimate rise to superpower status.
AHR 107: 1554-55; *HRNB* 31: 108; *JAH* 89: 1511-12; *PSQ* 117: 669-70; *VQR* 79: 18-19; *WMQ* 60: 660-63.

46 Leepson, Marc. *Saving Monticello: The Levy Family's Epic Quest to Rescue the House That Jefferson Built*. New York: Free Press, 2001. viii, 303 p. ISBN 074320106X; ISBN 9780743201063; OCLC 46822427; LC Call Number E332.74 .L44; Dewey 975.5/482. Citations: 2.
Describes what happened to Monticello between 1831 and its purchase by the Thomas Jefferson Memorial Foundation in 1923. Explains that members of the

Levy family owned the estate for most of that time and opened the grounds to sightseers, allowed limited tours of the house, reroofed the building, and made few changes to Jefferson's original design. Argues that the Levy family, though plagued by anti-Semitism, might very well have saved Monticello. Maintains that this fact "has been one of the best-kept secrets in the history of American preservation." States that once the Jefferson Foundation began restoration work in the late 1920s, all traces of the Levy period were purged.
JAH 89: 1517-18; *VMHB* 109: 343-44.

47 Mires, Charlene. *Independence Hall in American Memory*. Philadelphia: University of Pennsylvania Press, 2002. xviii, 350 p. ISBN 0812236653; ISBN 9780812236651; OCLC 49743696; LC Call Number F158.8.I3 M57; Dewey 974.8/11 21. Citations: 14.
Reviews the history of Independence Hall and of the Liberty Bell, noting that immediately after the Revolution neither occupied a particularly vaunted position in the national memory. Notes that during the early nineteenth century, the building served a primarily legislative function and that the second floor housed Charles Willson Peale's museum. Finds that the city government saved the building from destruction and remodeled the "Hall of Independence" in time for the 1824 visit of Marquis de Lafayette, marking the beginning of the building's use for historical commemoration. Explains that the building continued to be used for judicial space until the 1890s, after which time its primary function has been historical. Tells the story of the Liberty Bell, which near the end of the nineteenth century became a distinct icon of independence and freedom and one that traveled throughout the country.
AHR 109: 173-74; *JAH* 90: 1001-1002; *JER* 23: 105-108; *Penn Hist* 71: 388-90; *PMHB* 127: 231-32.

48 Morgan, Edmund S. *The Genuine Article: A Historian Looks at Early America*. New York: W.W. Norton, 2004. xi, 315 p. ISBN 0393059200; ISBN 9780393059205; OCLC 54425167; LC Call Number E188.5 .M67; Dewey 973.2. Citations: 7.
Presents 24 book reviews published in the *New York Review of Books* over the past quarter of a century. Traces Morgan's changing interests over the course of his career. Divides the essays into those dealing with New Englanders, with Southerners, and with Revolutionaries. Notes that the pieces represent a sort of "intellectual biography" and "a statement of what I have thought about early Americans during nearly 70 years in their company."
Booklist 100: 1344; *LJ* 129n11: 83.

49 Nash, Gary B. *First City: Philadelphia and the Forging of Historical Memory*. Philadelphia: University of Pennsylvania Press, 2002. viii, 383 p. ISBN 0812236300; ISBN 9780812236309; OCLC 47705387; LC Call Number F158.3 .N37; Dewey 974.8/11/0072073. Citations: 24.
Explores the ways in which Philadelphians remembered, celebrated, and neglected their past from the eighteenth century to the present. Examines how Philadelphia's museums (especially the Historical Society of Pennsylvania) and libraries (notably the Library Company of Philadelphia) collected items and thus

recovered and remembered the past. Explains that members of such institutions were largely drawn from Philadelphia's elite, and that class and status affected collection practices, which in turn reflected the accomplishments of elite males who attempted to disseminate "the values of genteel culture and impart a shared sense of identity among Philadelphians." Notes that "immigrants, laboring people, African Americans and others established alternative cultures that paralleled and sometimes challenged what leading citizens defined as the culture of America."
AHR 108: 515-16; *HRNB* 30: 100; *JAH* 89: 1517; *JER* 22: 315-18; *J Interdis Hist* 34: 652-53; *Penn Hist* 70: 215-18; *PMHB* 127: 342-44; *WMQ* 60: 254-57.

50   Purcell, Sarah J. *Sealed with Blood: War, Sacrifice, and Memory in Revolutionary America*. Philadelphia: University of Pennsylvania Press, 2002. x, 278 p. ISBN 0812236602; ISBN 9780812236606; OCLC 49226406; LC Call Number E209 .P93; Dewey 973.3. Citations: 34.
Examines public memory of the Revolutionary War through the first quarter of the nineteenth century. Explains that public displays promoted the ideals of sacrifice, duty, order, and national harmony, and that marginalized groups like African American veterans used the same celebrations to seek new rights in early national America. Finds that Loyalists had no alternative public memory of their own. Describes the failed attempt to form the independent state of Franklin in the 1780s and the controversy surrounding the Society of the Cincinnati.
AHR 108: 1441-42; *EAL* 39: 591-98; *FHQ* 82: 221-23; *JAH* 90: 1000-1001; *JER* 22: 696-98; *J Mil Hist* 67: 563-64; *NCHR* 80: 242-43; *PMHB* 127: 236-38; *RAH* 31: 356-62; *WMQ* 60: 251-54.

51   Schueller, Malini Johar and Edward Watts, eds. *Messy Beginnings: Postcoloniality and Early American Studies*. New Brunswick, N.J.: Rutgers University Press, 2003. vii, 267 p. ISBN 0813532329 (hbk.); ISBN 9780813532325 (hbk.); ISBN 0813532337 (pbk.); ISBN 9780813532332 (pbk.); OCLC 50422843; LC Call Number E188.5 .M39; Dewey 973. Citations: 17.
Argues that postcolonial methodologies should be applied to the study of early American culture, particularly as a way to escape unhelpful exceptionalism debates. Includes articles on William Apess and the search for postcolonial method, Indian "resurrection" in transatlantic colonial writings, rebelling children, disciplining Indians, and the critique of colonial authority in Puritan New England, the Whiskey Rebellion and the colonization of the West, decolonization in Crèvecoeur, the imagination of colonial space, internal colonialism and the rhetoric of U.S. nation building, missionary women and the race of true womanhood, the vernacular sociology of collectivity after the Haitian Revolution, Benjamin Franklin's antipodean cosmopolitanism, the "science of lying," and colonization, black freemasonry, and the rehabilitation of Africa. Contends that early settlements were neither American nor European, but rather an "entanglement of imperial and colonial experiences and identities" that postcolonial methods might be able to separate and make sense of. Concludes that "'colonized' and 'colonizing' are not mutually exclusive but rather simultaneous and contemporary" and that the "processes through which

colonial hegemony was formulated were, in fact, fuzzy and fluid, in short, messy."
AQ 57: 1223-29; *EAL* 39: 606-612.

52 Urofsky, Melvin I. *The Levy Family and Monticello, 1834–1923: Saving Thomas Jefferson's House.* Charlottesville, Va.: Thomas Jefferson Foundation, 2001. 256 p. ISBN 1882886151 (hbk.); ISBN 9781882886159 (hbk.); ISBN 188288616X (pbk.); ISBN 9781882886166 (pbk.); OCLC 46769097; LC Call Number E332.74 .U76; Dewey 973.4/6/092. Citations: 3.
Describes the Levy family's role in rehabilitating Monticello, noting its purchase by Uriah Phillips Levy, legal disputes over the estate, the work of Jefferson Monroe Levy, Maud Littleton's opposition to Levy family stewardship, and Levy's sale of the property to the Thomas Jefferson Memorial Foundation in 1923. Stresses the use of anti-Semitism among opponents of the Levy family, American interest in historic preservation since the mid-nineteenth century, government ambivalence toward Monticello, and the efforts of the Levy family to have its contributions to the preservation of the estate recognized.
JSH 69: 416-18; *VMHB* 109: 343-44; *VQR* 78: 395-412.

53 Vickers, Daniel, ed. *A Companion to Colonial America.* Malden, Mass.: Blackwell Publishing, 2003. xiii, 562 p. ISBN 0631210113; ISBN 9780631210115; OCLC 50072292; LC Call Number E187 .C75; Dewey 973.2. Citations: 25.
Presents twenty-three essays on topics and interpretations in American colonial history. Covers archaeological evidence, colonization, ecology, migration and settlement, empire, Native Americans, African Americans, economy, women and gender, children and families, class, politics, regionalism, consumption, religion, secular culture and the American enlightenment, borderlands, comparisons with the Caribbean, New Spain, New France, and Atlantic Canada, and causes of American revolutions.
JAS 37: 522-23; *JAS* 38: 173-74; *JSH* 70: 885-88; *WMQ* 63: 183-88.

54 Wills, Garry. *Henry Adams and the Making of America.* Boston, Mass.: Houghton Mifflin, 2005. viii, 467 p. ISBN 9780618134304; ISBN 0618134301; OCLC 57692101; LC Call Number E302.1 .A2538; Dewey 973.4/6. Citations: 8.
Sketches and life and work of Adams and contends that Adams's *History of the United States of America* represents a "non-fiction prose masterpiece" on the Adams and Madison administrations, a work that has either been misinterpreted or ignored by other historians. Contends that Adams viewed history as "far more complex than the interplay of two (or many) ideologies" and, in fact, previewed in his work many contemporary debates.
Booklist 101: 1988; *LJ* 130n13: 103; *NEQ* 79: 298-305.

3 Geography and Exploration

55 Ausband, Stephen Conrad. *Byrd's Line: A Natural History*. Charlottesville: University of Virginia Press, 2002. x, 187 p. ISBN 0813921341 (hbk.); ISBN 9780813921341 (hbk.); ISBN 081392135X (pbk.); ISBN 9780813921358 (pbk.); OCLC 49320313; LC Call Number F229 .A88; Dewey 508.755. Citations: 4.
Describes Byrd's role in the dividing line between Virginia and North Carolina, the natural features that he observed, such as the mountains, the Currituck Inlet, the Great Dismal Swamp, and the Meherrin, Dan, and Roanoke Rivers. Identifies the plants and animals that Byrd noted and discusses the hunting techniques of local Native Americans and cooking methods of backcountry settlers. Compares the land of Byrd's time to that of today.
VMHB 110: 402-403; *WMQ* 60: 904-907.

56 Bauer, Ralph. *The Cultural Geography of Colonial American Literatures: Empire, Travel, Modernity*. New York: Cambridge University Press, 2003. xiii, 295 p. ISBN 0521822025; ISBN 9780521822022; OCLC 52358738; LC Call Number PS185 .B38; Dewey 810.9001 21. Citations: 34.
Provides "exemplary case studies intended to illustrate the importance of cultural geography to literary history." Examines travel, shipwreck, piracy, captivity, and natural history narratives in their various contexts, describing their purposes, motives of authors and editors, and changes from edition to edition over time. Notes that these narratives provide "a way of knowing and representing the world in the globalizing economies of transoceanic empires" and show that "in the Spanish and British empires" the "early modern geo-political dialectic between imperial consolidation and Creole resistance was most manifest, resulting, in the late eighteenth and early nineteenth centuries, in a breakdown of the old imperial order."
Am Lit 77: 847-49; *EAL* 40: 545-53; *18c Stds* 38: 367-71; *WMQ* 62: 313-15.

57 Carlson, Laurie M. *Seduced by the West: Jefferson's America and the Lure of the Land Beyond the Mississippi.* Chicago, Ill.: Ivan R. Dee, 2003. xii, 226 p. ISBN 1566634903; ISBN 9781566634908; OCLC 50447619; LC Call Number F592 .C29; Dewey 978/.02 21. Citations: 6.
Surveys various French, Spanish, Russian, and British efforts to find the Northwest Passage. Views the Lewis and Clark expedition not as a "scientific venture," but rather as an American provocation of the Spanish, from whom Jefferson was seeking to take Florida and Louisiana. Contends that George Rogers Clark, Philip Nolan, and James Wilkinson were out for personal gain.
Booklist 99: 1444; *LJ* 128n8: 134; *WHQ* 35: 377-78.

58 Danson, Edwin. *Drawing the Line: How Mason and Dixon Surveyed the Most Famous Border in America.* New York: John Wiley, 2001. viii, 232 p. ISBN 0471385026; ISBN 9780471385028; OCLC 43790717; LC Call Number F157.B7; Dewey 974.8/802. Citations: 5.
Provides an account of the surveying of the Mason-Dixon Line, covering the long-standing family feud between the Calverts and the Penns, the vague character of English royal land grants, the 1763 emigration of Mason and Dixon to settle the feud by surveying the border between the colonies of Delaware, Pennsylvania, and Maryland, and the time required and the techniques that surveyors used. Relies heavily on the journal of Jeremiah Dixon and explains technical matters of longitude calculations, the employment of milestones along the Line, and the importance of geographical landmarks. Includes an appendix of mathematical calculations and diagrams.
Booklist 97: 906; *Penn Hist* 69: 441-43.

59 Davies, Wayne Kenneth David. *Writing Geographical Exploration: James and the Northwest Passage, 1631-33.* Calgary: University of Calgary Press, 2003. xvi, 318 p. ISBN 1552380629; ISBN 9781552380628; OCLC 54065751; LC Call Number G650 1631 .J26; Dewey 910/.9163/27. Citations: 1.
Recounts the story of Thomas James, commander of a 1631 expedition commissioned by the Company of Merchant Venturers of Bristol to find the Northwest Passage. Examines the context of the mission, including competition among trading companies and preparation for the voyage and studies James's account, the interpretations and representations in the narrative, and the impact of his descriptions. Argues that James deserves a special place in both Canadian and Anglo-Welsh literature because of his story-telling skills. Contends that James has been negatively portrayed because his narratives are constructed, rather than representing unmediated reporting, and traces James's bad reputation to the work of John Barrow (1818). Seeks to sort out from James's exploration journals real geographic information and to explain the influences that affect an explorer's perception of the environment.
CJH 40: 318-20.

60 Dening, Greg. *Beach Crossings: Voyaging Across Times, Cultures, and Self.* Philadelphia: University of Pennsylvania Press, 2004. ix, 376 p. ISBN 0812238494; ISBN 9780812238495; OCLC 55665305; LC Call Number GN671.M3; Dewey 996.3/1. Citations: 32.

Uses "the beach" as a metaphor for spaces of contact, negotiation, and transition, taking up, specifically, the geographical and temporal and the historical and personal. Focuses on the culture and post-contact history of the Marquesas Islanders of Eastern Polynesia ("Enata"), reconstructing the group ethnohistorically. Recounts some early encounters between Westerners and islanders, emphasizing the lack of certainties and the need for the use of imagination and contextualization. Relies heavily on the journals of foreign "beachcombers" who resided in the Marquesas in the late 1790s, such as English missionary William Crook, author of the first Marquesan-English dictionary, Edward Robarts, a cook on a whaling ship, Frenchman Joseph Kabris, artist Paul Gauguin, and author Herman Melville. Examines the ways in which Pacific Islanders understood arriving "Strangers" in terms of indigenous cultural contexts and social systems and how foreigners did the same.
AHR 111: 139-40; *WMQ* 63: 377-79.

61 Flint, Richard and Shirley Cushing Flint, eds. *The Coronado Expedition: From the Distance of 460 Years*. Albuquerque: University of New Mexico Press, 2003. xiii, 338 p. ISBN 0826329756; ISBN 9780826329752; OCLC 50809061; LC Call Number E125.V3 C725; Dewey 979/.01 21. Citations: 12.
Presents articles on various aspects of the Coronado expedition, including the context for Spanish exploration of the West, the financing and provisioning of the expedition, its muster roll, the ruins of southeastern Arizona, the trail from Sonora to Zuni, New Mexico, Barrionuevo's visit to Yuque Yunque, Coronado's route from the Pecos River to the Llano Estacado, the timeline of the expedition from Tiguex to the second Barranca (April and May 1541), bison hunters of the Llano, warfare on the South plains in the sixteenth and seventeenth centuries, various scholarly perspectives on the expedition, including archaeology of Spanish weaponry and tools in North America and Panama, the mapping, measuring, and naming of cultural spaces in Castañeda's *Relación de la Jornada de Cíbola*, and the lives of Francisco and Juan Vázquez de Coronado.
HAHR 85: 327-28; *16c J* 36: 1229-31.

62 Flint, Richard and Shirley Cushing Flint, eds. *Documents of the Coronado Expedition, 1539-1542: "They Were Not Familiar with His Majesty, Nor Did They Wish to be His Subjects"*. Dallas, Tex.: Southern Methodist University Press, 2005. x, 746 p. ISBN 0870744968; ISBN 9780870744969; OCLC 56955894; LC Call Number E125.V3 D66; Dewey 979/.01 22. Citations: 15.
Draws upon the collections of the Archivo General de Indias to present a collection of 34 documents on Coronado's expedition between 1532 and 1542. Corrects geographical errors regarding the expedition and provides five maps indicating Coronado's stopping points. Introduces each of the documents, clarifying characters and placing and analyzing where possible different versions and interpretations of the writings.
HAHR 88: 688-89; *SHQ* 110: 129.

63 Flint, Richard. *Great Cruelties Have Been Reported: The 1544 Investigation of the Coronado Expedition*. Dallas, Tex.: Southern Methodist University Press,

2002. xix, 647 p. ISBN 0870744607; ISBN 9780870744600; OCLC 47296232; LC Call Number E125.V3 F57; Dewey 979/.01/092. Citations: 9.

Provides the complete record of the investigation, including translations and transcriptions of documents from the proceedings and from witness testimony. Demonstrates that the investigation was carefully orchestrated to exonerate Coronado and his patron, Viceroy Antonio de Mendoza. Discusses the uses and limitations of the sources and the consequences of the Coronado expedition, particularly for its participants and for native peoples. Notes that Coronado's men raped native women, tortured native men, stole skins and textiles, burned captives at the stake, looted and destroyed native towns, and executed those who had been promised safe passage as a condition of surrender. Presents appendices of biographical and geographical data and a detailed index. Argues that the expedition's destruction and violence in the middle Rio Grande Valley profoundly disrupted the Tiwa Pueblos and led to the Keres Pueblo encroachment on the northern fringe of Tiwa territory.
SHQ 107: 333-34.

64   Foley, William E. *Wilderness Journey: The Life of William Clark.* Columbia: University of Missouri Press, 2004. xvi, 326 p. ISBN 0826215335; ISBN 9780826215338; OCLC 53953775; LC Call Number F592.7.C565; Dewey 917.804/2/092. Citations: 10.

Presents a biography of Clark for a general audience. Argues that the Lewis and Clark expedition was perhaps not even Clark's most significant contribution to American history. Examines Clark's early life, including his parents' 1784 migration from Virginia to Kentucky, his relationship with his elder brother George Rogers Clark, and the educational, business, and military experiences that prepared him to serve as co-captain of the expedition. Discusses the expedition itself and Clark's later careers as an Indian agent, a brigadier general in the militia of the upper Louisiana Territory, territorial governor, and entrepreneur. Notes that, though occasionally sympathetic to Native peoples, Clark favored Jackson's Indian removal policy and believed in making use of powerful fur merchants to combat British influence. Concludes that Clark was a "product of gentrified Virginia and backcountry Kentucky" and "mirrored his upbringing in both worlds."
Booklist 100: 1593; *IMH* 101: 373-75; *JAH* 92: 205-206; *JSH* 71: 672-73; *VMHB* 112: 195-97; *WHQ* 36: 372-73.

65   Foster, William C., ed. *The La Salle Expedition on the Mississippi River: A Lost Manuscript of Nicolas de La Salle, 1682.* Translated by Johanna S. Warren. Austin: Texas State Historical Association, 2003. xv, 175 p. ISBN 0876111967; ISBN 9780876111963; OCLC 52902581; LC Call Number F352 .L44; Dewey 977/.01/092 22. Citations: 14.

Prints a translation of the diary account, authored by Nicolas de La Salle, of the 1682 La Salle expedition on the Mississippi River. Describes Indian trade routes along the Mississippi and among various New Spain outposts at which were traded fruits, vegetables, weapons, horses, and other Spanish goods.
SHQ 108: 406-407.

66   Fresonke, Kris and Mark Spence, eds. *Lewis and Clark: Legacies, Memories, and New Perspectives.* Berkeley: University of California Press, 2004. vii, 290 p. ISBN 0520228391 (hbk.); ISBN 9780520228399 (hbk.); ISBN 0520238222 (pbk.); ISBN 9780520238220 (pbk.); OCLC 51848566; LC Call Number F592.7 .L6945; Dewey 917.8042. Citations: 9.
Presents the representation of the Lewis and Clark expedition by the American Philosophical Society, the idea of wilderness aesthetics, medicinal implications of the expedition, the legality of the Louisiana Purchase, the histories of the Mandan, Hidatsa, and Arikara Indians, Lewis and Clark in popular memory, Sacajawea as an object of frontier romance, twentieth-century commemorations of the expedition, the expedition's bicentennial, and issues of interpretation and preservation.
AHR 110: 475-76.

67   Galois, Robert, ed. *A Voyage to the North West Side of America: The Journals of James Colnett, 1786–89.* Vancouver: UBC Press, 2004. xiii, 441 p. ISBN 0774808551; ISBN 9780774808552; OCLC 52704635; LC Call Number F851.5 .C75; Dewey 917.11/1041 22. Citations: 3.
Publishes Colnett's 1786–1789 journals, which describe fur trading and exploration. Situates the journals in historical and comparative context, noting Native perspectives provided in oral traditions, and listing Northwest Coast place names. Discusses the role of violence in the maritime fur trade, arguing that violence reflected European and coastal indigenous societies and cultures, both of which saw violence as an acceptable means to assert power.
CHR 86: 733-34; *PHR* 75: 150-51.

68   Hann, John H., ed. *An Early Florida Adventure Story.* By Andrés de San Miguel. Gainesville: University Press of Florida, 2001. xiii, 109 p. ISBN 0813018765; ISBN 9780813018768; OCLC 44764222; LC Call Number F314 .A53; Dewey 975.9/01 21. Citations: 4.
Presents a first-person account of Andrés's voyage to Mexico in 1593, his shipwreck on the coast of Georgia when returning to Spain in 1595, and the English capture of Cádiz in 1596. Describes the Native Americans he met in La Florida and life at St. Augustine.
FHQ 80: 523-24; *HAHR* 82: 145; *16c J* 34: 931.

69   Hayes, Derek. *First Crossing: Alexander Mackenzie, His Expedition Across North America, and the Opening of the Continent.* Seattle: Sasquatch Books, 2001. 320 p. ISBN 1570613087; ISBN 9781570613081; OCLC 46835397; LC Call Number F1060.7.M1783; Dewey 917.1204/1. Citations: 4.
Describes the travel journal of the Scottish-born Alexander Mackenzie, who voyaged from Fort Chipewyan, Alberta, for the North West Company and became the first European to cross the North American continent from the East. Explains the motivations for the Canadian fur trade, the activities of the fur traders, and the discoveries that led to the opening of the Northwest.
Booklist 98: 45; *LJ* 126n17: 99.

70 Jenish, D'Arcy. *Epic Wanderer: David Thompson and the Mapping of the Canadian West*. Lincoln: University of Nebraska Press, 2004. 309 p. ISBN 0803226004; ISBN 9780803226005; OCLC 53796931; LC Call Number GA473.7.T48; Dewey 526/.092. Citations: 7.
Portrays Thompson as a hero, Canadian patriot, and a skilled explorer, trader, and surveyor. Claims that he accomplished a great deal, despite American expansionism and British colonial disinterest. Details Thompson's life from his arrival in North America in 1784 as an apprentice clerk in 1784, his time spent as a land surveyor in Williamstown and Montreal, adventures, and interactions with indigenous peoples. Contends that Thompson advanced British imperial and commercial interests in the Oregon territory, largely because of his talent as a cartographer.
PHR 74: 129-30.

71 Jones, Landon Y. *William Clark and the Shaping of the West*. New York: Hill and Wang, 2004. xii, 394 p. ISBN 0809030411; ISBN 9780809030415; OCLC 53987025; LC Call Number F592.7.C565; Dewey 973.5/092. Citations: 12.
Presents a chronological biography that traces Clark's life from the family's 1749 settlement in the Virginia Piedmont, to his supervision of his brother George Rogers Clark's financial affairs, to his 1789 enlistment into the Kentucky militia and selection by Meriwether Lewis to join the westward expedition.
Booklist 100: 1343; *IMH* 101: 373-75; *JAH* 92: 205-206; *LJ* 129n120; *RAH* 32: 365-73; *WHQ* 36: 372-73.

72 Kastor, Peter J. *The Nation's Crucible: The Louisiana Purchase and the Creation of America*. New Haven, Conn.: Yale University Press, 2004. xiv, 311 p. ISBN 0300101198; ISBN 9780300101195; OCLC 53162669; LC Call Number E333 .K37; Dewey 973.4/6; Dewey 973.5. Citations: 15.
Reviews the acquisition and incorporation of Louisiana, including background, territorial government, lawmaking, statehood, and the War of 1812. Rejects the idea that the Louisiana Purchase was merely one component of Manifest Destiny, noting that the acquisition was pragmatic and not part of an existing impulse toward national expansion. Emphasizes "attachment" of Louisiana to the United States, explaining that for residents of the region acceptance of the Union was a matter of practical self-interest, given the benefits gained in commerce, security, and institutional development. Discusses the uncertainties leaders faced in making non-Anglo-Saxons "Americans" and the ways in which persons of color and Native Americans asserted power through diplomacy and petitioning. Contends that slave revolts and free blacks' demands of the new territorial government led to the passage of Louisiana's repressive Black Code of 1806. Concludes that "The incorporation of Louisiana had defined an American nation."
AHR 110: 474-75; *JAH* 92: 964-65; *JAS* 39: 562-63; *JER* 25: 500-502; *JSH* 74: 950-51; *LJ* 129n6: 106-107; *WHQ* 36: 371.

73 Kukla, Jon. *A Wilderness So Immense: The Louisiana Purchase and the Destiny of America.* New York: Knopf, 2003. x, 430 p. ISBN 0375408126; ISBN 9780375408120; OCLC 50253149; LC Call Number E333 .K85; Dewey 973.4/6. Citations: 17.

Examines the acquisition of Louisiana Territory in the context of international events and American diplomatic efforts. Argues that the European concept of balance of power directly affected American trans-Mississippi expansion, as Spain valued the territory more for its use as a buffer between the United States and colonial Mexico than for its economic potential. Emphasizes the importance of the American union's volatility to westward expansion, since it was not clear in the early nineteenth century whether settlers would continue to be "American" or that the Union would survive. Contends that enhanced commercial ties between east and west cemented the union of the regions, that the flow of "British and American manufactured goods across the mountains in the 1790s ended the threat of separatism in the Ohio River Valley." Concludes that the Louisiana Purchase "was a turning point at America's halfway mark toward an inclusive national history," that "starting at New Orleans in 1803, five million Americans along the Atlantic Seaboard accelerated an encounter with diversity that had been sustained by geographic expansion and immigration in the nineteenth and twentieth centuries."
AHR 109: 519-20; *JAH* 91: 223-25; *LJ* 128n5: 97; *Penn Hist* 71: 241-43; *PMHB* 128: 317-19; *RAH* 32: 166-75; *VMHB* 111: 411-13.

74 MacMillan, Ken and Jennifer Abeles, eds. *John Dee: The Limits of the British Empire.* Westport, Conn.: Praeger, 2004. x, 150 p. ISBN 0275978230; ISBN 9780275978235; OCLC 56617325; LC Call Number DA10.5 .D44; Dewey 325/.32/0941 22. Citations: 3.

Presents an annotated edition of a manuscript compilation, written from 1577 to 1578 by John Dee. Includes a 33-page introduction and annotations. Reviews Dee's role in justifying Elizabethan claims to lands. Covers Dee's efforts to get the Crown to grant legitimacy to the New World voyages of Humphrey Gilbert, Martin Frobisher, and others.
16c J 37: 1183-85.

75 McCorkle, Barbara Backus, ed. *New England in Early Printed Maps, 1513 to 1800: An Illustrated Carto-Bibliography.* Providence, R. I.: The John Carter Brown Library, 2001. xx, 354 p. ISBN 091661753X; ISBN 9780916617530; OCLC 46947233; LC Call Number Z6027.U52; LC Call Number GA408.5.N37; Dewey 912.74. Citations: 2.

Lists and describes 800 maps of New England printed prior to 1800. Includes nautical charts and maps of individual states. Demonstrates progressively increasing knowledge of New England. Organizes chronologically entries that give the cartographer or engraver's name, complete title and size of the map, and source. Includes 455 black-and-white illustrations and provides lists of articles, books and carto-bibliographies for each map, and title and personal indexes.
WMQ 59: 710-15.

76 McGoogan, Kenneth. *Ancient Mariner: The Arctic Adventures of Samuel Hearne, the Sailor Who Inspired Coleridge's Masterpiece.* New York: Carroll and Graf, 2004. 333 p. ISBN 0786713046; ISBN 9780786713042; OCLC 53285176; LC Call Number F1060.7 .H495; Dewey 917.1904/22/092. Citations: 2.
Discusses the explorations of Samuel Hearne (1745-1792), the British sailor and famed North American adventurer who inspired Samuel Taylor Coleridge's "The Rime of the Ancient Mariner." Recounts Hearne's education, service in the Seven Years' War, work with the Hudson Bay Company, three-year exploration of northern Canada, and relationship with Native Americans, which included the haunting massacre of the Inuit at "Bloody Fall."
Booklist 100: 943.

77 Rodriguez, Junius P., ed. *The Louisiana Purchase: A Historical and Geographical Encyclopedia.* Santa Barbara, Calif.: ABC-CLIO, 2002. xxxv, 513 p. ISBN 157607188X; ISBN 9781576071885; OCLC 48784568; LC Call Number E333 .L69; Dewey 973.4/6. Citations: 2.
Includes an essay that provides the context for the Louisiana Purchase, the related politics and diplomacy, and the impact of the acquisition. Presents entries on those persons involved, Native American groups affected, and other important places and topics. Provides the full texts of 49 related documents, including Jefferson's message to Congress and the Purchase Treaty itself.
Booklist 99: 268; *LJ* 127n15: 56; *LJ* 128n7: 43.

78 Ronda, James P. *Finding the West: Explorations with Lewis and Clark.* Albuquerque: University of New Mexico Press, 2001. xxii, 138 p. ISBN 0826324177; ISBN 9780826324177; OCLC 46353317; LC Call Number F592.7 .R65; Dewey 917.804/2 21. Citations: 22.
Examines Jefferson's western vision, Lewis and Clark in the broader context of exploration, their expectations and surprises, and their expedition's contribution to scientific knowledge and geopolitics, and perspectives on indigenous peoples. Evaluates the successes and failures of the expedition, noting that it was largely irrelevant to westward expansion of the nineteenth and early twentieth centuries.
AHR 107: 1555; *IMH* 98: 321-22; *JER* 21: 706-707; *LJ* 126n13: 133; *PHR* 71: 317-18; *WHQ* 33: 349-50; *WMQ* 59: 697-709.

79 Seefeldt, Douglas, Jeffrey L. Hantman, and Peter S. Onuf, eds. *Across the Continent: Jefferson, Lewis and Clark, and the Making of America.* Charlottesville: University of Virginia Press, 2005. x, 222 p. ISBN 0813923131; ISBN 9780813923130; OCLC 55494879; LC Call Number F592 .A49; Dewey 917.804/2. Citations: 7.
Publishes essays that take up the Lewis and Clark expedition from the perspectives of Enlightenment science, global commerce, and geopolitics. Covers Jefferson's vision of the Pacific and plans for the "western perimeter," the Jeffersonian legacy in American archaeology, the physical measurement of the nation, and the landscapes and contested histories and memories in the Southwest.

JAH 93: 199-200; *JER* 26: 145-54; *JSH* 73: 168-69; *PHR* 75: 494-95; *VMHB* 114: 523-26; *WHQ* 37: 535-36.

80 Slaughter, Thomas P. *Exploring Lewis and Clark: Reflections on Men and Wilderness*. New York: Alfred A. Knopf, 2003. xxx, 231 p. ISBN 0375400788; ISBN 9780375400780; OCLC 49719275; LC Call Number F592.7 .S67; Dewey 917.804/2. Citations: 25.
Explores "the spiritual and mythological foundations of the journey and the journals" related to the expedition, seeking to "look beneath the explorers' narratives for different meanings than those they intended us to find." Asserts that Lewis was unaccustomed to failure and was loathe to write about his shortcomings. Notes that after Lewis's suicide, Clark and other editors were left to construct the journals, which was done to highlight the accomplishments of the Corps of Discovery. Downplays the importance of Lewis and Clark, concluding that their expedition serves as a guide to the soul of the nation, which "is why we will keep repeating their journey over and over again."
Ag Hist 78: 368-69; *Booklist* 99: 728; *EAL* 38: 527-32; *JAH* 92: 965-66; *JER* 23: 625-28; *LJ* 127n20: 152; *Penn Hist* 71: 106-108; *RAH* 31: 518-27; *VMHB* 111: 190-91; *WMQ* 60: 904-907.

81 Thomas, Hugh. *Rivers of Gold: The Rise of the Spanish Empire, from Columbus to Magellan*. New York: Random House, 2004. xxi, 696 p. ISBN 0375502041; ISBN 9780375502040; OCLC 53896784; LC Call Number E123 .T56; LC Call Number F1411 .T36; Dewey 980/.01. Citations: 15.
Outlines the early Spanish enterprise in North America from 1492 to 1522, noting the kingdom's difficulty in establishing royal authority in the New World, Spanish mistreatment of native peoples, the ineffectiveness of Spanish policy toward natives, and the Western Hemisphere's influence on Spain.
AHR 110: 1482-83; *Booklist* 100: 1691; *LJ* 129n13: 95-97; *WMQ* 64: 183-94.

82 Weddle, Robert S. *The Wreck of the* Belle, *the Ruin of La Salle*. College Station: Texas A&M Press, 2001. xviii, 327 p. ISBN 158544121X; ISBN 9781585441211; OCLC 45387000; LC Call Number   F352 .W4; Dewey 976.4/132; Dewey 923/.9/73. Citations: 17.
Investigates La Salle's involvement in the 1686 sinking of La Belle off the Texas coast. Explains that La Salle was indeed responsible for the ship's loss, arguing that "the wreck of the Belle and the tragic conclusion of the episode may now be seen as the natural culmination of La Salle's life and the way he lived it: a true reflection of the man himself." Contends that La Salle's career was "shrouded in deceit and obfuscation" and that he was driven by the desire for glory and had little regard for those who served him. Characterizes La Salle as a stubborn, paranoid, egotistical man and poor planner who was not above extortion and bribery to achieve his ends.
Booklist 97: 1531; *FHQ* 81: 84-86; *JAH* 89: 1020-21; *JSH* 68: 922-23; *16c J* 33: 892-94; *SHQ* 105: 688-89; *WHQ* 33: 100-101; *WMQ* 59: 490-94.

83 Williams, Patrick G., S. Charles Bolton, and Jeannie M. Whayne, eds. *A Whole Country in Commotion: The Louisiana Purchase and the American*

Southwest. Fayetteville: University of Arkansas Press, 2005. xviii, 228 p. ISBN 1557287848 (pbk.); ISBN 9781557287847 (pbk.); OCLC 57003621; LC Call Number E333 .W47; Dewey 976/.03. Citations: 7.

Contains papers on the impact of the Louisiana Purchase on the American southwest. Presents articles on Lewis and Clark as kidnappers, the mystery of the Red River, the possibility of Louisiana's having become an Hispano-Indian republic, Arkansas's frontier exchange economy and the Louisiana Purchase, Indian removal in the Arkansas Territory, the Louisiana Purchase and the Quapaws, the impact of the acquisition on black experience, courts and lawyers on the Arkansas frontier, and colonial legacies in modern Caddo Indian ceremony.

HRNB 33: 142-43; *JAH* 93: 199; *JSH* 72: 661-63; *PHR* 76: 470-71; *SHQ* 110: 131-32.

84 Wood, W. Raymond. *Prologue to Lewis and Clark: The Mackay and Evans Expedition*. Norman: University of Oklahoma Press, 2003. xviii, 234 p. ISBN 0806134917; ISBN 9780806134918; OCLC 50518989; LC Call Number F598 .W66; Dewey 978/.01. Citations: 10.

Recounts the Mackay and Evans expedition, which undertook an exploration of the Missouri River on behalf of Spain between 1795 and 1797. Places the expedition in the context of earlier journeys and of imperial negotiations among Britain, France, and Spain. Discusses the formation and operation of the Missouri Company and the roles of Scotsman James Mackay and Welsh nationalist John Evans, who were charged with finding a route to the Pacific and with scouting potential locations for Spanish forts. Notes that Mackay and Evans established trade with Indians along the Missouri River and traveled to Mandan and Hidatsa villages near the mouth of the Knife River. Explains that the expedition never ventured west of the Rocky Mountains, but that the experiences of Mackay and Evans were extremely useful to Lewis and Clark.

JER 24: 686-88; *WHQ* 36: 88-89.

85 Zug, James. *American Traveler: The Life and Adventures of John Ledyard, the Man Who Dreamed of Walking the World*. New York: Basic Books, 2005. xviii, 286 p. ISBN 0465094058; ISBN 9780465094059; OCLC 58749572; LC Call Number G226.L5; Dewey 910.92. Citations: 1.

Examines the life of Ledyard, who was present on James Cook's third voyage and was a business partner of both Robert Morris and John Paul Jones. Notes that Jefferson asked Ledyard to explore the North American continent from the west, which would have required Ledyard to cross at the Bering Strait, go south through Alaska, and eventually complete his journey in Virginia. Explains that the expedition failed after fifteen months, when Catherine the Great had Ledyard arrested in Siberia.

Booklist 101: 1053-54

4 Colonization

86 Campey, Lucille H. *After the* Hector*: The Scottish Pioneers of Nova Scotia and Cape Breton, 1733–1852*. Toronto, Ont.: Natural Heritage, 2004. xviii, 376 p. ISBN 1896219950; ISBN 9781896219950; OCLC 54692527; LC Call Number F1040.S4; Dewey 971.6/0049163. Citations: 2.
Describes Scottish migration to Canada, focusing on the ship *The Hector*, which brought arrivals to Nova Scotia and Cape Breton beginning in 1773. Finds that Cape Breton destination points were divided by religion, between Catholics and Presbyterian Scots and that immigrants were poor, but that they traveled aboard decent vessels. Concludes that, generally, Scottish migrants did not reach the economic status that they expected.
CHR 86: 389-90.

87 Canny, Nicholas. *Making Ireland British, 1580–1650*. Oxford: Oxford University Press, 2001. xvi, 633 p. ISBN 0198200919; ISBN 9780198200918; OCLC 45466134; LC Call Number DA940 .C26; Dewey 941.505 21. Citations: 54.
Attempts to "connect developments in Ireland with simultaneous happenings in England and Scotland" in the late sixteenth and early seventeenth centuries. Contends that the "conflagration of the 1590s" was not a straightforward religious struggle, but rather a "civil conflict both within the fledgling English community in Ireland, and within the Irish community." Explains that English administration of the plantation scheme was faulty and that Crown influence and protection of English interests fell short of settlers' expectations. Argues that there were no "passive sufferers" in Ireland, but rather a web of "working relationships" among the various constituencies until 1641. Finds that, until the 1640s, Catholics forged a loyalist coalition among the English and Irish as a bulwark against anti-Crown Puritans.

EHR 117: 910-13; *HRNB* 30: 152-55; *J Interdis Hist* 33: 625-26; *J Mod Hist* 75: 943-45; *16c J* 33: 1172-73; *WMQ* 60: 654-57.

88 Colley, Linda. *Captives: Britain, Empire, and the World, 1600–1850.* London: J. Cape, 2002. xxii, 438 p. ISBN 0224059254; ISBN 9780224059251; OCLC 50101146; LC Call Number DA16 .C65; Dewey 941. Citations: 132.

Takes a wide view of the British Empire from the seventeenth through the mid-nineteenth centuries. Looks at the increasing power of Britain in the Mediterranean, North America, and the Indian subcontinent, noting that the Empire was marked by extraordinary fragility and division, that it suffered from relative lack of direction, and that it was overstretched throughout the 250-year period. Traces expansion to Britain's smallness, which demanded an outward-looking mindset and encouraged greed and aggression. Points out that the strains of empire resulted in the taking of large numbers of captives, especially in North America where land hunger and the need for labor led to the enslavement of Africans and the mistreatment of Native Americans. Places Mary Rowlandson's captivity narrative (1682) in a transatlantic context and seeks out similar documents from "zones of imperial invasion and enterprise" in Africa and Asia. Documents the numbers and social origins of captives in each of these "zones of captivity," relating their meaning to Britain's imperial fortunes and to the basic work of empire.

CJH 34: 87-104; *EHR* 118: 719-21.

89 Fitzmaurice, Andrew. *Humanism and America: An Intellectual History of English Colonisation, 1500–1625.* Cambridge: Cambridge University Press, 2003. x, 216 p. ISBN 0521822254; ISBN 9780521822251; OCLC 50519310; LC Call Number E127 .F58; Dewey 325/.341/01 21. Citations: 38.

Examines the sixteenth and early seventeenth-century English intellectual justifications for empire, which were linked to the rise of the state, of Protestantism, of economic nationalism, and of emulation of the Spanish. Studies colonial discourse that reflected tense interaction between English culture and the New World. Points out that classical education (*studia humanitatis*) informed the rules of colonization, using humanistic concepts of moral philosophy, civic life, and private interest. Shows that various works often presented nuanced and conflicted discussions of virtue's transformation to greed or expediency and stresses that anxiety was prevalent partly because of the high stakes and partly because the classical—particularly Roman—models themselves indicated ways in which empire could both ennoble and corrupt.

EHR 118: 1327-29; *JAH* 91: 989-90; *J Mod Hist* 78: 188-90; *16c J* 36: 855-56; *WMQ* 61: 171-73.

90 Garate, Donald T. *Juan Bautista de Anza: Basque Explorer in the New World.* Reno: University of Nevada Press, 2003. xxi, 323 p. ISBN 0874175054; ISBN 9780874175059; OCLC 51293448; LC Call Number F799 .A74; Dewey 979/.01/092. Citations: 12.

Presents an account of Anza's life, beginning with the Basque origins of the name and the Roman conquest of Spain. Discusses his family, decision to emigrate to New Spain in 1712, arrival in Chihuahua, cavalry campaigns against

the Apaches, life on the eighteenth-century Sonoran frontier as a presidial captain, and death at the hands of the Apaches in 1740. Praises Anza's "outstanding accomplishments on one of the wildest, harshest, and least-tamed frontiers of the entire New World."
JAH 91: 603-604; *JAEH* 23: 117-18; *SHQ* 108: 259-60; *SHQ* 112: 216-17; *WHQ* 36: 223-24.

91 Goodfriend, Joyce D., ed. *Revisiting New Netherland: Perspectives on Early Dutch America.* Boston, Mass.: Brill, 2005. xiii, 345 p. ISBN 9004145079; ISBN 9789004145078; OCLC 61478845; LC Call Number F122.1 .R38; Dewey 974.7/020043931 22. Citations: 7.
Presents essays on Director Willem Kieft (1602-1647) and his Dutch relatives, the early years of Petrus Stuyvesant, including business and religious interests, the place of New Netherland in the West India Company's scheme, the importance of New Sweden, Walloons and Huguenots in New Netherland and seventeenth-century New York, Belgian versus Dutch origins of New Amsterdam, the status of and documents related to New Netherland studies, artisans and the making of New Amsterdam, municipal citizenship in New Amsterdam, New Netherland in the nineteenth century, the importance of genealogical studies in understanding the colony more fully, and relations between men and women in New Netherland.
AHR 111: 1472-73.

92   Gragg, Larry. *Englishmen Transplanted: The English Colonization of Barbados, 1627–1660.* New York: Oxford University Press, 2003. vii, 217 p. ISBN 0199253897; ISBN 9780199253890; OCLC 52327594; LC Call Number F2041 .G73; Dewey 972.98100421 21. Citations: 11.
Refutes the idea that Englishmen in Barbados abandoned the cultural norms of their native land, finding instead that institutions—though sometimes slightly modified—were often transplanted. Discusses the Barbadian environment and geography, the island's political history, institutional structures, its labor and economy, the financing of the sugar revolution and the creation of an orderly society, and the impact of the earlier period on the later colonial history of Barbados and other Caribbean islands. Rejects the importance of the Dutch, placing responsibility for the sugar revolution and the slave trade of Barbados with the English and the supply of capital derived from earlier staples of tobacco and cotton. Concludes that the English shippers supplied more slaves than the Dutch did.
HRNB 32: 145-46; *JAH* 92: 184; *WMQ* 61: 753-56.

93 Hofstra, Warren R. *The Planting of New Virginia: Settlement and Landscape in the Shenandoah Valley.* Baltimore, Md.: Johns Hopkins University Press, 2004. xv, 410 p. ISBN 0801874181 (hbk.); ISBN 9780801874185 (hbk.); ISBN 0801882710 (pbk.); ISBN 9780801882715 (pbk.); OCLC 52057399; LC Call Number F232.S5; Dewey 911/.7559. Citations: 19.
Investigates patterns of settlement and economic development in the northern Shenandoah Valley between the 1730s and the early 1800s. Traces changes in the region's evolution from a peripheral region to a "forecountry" that drew

upon commercial ties to the Atlantic trade. Discusses the forces and human agents that shaped the Valley, including the natural environment, the presence of Native American and European immigrants, provincial and British imperial policies, and the impact of trade. Examines property and survey tracts of European settlers in the lower valley during the 1730s and 1740s, noting that the shape of the tracts reflect both the historical effort to settle the region and the specific impact of immigration. Explains that the Virginia government relied upon German and Scots-Irish settlers to occupy the Valley quickly and thereby blunt French expansion.
Ag Hist 80: 129-30; *AHR* 110: 468; *Geog Rev* 96: 320-22; *JAH* 92: 186-87; *JER* 25: 289-92; *J Interdis Hist* 37: 466-68; *J Soc Hist* 39: 574-76; *JSH* 71: 666-67; *NCHR* 84: 99-100; *VMHB* 113: 80-82; *WMQ* 61: 759-61.

94 Horn, James. *A Land As God Made It: Jamestown and the Birth of America.* New York: Basic Books, 2005. xii, 337 p. ISBN 9780465030941; ISBN 0465030947; OCLC 60373719; LC Call Number F234.J3; Dewey 975.5/4251. Citations: 13.
Explores the founding of Jamestown, emphasizing the settlement's significance to American development. Downplays the importance of Pocahontas, noting that her "rescue" of Smith has become imbued with "mythic importance as the transcendent power of love over racial hatred." Reviews the March 1622 Powhatan attack that killed 347 colonists, arguing that it fundamentally altered the relationship between the English and the Native Americans. Discusses the introduction of slavery at Jamestown and the implementation of representative government.
AQ 60: 173-82; *Booklist* 102: 20; *JAH* 93: 493-94; *JSH* 73: 422-24; *LJ* 130n17: 68-69; *RAH* 34: 150-55; *VMHB* 114: 399-400; *WMQ* 63: 597-99.

95 Jasanoff, Maya. *Edge of Empire: Lives, Culture, and the Conquest in the East, 1750–1850.* New York: Alfred A. Knopf, 2005. ix, 404 p. ISBN 1400041678; ISBN 9781400041671; OCLC 57422682; LC Call Number DA16 .J33; Dewey 909/.097124107. Citations: 26.
Challenges the notion that the British imposed culture on its colonies, contending that the empire expanded and was stable because of the colonizers' capabilities to "find ways of accommodating difference." Looks at the objects collected in India and Egypt by diplomats, soldiers, aristocrats, and tourists who, by collecting artifacts, influenced British public perception of eastern colonies. Concludes that the Anglo-French imperial rivalry between 1750 and 1850 sparked the competition to acquire Indian and Egyptian antiquities.
AHR 112: 1140; *Booklist* 101: 1987; *J Brit Stds* 45: 670-72; *LJ* 130n13: 100; *WMQ* 63: 373-76.

96 Kamen, Henry. *Empire: How Spain Became a World Power, 1492–1763.* New York: HarperCollins, 2003. xxviii, 608 p. ISBN 0060194766; ISBN 9780060194765; OCLC 51782952; LC Call Number DP164 .K36; Dewey 946.03. Citations: 23.
Claims that Spanish-Portuguese rivalries dating to the fifteenth century inspired Spain to forge commercial ties with the East, leading to the discovery and

conquest of the Canary Islands and then the New World and that dynastic interests led Spain to compete with France for possession of Lombardy and Naples. Argues that the success of the Spanish resulted from cooperation with—not mere conquest of—various peoples. Explains that the building of the Spanish empire could not have happened without the help of Genoese bankers, Granadan Muslims, Africans, and indigenous American people. Concludes that "in war as in peace," the "power of Spain depended on its allies."
Booklist 99: 965; *LJ* 128n5: 97; *WMQ* 64: 183-94.

97 Price, David A. *Love and Hate in Jamestown: John Smith, Pocahontas, and the Heart of a New Nation.* New York: Alfred A. Knopf, 2003. 305 p. ISBN 0375415416; ISBN 9780375415418; OCLC 51306054; LC Call Number F234.J3; Dewey: 975.5/425101. Citations: 7.
Presents a biography of John Smith that largely covers his involvement in English colonization of North America between 1607 and 1620 and the relationships among Smith, Pocahontas, and Powhatan. Intended for a general readership.
AQ 60: 173-82; *Booklist* 100: 198; *HRNB* 32: 59-60; *JAH* 91: 602-603; *LJ* 128n13: 104; *RAH* 32: 317-28; *VMHB* 111: 413-14; *WMQ* 62: 774-81.

98 Restall, Matthew. *Seven Myths of the Spanish Conquest.* New York: Oxford University Press, 2003. xix, 218 p. ISBN 0195160770; ISBN 9780195160772; OCLC 51022823; LC Call Number F1230 .R47; Dewey 980/.013/072. Citations: 41.
Rejects the "myths" that (1) a limited number of "exceptional" persons (e.g., Christopher Columbus, Hernando Cortés, Francisco Pizarro) were responsible for the conquest; (2) the majority of conquest participants were trained and paid soldiers; (3) the conquistadors were nearly all white Europeans; (4) the conquest was "completed"; (5) the native response is largely unknown, due to problematic language differences and translation; (6) the native populations were virtually wiped out upon contact with the Spanish; and (7) the Spanish prevailed on the basis of cultural and religious superiority. Concludes that "the Conquest was a far more complex and protracted affair" than generally thought and that "the elements of native cultural vitality during the Conquest period" is notable.
AHR 109: 1271-72; *Ethnohistory* 52: 449-77; *HAHR* 87: 370-71; *LJ* 128n13: 104; *16c J* 35: 1208-1210.

99 Sarson, Steven. *British America, 1500–1800: Creating Colonies, Imagining an Empire.* London: Hodder Arnold, 2005. xix, 332 p. ISBN 0340760095 (hbk.); ISBN 9780340760093 (hbk.); ISBN 0340760109 (pbk.); ISBN 9780340760109 (pbk.); OCLC 60775108; LC Call Number JV1011 .S377; Dewey 970.02. Citations: 4.
Examines the tensions inherent in British state colonization and private settlement and emphasizes the importance of British identity in North America and the Caribbean. Contends that the seeds of the split of the United States from Britain were sown in the corporate and private approach to colonization, which was distinct from the Spanish model in which the state assumed an active role from the beginning. Points out that the result was a variety of colonial

experiments that emphasized settler self-government and the ultimate inability of the British state to gain control over eighteenth-century elites who were loyal to the Crown, not to Parliament, and who saw themselves as free British people who would not be ruled and who demanded that Parliament consult them on governance. Stresses the effect of the Glorious Revolution on later events, noting that eighteenth-century Americans were essentially seventeenth-century political creatures.
JSH 72: 909-910; *WMQ* 64: 199-202.

100 Schmidt, Benjamin. *Innocence Abroad: The Dutch Imagination and the New World, 1570–1670.* New York: Cambridge University Press, 2001. xxix, 450 p. ISBN 0521804086; ISBN 9780521804080; OCLC 46386144; LC Call Number PT5145.A47; Dewey 839.3/1093273. Citations: 45.
Investigates the influence of the New World on the formation of seventeenth-century Dutch national identity. Discusses impact on the Dutch of the notion of Spanish tyranny in America, of Bartolomé de Las Casas's critique of Spanish treatment of indigenous peoples, and of the failures of various Dutch enterprises in America. Contends that the American experience remained in the collective Dutch memory "as part of the very fabric of the commemorative tapestry of the Republic's foundation" and that the Dutch in turn influenced wider European images of America.
AHR 108: 800; *HAHR* 83: 567-68; *J Interdis Hist* 33: 650-51; *J Mod Hist* 75: 978-80; *RAH* 31: 14-23; *16c J* 35: 206-207.

101 Shorto, Russell. *The Island at the Center of the World: The Epic Story of Dutch Manhattan and the Forgotten Colony that Shaped America.* New York: Doubleday, 2004. xiv, 384 p. ISBN 0385503490; ISBN 9780385503495; OCLC 52477207; LC Call Number F128.4 .S56; Dewey 974.7/102. Citations: 21.
Studies the Dutch colonization in New Netherland in Atlantic context. Highlights the importance of New Amsterdam to the development of American culture, particularly in its "tolerance, openness, and free trade."
Booklist 100: 1262; *JAH* 92: 183-84; *LJ* 129n3: 142.

102 Stein, Stanley J. and Barbara H. Stein. *Apogee of Empire: Spain and New Spain in the Age of Charles III, 1759-1789.* Baltimore, Md.: Johns Hopkins University Press, 2003. ix, 464 p. ISBN 0801873398; ISBN 9780801873393; OCLC 50510850; LC Call Number HF3685 .S737; Dewey 382/.0946/08. Citations: 29.
Focuses on economic and political reforms undertaken in the reign of Charles III. Contends that these reforms had limited effects, largely due to opposition from traditional elites, because the reforms did not go far enough, because of inflexible policies regarding trade and colonies, and because of nearly constant conflict with other European powers.
AHR 113: 139-40; *CJH* 40: 504-506; *Econ Hist Rev* 58: 213-14; *18c Stds* 38: 539-45; *J Interdis Hist* 36: 96-97; *J Mod Hist* 78: 240-42.

5 Maritime

103 Bannister, Jerry. *The Rule of the Admirals: Law, Custom, and Naval Government in Newfoundland, 1699–1832.* Toronto: University of Toronto Press, for the Osgoode Society for Canadian Legal History, 2003. xix, 423 p. ISBN 0802088430 (hbk.); ISBN 9780802088437 (hbk.); ISBN 0802086136 (pbk.); ISBN 9780802086136 (pbk.); OCLC 53940063; LC Call Number KEN1365 .B35; LC Call Number JL205; Dewey 347.718. Citations: 15.
Studies Newfoundland government from its control by fishing admirals in 1699 to the beginning of representative government in 1832. Notes that under King William's Act of 1699, the master of the first fishing vessel to reach a Newfoundland port each spring became the admiral responsible for adjudicating fishing disputes. Argues that these admirals "did not play a central role in [Newfoundland's] legal development." Contends instead that by the mid-eighteenth century the Royal Navy was firmly in charge of the island and that rule by naval officers created in Newfoundland "a distinct legal culture" that relied heavily on customary and common law. Notes that whipping became "a hallmark of naval rule," but was largely applied to members of the lower orders, such as servants, laborers, and fishermen. Explains that planters and merchants who ran afoul of the law were typically given fines and that these wealthier sorts manipulated the justice system to protect property and control laborers and servants. Contends that class was the main determiner of punishments, but that anti-Catholic and anti-Irish sentiment constantly lurked below the surface. Concludes that Newfoundland's close connections to Britain brought about its transformation from naval to representative government.
AHR 110: 459-60; *CHR* 86: 356-59.

104 Davis, William C. *The Pirates Laffite: The Treacherous World of the Corsairs of the Gulf.* New York: Harcourt, 2005. xiv, 706 p. ISBN 015100403X;

ISBN 9780151004034; OCLC 57366449; LC Call Number F374.L2; LC Call Number G537.L35; Dewey 976.3/05/0922. Citations: 8.

Discusses the lives and work of pirate brothers Jean and Pierre Laffite, attributing their success to the tariffs and boycotts spawned by the Napoleonic Wars, which encouraged smuggling and legalized piracy. Argues that the two Laffites were essentially businessmen from a French middle-class merchant background who took advantage of the chaos in the Gulf of Mexico. Notes that pirates undercut legitimate merchants and that some feared that the Laffites would "dominate the economy of Louisiana." Demonstrates that pirates traded effectively in both goods and information and that the U.S. government used piracy as diplomatic leverage with Spain.

Booklist 101: 1338; *JAH* 93: 202-203; *JSH* 72: 921-22; *LJ* 130n8: 100-101.

105 Fisher, Vivian C., ed. *Esteban José Martínez: His Voyage in 1779 to Supply Alta California.* By Esteban José Martínez. Berkeley: Bancroft Library, University of California, 2002. xii, 269 p. ISBN 1893663159; ISBN 9781893663152; OCLC 50803619; LC Call Number F864 .M28; Dewey 979.4/02. Citations: 1.

Provides a translated and edited version of Martínez's diary, transcribed from the original in the Bancroft Library. Describes Martínez's command of the supply vessel Santiago, which sailed from San Blas on the Pacific coast of New Spain to Alta California and back again in 1779. Notes that the diary fulfilled the "functions of a log, journal, and report." Provides entries at sea from both outbound and inbound voyages that focus largely on daily challenges of navigation. Discusses faith in God, and divine credit for curing sick sailors, providing favorable winds, and keeping the vessel safe. Records impressions of the nascent communities of San Francisco, Monterey, and San Diego, focusing on physical structures and demographic profiles of the presidios and missions and the crops grown at the missions. Describes San Francisco as foggy, cold, and damp, and the entrance to the bay difficult to navigate. Explains difficulties in unloading cargo and transporting it to warehouses with insufficient local mules. Includes a glossary of maritime terms, annotations on flora and fauna, and appendices that list the ships that sailed up the coast from San Blas in the Spanish era (1769–1809) and the goods that they carried. Provides a transcription of the entire diary in readable Spanish that preserves most of the elements of the original.

HAHR 84: 521-22.

106 Gilje, Paul A. *Liberty on the Waterfront: American Maritime Culture in the Age of Revolution.* Philadelphia: University of Pennsylvania Press, 2003. xiv, 344 p. ISBN 0812237560; ISBN 9780812237566; OCLC 52980696; LC Call Number E182 .G55; Dewey 305.9/3875/097309033 22. Citations: 30.

Surveys the United States naval history from the Revolution through the 1840s, focusing on how sailors themselves viewed the politics of seafaring. Studies the concept of "liberty" among sailors, finding that it typically meant personal freedom (wandering, access to women, drinking). Discusses American sailors confined in British prisoner of war camps, whalers, explorers and adventurers,

and shipwrights and ship carpenters, arguing "that the boundary between those on board ship and on the docks was not that clear cut."
JAH 91: 1427-28; *JER* 24: 675-78; *J Interdis Hist* 36: 103-105; *J Soc Hist* 38: 1123-24; *J Soc Hist* 40: 731-43; *NEQ* 77: 651-53; *RAH* 32: 341-46; *WMQ* 62: 331-33.

107 Gwyn, Julian. *An Admiral for America: Sir Peter Warren, Vice Admiral of the Red, 1703-1752.* Gainesville: University Press of Florida, 2004. xiv, 228 p. ISBN 0813027098; ISBN 9780813027098; OCLC 53435220; LC Call Number DA87.1.W35; Dewey 973.2/6. Citations: 3.
Traces Warren's career from enlistment in the navy in 1716 to his death in 1752. Contends that "The most striking aspect of his life and career was his remarkable rise," which combined patronage and raw talent as a naval commander. Explains Warren's rise from a common Irish Catholic family to Parliament and status as an English country gentleman. Notes that Warren was very successful in capturing enemy prizes, including the French fortress of Louisbourg, and that he used the prize money to purchase real estate in America, Ireland, and England and invest in the English stock market. Finds that Warren's marriage to a New Yorker brought him the respect of the colonists and that his affection for the colonies influenced his desire to destroy French Canada so that British North America could expand. Uses "both the Royal Navy and Peter Warren as a lens through which to view the interconnectedness of the British Atlantic World."
EHR 120: 230-31; *JAH* 92: 196-97; *J Mil Hist* 68: 1251-53.

108 Lambert, Frank. *The Barbary Wars: American Independence in the Atlantic World.* New York: Hill and Wang, 2005. 228 p. ISBN 0809095335; ISBN 9780809095339; ISBN 0809028115; ISBN 9780809028115; OCLC 56329545; LC Call Number E335 .L36; Dewey 973.4/7. Citations: 12.
Argues that the Barbary Wars represented an American struggle for the exercise of free trade, not a battle between faiths or cultures. Reviews the challenges that the United States faced in navigating the dangers presented by French and British privateers, while attempting to build a viable navy and to bridge the gap between northern Federalist merchants and southern Jeffersonian farmers and planters. Discusses the conflicts between the United States and Morocco, Algiers, and Tripoli from 1784 to 1816, noting the domestic debates that these wars triggered, the relationship of these piracy conflicts to the War of 1812, and the impact of Barbary defeat on the long-term North African power decline. Explains that, for Americans, North African tyranny flowed directly from its lack of religious toleration and that tyranny, not Islam itself, was antithetical to the early republic's rhetoric of liberty.
AHR 111: 1475-76; *JAH* 93: 201-202; *J Mil Hist* 70: 509-510; *LJ* 130n13: 101.

109 Marsters, Roger. *Bold Privateers: Terror, Plunder, and Profit on Canada's Atlantic Coast.* Halifax, N.S.: Formac, 2004. 128 p. ISBN 0887806449 (pbk.); ISBN 9780887806445 (pbk.); OCLC 233646166; LC Call Number KZ6573 .M37; Dewey 910.4/5. Citations: 1.

Surveys French and Nova Scotian privateering from the 1680s until the end of the War of 1812. Provides background on the international conflicts that gave rise to privateering, noting that privateers such as Frenchmen Pierre LeMoyne d'Iberville, Pierre Maisonnat, Pierre Morpain, Jean-Vincent d'Abaddie and his son, Bernard Anselme d'Abaddie, the third and fourth Barons of Saint-Castin, Joannis-Galand d'Olabaratz, and Englishmen and New Englanders John Rous and Sylvannus Cobb played a variety of roles in colonial naval and military operations, ranging from full-scale attacks on fortifications and naval forces to shipping, transmitting messages, and collecting military intelligence. Intended for a general audience.
CHR 87: 353-54.

110 Rediker, Marcus. *Villains of All Nations: Atlantic Pirates in the Golden Age*. Boston, Mass.: Beacon Press, 2004. 256 p. ISBN 0807050245 (hbk.); ISBN 9780807050248 (hbk.); ISBN 9780807050255 (pbk.); ISBN 0807050253 (pbk.); OCLC 53186528; LC Call Number F106 .R42; Dewey 910.4/5. Citations: 26.
Focuses on European piracy in the years after Queen Anne's War, when governments turned their navies against pirates, which in turn resulted in greater violence and brutality on the part of the pirates. Notes that pirates were largely poor and often mutineers, who sought to control their own working conditions, that they usually acted collectively, and that there were significant examples of female pirates (e.g., Anne Bonny and Mary Read). Finds that pirates risked death rather than submit to authority and valued fraternity, equality, and inclusiveness.
JAH 92: 587-88; *JSH* 71: 868-69; *NEQ* 78: 142-44; *WMQ* 62: 334-36.

111 Vickers, Daniel and Vince Walsh. *Young Men and the Sea: Yankee Seafarers in the Age of Sail*. New Haven, Conn.: Yale University Press, 2005. xiii, 336 p. ISBN 0300100671 (hbk.); ISBN 9780300100679 (hbk.); ISBN 9780300123661 (pbk); ISBN 0300123663 (pbk); OCLC 56798950; LC Call Number F4 .V53; Dewey 387.5/09744/5. Citations: 17.
Examines the maritime aspects of Massachusetts, particularly Salem, noting that at its settlement it was an agricultural community and that it needed a decade or so to gain a maritime identity. Finds that most maritime ventures were small in scale and duration, that seaman were longtime acquaintances of those with whom they set sail, that vessel command was orderly and rarely challenged, that shipside deference was similar to that in effect on land, and that occupational mobility was limited by high mortality rates among sailors.
AHR 111: 1167-68; *JAH* 93: 186-87; *JER* 26: 164-67; *J Interdis Hist* 37: 463-65; *NEQ* 79: 134-36; *WMQ* 63: 416-18.

6 Native Americans

112 Allen, Paula Gunn. *Pocahontas: Medicine Woman, Spy, Entrepreneur, Diplomat*. San Francisco, Calif.: Harper Collins, 2003. xvi, 350 p. ISBN 006053687X; ISBN 9780060536879; OCLC 52455559; LC Call Number E99.P85; Dewey 975.5/01/092. Citations: 6.

Recounts the life of Pocahontas using the native narrative tradition that rejects western, academic rules of evidence and relies instead upon stories transmitted orally and upon "music, herbology, architecture, construction, cooking, pottery casting, etc." Seeks to remake "the entire life system: that community of living things, geography, climate, spirit people, and supernaturals" of Native Americans, including the myths of Pocahontas and "the worldview that informed her actions and character." Draws upon stories from a variety of Indian groups, including those of the Great Lakes and southwest regions. Claims that Pocahontas was not the daughter of Powhatan, but was rather a "shaman-priestess [and] sorcerer," who maintained membership in a secret society of medicine men and women. Interprets the rescue of John Smith as part of a traditional ceremony, a "ritual death and remaking" of Smith as a Powhatan Indian. Contends that Pocahontas had foreseen the coming of the English, was a political leader in her own right, and played a key role in the development of tobacco as a mainstay crop. Concludes that her husband John Rolfe poisoned her in order to prevent her from communicating to her tribesmen knowledge of English society.

AQ 60: 173-82; *LJ* 128n16: 88; *WMQ* 62: 774-81.

113 Barnes, Celia. *Native American Power in the United States, 1783–1795*. Madison, N.J.: Fairleigh Dickinson University Press, 2003. 250 p. ISBN 0838639585; ISBN 9780838639580; OCLC 50868257; LC Call Number E98.T77; Dewey 973.04/97. Citations: 4.

Examines the role of Native American power in shaping post-Revolutionary America, particularly the impact of Indian military and politics on the British and the Spanish. Discusses the settlement of trans-Appalachian lands, the American treatment of Indian allies of the British as conquered populations, Spain's use of Indian allies in the southwest and southeast, and the conflicts, negotiations, and treaties among Europeans, Americans, and Native Americans through 1795. Points out that the Native American tendency to decentralization presented special challenges to various nations in their negotiations with Indian officials. Contends that, despite these difficulties, "The influence and power of the Native Americans within the United States was pervasive," but that this power dissipated by 1795 in the wake of the treaties of Greenville and San Lorenzo.
AHR 109: 1224-25; *FHQ* 83: 195-97; *GHQ* 88: 99-101.

114 Bickham, Troy O. *Savages within the Empire: Representations of American Indians in Eighteenth-Century Britain.* New York: Oxford University Press, 2005. viii, 301 p. ISBN 0199286965; ISBN 9780199286966; OCLC 61151427; LC Call Number E77 .B584; Dewey 973.04/97. Citations: 10.
Traces British perceptions of Native Americans, as gleaned from material and print culture, travel narratives, speeches, sermons, government policy, missionary documents, and public reactions to the use of Indian allies in the Revolutionary War. Explains that, prior to the eighteenth century, the British regarded Native Americans as mere curiosities, but that by 1750 the British had begun to view Indians as "real peoples living in real places" and as "key players in a struggle that would determine whether or not the British nation would endure and prosper." Finds that the British public was fascinated by American Natives during the Seven Years' War and sought out accurate information on the various tribes, but that people generally disapproved of the British use of Indians as allies against the American rebels during the Revolutionary War. Concludes that "American Indians loomed larger in the eighteenth-century British imagination than any other non-Europeans."
J Brit Stds 46: 397-99; *WMQ* 67: 145.

115 Binnema, Thedore. *Common and Contested Ground: A Human and Environmental History of the Northwestern Plains.* Norman: University of Oklahoma Press, 2001. xvi, 263 p. ISBN 0806133619; ISBN 9780806133614; OCLC 46785408; LC Call Number E78.G73; Dewey 978/.00497. Citations: 32.
Examines the history of the northwestern plains from roughly 200 to 1806, focusing on plants, animals, native peoples, and the movement of settlers and fur traders westward. Discusses the impact of technology, from the bow and arrow to the horse and European weapons. Explains that a virulent smallpox strain from Santa Fe (1780) spread through trade and raiding parties northward to Hudson's Bay, destroying two-thirds of the indigenous population and restructuring tribal groups.
CHR 84: 108-110; *JAH* 90: 222; *PHR* 72: 450-51; *WHQ* 34: 80-81.

116 Blum, Rony. *Ghost Brothers: Adoption of a French Tribe by Bereaved Native America: A Transdisciplinary Longitudinal Multilevel Integrated*

Analysis. Montreal: McGill-Queen's University Press, 2005. xii, 448 p. ISBN 0773528288; ISBN 9780773528284; OCLC 69241607; LC Call Number F1030 .B68; Dewey 971.01/6. Citations: 3.

Studies the French relationship with Native American tribes in the seventeenth century, focusing on similarities and differences among them on matters of gender roles, law and politics, personal conduct, and subsistence. Uses "twinning" as an analytical device to show relationships among persons and ideas, particularly the notion of shared grief. Notes that Native American groups held memories of those killed by conflict and disease, while the French shared similar traumas and thus were able to form bonds with the Wendat, Innu, and Iroquois.

CHR 87: 507-509.

117   Borch, Merete Falck. *Conciliation—Compulsion—Conversion: British Attitudes towards Indigenous Peoples, 1763–1814*. New York: Rodopi, 2004. xvi, 318 p. ISBN 9042019425 9789042019423 9042019328 9789042019324; OCLC 57010857; LC Call Number JV1035 .F35; Dewey 305.8009171241. Citations: 5.

Studies British views of and policies toward natives in the American colonies, New South Wales, and the South African Cape, between the mid-eighteenth and early nineteenth centuries. Examines European legal notions of indigenous land rights and views on racial differences. Asserts that these ideas directly affected efforts to dispossess and marginalize natives.

EHR 120: 844-45; *JAH* 92: 958-59.

118   Brandão, José António, ed. *Nation Iroquoise: A Seventeenth-Century Ethnography of the Iroquois*. By René Cuillerier. Lincoln: University of Nebraska Press, 2003. xiii, 150 p. ISBN 0803213239; ISBN 9780803213234; OCLC 52107718; LC Call Number E99.I7 N3713; Dewey 974.7004/9755 21. Citations: 8.

Publishes an unsigned and undated manuscript found in the Bibliotheque Mazarine in Paris and in the National Archives of Canada in Ottawa. Provides a first-person account of society and of daily life among the seventeenth-century Oneida. Describes the role of women in tribal councils, Oneida religious beliefs and rituals, warfare, mortuary customs, the clan system, impact of alcohol, diplomacy, and the plants, animals, and lands of the territory controlled by the Oneida Iroquois. Presents the original French document and its English translation, the piece's background, and theories regarding authorship.

CHR 86: 144-45.

119   Bross, Kristina. *Dry Bones and Indian Sermons: Praying Indians and Colonial American Identity*. Ithaca, N.Y.: Cornell University Press, 2004. x, 257 p. ISBN 0801442060 (hbk.); ISBN 9780801442063 (hbk.); ISBN 0801489385 (pbk.); ISBN 9780801489389 (pbk.); OCLC 53098983; LC Call Number PS173.I6; Dewey 810.9/352997. Citations: 23.

Examines the idea of the "praying Indian" from the writings of John Eliot and others in the 1640s through the aftermath of King Philip's War. Places this image at the center of colonial discourse, noting that "the Praying Indian was a figure in transatlantic meditations on scriptural prophecy and colonial clashes over town boundaries; in colonial translation practices and the early Christian Indian church; in reports of the Antinomian controversy and in transatlantic debates over the New England Way; in experiments in early American fiction and English-Indian diplomacy; in war histories and captivity narratives." Calls the emphasis on Indian conversion the new Puritan errand, one that grew in importance after the failure of the Puritan Revolution in England. Concludes that "The presence of Indians, not just the idea of Indians as related to the frontier, savagism, natural nobility, or removal, shaped colonial evangelical literature." *AHR* 110: 1161; *EAL* 40: 375-85; *JAH* 92: 189-90; *NEQ* 78: 130-33; *WMQ* 61: 747-50.

120 Calloway, Colin G. *One Vast Winter Count: The Native American West before Lewis and Clark*. Lincoln: University of Nebraska Press, 2003. xx, 631 p. ISBN 0803215304 (hbk.); ISBN 9780803215306 (hbk.); ISBN 0803264658 (pbk.); ISBN 9780803264656 (pbk.); OCLC 51769031; LC Call Number E78.W5; Dewey 978/.01. Citations: 36.
Surveys Native American history through the early nineteenth century. Describes the rise and fall of various pre-Columbian empires in the Southwest and the Mississippi valley, the causes of their collapses, and their surviving legacies at the time of contact with Europeans. Emphasizes the role of environmental and biological causes in Indian demographic changes, particularly a smallpox epidemic that spread through the West in the 1770s and 1780s.
AHR 110: 136-37; *Booklist* 100: 196; *Ethnohistory* 52: 635-41; *FHQ* 83: 331-33; *HRNB* 32: 101; *IMH* 100: 393-94; *JAH* 91: 594-95; *J Mil Hist* 70: 225-26; *LJ* 128n14: 183; *PHR* 73: 504-505; *SHQ* 108: 110; *WHQ* 36: 71.

121 Calloway, Colin G. and Neal Salisbury, eds. *Reinterpreting New England Indians and the Colonial Experience*. Boston: Colonial Society of Massachusetts, distributed by the University of Virginia Press, 2003. 380 p. ISBN 0962073768; ISBN 9780962073762; ISBN 9780979466250; ISBN 0979466253; OCLC 54402725; LC Call Number F61 .C71 v.72; Dewey 974.004/9734. Citations: 18.
Presents ten essays covering the Native American response to European animals in New England, translation and interculturism in the John Eliot tracts, colonization and consciousness, late seventeenth- and early eighteenth-century Indian slavery, slavery among Native American children in Rhode Island, Wheelock's Indians and Christian identity in the decade prior to the American Revolution, Native American women, churches and Indians on Cape Cod, Mashpee autonomy in the late eighteenth and early nineteenth centuries, and crafts among New England Indians.
HRNB 33: 104; *JAEH* 25: 105-106; *JAH* 91: 1424-25; *WMQ* 62: 319-24.

122 Carpenter, Roger M. *The Renewed, the Destroyed, and the Remade: The Three Thought Worlds of the Iroquois and the Huron, 1609-1650*. East Lansing: Michigan State University Press, 2004. xxii, 179 p. ISBN 087013728X (pbk.);

ISBN 9780870137280 (pbk.); OCLC 55597142; LC Call Number E99.I7 C37; Dewey 973.04/9755. Citations: 4.

Focuses on "thought worlds"—culturally adapted modes of thought—which explain human behavior. Argues that the modes of thinking of the Five Nations Iroquois and the Hurons defined the ways in which the groups responded to European incursions. Explains that "renewal" was a key theme to both groups, but that this trope placed limits on "technological imagination" and virtually precluded innovation. Finds that Huron demand for European goods led to rapid transformation of the group's hunting habits and view of the world, which led to disunity and domination of the Hurons by the Five Nations Iroquois, who had become remade in such a way as to bring "other peoples into their confederacy." *AHR* 111: 821-22; *CJH* 41: 204-206; *Ethnohistory* 54: 764-66.

123 Clark, Michael P., ed. *The Eliot Tracts: With Letters from John Eliot to Thomas Thorowgood and Richard Baxter.* Westport, Conn.: Praeger Publishers, 2003. vi, 452 p. ISBN 0313304882; ISBN 9780313304880; OCLC 51615317; LC Call Number E78.N5; Dewey 266.008997074. Citations: 4.

Describes the history of New England Protestant mission work and the millennial theology motivating it, the so-called "Praying Towns," and the specific vision of John Eliot, which was imperialistic in nature. Notes that the eleven pamphlets making up the Eliot Tracts were "cobbled together hurriedly by authors and editors struggling to provide support for various measures in Parliament related to the missionary efforts." Explains that Eliot primarily authored four of the tracts and that the other authors included Thomas Shepard, Edward Winslow, Henry Whitfield, and Thomas Mayhew, Jr. Reprints the eleven pamphlets and letters from Eliot to Thomas Thorowgood and to Richard Baxter and concludes that the Tracts "serve as a comparatively modest but important counterpart to the *Jesuit Relations in New France* and to the missionary work described as part of the conquistador narratives of New Spain." *EAL* 40: 375-85; *NEQ* 78: 127-30.

124 Deeds, Susan M. *Defiance and Deference in Mexico's Colonial North: Indians under Spanish Rule in Nueva Vizcaya.* Austin: University of Texas Press, 2003. xiii, 300 p. ISBN 0292705204 (hbk.); ISBN 9780292705203 (hbk.); ISBN 0292705514 (pbk.); ISBN 9780292705517 (pbk.); OCLC 51041275; LC Call Number F1219.1.C46; Dewey 972/.150049745. Citations: 1.

Examines five semi-sedentary and non-sedentary indigenous groups in Nueva Vizcaya, from the first Spanish missionary efforts among them in the late sixteenth century through the mid-eighteenth century. Concludes that the groups that maintained the most cohesive ethnic identities were those most physically isolated from the Spanish. *AHR* 109: 1611-12; *Ethnohistory* 52: 494-96; *HAHR* 84: 527-28; *J Soc Hist* 37: 1107-1109; *16c J* 35: 945-47; *SHQ* 108: 112-13; *WHQ* 35: 519-20.

125 Dixon, David. *Never Come to Peace Again: Pontiac's Uprising and the Fate of the British Empire in North America.* Norman: University of Oklahoma Press, 2005. xvii, 353 p. ISBN 0806136561; ISBN 9780806136561; OCLC 469780473; LC Call Number E83.76 .D595; Dewey 973.27. Citations: 10.

Places the Pontiac's War in the context of the frontier settlement of the Ohio country prior to the Seven Years' War, and traces Anglo-Indian relations from the French and Indian War through the end of Pontiac's Uprising in the winter of 1764–65. Extends the narrative through the American Revolution and the history of the Ohio country through the Battle of Fallen Timbers. Points out that Pontiac's War was a successful Indian uprising in that it delayed European settlement of the Ohio country until the 1790s. Argues that perceived failure of British and colonial frontier policy served to radicalize the backcountry and move its settlers to revolution much sooner than coastal and urban areas. Concludes that Pontiac's War had a much greater impact on American government than previous historians have suggested.
AHR 111: 1505-1506; *IMH* 102: 381-82; *JAH* 93: 187-88; *JER* 26: 125-28; *J Mil Hist* 70: 1118-19; *VMHB* 114: 297-99; *WMQ* 63: 870-72.

126 Dowd, Gregory Evans. *War under Heaven: Pontiac, the Indian Nations, and the British Empire*. Baltimore, Md.: Johns Hopkins University Press, 2002. xviii, 360 p. ISBN 0801870798; ISBN 9780801870798; OCLC 48876479; LC Call Number E83.76 .D69; Dewey 973.2/7. Citations: 41.
Maintains that Pontiac's War demonstrates the British failure to grasp the implications of victory in the Seven Years' War and set the stage both for early republican denial of sovereign nation status to Native Americans and for their westward removal. Contends that, after 1763, subjects of the British Empire in North America maintained a belief in their own cultural superiority, which encouraged the Pontiac uprising. Points out that specific triggers included the elimination of traditional gifts from diplomatic transactions, British occupation of former French posts, and personal insults against Algonquian peoples. Explains that these mundane causes were compounded by Native spiritual awakenings. Finds that both the Natives and the British were losers, the former because the way was cleared for status as "domestic dependent nations" and the latter because the imperial government essentially surrendered to the colonists the management of Indian affairs.
AHR 109: 891; *18c Stds* 42: 458-62; *EHR* 120: 787-89; *Ethnohistory* 52: 635-41; *IMH* 100: 258-60; *JAH* 90: 994-95; *J Mil Hist* 67: 559-60; *LJ* 127n18: 104; *RAH* 31: 363-71; *WHQ* 35: 240-41; *WMQ* 60: 865-69.

127 Ellingson, Ter. *The Myth of the Noble Savage*. Berkeley: University of California Press, 2001. xxii, 445 p. ISBN 0520222687 (hbk.); ISBN 9780520222687 (hbk.); ISBN 0520226100 (pbk.); ISBN 9780520226104 (pbk.); OCLC 42960588; LC Call Number GN33 .E44; Dewey 301/.01 21. Citations: 36.
Views the term "noble savage" as a rhetorical construct rather than a substantive object and contends that the construction was a mythic hoax perpetrated for political reasons. Finds that the myth became embedded in anthropological and popular thought and continues today, but that it originated from a misinterpretation of Rousseau, who merely referred to the "savage" way of life as a prop to criticize aspects of European civilization. Explains that Rousseau saw the "savage" as free from the complexities of more developed societies and

thus happier and in some ways more fortunate. Concludes that Rousseau did not, however, extend his argument to include the nobility of "savages."
JAH 88: 1499-1500; *JHG* 28: 622-26.

128 Ethridge, Robbie. *Creek Country: The Creek Indians and Their World.* Chapel Hill: University of North Carolina Press, 2003. xiv, 369 p. ISBN 0807828270 (hbk.); ISBN 9780807828274 (hbk.); ISBN 0807854956 (pbk.); ISBN 9780807854952 (pbk.); OCLC 52312190; LC Call Number E99.C9; Dewey 976.004973. Citations: 29.
Surveys Creek history from late prehistory to removal to Oklahoma. Relies upon the testimony of Benjamin Hawkins on Creek society, based on his career in Creek country from1796 to 1816. Focuses on the environment and lifeways connected with subsistence, and on changes brought about by European and American influences. Examines the flora and fauna and geographical features of Creek territory, Creek social organization and towns, hunting and gathering, and the development of a gendered division of labor. Finds that by the nineteenth century the Creek reliance on farming and adoption of European values regarding property resulted in relatively wide dispersal of Creek settlements. Notes that American encroachment on Creek lands triggered Creek retaliation and American revenge, increasing frontier tensions and leading eventually to war that spelled the end of Creek country.
AHR 110: 783-84; *Ethnohistory* 53: 753-64; *GHQ* 88: 433-34; *JER* 25: 674-77; *JAH* 91: 1443-44; *JSH* 71: 433-34; *NCHR* 81: 343-44; *RAH* 32: 374-79.

129 Ethridge, Robbie, Marvin T. Smith, and Charles Husdon, eds. *The Transformation of the Southeastern Indians, 1540–1760.* Jackson: University Press of Mississippi, 2002. xl, 369 p. ISBN 1578063515; ISBN 9781578063512; OCLC 50418218; LC Call Number E78.S65; Dewey 975/.00497. Citations: 39.
Presents articles on population movements in the post-contact Southeast, the smallpox epidemic of 1696–1700, the persistence of chiefly power under the Spanish mission system, the influence of seventeenth-century Virginia, the Carolina Creek Indians in the late seventeenth and eighteenth centuries, Indians in the Ohio Valley from the mid-sixteenth through the mid-eighteenth centuries, the North Carolina piedmont "cultural landscape" at the point of contact, the coalescence of Cherokee communities in southern Appalachia, the long sweep of history in the northern lower Mississippi Valley, the Mississippi Indian communities in the colonial period, and sixteenth- and seventeenth-century social changes among the Caddo Indians.
Ethnohistory 51: 171; *JAH* 89: 1498-99; *JSH* 69: 667-69; *NCHR* 79: 465.

130 Gallay, Alan. *The Indian Slave Trade: The Rise of the English Empire in the American South, 1670–1717.* New Haven, Conn.: Yale University Press, 2002. xviii, 444 p. ISBN 0300087543 (hbk.); ISBN 9780300087543 (hbk.); ISBN 0300101937 (pbk.); ISBN 9780300101935 (pbk.); OCLC 48013653; LC Call Number HT1162 .G35; Dewey 381/.44/0975 21. Citations: 46.
Explores nations' competition for slave labor, starting with the Mississippian chiefdoms, noting that there was a long, pre-Columbian history of slave raiding among tribes in the South. Discusses Indian slave trade, particularly among the

English, and the trade's influence on personal wealth, colonial policies, and Indian alliances and enmities. Explains that the English success with Indians in the South came from the protection that English alliances offered vis-à-vis slave raids (i.e., only captured enemies could be legitimate slaves, in the eyes of the English). Traces the creation of Indian confederacies for defensive purposes, and thus the development of tribal systems, and discusses South Carolina Indian policy in the context of the imperial Whig-Tory political divide. Contends that, at the beginning of the eighteenth century, the Indian slave trade created a distinct region that connected southern peoples, both European and Native Americans, in diplomatic, economic, and cultural activity in the South.
AHR 108: 823-24; *Ethnohistory* 51: 171; *FHQ* 82: 91-93; *GHQ* 86: 288-90; *HRNB* 30: 102; *JAH* 89: 1506-1507; *J Soc Hist* 37: 265-66; *JSH* 69: 670-71; *NCHR* 79: 466-67; *RAH* 31: 192-203; *WMQ* 60: 677-80.

131 Gallivan, Martin D. *James River Chiefdoms: The Rise of Social Inequality in the Chesapeake*. Lincoln: University of Nebraska Press, 2003. xvii, 295 p. ISBN 080322186X; ISBN 9780803221864; OCLC 51769017; LC Call Number E99.P85 G35; Dewey 975.5004/973 21. Citations: 8.
Traces the evolution of social hierarchy among the Powhatan Indians of Virginia, through James River valley archaeology and accounts of early colonists. Finds that between 1200 and 1500 the Powhatans moved from a foraging, egalitarian, nomadic culture to one that relied upon crop cultivation and that created permanent villages ruled by a group of elites. Argues that chiefs exercised cultural authority, but that village councils comprised of commoners made the decisions. Explains that the evolution of hierarchy accompanied a decrease in inter-village communication, resulting in clear differentiation between the peoples of the Coastal Plain and those of the Piedmont and Ridge and Valley, who were in constant conflict by the seventeenth century. Argues that no single cause can account for these changes, but that cultural choices and actions played a major part.
JAS 39: 316-17; *VMHB* 112: 64-66.

132 Hackel, Steven W. *Children of Coyote, Missionaries of Saint Francis: Indian-Spanish Relations in Colonial California, 1769–1850*. Chapel Hill: University of North Carolina Press, published for the Omohundro Institute of Early American History and Culture, 2005. xx, 476 p. ISBN 0807829889 (hbk.); ISBN 9780807829882 (hbk.); ISBN 0807856541 (pbk.); ISBN 9780807856543 (pbk.); OCLC 58050671; LC Call Number E78.C15; Dewey 979.4/7602. Citations: 34.
Explores power and religion at Mission San Carlos in the Monterey region, discussing the Costanoan and Esselen linguistic groups. Notes that California Indians were not agricultural at the time of European arrival because they were able to support a fairly dense population through trade and the production of local berry bushes and nut trees. Explains that Indians came to missions because of European diseases and increased reliance upon European plants and animals for food. Notes that the missions organized Indian labor into agricultural production efficiently and that Franciscans encouraged mission settlement by focusing on practice over doctrine. Points out that religious art, priestly

vestments, music, and elaborate holy day processions gave mission Indians and Franciscans a shared sense of the sacred, despite disagreements on meanings. Finds that Franciscans were very strict in matters of sexuality and other matters, but that "Indians pursued a variety of survival strategies rooted in their cultures," which "often unintentionally reinforced colonists' hold on the region." Contends that, despite the strong influence of the Spaniards, Indians influenced the missions and helped the mission system succeed and eventually effect cultural change.

AHR 112: 901-902; *HAHR* 86: 827-28; *JAH* 93: 855-56; *JAEH* 25: 174-77; *JER* 26: 489-92; *J Interdis Hist* 38: 131-33; *J Relig Hist* 32: 377-79; *PHR* 76: 273-74; *RAH* 34: 259-69; *SHQ* 110: 292-93; *WHQ* 38: 73-74; *WMQ* 64: 194-99.

133 Haefeli, Evan and Kevin Sweeney. *Captors and Captives: The 1704 French and Indian Raid on Deerfield.* Amherst: University of Massachusetts Press, 2003. xv, 376 p. ISBN 1558494197; ISBN 9781558494190; ISBN 1558495037; ISBN 9781558495036; OCLC 52134728; LC Call Number E99.A13; Dewey 973.2/5. Citations: 29.
Describes and analyzes the February 1704 raid on Deerfield, Massachusetts, examining the fate of the residents, and the causes and effects of the attack. Explores the various interests of Canadian colonists, French officials, New Englanders, Kahnawake Mohawks, and the Iroquois and the ways in which captors and victims related to one another. Finds that competition for captives "helped drive the war and undercut it" in that it resulted in ransom money, while creating contention that alienated traditionalist Indians and precluded continued cooperation.

AHR 110: 128-29; *J Brit Stds* 44: 574-75; *CJH* 40: 131-32; *JAH* 91: 991-92; *J Brit Stds* 44: 574-75; *LJ* 128n20: 138; *NEQ* 77: 653-55; *RAH* 32: 151-58; *WMQ* 62: 315-18.

134 Hahn, Steven C. *The Invention of the Creek Nation, 1670–1763.* Lincoln: University of Nebraska Press, 2004. xii, 338 p. ISBN 0803224141; ISBN 9780803224148; OCLC 53903769; LC Call Number E99.C9; Dewey 975.004/97385. Citations: 16.
Surveys the development of the Creek Nation, from its origins and demographic collapse after contact with Spanish explorers, through the end of the Seven Years' War. Focuses on the town of Coweta, arguing that the Nation came into existence between 1670 and 1763 through the responses to Spanish and English colonial pressure, which made use of the strategic Creek geographical position to control land and resources. Explains that this strategy required a continuity of power found in nationhood and an ability to adapt to changing conditions, which was unsuccessful.

AHR 111: 153; *Ethnohistory* 53: 753-64; *GHQ* 88: 545-47; *JAEH* 24: 107-108; *JAH* 92: 584-85; *JSH* 71: 662-63; *NCHR* 82: 96-97; *WHQ* 37: 229-30.

135 Havard, Gilles. *Empire et Métissages: Indiens et Français dans le Pays d'en Haut, 1660-1715.* Sillery, Que.: Septentrion, 2003. 858 p. ISBN 289448321X; ISBN 9782894483213; ISBN 284050281X; ISBN

9782840502814; OCLC 52031607; LC Call Number F1030 .H37; Dewey 971.01/6. Citations: 11.

Describes contact between the French and Native Americans through 1715, including its consequences for the region and for each group. Discusses Native inhabitants of the region, French exploration and settlement in the *pays d'en haut*, and relationships that developed between various tribes and the French. Points out that French interest in trade, rather than settlement, and the relatively small numbers of Europeans, created a strong basis for a   French-Native alliance. Explains that the French traded well with the Ottawa, Potawatomi, and Ojibwa, but that both the Natives and the French sought to advance economic and political agendas at the expense of the other. Notes that increasing conflict led to the French assumption of a mediating role, which in turn led to increased entrenchment region among the French. Examines the effects of cultural and biological intermingling among the Natives and the French, noting that each affected the other's beliefs and practices. Concludes that the low French population intensified the influence of the Natives and limited the French ability to fulfill imperial goals for the region.

CHR 85: 783-86.

136 Havard, Gilles. *The Great Peace of Montreal of 1701: French-Native Diplomacy in the Seventeenth Century*. Translated by Phyllis Aronoff and Howard Scott. Kingston, Ont.: McGill-Queen's University Press, 2001. xvi, 308 p. ISBN 0773522093 (hbk.); ISBN 9780773522091 (hbk.); ISBN 0773522190 (pbk.); ISBN 9780773522190 (pbk.); OCLC 46629368; LC Call Number F1030 .H3813; Dewey 971.01/8. Citations: 22.

Surveys French-Indian diplomatic transactions and interactions in the last few decades of the seventeenth century. Draws heavily from annual correspondence sent from New France to authorities in Paris. Describes gift-giving ceremonies, chiefs' speeches, and Indian diplomatic protocol. Provides brief biographies of the main actors and a glossary of the names of Indian nations and a bibliography of French and English sources.

CHR 83: 430-31; *J Mil Hist* 66: 549-51; *WMQ* 60: 222-25.

137 Hudson, Charles M. *Conversations with the High Priest of Coosa*. Chapel Hill: University of North Carolina Press, 2003. xxii, 222 p. ISBN 0807827533 (hbk.); ISBN 9780807827536 (hbk.); ISBN 0807854212 (pbk.); ISBN 9780807854211 (pbk.); OCLC 50291057; LC Call Number PS3608.U343; Dewey 813/.6. Citations: 3.

Combines history, ethnography, archaeology, and fiction into "fictionalized ethnography." Tells the story of the visit to Coosa by Tristan de Luna's detachment almost twenty years after De Soto and Spanish priest Domingo de la Anuciacion's learning about the worldview of the Coosa Indians from a fictional tribal elder, Raven, whose stories are translated by Teresa, a character modeled after the translator who accompanied the Luna expedition.

FHQ 83: 71-73; *WMQ* 60: 861-65.

138 Ingersoll, Thomas N. *To Intermix with Our White Brothers: Indian Mixed Bloods in the United States from Earliest Times to the Indian Removals.*

Albuquerque: University of New Mexico Press, 2005. xxii, 450 p. ISBN 0826332870; ISBN 9780826332875; OCLC 60373661; LC Call Number E98.M63; Dewey 323.11/0597/000973. Citations: 11.

Examines "mixed bloods," persons of Indian and European or African descent, in the part of colonial North America east of the Mississippi River. Explores the context of intermixture, prejudice against mixed bloods, and the roles that mixed bloods played in the Indian removals of the 1830s. Finds that the racial policies of the Spanish, Russian, French, and British colonizers in North America differed little from one another and that the children of Indians and Europeans were rarely accepted in the mother countries or in colonial centers. Distinguishes between mostly white areas and the frontier where racial mixing was tolerated and sometimes even encouraged for economic and political reasons. Notes that social practice and then law discouraged racial mixing in order to maintain property succession, class integrity, and pure white bloodlines, particularly among women, who needed to keep eligibility in the mainland Europe marriage market. Explains that, despite mixed bloods' physical characteristics and cultural affinities, members of white society viewed mixed bloods as Indians. Indicates that assimilation of Indians was never an aim of Jeffersonian and Jacksonian policy, despite Jefferson's suggestions of incorporation. Notes that, instead, both presidents believed that racial separation and removal was the only solution to the Indian problem. Points out that mixed bloods became the strongest advocates for tribal rights and most ardent resisters to removals.
AHR 112: 846-47; *JAEH* 26: 100-101; *JAH* 93: 512-13; *JER* 27: 180-84; *JSH* 73: 424-25.

139 Jackson, Robert H. *Missions and the Frontiers of Spanish America: A Comparative Study of the Impact of Environmental, Economic, Political, and Socio-Cultural Variations on the Missions in the Río de la Plata Region and on the Northern Frontier of New Spain.* Scottsdale, Ariz.: Pentacle Press, 2005. xxii, 568 p. ISBN 0976350009; ISBN 9780976350002; OCLC 61452103; LC Call Number F864 .J28; Dewey 266/.28. Citations: 15.

Compares the Río de la Plata in South America to the north Mexican frontier (specifically Alta and Baja California) in terms of environmental, economic, and political impacts and sociocultural variations. Compares the activities of Jesuit, Franciscan, and Dominican missionaries in each of the geographical areas. Finds that epidemic disease caused Native populations on the northern frontier to suffer catastrophic declines, while in the Río de la Plata region, indigenous populations remained relatively healthy. Argues that moving small populations of hunter-gatherers into missions disrupted Native social order and increased the risk of disease and made recovery less likely, while in the Río de la Plata, Jesuit practices were much less disruptive and Native social structures remained intact.
AHR 111: 787; *HAHR* 87: 418-19; *SHQ* 110: 291-92.

140 Kawashima, Yasuhide. *Igniting King Philip's War: The John Sassamon Murder Trial.* Lawrence: University Press of Kansas, 2001. xii, 201 p. ISBN 0700610928 (hbk.); ISBN 9780700610921 (hbk.); ISBN 0700610936 (pbk.); ISBN 9780700610938 (pbk.); OCLC 45634538; LC Call Number KF8205 .K38; Dewey 973.2/4. Citations: 4.

Recounts the murder of Christian Wampanoag Indian John Sassamon and the ensuing trial, conviction, and execution of his alleged assailants. Explains that Plymouth authorities diminished Wampanoag autonomy by assuming jurisdiction and dismissing Indian legal traditions. Places the episode in the broader context of New England Anglo-Indian relations, noting in particular the parallels with the Pequot War. Explores the crime, using evidence gleaned as part of the coroner's inquest and examines the unusual trial, which involved a jury of English men and an adjunct body of six Christian Indians. Asserts that "The Sassamon case, which sparked King Philip's War, was not merely a triggering incident but a legal manifestation of the primary cause of the war." *BHM* 77: 947-48; *CH* 71: 892; *J Mil Hist* 66: 548-49; *WMQ* 59: 986-89.

141 Kessell, John L., ed. *A Settling of Accounts: The Journals of Don Diego de Vargas, New Mexico, 1700-1704.* Albuquerque: University of New Mexico Press, 2002. xvi, 446 p. ISBN 0826328679; ISBN 9780826328670; OCLC 48550873; LC Call Number F799 .V2843; Dewey 978.9/02/092. Citations: 3.
Presents a translation of Diego de Vargas's journals. Includes accounts of disputes with New Mexico governors, his defense against charges of embezzlement, reunion with his only legitimate son, and the death of his son. Summarizes Diego de Vargas's accomplishments, life among the Pueblos, and the Reconquista, including the distinct groups of Hispanic participants. Recounts the long-lasting accommodations between Hispanics and Pueblos, which were due more to external pressure—namely the threats from Comanches, Apache, and Ute raids—than to increasing cultural tolerance. Concludes that accommodation did not result in a multiracial society like that in New Spain, as the cultural divide between Pueblos and Hispanics remained.
HAHR 84: 523-25.

142 Krieger, Alex D. and Margery H. Krieger, eds. *We Came Naked and Barefoot: The Journey of Cabeza de Vaca across North America.* Austin: University of Texas Press, 2002. xvii, 318 p. ISBN 0292743505; ISBN 9780292743502; OCLC 49576828; LC Call Number E125.N9; Dewey 970.01/6. Citations: 7.
Analyzes Cabeza de Vaca's route, supplementing information contained in *La Relación de los Naufragios* with facts on Texas geography, archaeology, geology, and ethnology. Stresses that understanding Cabeza de Vaca's route is the key to understanding the "unique information on customs and beliefs of many Indian peoples over a vast area of the southeastern United States and northern and western Mexico in the first part of the sixteenth century." Explains that Native American belief in the curative powers of Cabeza de Vaca and his men was vital to the Spaniards' cultural power, the sustaining of diplomatic relations, and the continuing of a good food supply.
JSH 70: 637-39; *SHQ* 107: 615-17.

143 Mann, Barbara Alice. *George Washington's War on Native America.* Westport, Conn.: Praeger, 2005. xi, 295 p. ISBN 0275981770; ISBN 9780275981778; OCLC 57283655; LC Call Number E230.5.N67; Dewey 973.3/3/0977. Citations: 4.

Recounts Colonel Goose Van Schaick's 1779 attack on the Onondagas in New York, and General John Sullivan's and Colonel Daniel Brodhead's 1779 campaigns against Iroquois in New York and Pennsylvania, as well as the Ohio expeditions of George Rogers Clark and Brodhead in 1781. and Colonel David Williamson's murder of 128 Moravian Indians at Gnadenhutten, Ohio in 1782. Notes that American officials explained these attacks as responses to Indian atrocities, efforts to make the frontier safe for settlement, and attempts to take British allies out of the war. Contends that the real reasons were to acquire Indian land for the United States and to exterminate the entire Indian population. Points out that the commanding officers' official reports exaggerated Indian resistance and even claimed that American forces had to overcome superior numbers of Indian warriors. Concludes that "Washington actually lost the Revolutionary War in the west" because unwarranted attacks drove the Indians into alliance with the British and led to significant frontier raids.
EHR 122: 261-63; *JAEH* 30: 81-82; *JAH* 93: 501-502; *JER* 31: 529-33; *J Mil Hist* 70: 501-502.

144 McCollough, Martha. *Three Nations, One Place: A Comparative Ethnohistory of Social Change Among the Comanches and Hasinais During Spain's Colonial Era, 1689–1821.* New York: Routledge, 2004. viii, 140 p. ISBN 0415943949; ISBN 9780415943949; OCLC 51553739; LC Call Number E99.C85; Dewey 978.0049745. Citations: 4.
Argues that the nomadic Comanches and Hasinai farmers in Texas deliberately changed their societies in order to resist Spanish domination and to profit from the horse and gun trade. Contrasts the power of the Comanches to the relative weakness of the Hasinais. Contends that the Spanish in Texas were too weak to control the Comanches or Hasinais, that both native groups developed distinct strategies to exploit the European demand for horses, and that the Indians sought to secure firearms. Finds that "the Comanches and Hasinais relied on alliances, spatial locations, and force to ensure themselves not only access but also increasing control over the distribution of firearms and horses."
AHR 110: 127-28; *Ethnohistory* 53: 248-51.

145 Merritt, Jane T. *At the Crossroads: Indians and Empires on a Mid-Atlantic Frontier, 1700–1763.* Chapel Hill: University of North Carolina Press, for the Omohundro Institute for Early American History and Culture, 2003. xii, 338 p. ISBN 0807827894 (hbk.); ISBN 9780807827895 (hbk.); ISBN 080785462X (pbk.); ISBN 9780807854624 (pbk.); OCLC 50511376; LC Call Number E78 .P4; Dewey 305.897/0748/09032. Citations: 41.
Focuses on land, trade, kinship, diplomacy, warfare, missionization, frontier violence, and racialization in early eighteenth-century Pennsylvania. Finds that Moravians missionaries were relatively successful among the Indians because their proselytizing messages included emotional and even graphic aspects of Christian practice and that they found common interest with natives in emphasis on dreams, the healing properties of blood, and the roles of women. Views the frontier as constantly shifting, as a place where colonial roads and Indian paths "both literally and figuratively passed through and between communities, connecting their lives and histories." Contends that racial polarization of the

frontier did not occur until the mid-eighteenth century, when "the differences among Pennsylvania immigrants—whether political, economic, social, religious, ethnic, or racial—once negotiable and often tolerated at a local level, became increasingly characterized by race ('Indianness')."

AHR 109: 175-76; *18c Stds* 39: 120-30; *JAEH* 24: 108-10; *JAH* 91: 213-14; *J Interdis Hist* 35: 143-45; *PMHB* 128: 199-200; *RAH* 31: 511-18; *SCHM* 106: 66-70; *WHQ* 35: 521-22; *WMQ* 60: 870-75.

146 Milton, Giles. *Big Chief Elizabeth: The Adventures and Fate of the First English Colonists in America*. New York: Picador, 2001. x, 358 p. ISBN 0312420188; ISBN 9780312420185; OCLC 48157974; LC Call Number E98.F39; Dewey 970/.00497. Citations: 7.

Focuses on the efforts of Sir Walter Ralegh to colonize Virginia. Describes his voyages, encounters with natives, and shipwrecks, instances of murder and cannibalism, the "lost colony" of Roanoke, the founding of Jamestown, the tale of Pocahontas, John Rolfe, and John Smith, and the fate of Ralegh. Presents an interpretation favorable to Ralegh.

Booklist 97: 607-608; *JSH* 69: 669-70; *LJ* 125n16: 122; *NCHR* 79: 97-98; *VMHB* 109: 87-88; *VQR* 77: 43.

147 Morrison, Kenneth M. *The Solidarity of Kin: Ethnohistory, Religious Studies, and the Algonkian-French Religious Encounter*. Albany: State University of New York Press, 2002. x, 243 p. ISBN 0791454053 (hbk.); ISBN 9780791454053 (hbk.); ISBN 0791454061 (pbk.); ISBN 9780791454060 (pbk.); OCLC 47717969; LC Call Number E99.A35; Dewey 266/.2/089973. Citations: 17.

Examines Algonkian conversions to Christianity, stressing that the very notion of conversion cannot capture adequately the changes that European contact brought to Algonkian spirituality. Contends that Algonkian changes ought to be viewed as adaptations, not conversions, as they represent reactions to the intersection of cosmologies rather than the replacement of one system of beliefs with another. Charges that most historians have not appreciated the fact that Native American spirituality held "a relational, pragmatic character all its own," one that has been misinterpreted because of reliance on Euro-centric source material. Notes instead that native peoples were aware that Christian missionary teachings challenged their identity and social solidarity and therefore turned to their own traditions and rituals for guidance. Focuses on the Wabanaki (Abenaki, including Penobscot, Passamaquoddy, and Kennebec), Mi'kmaq, Montagnais, and Ojibwa. Points out that major differences between Europeans and Native Americans included the relative scale of their societies, the nature of their politics (European authoritarian versus the more consensual natives), economic values (profit versus sharing), and ideological orientations (European reliance on the dogmatic versus Native American openness to experience). Concludes that scholars generally have failed "to understand Algonkian religious life in its own terms," which has resulted in a "long tradition of ethnocentrically misinterpreting Alongkian religious life."

AHR 109: 170; *JAH* 90: 613.

148   Motsch, Andreas. *Lafitau et l'émergence du discours ethnographique.* Sillery: Septentrion, 2001. 295 p. ISBN 2894481845; ISBN 9782894481844; ISBN 2840501961; ISBN 9782840501961; ISBN 2840501619; ISBN 9782840501619; OCLC 47788403; LC Call Number E58.L162; Dewey 970.004/97. Citations: 16.

Describes French Jesuit missionary Joseph-Franfois Lafitau's ethnographic influence, particularly his analysis of kinship systems and the matriarchal dimensions of Indian societies and his anticipation of modern anthropology. Explains that Lafitau sought to prove that Native Americans shared in an original divine revelation known to all peoples. Discusses the historical context of Lafitau's work, his categories of time, space, and agency, and his view of native institutions.

EAL 38: 495-504; *JAH* 89: 1505-1506.

149   Oberg, Michael Leroy. *Uncas: First of the Mohegans.* Ithaca, N.Y.: Cornell University Press, 2003. xii, 268 p. ISBN 0801438772; ISBN 9780801438776; OCLC 50684195; LC Call Number E99.M83; Dewey 974.6/02/092. Citations: 13.

Presents a biography of the Mohegan sachem Uncas, noting his complexity and Indian ways of life in southern New England. Explains that Uncas endured the coming of Dutch and English traders, devastating epidemics, waves of English immigration, and eventual pressures from the English for Mohegans to sell lands, convert to Christianity, and alter traditional practices. Discusses Uncas's decision to ally with the English against the Pequots, rivalry of the Mohegans with the Narragansetts for "networks of tribute and obligation," and the assassination of the Narragansett sachem Miantonomi in 1643. Contends that Uncas did what he thought was best for the Mohegan people in a rapidly changing world.

CJH 40: 554-56; *Ethnohistory* 52: 644-46; *HRNB* 31: 149-50; *JAH* 91: 210-11; *LJ* 128n6: 110; *NEQ* 76: 640-42; *WMQ* 61: 559-62.

150   O'Brien, Greg. *Choctaws in a Revolutionary Age, 1750–1830.* Lincoln: University of Nebraska Press, 2002. xxx, 158 p. ISBN 0803235690; ISBN 9780803235694; OCLC 48810240; LC Call Number E99.C8; Dewey: 976.004/973. Citations: 15.

Discusses Choctaw ideology in 1750, changes in the view of authority that resulted from a tribal civil war, notions of political and spiritual power, and Choctaw leadership over time. Finds that frontier settlement pressures and rising capitalism, which provided the context for gifts to tribal leaders, obliterated the former system of relations between whites and Native Americans, and made sovereignty within defined boundaries impossible to maintain.

AHR 108: 1441; *FHQ* 82: 492-94; *GHQ* 87: 455-57; *JAEH* 26: 101-103; *JAH* 90: 1012; *JER* 23: 485-87; *JSH* 70: 130-31; *NCHR* 80: 91-93; *WHQ* 34: 372; *WMQ* 60: 874-77.

151   Odell, George H. *La Harpe's Post: A Tale of French-Wichita Contact on the Eastern Plains.* Tuscaloosa: University of Alabama Press, 2002. xx, 369 p.

ISBN 0817311629 (pbk.); ISBN 9780817311629 (pbk.); OCLC 48906403; LC Call Number F697 .O4; Dewey 976.6004/979. Citations: 2.

Explores the initial contact between the party of French commander Jean-Baptist Benard, Sieur de la Harpe, and the Plains Indians in 1719 in what is now eastern Oklahoma. Focuses on the characteristics of the Tawakoni village, finding that the Plains Indians were likely at least part-time farmers, were semi-sedentary, occasionally hunted bison, likely traded with faraway tribes, and that the Indians probably left the village quickly and involuntarily around 1750.
J Econ Hist 63: 272.

152 O'Donnell, James H. *Ohio's First Peoples*. Athens: Ohio University Press, 2004. xii, 176 p. ISBN 0821415247 (hbk.); ISBN 9780821415245 (hbk.); ISBN 0821415255 (pbk.); ISBN 9780821415252 (pbk.); OCLC 52858409; LC Call Number E78.O3; Dewey 977.1004/97. Citations: 1.

Surveys Native American settlements in Ohio from approximately ten thousand years ago to the removal of the Wyandots from the state in 1843. Studies the archaeological work of Rufus Putnam, who speculated in Ohio land after the American Revolution and established the moundbuilder myth, which suggested that a lost European civilization built the mounds rather than the Adena and Hopewell peoples who dominated Ohio for a millennium. Notes that Putnam denigrated native capabilities in order to support white interests and justify American land acquisition from the Shawnees and other Ohio Indians. Discusses fighting in Ohio from 1763 to 1813, focusing on the roles of the Shawnees, Delawares, and Wyandots, Notes that Tecumseh's death in 1813 effectively accelerated Indian removal.
IMH 102: 50-51; *JAH* 92: 597-98.

153 Oliphant, John. *Peace and War on the Anglo-Cherokee Frontier, 1756–63*. Baton Rouge: Louisiana State University Press, 2001. xviii, 269 p. ISBN 0807126373; ISBN 9780807126370; OCLC 47203434; LC Call Number E83.759 .O45; Dewey 973.2/6. Citations: 11.

Analyzes relations between the Cherokee and colonists in South Carolina, leading up to and immediately after the Cherokee War of 1760–61. Blames South Carolina Governor William Henry Lyttelton for the outbreak of hostilities and credits Colonel James Grant and Cherokee leader Attakullakulla for restoring the peace. Contends that dispersal of power on each side meant that "strong-willed individuals on the ground could exercise disproportionate influence" over events. Views the Proclamation of 1763 as mercantilistic in nature, "not a desperate attempt to stave off disaster in the American backwoods."
AHR 107: 872-73; *GHQ* 86: 118-19; *HRNB* 30: 146; *JAH* 89: 615-16; *JSH* 69: 674-75; *NCHR* 80: 481-82; *RAH* 30: 373-80; *SCHM* 103: 181-83; *WMQ* 60: 229-31.

154 O'Toole, Fintan. *White Savage: William Johnson and the Invention of America*. New York: Farrar, Straus and Giroux, 2005. x, 402 p. ISBN 0374281289; ISBN 9780374281281; OCLC 59360234; LC Call Number E195.J63; Dewey 973.2/092. Citations: 13.

Discusses Johnson's work among the Iroquois, his successes in recruitment of Native Americans during the French and Indian War, work as British Superintendent of Indian Affairs, and his promotion of peace between the British and Native Americans. Seeks to explain Johnson's actions among the Iroquois on the basis of his Gaelic cultural norms and suppressed Catholicism. Contends that there were "aspects of [Johnson's] Irish background that made him peculiarly sensitive to the nature of Indian culture."
Booklist 101: 1987; *JAS* 41: 489-90; *J Mil Hist* 71: 916-17; *LJ* 130n15: 73.

155 Pencak, William A. and Daniel K. Richter, eds. *Friends and Enemies in Penn's Woods: Indians, Colonists, and the Racial Construction of Pennsylvania.* University Park: Pennsylvania State University Press, 2004. xxi, 336 p. ISBN 0271023848 (hbk.); ISBN 9780271023847 (hbk.); ISBN 0271023856 (pbk.); ISBN 9780271023854 (pbk.); OCLC 54817208; LC Call Number F152 .F865; Dewey 974.8/02. Citations: 24.
Presents articles on New Sweden and natives, the discursive antecedents of Penn's treaty with the Indians, Quaker and Native American dream stories, Indian, metis, and European-American women on the frontiers, female relationships and intercultural bonds in Moravian Indian missions, the death of Sawantaeny and the problem of justice on the frontier, justice and retribution in the case of John Toby, the diplomatic career of Canasatego, Delawares and Pennsylvanians after the Walking Purchase, squatters, Indians, proprietary government, and land in the Susquehanna Valley, metonymy, violence, patriarchy, and the Paxton boys, Indians, "white" Indians, and the struggle for the Wyoming Valley, and whiteness and warfare on the revolutionary frontier.
AHR 111: 471-72; *HRNB* 33: 102-103; *JAEH* 25: 313-15; *JAH* 92: 583-84; *Penn Hist* 72: 249-50; *PMHB* 130: 331-32; *WMQ* 62: 795-98.

156 Perdue, Theda. *"Mixed Blood" Indians: Racial Construction in the Early South.* Athens: University of Georgia Press, 2003. xiv, 135 p. ISBN 0820324531; ISBN 9780820324531; OCLC 49805922; LC Call Number E78.S65; Dewey 975/.00497. Citations: 29.
Explores racial definitions among southeastern Native Americans and the change in Indian-white relations over the course of the eighteenth and nineteenth centuries. Discusses ways in which Indians used or ignored concepts of race, explaining that flexible kinship and cultural categories allowed southeastern tribes to absorb outsiders. Notes that white men who married Native American women gained access to Indian resources, but conformed to native norms and generally were marginalized as persons without clan affiliation. Finds that native women controlled land and that mixed-race children moved between Indian and white worlds, resisted Anglo-American Christian education and values, and increasingly became political and economic go-betweens as white population eroded Indian autonomy. Explains that many natives accumulated wealth, including African American slaves, and engaged in entrepreneurial opportunities, but that Americans emphasized biological notions of race, stigmatizing "half-breeds" in preparation for the federal removal policies of the 1830s.

FHQ 83: 204-206; *GHQ* 88: 251-52; *JAEH* 24: 110-15; *JAH* 90: 1011-12; *JER* 23: 272-75; *J Interdis Hist* 35: 148-49; *JSH* 70: 125-26; *NCHR* 80: 242-43; *SCHM* 105: 310-12.

157 Piker, Joshua. *Okfuskee: A Creek Indian Town in Colonial America.* Cambridge, Mass.: Harvard University Press, 2004. xiv, 270 p. ISBN 0674013352; ISBN 9780674013353; ISBN 0674013417; ISBN 9780674013414; OCLC 53992896; LC Call Number E99.C9; Dewey 976.1/64; Dewey 976.17405. Citations: 20.
Describes the Creek town of Okfuskee as a commercial crossroads between the natives and the eastern British colonies. Examines Creek relations with South Carolina and Georgia settlers and explains that trade from Georgia grew in prominence in the mid-eighteenth century and caused increased tensions between the Creeks and South Carolinians. Points out that Creeks and colonists shared relative autonomy from centralized governments, vulnerability to cross-cultural warfare, settler mobility because of land and game exhaustion, and participation in frontier exchange economies. Finds that Native Americans had limited access to markets and that "boundaries were increasingly set not by market forces or Indian culture but by the political requirements of colonial and imperial life."
AHR 111: 472-73; *Ethnohistory* 53: 753-64; *FHQ* 84: 132-34; *GHQ* 89: 111-13; *JAH* 92: 585; *J Soc Hist* 39: 549-50; *JSH* 73: 148-49; *SCHM* 106: 263-65; *WHQ* 36: 510-11.

158 Pulsipher, Jenny Hale. *Subjects unto the Same King: Indians, English, and the Contest for Authority in Colonial New England.* Philadelphia: University of Pennsylvania Press, 2005. 361 p. ISBN 0812238761; ISBN 9780812238761; OCLC 58042990; LC Call Number E78.N5; Dewey 974.4/02. Citations: 11.
Reviews Indian-English relationships in seventeenth-century New England, noting that Native Americans actually saw themselves as subjects to the same king as the English colonists and therefore their equals. Explains that over time Indians discovered that the English king, to whom they swore allegiance in order to resist colonial authority, did not recognize Massachusetts colonial authorities. Contends that imperial-colonial disagreements gave tribes space in which to operate and provided Metacom encouragement to initiate war against New England colonists in the belief that Charles II would support him. Concludes that King Philip's War allowed the Crown to tighten its control over New England, while the colonists asserted authority over local tribes.
EHR 122: 254-55; *Hist Teach* 39: 413-14; *JAH* 93: 177-78; *NEQ* 79: 306-311; *WMQ* 63: 195-97.

159 Richter, Daniel K. *Facing East from Indian Country: A Native History of Early America.* Cambridge, Mass.: Harvard University Press, 2001. x, 317 p. ISBN 0674006380 (hbk.); ISBN 9780674006386 (hbk.); ISBN 0674011171 (pbk.); ISBN 9780674011175 (pbk.); OCLC 46974998; LC Call Number E98.F39; Dewey 970/.00497. Citations: 95.
Presents a historical synthesis of eastern North American native peoples from the sixteenth through the early nineteenth century, largely from the Indian

perspective. Discusses Europeans' initial encounters with Native Americans, noting that Indians were curious and open to exchanges and incorporation of European materials and people. Finds that, over time, Indians refined traditional crafts using European iron tools, that "Indian customers' demand for inexpensive, lightweight, easily portable items stretched European technological capabilities to their limits," and that Europeans misjudged Indian conversion narratives because of Native Americans' emphases on outward behavior rather than inner spirituality.

AHR 107: 872; *Ethnohistory* 52: 635-41; *FHQ* 82: 87-89; *IMH* 101: 183-84; *JAH* 89: 1018-19; *JER* 23: 101-102; *J Econ Hist* 63: 1169-70; *J Soc Hist* 36: 808-809; *LJ* 126n17: 93; *NEQ* 75: 507-509; *NCHR* 79: 378-79; *PHR* 72: 150-52; *Penn Hist* 70: 445-49; *PMHB* 127: 104-106; *RAH* 31: 184-91; *SCHM* 105: 59-61; *VMHB* 110: 101-102; *WHQ* 34: 82-83; *WMQ* 60: 672.

160 Rountree, Helen C. *Pocahontas, Powhatan, Opechancanough: Three Indian Lives Changed by Jamestown.* Charlottesville: University of Virginia Press, 2005. xii, 292 p. ISBN 0813923239; ISBN 9780813923239; OCLC 56058105; LC Call Number E99.P85; Dewey 975.5/4251. Citations: 15.

Presents biographies of Pocahontas, her father Powhatan, and Powhatan's brother and successor Opechancanough and tells the story of Jamestown from their perspectives, covering the period from 1607 to 1646. Describes the Powhatan environment, family, dwelling places, reaction to English settlers, and Indian motivations. Finds that Powhatan gradually increased his power by building a confederacy and by limiting the power traditionally granted women. Notes that overconfidence in his expansive power caused Powhatan not to take action to wipe out Jamestown. Lauds Opechancanough's diplomatic skills and suggests that Pocahontas's role was remarkably small.

AHR 111: 821; *AQ* 60: 173-82; *JAH* 93: 494; *JSH* 73: 674-75; *NCHR* 83: 105; *16c J* 40: 1354-56; *VMHB* 114: 292-93; *WMQ* 62: 774-81.

161 Rubertone, Patricia E. *Grave Undertakings: An Archaeology of Roger Williams and the Narragansett Indians.* Washington, D. C.: Smithsonian Institution Press, 2001. xxii, 248 p. ISBN 1560989750; ISBN 9781560989752; OCLC 44885158; LC Call Number E99.N16; Dewey 974/.00497. Citations: 25.

Studies evidence from a Narraganett cemetery near present-day Kingston, Rhode Island and questions the widely held view that Williams was "a folk-hero, who has been endowed with an uncanny ability to understand not only his own society but also that of the Narragansett Indians." Finds instead that Williams did not comprehend the depth of the Narragansett connection to their lands nor did he understand the lives and roles of native women and children. Notes that the archeological evidence reveals a Narrangansett community in distress, as about 40 percent of children died before the age of three and tuberculosis ravaged the Indian settlements. Explains that the graves also indicate a great deal about the status of Narragansett women and that the "presence of separate burial areas close to each other reveals a kind of sacredness and sociability that Williams poorly understood and paints a picture different from that which might be conjured."

AHR 110: 468-69; *Ethnohistory* 51: 817-23; *JAH* 89: 1503; *WMQ* 60: 213-16.

162 Sandos, James A. *Converting California: Indians and Franciscans in the Missions*. New Haven, Conn.: Yale University Press, 2004. xx, 251 p. ISBN 0300101007 (hbk.); ISBN 9780300101003 (hbk.); ISBN 9780300136432 (pbk.); ISBN 0300136439 (pbk.); OCLC 54005473; LC Call Number E78.C15; Dewey 266/.2794. Citations: 21.

Studies the impact of Franciscan missions on Native groups in California and various approaches to conversion, including the use of music. Contends that, though the goal for the Franciscans was "conversion," their view of the concept was that baptism indicated agreement to learn about Catholicism and assent to "spiritual debt peonage," meaning that the Indian "bound to the mission spiritually and physically and was not free to be a pagan." Notes that this concept led to Spanish military expeditions to recapture runaways and influenced Franciscan relations with secular officials, who were of a more "Enlightenment mind" and sought to liberate natives from the paternalism of Franciscan priests. Concludes that Franciscans were not responsible for genocide in California.

AHR 110: 1160; *CH* 74: 391-92; *Ethnohistory* 52: 646-48; *HAHR* 86: 363-64; *HRNB* 33: 17; *JAH* 92: 190-91; *J Interdis Hist* 37: 301-302; *RAH* 34: 259-69; *WHQ* 36: 506-507.

163 Seed, Patricia. *American Pentimento: The Invention of Indians and the Pursuit of Riches*. Minneapolis: University of Minnesota Press, 2001. xii, 299 p. ISBN 0816637660; ISBN 9780816637669; OCLC 46642157; LC Call Number E59.L3; Dewey 970/.00497. Citations: 20.

Examines land use, labor, British hunting, tribute traditions, Iberian mining, cannibalism, and the various approaches of Europeans to the New World. Argues that the British were obsessed with land, while Iberians focused on precious metals and, to some extent, social dominance, and that these lenses determined the course of colonization and Euro-Indian relations. Explains that, in the English view, land had to be occupied and worked in order to be possessed, and therefore found that Indians were "wasting" the lands. Finds that the Spanish viewed natives as subordinates to be demeaned because of signs of practicing cannibalism and savagery and that the Spanish continued an old practice of giving mines to the state.

AHR 108: 155-56; *HAHR* 84: 505-506; *IMH* 99: 60-61; *J Interdis Hist* 33: 655-57.

164 Shoemaker, Nancy, ed. *Clearing a Path: Theorizing the Past in Native American Studies*. New York: Routledge, 2002. xiv, 215 p. ISBN 0415926742 (hbk.); ISBN 9780415926744 (hbk.); ISBN 0415926750 (pbk.); ISBN 9780415926751 (pbk.); OCLC 46449115; LC Call Number E76.8 .C54; Dewey 970/.00497/0072. Citations: 19.

Includes articles on Native American historiography about the Yukon Territory, Canada, categories of tribal analysis, gender and Native American history, political economy, Marxism, and historical materialism in American Indian history, Indian goods, the history of American colonialism, and the nineteenth-century reservation, the development and presentation of tribal histories, and hybridity among indigenous peoples.

Ethnohistory 52: 492-94; *JAH* 90: 737; *J Interdis Hist* 33: 654-55; *WHQ* 34: 220-21; *WMQ* 60: 861-65.

165 Shoemaker, Nancy. *A Strange Likeness: Becoming Red and White in Eighteenth-Century North America.* Oxford: Oxford University Press, 2004. viii, 211 p. ISBN 0195167929; ISBN 9780195167924; OCLC 52412276; LC Call Number E98.F39; Dewey 306/.089/97. Citations: 43.
Examines the relationships between Europeans (French, Dutch, Swedes, Germans, Spanish, and British) and Indians (Shawnees, Mahicans, Mohegans, Miamis, Creeks, Natchez, Yuchis, Catawbas, Chickasaws, the Iroquois, and the Cherokee) along "both sides of the Appalachian mountain chain from the Great Lakes to the Gulf of Mexico." Discusses perceptions of land and boundaries, hierarchy and politics, oral and written communication, alliances, gender, and bodily metaphors. Argues that Native Americans and Europeans at first held similar worldviews, but that by the beginning of the nineteenth century had together developed a "fiction of irresolute difference" underscored by "red" and "white" racial constructs.
AHR 110: 469-70; *Ethnohistory* 52: 491-92; *Hist Teach* 38: 431-22; *JAH* 92: 188-89; *J Interdis Hist* 36: 101-102; *J Soc Hist* 38: 827-29; *JSH* 71: 663-64; *RAH* 33: 29-40; *WHQ* 36: 509-510; *WMQ* 62: 540-42.

166 Silverman, David J. *Faith and Boundaries: Colonists, Christianity, and Community among the Wampanoag Indians of Martha's Vineyard, 1600–1871.* New York: Cambridge University Press, 2005. xxiv, 303 p. ISBN 0521842808; ISBN 9780521842808; OCLC 57211173; LC Call Number E99.W2; Dewey 305.897/348074494. Citations: 21.
Examines the roles of Christianity in Wampanoag culture and of sachems, the nature of indentured servitude on Martha's Vineyard, community problems like disease, racism, land loss, and debt peonage, and cultural persistence. Finds that the Wampanoags on the island did not fit "the pattern of total Indian dispossession and removal in the face of Anglo-American expansion" found elsewhere. Concludes that adaptive Wampanoags fared reasonably well, but "swallowed hard on their pride to compromise several times over, and in the process adopted many of the social and cultural behaviors of the colonists who pressed upon them."
AHR 112: 495-96; *JAH* 93: 495-96; *NEQ* 79: 306-311; *WMQ* 63: 407-409.

167 Sleeper-Smith, Susan. *Indian Women and French Men: Rethinking Cultural Encounter in the Western Great Lakes.* Amherst: University of Massachusetts Press, 2001. xviii, 234 p. ISBN 1558493085 (hbk.); ISBN 9781558493087 (hbk.); ISBN 1558493107 (pbk.); ISBN 9781558493100 (pbk.); OCLC 47023498; LC Call Number E78.N76; Dewey 977/.01/082. Citations: 54.
Asserts that previous historians have not properly acknowledged Indian peoples' perseverance in the face of European colonization. Considers the process of Catholic conversion and gender dynamics among the Illini people in seventeenth-century Kaskaskia, the use of agricultural surpluses by the Potawatomi people of the St. Joseph River valley, the Miami removal from northwestern Indiana, and the survival of Indian communities in Michigan

during the period of statehood. Investigates adaptive strategies that Native Americans used from the seventeenth through the nineteenth centuries in their dealings with friendly and hostile strangers alike, including intermarriage with fur traders, adoption of Catholicism and its incorporation into traditional cultural practice, and the maintenance of extensive kin networks. Contends that continuity and persistence better than decline and disappearance characterize Great Lake Native American cultures.

Ethnohistory 51: 799-803; *IMH* 99: 173-74; *JAH* 90: 204; *JAEH* 22: 128-29; *JER* 23: 275-77; *WMQ* 61: 750-53.

168   Smith, F. Todd. *From Dominance to Disappearance: The Indians of Texas and the Near Southwest, 1786–1859.* Lincoln: University of Nebraska Press, 2005. xviii, 314 p. ISBN 0803243138; ISBN 9780803243132; OCLC 58789419; LC Call Number E78.T4; Dewey 976.004/97. Citations: 17.

Studies the area east of the High Plains, focusing on Native American tribes prior to 1786, relations among the Spanish and Indians before the Louisiana Purchase, the boundary dispute between Spain and the United States after the Purchase, Native American fortunes after the decline of Spanish influence (e.g., reactions to the Hidalgo revolt of 1810–1811, Mexican independence, and Texas freedom), and antebellum federal Indian policy, particularly in Texas and the Comanche and Brazos reserves. Concludes that "Within a quarter of a century of gaining independence from Mexico, the citizens of Texas had caused almost all of the Indians to disappear from the region entirely."

Ethnohistory 54: 768-69; *HAHR* 87: 173-74; *JAH* 93: 864-65; *JER* 27: 740-45; *J Mil Hist* 71: 505-511; *JSH* 75: 137-38; *SHQ* 110: 549-50; *WHQ* 38: 229.

169   Steckley, John, ed. *De Religione: Telling the Seventeenth-Century Jesuit Story in Huron to the Iroquois.* Norman: University of Oklahoma Press, 2004. 213 p. ISBN 0806136170; ISBN 9780806136172; OCLC 53823373; LC Call Number E99.H9; Dewey 277.13/07/0899755. Citations: 0.

Translates and publishes a Jesuit-written, Huron-language catechism, which "bears the verbal soul of the Wendat language." Examines Christianity from the Huron perspective, explaining the intricacies of translation, such as "sin" as "to be mistaken in some matter" and "God" as "Great Voice."

EAL 41: 129-44.

170   Stevens, Laura M. *The Poor Indians: British Missionaries, Native Americans, and Colonial Sensibility.* Philadelphia: University of Pennsylvania Press, 2004. 264 p. ISBN 0812238125 (hbk.); ISBN 9780812238129 (hbk.); ISBN 0812219678 (pbk.); ISBN 9780812219678 (pbk.); OCLC 54966622; LC Call Number E98.M6; Dewey 266/.02341/008997. Citations: 17.

Focuses on Protestant missionary rhetoric in seventeenth- and eighteenth-century English writings, noting the tropes of trade, husbandry, and epistolarity, biographies of missionaries David Brainerd and John Sergeant, and the shift in concern from "poor Indian" to self-sacrificing missionary during the eighteenth century and then back to the Romantic, dying Indian in the nineteenth century. Contends that such writings created in the colonies a single, national community of like-minded persons and "an optimistic moral philosophy intertwined with a culture of sensibility" that founded "a benevolent imperialist rhetoric" and provided "justification for colonialism." Concludes that missionary efforts in New England largely failed from the perspective of conversions and adverse impacts on Indian communities, but that such work had significant rhetorical effects.

EAL 41: 145-48; *18c Stds* 42: 458-62; *NEQ* 78: 328-30.

171 Sweet, Julie Anne. *Negotiating for Georgia: British-Creek Relations in the Trustee Era, 1733 –1752.* Athens: University of Georgia Press, 2005. x, 267 p. ISBN 0820326755; ISBN 9780820326757; OCLC 56493626; LC Call Number E99.C9; Dewey 975.8/02. Citations: 5.

Seeks to provide "a new colonial history that documents the ways in which all cultures play a part" with special focus on British Georgia in the mid-eighteenth century. Examines colonists' relations with Lower Creek Indians, the views of James Oglethorpe and Tomochichi, disputes between the English and the Creeks over trade, land, and religion, the impact of Tomochichi's death on Anglo-Creek relations, cooperation against the Spanish, changes in colonial leadership, and the activities of Mary Musgrove. Finds that early accommodation and amity soured with increased English immigration to the colony, which brought more land pressure, demands for unfree labor, and expanded deerskin trade.

AHR 112: 496-97; *18c Stds* 43: 117-20; *FHQ* 84: 266-68; *GHQ* 90: 125-28; *JAH* 92: 1412-13.

172 Townsend, Camilla. *Pocahontas and the Powhatan Dilemma.* New York: Hill and Wang, 2004. xi, 223 p. ISBN 0809095300; ISBN 9780809095308; OCLC 60341383; LC Call Number E99.P85; Dewey 975.5/01/092. Citations: 14.

Explains that Pocahontas lived in a world in which Indians valued openness to people, technology, and ideas. Characterizes Pocahontas as a youthful, energetic, assertive woman who played an important role—via marriage—in the Powhatan Confederacy's diplomatic strategy. Examines her initial marriage to a Powhatan warrior, capture by Samuel Argall, marriage to John Rolfe, visit to London, death, progeny, the attacks of 1622 and 1644, and the end of the Powhatan Confederacy. Asserts that the supposed rescue of John Smith was a fiction devised by Smith himself and concludes that there was nothing that Pocahontas could have done "that would have dramatically changed the outcome: a new nation was going to be built on their people's destruction—a destruction that would be either partial or complete."

AQ 60: 173-82; *Hist Teach* 39: 137-38; *JAEH* 25: 289-93; *JAH* 92: 949; *JSH* 71: 866-67; *VMHB* 112: 419-20; *WMQ* 62: 774-81.

173 Warren, Stephen. *The Shawnees and Their Neighbors, 1795–1870.* Urbana: University of Illinois Press, 2005. xii, 217 p. ISBN 025202995X; ISBN 9780252029950; OCLC 58423161; LC Call Number E99.S35; Dewey 974.004/97317. Citations: 8.

Traces the experience of the Shawnees from their removal from Ohio to the tribe in Oklahoma in the 1870s. Studies divisions in Shawnee communities that resulted from differences in approaches to resettlement and examines

governance structures, kinship groups, ethnic compositions, and the ways in which Shawnee culture and identity persisted. Finds that traditionalist Shawnees sought to transform western reservations into "multitribal commons" based on their ancestral Ohio villages, which accepted other Native Americans who had been removed from their eastern homelands. Contrasts this group with elite Shawnees who embraced Christianity, spoke English, intermarried with whites, and owned slaves. Concludes that variations among Shawnees resulted in the failure of the U.S. government's attempt to create a single Shawnee reservation with a single tribal council and led instead to several federally recognized Shawnee tribes.
AHR 112: 1164-65; *CJH* 42: 540-42; *JAH* 93: 513-14; *JER* 26: 508-511; *JSH* 73: 161-62; *WHQ* 38: 232-33.

174 Weber, David J. *Bárbaros: Spaniards and Their Savages in the Age of Enlightenment*. New Haven, Conn.: Yale University Press, 2005. xviii, 466 p. ISBN 0300105010 (hbk.); ISBN 9780300105018 (hbk.); ISBN 0300119917 (pbk.); ISBN 9780300119916 (pbk.); OCLC 57434218; LC Call Number E59.C58; Dewey 323.1197/0171246/09033. Citations: 46.
Examines Bourbon Spanish policies toward resurgent Native Americans, focusing on missionary efforts, military action, commerce, and diplomacy. Explains that the Enlightenment influenced treatment of Indians and dictated the division of action between the missionary (spiritual) and governmental (economic, political, and cultural) realms. Characterizes reforms during the eighteenth century as inefficient and ineffective and often mere rehashings of failed Habsburg policies toward Indians. Finds that "It was power, then, more than the power of ideas that had determined how enlightened Spaniards would treat savages."
AHR 111: 433-34; *CH* 76: 439-41; *18c Stds* 39: 542-46; *HAHR* 87: 584-85; *JAEH* 25: 174-77; *JAH* 93: 188-89; *JER* 27: 560-63; *J Interdis Hist* 37: 288-90; *PHR* 76: 95-97; *RAH* 34: 270-75; *SHQ* 110: 288-89; *WHQ* 38: 511-12; *WMQ* 64: 183-94.

175 Williamson, Margaret Holmes. *Powhatan Lords of Life and Death: Command and Consent in Seventeenth-Century Virginia*. Lincoln: University of Nebraska Press, 2003. xiv, 323 p. ISBN 0803247982 (hbk.); ISBN 9780803247987 (hbk.); ISBN 9780803260375 (pbk.); ISBN 0803260377 (pbk.); OCLC 50155440; LC Call Number E99.P85; Dewey 975.5004/973. Citations: 10.
Explains that Powhatans made power distinctions between "the right to say what shall be done" and the ability to carry out whatever is authorized. Notes that religious authority was held by priests, while political power was exercised by chiefs and councilors, but that most leaders exercised some degree of both sorts of power.
JAH 91: 211-12; *JSH* 70: 641-42; *VMHB* 111: 300-301.

7 Race and Slavery

176 Basker, James G., ed. *Amazing Grace: An Anthology of Poems about Slavery, 1660–1810*. New Haven, Conn.: Yale University Press, 2002. lvii, 721 p. ISBN 0300091729; ISBN 9780300091724; OCLC 49743685; LC Call Number PR1195.S44; Dewey 821.008/0355. Citations: 15.

Provides approximately 400 examples of poetic works about slavery by more than 250 writers, including John Dryden, Samuel Butler, Michael Wigglesworth, Aphra Behn, Thomas Tryon, Daniel Defoe, Samuel Sewall, Alexander Pope, William Pattison, Robert Blair, Samuel Johnson, John Hawkesworth, James Grainger, Phillis Wheatley, Thomas Thistlethwaite, Daniel Bliss, John Wesley, Lemuel Haynes, John Trumbull, Philip Freneau, Joel Barlow, Thomas Bellamy, William Blake, Olaudah Equiano, Francis Hopkinson, William Hutchinson, Joanna Baillie, Charles Dunster, John Marriott, Joseph Mather, Susanna Pearson, Joseph Sansom, Benjamin Banneker, Mary Birkett, Robert Burns, Samuel Taylor Coleridge, Samuel Rogers, Timothy Dwight, David Humphreys, John Leyden, Joseph Dennie, John Quincy Adams, Susanna Watts, William Wordsworth, Thomas Branagan, Joshua Marsden, and many others, including anonymous authors. Arranges pieces chronologically and argues that, through the eighteenth century slavery in poetry was approached with relative uniformity and that the subject itself carried little significance, but that after the beginning of the nineteenth century "slavery in British and American cultural life became two different stories."
EAL 40: 565-74; *WMQ* 62: 299-307.

177 Bennett, Herman L. *Africans in Colonial Mexico: Absolutism, Christianity, and Afro-Creole Consciousness, 1570–1640*. Bloomington: Indiana University Press, 2003. xii, 275 p. ISBN 0253342368 (hbk.); ISBN 9780253342362 (hbk.); ISBN 025321775X (pbk.); ISBN 9780253217752 (pbk.); OCLC 50868255; LC Call Number F1386.9.B55; Dewey 972/.00496. Citations: 39.

Traces the treatment of free and enslaved Africans in late sixteenth- and early seventeenth-century Mexico, taking up their relationship to government and religious authorities, the effects of the Inquisition and ecclesiastical courts, the legal status of African marriage, and Africans' roles as Christian subjects of the Spanish monarch. Suggests that plantation slavery has occupied large portions of the historiography, while the influence of slavery in urban areas like Mexico City has generally been ignored. Notes that, despite the absolutist Spanish government and the autocratic tendencies of the Roman Catholic Church, Africans were able to use the legal machinery of both church and state, modify their cultural identities, and draw upon significant psychological resources to carve out a measure of autonomy. Explains that the Church upheld slaves' conjugal rights and marriages and that Africans increasingly asserted rights against their owners using knowledge of the Church, morality, the judicial system, and masculine honor and prestige.
AHR 109: 1275-76; *Ethnohistory* 52: 651-52; *HAHR* 84: 730-31; *WMQ* 61: 349-52.

178 Berlin, Ira. *Generations of Captivity: A History of African-American Slaves.* Cambridge, Mass.: Belknap Press of Harvard University Press, 2003. x, 374 p. ISBN 0674016246 (pbk.); ISBN 9780674016248 (pbk.); OCLC 424101194; LC Call Number E441 B47; Dewey 306.362 0973. Citations: 56.
Surveys slavery in America from the seventeenth century through the Civil War. Identifies five generations of slaves, each of which adapted to the unique conditions of its captivity and renegotiated the terms of servitude. Notes that the "charter" generation represented the initial seventeenth-century wave, the "plantation" generation built colonial society in the early eighteenth century, the "Revolutionary" generation negotiated upheaval, the "migration" generation aided American nineteenth-century expansionism, and the "freedom" generation saw the end of the institution. Asserts that the slave economy was remarkably efficient and profitable and grew more so over time, that negotiation and renegotiation constantly modified the conditions of production (e.g., the practices of "overwork" and "hiring out"), and that class and color distinctions among slaves were significant. Contends that "matters touching upon the slaves' spiritual world" were of primary importance in the nineteenth century and that many planters paid Christian missionaries to attend to their slaves and even built plantation chapels for slaves.
Ag Hist 81: 275-77; *AHR* 109: 183-84; *Booklist* 99: 1037; *EHR* 122: 207-209; *IMH* 100: 266-68; *JAH* 90: 1432-33; *JAS* 38: 498; *LJ* 128n2: 100; *NCHR* 81: 110-11; *WMQ* 61: 544-55.

179 Blumrosen, Alfred W. and Ruth G. Blumrosen. *Slave Nation: How Slavery United the Colonies and Sparked the American Revolution.* Naperville, Ill.: Sourcebooks, 2005. xv, 336 p. ISBN 1402204000 (hbk.); ISBN 9781402204005 (hbk.); ISBN 1402206976 (pbk.); ISBN 9781402206979 (pbk.); OCLC 57007982; LC Call Number E446 .B58; Dewey 973.3/11 22. Citations: 3.
Contends that slavery was the primary issue in the run-up to the American Revolution. Suggests that southerners were sensitive to British court rulings against slavery and to Parliament's claims of supremacy over the colonies.

Emphasizes the importance of Lord Mansfield's ruling in the Somerset case (1772), which found that English common law did not protect slavery. Claims that this decision caused southerners to push for independence and for assurances from northerners that slavery would be protected in a new government scheme. Argues that the Constitution hinged upon the informal compromise of three-fifths representation in exchange for the banning of slavery north of the Ohio River.

Booklist 101: 933; *JAH* 92: 1415-16; *JER* 27: 546-55; *JSH* 72: 922-23; *LJ* 130n5: 94.

180   Bontemps, Alex. *The Punished Self: Surviving Slavery in the Colonial South*. Ithaca, N.Y.: Cornell University Press, 2001. x, 224 p. ISBN 0801435218; ISBN 9780801435218; OCLC 45500151; LC Call Number E443 .B66; Dewey 975/.00496. Citations: 15.

Explains that masters' depictions of slavery were highly fictionalized and avoided reference to slaves as conscious human beings. Notes that slave invisibility in the writings of slaveholders "seems repressed rather than merely overlooked or consciously ignored" and that runaway slave ads suggest that physical abuse of slaves was more common and more severe than previously thought. Describes slave marginalization as a psychological process, one that depended upon internalization of subservience. Discusses the transition of slaves from "New Negroes" to "sensible Negroes," whereby slaves were "seasoned" and became productive workers.

AHR 107: 1559-60; *GHQ* 86: 449-53; *JAEH* 22: 116-18; *JAH* 89: 611; *J Interdis Hist* 33: 484-85; *J Soc Hist* 37: 545-47; *JSH* 69: 143-44; *NCHR* 79: 381-82.

181   Brooks, James F. *Captives and Cousins: Slavery, Kinship, and Community in the Southwest Borderlands*. Chapel Hill: University of North Carolina Press, published for the Omohundro Institute of Early American History and Culture, 2002. xii, 419 p. ISBN 0807827142 (hbk.); ISBN 9780807827147 (hbk.); ISBN 0807853828 (pbk.); ISBN 9780807853825 (pbk.); OCLC 48550954; LC Call Number F790.A1; Dewey 305.8/00976. Citations: 101.

Studies the origins, development, and impact of the captive labor exchange economy among Native American tribes and European settlers in the southwest borderlands from the sixteenth century through the end of the nineteenth century. Explains that Apaches, Comanches, Kiowas, Navajos, Utes, and Spaniards raided and traded slaves and livestock, resulting in the redistribution of wealth, the development of kinship connections, and the integration of various antagonistic groups. Contends that "Native and European men fought to protect their communities and preserve personal repute yet participated in conflicts and practices that made the objects of their honor, women and children, crucial products of violent economic exchange." Argues that in the Southwest "a unifying web of intellectual, material, and emotional exchange" developed "with which Native and Euramerican men fought and traded to exploit and bind to themselves women and children of other peoples." Concludes that, over time, captives "became agents of conflict, conciliation, and cultural redefinition."

AHR 108: 182-83; *Am Stds* 43: 115-16; *Ethnohistory* 51: 838-40; *HAHR* 83: 578-79; *JAH* 90: 205; *JSH* 70: 639-41; *PHR* 72: 301-302; *SHQ* 107: 138-39; *WHQ* 34: 364-65; *WMQ* 60: 436-39.

182 Burnard, Trevor. *Mastery, Tyranny, and Desire: Thomas Thistlewood and His Slaves in the Anglo-Jamaican World.* Chapel Hill: University of North Carolina Press, 2004. xii, 320 p. ISBN 0807828564 (hbk.); ISBN 9780807828564 (hbk.); ISBN 0807855251 (pbk.); ISBN 9780807855256 (pbk.); OCLC 53231206; LC Call Number HT1096 .B86; Dewey 306.3/62/097292 22. Citations: 30.
Uses Thistlewood's diaries to study the various worlds of eighteenth-century Jamaican slaveholders. Explains that Thistlewood started out as an overseer and at his death in 1786 owned thirty-four slaves. Describes the entries in Thistlewood's diaries, which included slave tasks and punishments, his business transactions and social life, intellectual pursuits, and sex life. Asserts that "No other eighteenth-century diary contains the wealth of material that Thistlewood's diaries offer about Africans and people of African descent." Contends that, despite extraordinary repression and uncertainty, slaves "developed a rich cultural life, exemplified by their language, music, and religion." Finds that whites in Jamaica were much wealthier than their counterparts in England. Characterizes Thistlewood as a "brutal slave owner, an occasional rapist, and torturer."
AHR 110: 832-33; *EAL* 40: 202-205; *JAH* 92: 1414; *J Brit Stds* 45: 169-71; *J Mod Hist* 78: 483-84; *NCHR* 83: 109-110; *WMQ* 62: 533-36.

183 Carretta, Vincent. *Equiano the African: Biography of a Self-Made Man.* Athens: University of Georgia Press, 2005. xviii, 436 p. ISBN 9780820325712; ISBN 0820325716; OCLC 60323361; LC Call Number HT869.E6; Dewey 306.3/62/092. Citations: 52.
Presents a full biography of Equiano whose *Narrative* made him famous and was, at once, a "spiritual biography, captivity narrative, travel book, adventure tale, slave narrative, rags-to-riches saga, economic treatise, apologia, [and] testimony." Questions the veracity of several parts of the *Narrative*, including Equiano's accounts of Africa and the Middle Passage and finds that his image was constructed in order to make him a more credible critic of slavery and commentator on Africa. Claims that at his death in 1797 Equiano, as a result of the publication of the *Narrative*, "was probably the wealthiest and certainly most famous person of African descent in the Atlantic world."
AHR 111: 795-96; *Booklist* 102: 9; *EAL* 41: 600-603; *18c Stds* 39: 571-73; *GHQ* 91: 219-22; *HRNB* 34: 65-66; *JAH* 93: 840-41; *JER* 28: 669-74; *JSH* 73:150-51; *NCHR* 83: 272-73; *RAH* 34: 12-17.

184 Carrington, Selwyn H.H. *The Sugar Industry and the Abolition of the Slave Trade, 1775–1810.* Gainesville: University Press of Florida. 2002. xxii, 362 p. ISBN 0813025575; ISBN 9780813025575; OCLC 49383583; LC Call Number HD9114.W42; Dewey 972.9/03. Citations: 16.
Argues that the American Revolution virtually destroyed the illegal inter-colonial trade that supported the British Caribbean sugar industry and that, by

enforcing strictly the Navigation Acts, the imperial government increased supply, shipping, and tax costs for sugar producers, many of whom were already heavily in debt. Contends that the negative effects were not limited to plantation owners and merchants, but also reached free and unfree colonists in the form of poorer diets, lower fertility rates and life expectancies, and less productivity.
AHR 109: 145-46; *HAHR* 84: 525-26; *J Econ Hist* 64: 255-57; *J Interdis Hist* 34: 489-91.

185 Cecelski, David S. *The Waterman's Song: Slavery and Freedom in Maritime North Carolina*. Chapel Hill: University of North Carolina Press, 2001. xx, 304 p. ISBN 080782643X (hbk.); ISBN 9780807826430 (hbk.); ISBN 0807849723 (pbk.); ISBN 9780807849729 (pbk.); OCLC 45951690; LC Call Number E444.N8 C43; Dewey 975.6/00496 21. Citations: 23.
Studies the work performed by slave fishermen, boatmen, pilots, sailors, sail makers, and nautical tradesmen, the various tools of their trades, and the use of water as a symbol of freedom. Explains that maritime slaves were away from farms and plantations for days, weeks, or months at a time, were often hired out by their owners, and were occasionally able to negotiate the conditions of their own employment. Describes the brutally difficult work of canal digging and finds that, although "Most black maritime laborers never led a slave rebellion," they still "had a powerful hand in building a culture of slave resistance that shaped African American freedom struggles before, during, and after the Civil War."
AHR 109: 526-27; *GHQ* 86: 449-54; *JAH* 89: 628-29; *JER* 22: 534-36; *J Interdis Hist* 33: 663-64; *J Soc Hist* 36: 800-802; *JSH* 69: 424-25; *WMQ* 60: 439-43.

186 Chambers, Douglas B. *Murder at Montpelier: Igbo Africans in Virginia*. Jackson: University Press of Mississippi, 2005. x, 325 p. ISBN 1578067065; ISBN 9781578067060; OCLC 58392553; LC Call Number F232.O6 C457; Dewey 975.5/372/08625 22. Citations: 11.
Investigates the 1732 alleged poisoning by slaves of Ambrose Madison, grandfather of James Madison. Reconstructs slave community at Montpelier and blames Madison's murder on Igbo slaves from Calabar, who exerted extraordinary influence on eighteenth-century Afro-Virginian culture. Notes that the plantation community was relatively stable, but that Madison's slaves would have had special knowledge of poisons and a motive for murder.
AHR 111: 793-94; *GHQ* 90: 283-85; *JAH* 92: 1413-14; *JSH* 72: 651-52; *NCHR* 83: 106-107; *VMHB* 114: 403-405.

187 Coates, Eyler Robert, ed. *The Jefferson-Hemings Myth: An American Travesty*. Charlottesville, Va.: Thomas Jefferson Heritage Society, 2001. 207 p. ISBN 0934211663; ISBN 9780934211666; OCLC 46474068; LC Call Number E185.62 .J43; Dewey 973.4/6/092. Citations: 4.
Undertakes "an independent and objective review of all the facts" related to the relationship of a Jefferson male to Thomas Jefferson's slave Sally Hemings. Seeks to defend the third President's reputation from his "politically correct, revisionist critics" by arguing that a DNA test shows only a relationship between

Thomas Jefferson's uncle, Field Jefferson, and the descendants of Sally Hemings' son Eston Hemings, who could have been the son of any of the twenty-five male Jeffersons in Virginia at the time. Contends that the most likely father of Eston was Randolph Jefferson, Thomas's younger brother, who was known to have sexual relationships with female slaves and who had been invited to Monticello at the time when Eston would have been conceived. Asserts that a smear campaign against Jefferson began in his first term as President, orchestrated by journalist James T. Callender, who was famous for his attacks and exaggerations. Calls the 1873 testimony of Sally Hemmings' son Madison "hearsay" and attributes the document to the politically motivated newspaper editor Samuel Wetmore.
WMQ 58: 1039-46.

188   Coleman, Deirdre. *Romantic Colonization and British Anti-Slavery*. Cambridge: Cambridge University Press, 2005. xv, 273 p. ISBN 0521632137; ISBN 9780521632133; OCLC 55019231; LC Call Number DA16 .C627; Dewey 325/.341/09033 22. Citations: 17.
Contends that the idea of a moral colony was deeply rooted in late eighteenth-century British culture and influenced—and was influenced by—the abolitionist movement. Focuses on the foundation of New South Wales, including its "etiquettes of colonization and dispossession" and the work of Henry Smeathman, a West African entomologist in West Africa who viewed termite colonies as ideal models for human imperialism and who argued for a West African colony settled by freed slaves and based upon "rational commerce" that would make Africa a shining example for the rest of the world. Examines Swedenborgian ideas about Africa as a lost paradise and the early years of the evangelical colony of Sierra Leone, which was marked by conflict between colonial masters and black loyalists. Explains that the flaws in romantic notions of Sierra Leone and New South Wales ultimately resulted in the brutalization of black settlers and indigenous Australians. Suggests that "labour schemes are crucial to understanding the tensions between slavery and freedom inherent in all Romantic colonization plans, especially those of plantation-scale proportions."
J Interdis Hist 36: 233-40; *WMQ* 65: 191-96.

189 Dain, Bruce. *A Hideous Monster of the Mind: American Race Theory in the Early Republic*. Cambridge, Mass.: Harvard University Press, 2002. x, 321 p. ISBN 0674009460; ISBN 9780674009462; OCLC 50132276; LC Call Number GN269 .D34; Dewey 305.8/009 21. Citations: 37.
Offers "an integrated intellectual history of the emergence in the United States, from the American Revolution to the Civil War" of the "first major rationalizations of race." Views the late eighteenth-century and early nineteenth-century American concern about race as the product of a transatlantic discussion among British, French, German, and white American intellectuals, contending that "ideas on race did not fall into neat, self-contained, racially determined categories." Examines the thought about race of Thomas Jefferson, Samuel Stanhope Smith, Samuel G. Morton, Josiah Nott, a number of black thinkers like David Walker and the editors of the *Freedom's Journal*, and Alexander Everett,

who wrote that Africans "had enjoyed a decided predominance throughout the whole ancient western world." Finds that racial views changed over time (e.g., *Freedom's Journal*'s initial critique of colonization schemes that later became an endorsement and Haiti's development in the 1820s as a temporary refuge for American blacks) and that black intellectuals like Hosea Easton and James McCune Smith developed racial formulations to critique the dominant racial thought of the era.
AHR 108: 1444-45; *Am Lit* 78: 613-15; *EAL* 43: 511-16; *JAH* 90: 1433-34; *JSH* 71: 147-48; *LJ* 127n20: 157; *NEQ* 77: 155-57; *PMHB* 128: 324-25; *RAH* 32: 27-32; *WMQ* 60: 895-99.

190 Doolen, Andy. *Fugitive Empire: Locating Early American Imperialism.* Minneapolis: University of Minnesota Press, 2005. xxvii, 254 p. ISBN 0816644535 (hbk.); ISBN 9780816644537 (hbk.); ISBN 0816644543 (pbk.); ISBN 9780816644544 (pbk.); OCLC 60515018; LC Call Number E179.5 .D66; Dewey 325/.32/097309033 22. Citations: 11.
Contends that, despite democratic ideals, eighteenth-century, pre-Revolution notions of race persisted in America after nationhood, prompting aggressive, coercive action, both at home and abroad. Begins with the 1741 New York Conspiracy trial, arguing that the execution of thirty suspected slave rebels demonstrated both imperial overreach and increased racialization of domestic and foreign threats (e.g., belief that Spain sought to incite slave insurrection). Reviews the writings of Charles Brockden Brown, James Fenimore Cooper, William Apess, and Herman Melville, arguing that they show, ironically, the dependence of an imperialistic, majority identity on the images of helpful, threatening, or vanishing racial "others."
Am Lit 79: 612-15; *EAL* 41: 592-600; *WMQ* 63: 615-18.

191 Dresser, Madge. *Slavery Obscured: The Social History of the Slave Trade in an English Provincial Port.* London: Continuum, 2001. xii, 242 p. ISBN 0826448755 (hbk.); ISBN 9780826448750 (hbk.); ISBN 0826448763 (pbk.); ISBN 9780826448767 (pbk.); OCLC 45320833; LC Call Number HT1164.B74; Dewey 382/.44/0942393. Citations: 16.
Claims that recent histories of Bristol have "obscured" the importance of the slave trade to the city's wealth and development. Argues instead that Bristol relied a great deal on the exploitation of black labor and notes that 90,000 Africans died aboard Bristol ships while crossing the Atlantic. Discusses the particulars of the slave trade and how it came to influence Bristol material culture and mental and social worlds, and how, when the city began to decline, abolitionist movements and emancipation campaigns increased. Explores issues of identity, representation, gender, and middle-class consumption.
Econ Hist Rev 55: 764-65; *WMQ* 62: 307-10.

192 Dubois, Laurent. *A Colony of Citizens: Revolution & Slave Emancipation in the French Caribbean, 1787–1804.* Chapel Hill: University of North Carolina Press, published for the Omohundro Institute of Early American History and Culture, 2004. x, 452 p. ISBN 0807828742 (hbk.); ISBN 9780807828748 (hbk.); ISBN 0807855367 (pbk.); ISBN 9780807855362 (pbk.); OCLC 53002644; LC Call Number F2151 .D83; Dewey 326/.8/0972976. Citations: 76.

Contends that slave rebellion in the French Caribbean with the aim of freedom and citizenship changed the Enlightenment notion of universalism. Argues that, as such, and discussion of the French Revolution is incomplete if divorced from the imperialism of the Caribbean. Traces the flow of persons and communications throughout the French empire, focusing on slaves' struggles for freedom and the diplomatic implications of revolution. Notes the anomalous, unprecedented, violent, and tragic reinstatement of slavery in Guadeloupe and concludes that the new, supposedly more egalitarian version of universalism fell short in practice.

AHR 110: 521-22; *J Interdis Hist* 36: 310-11; *J Mod Hist* 78: 213-15; *WMQ* 63: 197-202.

193 Eltis, David, Frank D. Lewis, and Kenneth L. Sokoloff, eds. *Slavery in the Development of the Americas*. New York: Cambridge University Press, 2004. x, 372 p. ISBN 0521832772; ISBN 9780521832779; OCLC 54001509; LC Call Number HT1048 .S55; Dewey 306.3/62/097. Citations: 32.

Includes articles on the development of African slavery in the Americas, the Dutch role in American slavery, colonial Chesapeake economy in transatlantic perspective, the use of slavery in the production of subsistence crops in nineteenth-century São Paulo, comparative manumission in the United States and Guadeloupe, changes in prices of newly arrived slaves in the Americas between 1673 and 1865, slave markets in 1850s United States, Cuba, and Brazil, efficiencies of free and slave agriculture in antebellum United States, wealth accumulation in Virginia in the century prior to the Civil War, slavery in early America, and the differences in northern and southern wages before and after the Civil War.

J Interdis Hist 36: 99-100; *JAH* 92: 585-86; *JSH* 71: 660-62.

194 Ely, Melvin Patrick. *Israel on the Appomattox: A Southern Experiment in Black Freedom from the 1790s through the Civil War*. New York: Alfred A. Knopf, 2004. x, 640 p. ISBN 0679447385; ISBN 9780679447382; OCLC 53483636; LC Call Number F232.P83; Dewey 975.5/63200496073. Citations: 12.

Tells the story of ex-slaves, freed in 1796 after the death of their master, Richard Randolph, a cousin of Thomas Jefferson, who established a free black community in rural Prince Edward County, Virginia. Discusses Randolph's 1796 will, in which he expresses remorse for having inflicted a "monstrous tyranny" over other human beings "in violation of every sacred Law of nature." Explains that Randolph willed land to the ex-slaves, who built, with others, a settlement named Israel Hill. Finds that "black and white people related to one another in a stunning variety of ways" and explains that free blacks made tremendous advances, earning equal wages, doing business with white neighbors, and suing white people in court. Claims that the presence of free blacks threatened neither slavery nor white supremacy because the ex-slaves were disfranchised, second-class citizens and the vast majority of African Americans were held in bondage. Focuses on the activities of daily life, noting

that, although they were outnumbered nine-to-one by whites and twelve-to-one by slaves, the free blacks of Prince Edward County, Virginia, left remarkably rich documentation. Asserts that the norm was "civil relationships between white and free black people in a society whose fundamental assumptions about race seemed to dictate the opposite." Finds that, even as the sectional crisis intensified, local courts "still gave black defendants fairer hearings by far than would generally be the case from the latter nineteenth century to the 1960s." Concludes that the main focus of the time was slavery, not race and that southern whites in the late antebellum era were not uniformly proslavery, but that some in fact had reservations "about the morality of human bondage."
AHR 111: 169-70; *Booklist* 100: 1893; *HRNB* 33: 100; *JAH* 92: 978-79; *JSH* 71: 879-81; *LJ* 129n12: 96-97; *VMHB* 112: 428-29.

195 Fehrenbacher, Don E. *The Slaveholding Republic: An Account of the United States Government's Relations to Slavery.* New York: Oxford University Press, 2001. xii, 465 p. ISBN 0195141776; ISBN 9780195141771; OCLC 44427242; LC Call Number E446 .F45; Dewey 326/.0973 21. Citations: 47.
Discusses the evolution of the American government's relation to the issue of slavery, from the Constitutional Convention and ratification debates through the beginning of the Civil War. Reviews the fight over slavery in Washington, D.C., American foreign relations and the issue of slavery, the African slave trade in the early republic, the fugitive slave law, and the issue of slavery in the territories. Asserts that the initial Constitution was neutral on the question of slavery and that the perception of the Constitution's proslavery intent grew after the ratification debate and became a divisive national issue from that point to Lincoln's election in 1860, which southerners believed would trigger repeal of fugitive slave laws, the overturn of the Dred Scott case, the end of slavery in the territories, and the prohibition of slavery in the District of Columbia. Examines the Confederacy's Constitution, which explicitly sanctioned racial slavery in a way that the United States Constitution did not and emphasizes other differences between the two documents.
Booklist 97: 1097; *JSH* 68: 957-59; *LJ* 126n5: 93; *VMHB* 110: 496-97.

196 Foote, Thelma Willis. *Black and White Manhattan: The History of Racial Formation in Colonial New York City.* New York: Oxford University Press, 2004. x, 334 p. ISBN 0195088093 (hbk.); ISBN 9780195088090 (hbk.); ISBN 0195165373 (pbk.); ISBN 9780195165371 (pbk.); OCLC 50913091; LC Call Number F128.9.A1 F66; Dewey 305.8/009747/1 21. Citations: 11.
Looks at the history of colonial New York City through the lens of race, asserting that previous studies have focused on ethnicity and religion to the exclusion of race. Argues that white elite construction of whiteness in order to unite disparate communities shaped the colony. Studies Dutch New Amsterdam, noting that colony-building, especially labor demands, fostered pluralism and required the importation of African slaves, which brought whites and blacks into close contact with one another. Finds the origins of anti-black racism in the English takeover of the Dutch colony, noting that New York authorities extended citizenship to nearly all whites while denying citizenship to free blacks. Describes the legal codes that legitimized brutal punishments of and

strict control of black slaves and cites the importance of official treatments of the 1711 slave insurrection and the 1741 conspiracy, events that brought whites together in a common cause. Discusses other ways in which white elites created unity among diverse white groups, including the publication of a racial taxonomy that reclassified most whites as Anglo-Saxons, the official use of the English language, and the promotion of the Church of England's power to encourage non-English whites to identify themselves as British subjects. Traces the use of race through the American Revolution, in which blacks embraced revolt to create opportunities in British-occupied New York. Concludes that this situation was temporary, as after the war white revolutionaries reinstated a racial order in the new American nation.

AHR 111: 825-26; *JAH* 93: 498-99; *J Soc Hist* 41: 204-206; *RAH* 33: 501-509.

197   Fox-Genovese, Elizabeth and Eugene D. Genovese. *The Mind of the Master Class: History and Faith in the Southern Slaveholders' Worldview.* Cambridge: Cambridge University Press, 2005. xiv, 828 p. ISBN 0521850657 (hbk.); ISBN 9780521850650 (hbk.); ISBN 0521615623 (pbk.); ISBN 9780521615624 (pbk.); OCLC 60188223; LC Call Number F213 .F69; Dewey 306.3/62/0975. Citations: 39.

Rejects the notion that southern slaveholders were provincials, noting that most were well-educated and took seriously their studies in theology, philosophy, politics, and history. Contends that slaveholders, increasingly under attack by proponents of "modernity" and liberalism, sought to justify slaveholding society intellectually and to critique revolutionary-era notions of freedom. Explains that Enlightenment thinkers were confronted by the moral philosophy of southern clergymen and academics, who also attacked German and transcendentalist idealism. Finds that the North and South held "incompatible visions of the social relations necessary to sustain Christianity in a sinful world" and that southerners "reflected on the world they lived in and on the bearing of history and Christian faith on their lives as masters in a slaveholding society." Explains that classical history became particularly important for southerners to attack potential excesses of democracy and to support the idea that "inferiors" required the protection of white men and in return had to accept certain restrictions. Emphasizes that southerners were extraordinarily religious, subscribed to denominational periodicals, read widely from theological tracts, and held tightly to Calvinist doctrines like human depravity, the Trinity, the Holy Ghost, and the concept of heaven and hell.

AHR 111: 834-35; *JAH* 93: 1226-27; *J Soc Hist* 40: 788-90; *JSH* 73: 444-47; *NCHR* 83: 274-75; *RAH* 34: 332-41; *VMHB* 114: 498-99.

198   Geggus, David Patrick. *Haitian Revolutionary Studies.* Bloomington: Indiana University Press, 2002. xii, 334 p. ISBN 0253341043; ISBN 9780253341044; OCLC 50392054; LC Call Number F1923 .G34; Dewey 972.94/03. Citations: 36.

Presents several revised, previously published and new articles on the origins, development, and consequences of the revolution in Saint Domingue for persons of color. Claims that "too much in the historiography of the Haitian Revolution has gone without critical appraisal," which has impeded our understanding of

"this greatest of all slave revolts." Explains that historians have attributed slave revolts to ideology or economics, but argues that too little is known to make meaningful generalizations. Contends that leaders of the slave rebellion based claims to freedom not on republican ideology, but on rumors that the king had already granted it. Rejects as overdrawn claims that vodou was effectively an anti-white, revolutionary ideology that inspired revolt, pointing to the August 1791 Bois Caiman ceremony as a non-religious event and noting that vodou's incorporation of Christian elements could have had a stabilizing effect on slave society, rather than a disruptive one. Explores the relationship between free and enslaved persons of color and asserts that "Although the destruction of slavery constitutes [the Revolution's] core, only the simultaneous struggle of free and enslaved nonwhites explains its outcome." Examines the Spanish reactions to the revolt and concludes that the choice of the native word "Haiti" as the name for the new republic in 1804 was meant to diminish factionalism among the nonwhite population.
18c Stds 37: 113-22; *WMQ* 60: 877-79.

199   Gould, Philip. *Barbaric Traffic: Commerce and Antislavery in the Eighteenth-Century Atlantic World.* Cambridge, Mass.: Harvard University Press, 2003. viii, 258 p. ISBN 067401166X; ISBN 9780674011663; OCLC 51878852; LC Call Number E446 .G68; Dewey 306.3/62/097309033 21. Citations: 28.
Explores the "cultural discourses about the slave trade circulating throughout the late eighteenth-century Atlantic world," with a focus on how "transatlantic ideologies about the relations among commerce, consumption, and cultural health lent discursive power to these subjects." Concentrates on the "poetics of antislavery" from the 1770s to about 1810, emphasizing the shift from discussions of liberalism and republicanism to those of manners, civilization, and barbarity. Argues that "Antislavery sentimentalism" both "denounces and requires the rational calculation of market capitalism" and that black Atlantic autobiography provides a "rhetorical mix of liberty, property, and humanity" that "both empowers and undermines early Black Atlantic writing." Finds "mutually constitutive relations of sentiment and capitalism," noting that the two elements developed together, but remained in tension to one another. Concludes that the arguments against 'barbaric traffic' became increasingly more difficult to sustain in an era characterized by the development of liberal capitalism."
AHR 110: 443; *Am Lit* 77: 847-49; *EAL* 40: 199-202; *JAS* 39: 122-23; *JSH* 71: 423-24.

200   Hadden, Sally E. *Slave Patrols: Law and Violence in Virginia and the Carolinas.* Cambridge, Mass.: Harvard University Press, 2001. xii, 340 p. ISBN 0674004701; ISBN 9780674004702; OCLC 44860794; LC Call Number E443 .H33; Dewey 326/.09757 21. Citations: 38.
Focuses on slave patrols in Virginia and the Carolinas from about 1700 until the Civil War era. Refutes the notion "that patrollers came primarily from the lower social classes, often called 'poor whites' in Southern communities." Contends that the characterization of patrollers as "destitute non-slave-owning men" comes from historians' overreliance "on the 1930's WPA interviews conducted

with former slaves." Analyzes property ownership, including slaves, among various groups of patrollers, finding that patrol membership varied by location, and tended to be drawn less from the slaveholding class in the nineteenth than in the eighteenth century. Argues that participants came from a cross-section of southern society and included a significant percentage of slave owners. Discusses the influence of Barbadian laws on the formation of slave codes in the colonial South, early attempts to use Indians to pursue runaway slaves, and the 1727 Virginia laws that created patrols. Notes that the 1738 expanded statutes directed patrollers to visit "'all negro quarters, and other places suspected of entertaining unlawful assemblies of slaves, servants or other disorderly persons.'" Explains that Virginia county courts were authorized to pay patrollers a per diem in tobacco and that, from a legal perspective, the Virginia system was "largely unchanged until the Civil War." Describes the ways in which white attitudes were reflected in the patrol system, the nature of rural and urban patrols, relationships between patrols and police, constables, and sheriffs, variations in patrols in areas with large and small slave populations, and the legacy of patrols during Reconstruction.
AHR 107: 195-96; *AJLH* 44: 455-56; *Booklist* 97: 1024-25; *18c Stds* 39: 130-34; *FHQ* 81: 90-92; *GHQ* 85: 633-35; *JAH* 89: 627-28; *JAS* 37: 331; *JAS* 39: 319; *JER* 21: 554-56; *J Interdis Hist* 33: 135; *JNH* 86: 189-91; *J Soc Hist* 36: 220-21; *JSH* 68: 932-33; *LJ* 126n4: 113; *NCHR* 78: 380-81; *RAH* 30: 245-51; *SCHM* 103: 379-81; *VMHB* 109: 224-26; *VQR* 77: 122; *WMQ* 59: 799-803.

201 Harms, Robert W. *The* Diligent: *A Voyage through the Worlds of the Slave Trade.* New York: Basic Books, 2001. xxx, 466 p. ISBN 0465028713 (hbk.); ISBN 9780465028719 (hbk.); ISBN 0465028721 (pbk.); ISBN 9780465028726 (pbk.); OCLC 47767151; LC Call Number HT1177 .H37; Dewey 380.1/44/096 21. Citations: 16.
Examines the French slave trade of the early eighteenth century, particularly the activities of the French slave ship, the *Diligent*, in 1731-1732. Describes the voyage of the *Diligent* from the small Atlantic French port of Vannes to the West African coast and then on to Martinique and back to Vannes. Bases observations on the ship's journal, which was kept by Robert Durand, first lieutenant of the *Diligent*, on his first voyage to Africa. Notes that the *Diligent* delivered 256 African captives to Martinique, nine of whom died during the Atlantic crossing, along with four of the thirty-seven crew members of the ship. Reveals "the various 'worlds' through which it passed and the various local interests that conditioned its impact and outcome."
AHR 109: 144-45; *EHR* 118: 517-18; *LJ* 126n20: 143; *VQR* 78: 81-82; *WMQ* 61: 161-66.

202 Harris, Leslie. *In the Shadow of Slavery: African Americans in New York City, 1626–1863.* Chicago: University of Chicago Press, 2003. xii, 380 p. ISBN 0226317749; ISBN 9780226317748; OCLC 50143193; LC Call Number F128.9.N4; Dewey 305.896/07307471/09. Citations: 36.
Asserts that "Central to the story of freedom in New York is the development of class relations and community among blacks," especially class formation and the impact of class divisions on community reform strategies. Contends that

"compared to whites, cultural, political, and social markers became more important points of difference between the black middle class and the black working class than economic and occupational factors alone." Finds that, in the era of freedom for blacks, the black family was devalued, as whites used blacks for domestic labor. Describes the anti-abolitionist and anti-black riot of 1834, noting that it significantly shaped black and white abolitionists' views for many years afterward. Concludes that the generation led by Frederick Douglass, Henry Highland Garnet, and James W. C. Pennington, among others, developed a new "black working-class activism" that spurred activities such as manual labor schools and the black-led mass insurrection against the Fugitive Slave Law.
AHR 109: 1230-31; *JAH* 90: 1435-36; *JER* 23: 295-98; *J Soc Hist* 39: 558-60; *JSH* 73: 452-53; *LJ* 128n2: 101; *WMQ* 60: 899-905.

203 King, Stewart R. *Blue Coat or Powdered Wig: Free People of Color in Pre-Revolutionary Saint Domingue.* Athens: University of Georgia Press, 2001. xxvi, 328 p. ISBN 0820322334; ISBN 9780820322339; OCLC 44541818; LC Call Number F1911 .K56; Dewey 972.94/00496. Citations: 20.
Studies the free persons of color in Saint Domingue on the eve of the Haitian Revolution, focusing on the society's structure and prospects for and impacts of social mobility. Finds in free colored society two higher orders, a planter elite and a military leadership group. Notes that the former group had close connections to wealthy whites, who often provided start-up capital, a penchant for conservative investments and rural land ownership, and a fairly cosmopolitan worldview, while the latter formed connections to the militia, the police, or the army, participated in manumission efforts, and had relatively few ties to whites, but extensive connections to other free colored persons. Explains that the military group generally led the population and was more entrepreneurial than their planter counterparts, that they remained risk-tolerant and distinct, and that they had a greater affinity for African surnames and for African cultural practices.
AHR 107: 1604-1605; *18c Stds* 37: 113-22; *HAHR* 83: 381-83; *J Soc Hist* 36: 811-13.

204 Lemire, Elise Virginia. *"Miscegenation": Making Race in America.* Philadelphia: University of Pennsylvania Press, 2002. 204 p. ISBN 0812236645 (hbk.); ISBN 9780812236644 (hbk.); ISBN 9780812220643 (pbk.); ISBN 0812220641 (pbk.); OCLC 49011195; LC Call Number PS217.M57; Dewey 810.9/355. Citations: 21.
Explores relationships between black and white characters in fiction, including those of James Fenimore Cooper's *The Last of the Mohicans* (1826), Edgar Allan Poe's "Murders in the Rue Morgue" (1844), Herman Melville's "Benito Cereño" (1856), and Louisa May Alcott's "L. M." (1864). Argues that the modern usage of "race" comes from whites' desires to define in the years between the American Revolution and the Civil War "a set of traits that are more or less sexually desirable." Finds that in the North, movements after the Revolution to expand blacks' political rights increased white anxiety that social equality and intermarriage might result, leading to depictions of blacks as physically distasteful and socially inferior in order to discourage interracial

relationships. Explores texts and images produced in Massachusetts, New York, and Pennsylvania, including poetry on Jefferson's relations with Sally Hemings, anti-abolitionist tracts of the 1830s, and pamphlets condemning Abraham Lincoln's reelection in 1864 as certain to lead to race mixing.
AHR 108: 827-28; *Am Lit* 78: 613-15; *AQ* 55: 323-31; *JAH* 90: 1019; *Penn Hist* 71: 243-45; *PMHB* 127: 441-42.

205   Lepore, Jill. *New York Burning: Liberty, Slavery, and Conspiracy in Eighteenth-Century Manhattan.* New York: Alfred A. Knopf, 2005. xx, 323 p. ISBN 1400040299; ISBN 9781400040292; OCLC 56334128; LC Call Number F128.4 .L47; Dewey 974.7/102. Citations: 25.
Analyzes the so-called New York Conspiracy, or "Negro Plot" of 1741. Seeks to distinguish between the kind of liberty achieved by literate whites (e.g., freedom of the press) and that which blacks aspired to. Argues that the episode might have been colored by a white populace that was very aware of its oppression of blacks and drenched in factional politics. Suggests that whites' fear of black rebellion led them to blame any threat to the colony on the activity of slaves.
Concludes that "It is impossible to understand how faction and party worked in New York . . . without considering slavery, and how real and imagined slave conspirators functioned as a phantom political party" and that "in eighteenth-century New York, slavery made liberty possible."
AHR 111: 1503-1504; *Booklist* 101: 1745; *Booklist* 102: 20; *JAH* 93: 184-85; *LJ* 130n7: 138; *LJ* 130n13: 100-102; *Penn Hist* 73: 263-65; *RAH* 34: 281-90; *WMQ* 63: 611-15.

206   Levy, Andrew. *The First Emancipator: The Forgotten Story of Robert Carter, the Founding Father Who Freed His Slaves.* New York: Random House, 2005. xviii, 310 p. ISBN 0375508651 (hbk.); ISBN 9780375508653 (hbk.); ISBN 9780375761041 (pbk.); ISBN 0375761047 (pbk.); OCLC 56413293; LC Call Number F229.C34; Dewey 973.3/092. Citations: 7.
Examines the life of Robert Carter III, one of the wealthiest men in eighteenth-century America, and his monumental "Deed of Gift," recorded in 1791, which allowed for the largest single emancipation of slaves until the Emancipation Proclamation. Describes Carter's employment of a system of gradual emancipation, which was strongly opposed by family, neighbors, and local officials and which was carried out by his lawyers and agents. Traces Carter's spiritual evolution "from traditional Episcopalian to radical Baptist reformer to Swedenborgian" and how it influenced his views on slavery.
Booklist 101: 1426; *JAH* 93: 194; *JSH* 72: 656-57; *LJ* 130n8: 101; *VMHB* 113: 414-15.

207   Libby, David J. *Slavery and Frontier Mississippi, 1720–1835.* Jackson: University Press of Mississippi, 2004. xvii, 163 p. ISBN 1578065992; ISBN 9781578065998; OCLC 52251140; LC Call Number E445.M6; Dewey 306.3/62/0976209032. Citations: 4.
Traces the development of "plantation society and economy established in eighteenth-century Natchez." Notes that the area was significant economically in the early nineteenth century, particularly as cotton and American political power

were rising and becoming more important elements of the Atlantic economy. Examines the transition from an exchange economy of hides, lumber, and other raw materials to the cultivation of tobacco, indigo, and finally cotton. Indicates that the regional economy was closely tied to Louisiana and suggests that many western settlers were ready to swear allegiance to Spain in order to secure safe navigation of the Mississippi River and therefore have access to overseas markets. Notes a change in relationship between planters and their slaves, from benevolence early on to greed, and then "a sense of humanitarianism" and accommodation after the War of 1812, when laws aimed at reducing cruelty were implemented to reduce the risks of slave rebellion, followed by more severe treatment brought on by the rise of cotton, and finally, in the mid-1830s, ideological defenses of slavery brought on by hysteria over slave conspiracy. *JAH* 92: 210-11; *J Soc Hist* 40: 239-41.

208   Lockley, Timothy. *Lines in the Sand: Race and Class in Lowcountry Georgia, 1750–1860*. Athens: University of Georgia Press, 2001. xx, 280 p. ISBN 0820322288; ISBN 9780820322285; OCLC 43751741; LC Call Number F290 .L63; Dewey 975.8. Citations: 14.
Examines the relationships between nonslaveholding whites and slaves in the Georgia lowcountry, noting that interactions were extensive from the colonial era through the Civil War and were shaped by many factors other than race and racism. Demonstrates that racial barriers between whites and blacks in Georgia, though real, were permeable because individuals in both groups recognized commonalities in class and in exclusion from power centers. Acknowledges that whites, regardless of class, held a privileged status in law and society that African Americans could never attain, and tensions and hostility between poor whites and slaves were clear. Notes that, nonetheless, some poor whites "carried on a normal day-to-day existence with African Americans that was not characterized by hatred and suspicion." Finds that members of the two groups, especially in rural areas of the lowcountry during the early national period, worshiped together in mixed evangelical churches, which "to some extent blurred the racial distinction between poor whites and African Americans." Points out that poor whites and slaves also worked together, met in brothels, taverns, and gambling dens, engaged in underground trade, and occasionally committed crimes together. Concludes that "the similar social condition of nonslaveholding whites and African Americans in these situations destroyed the concept of whiteness as a trait that naturally and innately elevated the European above the African."
AHR 107: 535-36; *GHQ* 86: 620-34; *JAH* 88: 1511-12; *JSH* 68: 679-80; *WMQ* 59: 302-304.

209   Lowance, Mason I., ed. *A House Divided: The Antebellum Slavery Debates in America, 1776–1865*. Princeton, N.J.: Princeton University Press, 2003. lxxi, 492 p. ISBN 0691002274 (hbk.); ISBN 9780691002279 (hbk.); ISBN 0691002282 (pbk.); ISBN 9780691002286 (pbk.); OCLC 50064944; LC Call Number E441 .H86; Dewey 326/.0973/09033 21. Citations: 3.
Presents excerpts of documents covering the public national debates over slavery in antebellum America. Reviews arguments on both sides, which were

forwarded by essayists, fiction writers, activists, politicians, and judges. Highlights biblical, economic, literary, and scientific arguments, introducing each with biographic information about the writers. Discusses the ways in which writers used race theory, phrenology, and ethnography to advance their positions.
JSH 70: 648-49.

210   Mackenthun, Gesa. *Fictions of the Black Atlantic in American Foundational Literature*. New York: Routledge, 2004. x, 214 p. ISBN 0415333024; ISBN 9780415333023; ISBN 9780203412640; ISBN 0203412648; OCLC 54046951; LC Call Number PS217.B55; Dewey 810.9/3552/09034. Citations: 5.
Examines the nineteenth-century "postcolonial" corpus made up of texts written between American independence and the Civil War. Includes many texts that are set on or near the ocean and that comment on the complex relationship of postcolonial America to Atlantic commerce and the transatlantic slave trade.
JAS 39: 565-66.

211   McBride, Dwight A. *Impossible Witnesses: Truth, Abolitionism, and Slave Testimony*. New York: New York University Press, 2001. xvi, 205 p. ISBN 0814756042 (hbk.); ISBN 9780814756041 (hbk.); ISBN 0814756050 (pbk.); ISBN 9780814756058 (pbk.); OCLC 47044779; LC Call Number PS366.A35; Dewey 306.3/62/0973. Citations: 18.
Discusses the rhetorical strategies and discursive contexts of early nineteenth-century British antislavery tracts, novels, and selected writings of former slaves Mary Prince, Phillis Wheatley, Olaudah Equiano, and Frederick Douglass. Argues that personal slave narratives used a rhetorical appeal based on the inadequacy of language to share lived experience and thereby secured undeniable authority of interpretation over a condition that was inherently impossible to narrate (slavery). Explains that "In these moments of unspeakable horror the narrative is denied to us and is reduced to the sheer personal memory of the witness, which we can witness only as that which is unspeakable." Reviews the subject of slavery as a major topic of Romanticism, particularly in the works of Margaret Fuller, Ralph Waldo Emerson, William Lloyd Garrison, and Maria Edgeworth.
Am Lit 76: 177-79; *JAEH* 22: 72-76; *JAH* 89: 1032.

212   McMillin, James A. *The Final Victims: Foreign Slave Trade to North America, 1783–1810*. Columbia: University of South Carolina Press, 2004. xiv, 207 p. ISBN 1570035466; ISBN 9781570035463; OCLC 54415883; LC Call Number HT1049 .M35; Dewey 306.3/62/097. Citations: 11.
Examines the Atlantic slave trade between the end of the Revolutionary War and the federal ban of the trade beginning in 1808, focusing on the extent of the trade, changes in the origins of the new generation of forced migrants and the merchants who owned the ships that carried slaves, and the variations in treatment of the human cargo. Concludes that the number of foreign slaves brought to America between 1783 and 1808 was on the order of 170,000. Finds that after the Revolution, European (particularly British) merchants gained a

larger share of the slave trade, largely because of their positions as creditors, displacing many southerners. Emphasizes the horrors of the post-revolutionary middle passage, arguing that the trade's brutalities exceeded those of the colonial era.

AHR 111: 166-67; *GHQ* 89: 113-14; *JAH* 92: 598-99; *JER* 25: 130-33; *J Soc Hist* 40: 237-39; *JSH* 71: 670-71; *NCHR* 82: 264-65; *SCHM* 107: 351-53.

213 Menard, Russell R. *Migrants, Servants, and Slaves: Unfree Labor in Colonial British America.* Burlington, Vt.: Ashgate, 2001. 302 p. ISBN 0860788385; ISBN 9780860788386; OCLC 45339150; LC Call Number E446 .M48; Dewey 973.2 21. Citations: 6.

Presents eleven essays originally published between 1973 and 1995. Includes two general pieces, five on Maryland, and four on South Carolina covering, generally, demography, the transition of the colonial labor force from white indentured servants to black slaves, and long-term social change.

Econ Hist Rev 55: 375-76; *J Econ Hist* 61: 1135-37.

214 Morrison, Michael A. and James Brewer Stewart, eds. *Race and the Early Republic: Racial Consciousness and Nation-Building in the Early Republic.* Lanham, Md.: Rowman and Littlefield, 2002. iv, 203 p. ISBN 0742521303 (hbk.); ISBN 9780742521308 (hbk.); ISBN 0742521311 (pbk.); ISBN 9780742521315 (pbk.); LC Call Number E302.1 .R33; Dewey 323.1/73/09. Citations: 5.

Presents essays on the role of race formation in the making of the American nation, including pieces that cover "whiteness studies," racial polarities in the eighteenth and nineteenth centuries, and Baltimore Quakers in late eighteenth- and early nineteenth-century Indian country.

JER 23: 471-74.

215 Mouser, Bruce L., ed. *A Slaving Voyage to Africa and Jamaica: The Log of the "Sandown," 1793–1794.* Bloomington: Indiana University Press, 2002. xxiv, 156 p. ISBN 0253340772; ISBN 9780253340771; OCLC 48241320; LC Call Number HT1162 .M68; Dewey 380.1/44/094. Citations: 9.

Publishes the log of Captain Samuel Gamble, commander of the London ship *Sandown*'s 1793–94 Guinea venture. Tells the story of the sixteen-month voyage to Rio Nunez and Kingston and the captain's eighty-day return passage to Liverpool on the ship *Benson*. Contains journal entries and sea logs from 23 January 1793 in London to 11 October 1794, when Gamble disembarked at Liverpool. Includes information on navigation, convoys, maritime art history, African history, medical history, and the slave trade.

WMQ 61: 161-66.

216 Murphy, Thomas. *Jesuit Slaveholding in Maryland, 1717–1838.* New York: Routledge, 2001. xxv, 258 p. ISBN 0815340524; ISBN 9780815340522; OCLC 46976486; LC Call Number BX3709.M3; Dewey 271/.530752. Citations: 6.

Finds that the Jesuit order in Maryland held nearly four hundred slaves by the early nineteenth century. Describes the moral and religious assumptions that led

Jesuits to acquire slaves, affected their treatment of and attitude toward slaves, and finally led to the sale of the slaves in 1838. and that sent hundreds of African Americans to Louisiana. Argues that Jesuit slaveholders were caught between conflicting worlds of Jesuit ethics and Anglo-American culture. Contends that the Jesuits sold the slaves due to "the desire to fit in," to be accepted in a non-Catholic world. Concludes that Jesuit slaveholders, like their Protestant neighbors, became more racist and profit-oriented in the early nineteenth century and that even after divesting their slaves, the order did not explicitly condemn slavery.

AHR 108: 824-25; *JSH* 70: 898-99.

217   Newman, Richard S. *The Transformation of American Abolitionism: Fighting Slavery in the Early Republic*. Chapel Hill: University of North Carolina Press, 2002. xiv, 256 p. ISBN 0807826715 (hbk.); ISBN 9780807826713 (hbk.); ISBN 0807849987 (pbk.); ISBN 9780807849989 (pbk.); OCLC 47023536; LC Call Number   E446 .N58; Dewey 326.8/0973. Citations: 39.

Traces the transformation of abolitionist movements from relatively mild post-Revolutionary form to the more radical and fiery approach of the 1830s. Attributes the character of the milder movement to the upper-class benevolence that held sway in the 1790s and that sought change incrementally through established institutions, particularly the courts. Notes that groups like the Quaker-based Pennsylvania Abolition Society rejected zealotry and confrontation in favor of means that were respectable and aimed at amelioration of harm. Connects radicalization of the movement to the shift from elitism to egalitarianism and rationalism to emotionalism, which sought more immediate results and greater racial integration. Stresses the important role of African Americans in both pre- and post-1830 abolitionism, noting that they adopted a moral and emotional approach to antislavery because conservative abolitionists excluded them.

AHR 108: 522-23; *GHQ* 86: 455-57; *JAH* 89: 1514-15; *JER* 23: 119-23; *J Interdis Hist* 33: 664-66; *JSH* 70: 913-14; *NEQ* 75: 656-62; *RAH* 31: 220-27; *VQR* 79: 8; *WMQ* 59: 1040-46.

218   Parent, Anthony S., Jr. *Foul Means: The Formation of a Slave Society in Virginia, 1660–1740*. Chapel Hill: University of North Carolina Press, published for the Omohundro Institute of Early American History and Culture, 2003. xiv, 291 p. ISBN 0807828130 (hbk.); ISBN 9780807828137 (hbk.); ISBN 0807854867 (pbk.); ISBN9780807854860 (pbk.); OCLC 51454240; LC Call Number E445.V8; Dewey 326/.09755/09032. Citations: 20.

Characterizes early settlers in Virginia as ruthlessly land-hungry, deceitful in their relations with local Indian tribes, and willing to use political positions, bribery, and imported labor to secure and benefit from their large landholdings. Focuses on William Byrd I and William Fitzhugh as the primary proponents of the shift from indentured servants to slaves and notes the role of tobacco market fluctuations in colonists' labor decisions. Contends that planters were intentional in the movement to racial slavery and sought to mitigate class differences through the passage of laws that emphasized race, but that the development of slavery had the opposite effect, resulting in class and racial conflict (e.g., Bacon's Rebellion and organized slave resistance). Explains that planters responded to strife by developing an ideology of patriarchalism in the 1720s and 1730s, which entailed emphases on social order through hierarchy, provincialism, and efforts to convert slaves to Christianity.

AHR 110: 782-83; *18c Stds* 38: 361-67; *GHQ* 88: 253-55; *JAH* 91: 990; *J Soc Hist* 39: 556-58; *JSH* 71: 138-40; *NCHR* 82: 389-90; *VMHB* 111: 299-300; *WMQ* 62: 310-12.

219 Paton, Diana, ed. *A Narrative of Events, since the First of August, 1834, by James Williams*. Durham, N. C.: Duke University Press, 2001. x, 141 p. ISBN 0822326582 (hbk.); ISBN 9780822326588 (hbk.); ISBN 0822326477 (pbk.); ISBN 9780822326472 (pbk.); OCLC 45065984; LC Call Number F1886 .W56; Dewey 972.92/04. Citations: 5.

Presents information related to a short slave narrative published in 1837, which influenced the abolition of the apprenticeship system in Jamaica. Notes that the pamphlet sparked debates throughout Britain and Ireland, due to its graphic portrayal of punishments that Afro-Jamaicans endured.

HAHR 83: 170-71; *WMQ* 59: 809-812.

220 Paton, Diana. *No Bond but the Law: Punishment, Race, and Gender in Jamaican State Formation, 1780–1870*. Durham, N.C.: Duke University Press, 2004. xv, 291 p. ISBN 0822334011 (hbk.); ISBN 9780822334019 (hbk.); ISBN 0822333988 (pbk.); ISBN 9780822333982 (pbk.); OCLC 54882131; LC Call Number HV9323.A5; Dewey 364.97292/09/034. Citations: 16.

Traces the aftermath of slavery's abolition in Jamaica. Discusses conflicts between imperial elites, including absentee sugar plantation owners and resident planter elites over conventions of treatment of black laborers. Describes conflicts between African laborers and magistrates and how various interests shaped the penal system, including the punishment of women. Explains the eighteenth-century Jamaican expansion of prisons and the commitment of runaway slaves to workhouses by planters, who sought to guarantee dominance and an adequate supply of slave labor. Notes that the apprenticeship system officially replaced slavery in the 1830s, but that it amounted to slavery under another name and made use of stipendiary magistrates to enforce discipline on behalf of the planters. Argues that in the place of slavery, whites expanded prisons as a means of "enlightened" and "humanitarian" social control.

AHR 110: 1222; *HAHR* 86: 844-46; *HRNB* 34: 32-33; *J Soc Hist* 42: 501-503.

221 Rothman, Adam. *Slave Country: American Expansion and the Origins of the Deep South*. Cambridge, Mass.: Harvard University Press, 2005. xi, 296 p. ISBN 0674016742; ISBN 9780674016743; OCLC 56191767; LC Call Number E446 .R67; Dewey 306.3/62/0973. Citations: 29.

Explores the period from ratification of the Constitution to the Missouri Compromise in an effort to find when slavery transitioned from "necessary evil" to "positive good." Finds that the shift occurred early on, with the expansion of the institution to the Deep South, which "emerged from contingent global forces, concrete policies pursued by governments, and countless small choices made by thousands of individuals in diverse stations of life." Notes that the enlargement of territory in which slavery was utilized was encouraged by demographic and economic shifts, including southwesterly migration, increased demand for cotton from a rapidly expanding textile industry, and need to supplement Caribbean sugar supplies. Contends that Jefferson's agrarian vision for the nation encouraged the expansion and that Jackson "carried forward the Jeffersonian idea that converting Indian land into private property would invite migration, strengthen security, and ultimately guarantee US sovereignty in the Deep South."

Ag Hist 81: 141-43; *AHR* 111: 167-68; *JAH* 92: 1425-26; *JAS* 40: 675-76; *JER* 27: 745-56; *JSH* 72: 665-66; *RAH* 34: 18-23; *Soc Hist* 32: 82-115; *WMQ* 63: 206-208.

222 Rothman, Joshua D. *Notorious in the Neighborhood: Sex and Families across the Color Line in Virginia, 1787–1861.* Chapel Hill: University of North Carolina Press, 2003. xvii, 341 p. ISBN 0807827681 (hbk.); ISBN 9780807827680 (hbk.); ISBN 0807854409 (pbk.); ISBN 9780807854402 (pbk.); OCLC 49824701; LC Call Number HQ1031 .R695; Dewey 306.84/6/09755. Citations: 25.

Takes up Virginians' toleration of interracial relationships, while maintaining the notion of white supremacy. Focuses in particular on the Hemings case and the Jewish community in Richmond, which maintained a zone of tolerance within in the city until the 1850s. Discusses tightened regulation of racial intermixing, which is revealed in divorce petitions that allege interracial adultery and in efforts to define race by ancestry. Concludes that "interracial sex was ubiquitous in urban, town, and plantation communities throughout the state" and that "bending to the winds of social and legal contradiction helped keep early national and antebellum Virginia from breaking."

AHR 110: 1178-79; *FHQ* 83: 78-79; *GHQ* 88: 101-105; *JAH* 91: 231; *JER* 24: 500-503; *J Interdis Hist* 38: 133-34; *JSH* 71: 143-44; *NCHR* 80: 379-80; *PMHB* 128: 322-24; *RAH* 32: 20-26; *VMHB* 111: 191-92; *WMQ* 61: 371-75.

223 Schama, Simon. *Rough Crossings: Britain, the Slaves, and the American Revolution.* London: BBC, 2005. 447 p. ISBN 0563487097; ISBN 9780563487098; OCLC 60741030; LC Call Number E269.N3; Dewey 326.0973/09033; Dewey 973.31. Citations: 41.

Investigates the founding of Sierra Leone as a refuge for London's "black poor," black loyalists, and the Maroons of Jamaica. Discusses the Somerset decision (1772), the effect of Lord Dunmore's proclamation (1775), the Revolutionary War in the South, efforts to settle free blacks at Granville Town (1787), the movement of black loyalists to Canada, the founding of Freetown in 1792, the departure of blacks from Nova Scotia, the life and work of John Clarkson, the governorships of Zachary Macaulay and Thomas Ludlam, French attacks, and Sierra Leone's transition to British colony.

AHR 111: 1504-1505; *Booklist* 102: 4; *JER* 27: 546-55; *LJ* 131n5: 83; *NEQ* 80: 144-47; *VMHB* 115: 123-25.

224 Schwarz, Philip J.,ed. *Slavery at the Home of George Washington.* Mount Vernon, Va.: Mount Vernon Ladies' Association, 2001. iii, 182 p. ISBN 0931917387; ISBN 9780931917387; OCLC 50446772; LC Call Number E312.17 .S43; Dewey 973.4. Citations: 7.

Presents essays on George Washington as slaveowner. Covers the particulars of the plantation at Mount Vernon, slavery and agriculture, private lives of slaves, the archeology of slavery at Mount Vernon, Washington's emancipated laborers and their descendants, and the various historical interpretations of slave life on the Mount Vernon plantation. Points out that "Mr. Washington may have spent more of his lifetime overseeing enslaved laborers than he did supervising soldiers or government officials."

JSH 70: 131-32; *VMHB* 111: 81-82.

225 Sensbach, Jon F. *Rebecca's Revival: Creating Black Christianity in the Atlantic World.* Cambridge, Mass.: Harvard University Press, 2005. 318 p. ISBN 0674016890 (hbk.); ISBN 9780674016897 (hbk.); ISBN 9780674022577 (pbk.); ISBN 0674022572 (pbk.); OCLC 56198689; LC Call Number BV3785.P74; Dewey 269/.2/092. Citations: 23.

Tells the story of Rebecca Protten, an eighteenth-century mixed-race woman who was enslaved in the West Indies, proselytized in central Europe with the Moravians, and then worked on the Gold Coast of West Africa. Concludes that Protten played an extraordinary role in "the origins of the black church."

AHR 111: 794-95; *Booklist* 101: 1039; *CJH* 40: 594-95; *18c Stds* 39: 573-74; *JAAR* 75: 182-85; *JAH* 92: 1409-1410; *JAS* 40: 450-51; *JER* 26: 349-52; *NCHR* 82: 508-509; *WMQ* 65: 378-84.

226 Sparks, Randy J. *The Two Princes of Calabar: An Eighteenth-Century Atlantic Odyssey.* Cambridge, Mass.: Harvard University Press, 2004. 189 p. ISBN 0674013123; ISBN 9780674013124; OCLC 53038067; LC Call Number DA125.N4; Dewey 909/.049607/092266944. Citations: 16.

Traces the journeys of two enslaved Africans, Little Ephraim Robin John and Ancona Robin Robin John, from the slave ports of Old Calabar to Dominica and Virginia, then Britain, and finally back to West Africa. Explains that both were members of the ruling slave-trading family of Old Town in Old Calabar before being enslaved themselves. Examines the complexities of the Euro-African trade relationship and the impact of that trade on African economies and societies, particularly in the displacement of traditional leaders by emerging mercantile elites. Describes the Robin Johns legal efforts in Britain to gain freedom in the wake of the Somerset case, their conversion to Methodism, and their exploitation of linguistic and cultural knowledge and of personal connections.

AHR 110: 759-60; *Booklist* 100: 1125; *JAH* 92: 196; *JAS* 40: 452-53; *JSH* 73: 151-53.

227 Sweet, John Wood. *Bodies Politic: Negotiating Race in the American North, 1730–1830.* Baltimore, Md.: Johns Hopkins University Press, 2003. xii, 486 p. ISBN 0801873789; ISBN 9780801873782; OCLC 50913507; LC Call Number F7 .S88; Dewey 305.896/073074/09033. Citations: 32.

Discusses the connection between race and American nationalism, using Rhode Island as a case study. Notes that citizenship became defined as something reserved for whites only, even though Native Americans, African Americans, and European Americans lived and worked together and that, over time, non-white groups were continuously redefined as outsiders. Asserts that "In many ways, America came to present itself as a white nation when it was, and had been from the start, diverse, hybrid, and multiracial." Finds that by the post-revolutionary period white authorities had supplanted culture "with the more stubborn, essentialist, identities of race."
AHR 110: 793-94; *HRNB* 32: 97; *JAH* 92: 208-209; *JAS* 39: 138-39; *JER* 24: 680-82; *NEQ* 78: 125-27; *RAH* 32: 347-51; *WMQ* 62: 791-94.

228 Waldstreicher, David. *Runaway America: Benjamin Franklin, Slavery and the American Revolution.* New York: Hill and Wang, 2004. xv, 315 p. ISBN 0809083140; ISBN 9780809083145; OCLC 54022435; LC Call Number E302.6.F8; Dewey 973.3/092. Citations: 27.
Uses "running away" as a principal theme for Franklin's life and for the early American nation. Points out that a young apprenticed Franklin escaped from his master and then from legal dependence upon his brother James to find opportunity in Philadelphia. Makes the connection between Franklin's running away and others who similarly sought their freedom (e.g., slaves, bound laborers) and the attempt of the colonies to escape from the grip of Great Britain. Notes that Franklin, as colonial agent, adjusted his rhetoric on servitude and freedom to meet the needs of the moment and that he often had to deny or downplay slavery in public exchanges with Europeans. Concludes that Franklin was "a runaway who made good but who never escaped the lessons painfully learned" and that his antislavery, "like that of the American Revolution, was a runaway's antislavery: compromised and compromising."
EAL 41: 535-53; *JAH* 93: 502-503; *JER* 27: 788-91; *J Soc Hist* 39: 1240-44; *LJ* 129n12: 94; *NEQ* 78: 653-55; *PMHB* 130: 236-37; *RAH* 33: 1-7; *WMQ* 62: 745-64.

229 White, Shane. *Stories of Freedom in Black New York.* Cambridge, Mass.: Harvard University Press, 2002. x, 260 p. ISBN 0674008936; ISBN 9780674008939; OCLC 50028767; LC Call Number F128.9.N4; LC Call Number ML3800; Dewey 974.7/100496073. Citations: 23.
Studies manifestations of African American freedom in New York City during roughly the first three decades of the nineteenth century, with special focus on the African Company, a theatrical troupe that performed for mixed-race audiences. Contends that, in its two years (1821–23), the Company performed Shakespeare and other popular plays and thereby asserted an African American claim to mainstream American culture. Describes the roles of various actors, theater managers, and critics and finds that many whites were attracted to African American culture, while others reviled it. Notes that the "resulting conjunction between black creative activity and white voyeurism was unprecedented, and would not recur until the Harlem Renaissance" and concludes that "black life in these awkward transition decades possessed a distinct edge, a particular kind of restless vitality."

AHR 109: 1567-68; *Booklist* 99: 299; *JAH* 90: 1435-36; *JER* 23: 295-98; *JSH* 70: 138-39; *LJ* 128n1: 134; *PMHB* 128: 92-93; *WMQ* 60: 899-904.

230 Wiencek, Henry. *An Imperfect God: George Washington, His Slaves, and the Creation of America.* New York: Farrar, Straus and Giroux, 2003. 416 p. ISBN 0374175268; ISBN 9780374175269; OCLC 51942552; LC Call Number E312.17 .W6; Dewey 973.4/1/092. Citations: 30.

Underscores Washington's ambivalence about slavery, noting his embrace of the institution for economic purposes, but his concerns about it morally. Explains that Washington the Enlightenment figure condemned slavery, while Washington the planter traveled with his slaves and condoned his wife's strict treatment of them. Concludes that Washington only rejected slavery outright late in life, after 1789, that before the Revolution Washington "was just another striving young planter, blithely ordering breeding wenches for his slave trade, blithely exiling a man to a likely death at hard labor," while at the end of his life Washington was "sickened by slavery" and was "willing to sacrifice his own substance to end it."

Booklist 100: 297; *JAH* 91: 997-98; *LJ* 128n14: 38; *LJ* 128n15: 73; *LJ* 129n1: 50; *VMHB* 111: 414-16; *WMQ* 62: 745-64.

231 Wilkins, Roger. *Jefferson's Pillow: The Founding Fathers and the Dilemma of Black Patriotism.* Boston: Beacon Press, 2001. 163 p. ISBN 0807009563; ISBN 9780807009567; OCLC 46343100; LC Call Number E302.5 .W68; Dewey 973/.09/9. Citations: 9.

Investigates the interactions with slavery of Thomas Jefferson, George Mason, George Washington, and James Madison, acknowledging that all benefited greatly from bound labor and all fought to defend the institution. Recognizes that Virginia planters held to "a hierarchical and paternalistic world where the weight and worth of human beings were always tied tightly to property," but that they set in motion the arc of applied natural rights that eventually resulted in the fulfillment of the American principle of equality.

Booklist 97: 1834; *JSH* 69: 408-409; *WMQ* 59: 802-805.

232 Wills, Garry. *Negro President: Jefferson and the Slave Power.* Boston, Mass.: Houghton Mifflin, 2003. xiv, 274 p. ISBN 0618343989; ISBN 9780618343980; OCLC 52902750; LC Call Number E332.2 .W57; Dewey 326/.0973; Dewey 973.460922. Citations: 27.

Links Jefferson's career to the "protection and extension of the slave power," the policies and constitutional provisions (e.g., the Three-Fifths Compromise) that led to the expansion of the institution and an electoral advantage for the South. Compares Jefferson to the Federalist Timothy Pickering of Massachusetts and indicates that the Federalists were typically more liberationist than were the Jeffersonians. Emphasizes Pickering's role in securing diplomatic and military aid for Toussaint L'Ouverture and Jefferson's opposition to the Haitian Revolution and to diluted southern power.

Booklist 100: 179; *HRNB* 32: 98; *JSH* 72: 871-908; *LJ* 128n16: 97-98.

233 Winch, Julie. *A Gentleman of Color: The Life of James Forten.* New York: Oxford University Press, 2002. x, 501 p. ISBN 0195086910; ISBN 9780195086911; OCLC 47216859; LC Call Number E185.97.F717; Dewey 326/.092. Citations: 23.

Presents a biography of Forten, a "gentleman of color," who was a privateer during the Revolution, an apprentice to a Philadelphia sailmaker, and an entrepreneur. Describes Forten's business and political careers, noting his leadership in the antislavery and African American convention movements. Asserts that "what he wanted, and what he felt he deserved, was the title he would never in fact be given: American citizen."

AHR 107: 1550-51; *JAH* 90: 1005; *LJ* 126n19: 77; *NEQ* 75: 647-55; *PMHB* 126: 654-57.

234 Winter, Kari J. and Benjamin F. Prentiss, eds. *The Blind African Slave, or, Memoirs of Boyrereau Brinch, Nicknamed Jeffery Brace.* Madison: University of Wisconsin Press, 2004. xvi, 244 p. ISBN 0299201406 (hbk.); ISBN 9780299201401 (hbk.); ISBN 0299201449 (pbk.); ISBN 9780299201449 (pbk.); OCLC 54966234; LC Call Number E444.B86; Dewey 306.3/62/092. Citations: 4.

Presents a first-hand account of eighteenth-century New England slavery in the form of the memoir of Jeffery Brace, who suffered under the harsh treatment of master John Burwell and his wife. Demonstrates that slavery among Puritans could be every bit as inhumane as it was in the South and shows that earning one's freedom through service in the Revolution was difficult. Places in stark relief the racism that Brace faced after he became a free man and notes Vermont's system of involuntary child labor that masqueraded as apprenticeship.

Am Lit 77: 873-81; *JAS* 40: 203; *NEQ* 79: 136-38.

235 Woodson, Byron W., Sr. *A President in the Family: Thomas Jefferson, Sally Hemings, and Thomas Woodson.* Westport, Conn.: Praeger, 2001. xviii, 271 p. ISBN 0275971740; ISBN 9780275971748; OCLC 44812116; LC Call Number E332.2 .W66; Dewey 921; Dewey 973.4/6/092/2. Citations: 7.

Investigates the claim that Thomas Jefferson was the father of Sally Hemings' first child, Thomas Woodson, and thus the progenitor of the Woodson family. Discusses the life of Jefferson and the Woodson family legend and critiques the DNA testing of 1997, which failed to show a genetic link between the Woodsons and Jefferson.

Booklist 97: 1446; *JAH* 89: 206-207; *LJ* 126n7: 108-109; *WMQ* 58: 1039-46.

8 Gender

236 Anzilotti, Cara. *In the Affairs of the World: Women, Patriarchy, and Power in Colonial South Carolina.* Westport, Conn.: Greenwood Press, 2002. x, 216 p. ISBN 0313320314; ISBN 9780313320316; OCLC 48177307; LC Call Number HQ1438.S6; Dewey 305.4/09757. Citations: 7.

Reconsiders the image of South Carolina women, arguing that those of the planter class did not seek autonomy, but rather sought to advance the material positions of their families. Notes that, due to disease, even among the young, widows often were left to manage plantations. Finds that this role did not translate to real power, but merely advanced the aspirations of male relatives. Argues that women understood their temporary management of property to be a "stopgap, a necessary expedient" and that, seeing women as "frail, frivolous, extravagant, fickle, and none too bright," planter men still expected women to be obedient. Concludes that colonists' retention of gender norms flowed from their desire to re-create English society and therefore that females never sought "financial independence as an end in itself." Rather, women reassured their male kin that females could never threaten patriarchy, even though this assurance often took the form of "formulaic self-deprecation." Suggests that such differences between public expressions and private motivations regarding gender norms reveal complications in social relationships and structures.
JAH 90: 995-96; *JSH* 69: 873-74; *WMQ* 60: 225-29.

237 Berkin, Carol. *Revolutionary Mothers: Women in the Struggle for America's Independence.* New York: Random House, 2005. xviii, 194 p. ISBN 1400041635; ISBN 9781400041633; OCLC 54826129; LC Call Number E276.B47 B505; Dewey 973.3/082. Citations: 6.

Outlines the roles that women played in the Revolutionary era, noting that they organized boycotts of British goods, managed businesses, followed their husbands' military units, acted as spies, saboteurs, and couriers, and even fought as Margaret Corbin did at the Battle of Monmouth. Explains that, though their roles expanded slightly during the War, afterwards women "returned to their kitchens and parlors, to nurseries and gardens—and to the anonymity their society considered appropriately feminine." Finds similarly that "Many African American women who won their freedom lost it again through violence and trickery and the venality of men entrusted with their care." Reviews the lives of both loyalists and patriots and women of various races and social levels. Contends that, after the Revolution, women were not perceived as "morally and mentally inferior to men," a view that grew into the notion of Republican Motherhood.

AHR 111: 827-28; *Booklist* 101: 805; *JAH* 93: 191; *JSH* 72: 653-54; *NEQ* 78: 651-53; *Penn Hist* 73: 113-15; *RAH* 33: 309-13.

238 Bloch, Ruth H. *Gender and Morality in Anglo-American Culture, 1650–1800*. Berkeley: University of California Press, 2003. x, 225 p. ISBN 0520234057 (hbk.); ISBN 9780520234055 (hbk.); ISBN 0520234065 (pbk.); ISBN 9780520234062 (pbk.); OCLC 49415634; LC Call Number HQ1416 .B53; Dewey 305.4/0973 21. Citations: 21.

Collects eight articles written between 1978 and 2001 covering feminist theory, changes in sex roles over time, the post-Revolutionary notion of the "moral mother," the eighteenth-century law of courtship, perspectives on women and love in the work of Edwards and Franklin, literary sentimentalism and religion in Revolutionary ideology, gendered meanings of virtue in the Revolutionary era, and gender and the public-private dichotomy in the Revolutionary period. Focuses on "the relationship between notions of masculinity and feminity and wide cultural systems of value," including "the role of symbols and ideas in shaping definitions of gender."

AHR 109: 479-80; *Am Lit* 76: 603-605; *WMQ* 60: 892-95.

239 Boylan, Ann. *The Origins of Women's Activism: New York and Boston, 1797–1840*. Chapel Hill: University of North Carolina Press, 2002. xiv, 343 p. ISBN 0807827304 (hbk.); ISBN 9780807827307 (hbk.); ISBN 0807854042 (pbk.); ISBN 9780807854044 (pbk.); OCLC 48958410; LC Call Number HQ1904 .B69; Dewey 305.4/06/073. Citations: 26.

Discusses female volunteer associations, including those of various religious groups, races, and classes. Covers more than seventy organizations in New York and Boston, describing their leadership, structure, fundraising, and political influence. Argues that prior to the 1820s, women reached political goals through their relationships with powerful men, thereby maintaining "the mantle of domesticity." Asserts that during the 1820s and 1830s "deferential politics" declined, leading women to shift to a more direct approach that depended upon influencing votes through conventions and petitions. Explains that this new strategy allowed lower orders of women to participate in the process. Includes profiles of Elizabeth Bayley Seton, Mary Morgan Mason, and Henrietta Green Regulus Ray.

AHR 108: 1443-44; *JAH* 90: 1023-24; *J Interdis Hist* 35: 310-11; *NEQ* 76: 141-43; *RAH* 31: 379-88.

240 Branson, Susan. *These Fiery Frenchified Dames: Women and Political Culture in Early National Philadelphia*. Philadelphia: University of Pennsylvania Press, 2001. 218 p. ISBN 0812236092; ISBN 9780812236095; ISBN 0812217772; ISBN 9780812217773; OCLC 45700503; LC Call Number HQ1236.5.U6; Dewey 305.42/09748/11. Citations: 4.

Shows that a number of Philadelphia women created a republican salon culture and were able to bring together men of different views, thereby mediating party conflict. Notes that women's activities helped them gain "a foothold in the world of politics." Argues that in the early republic women were both "the civic glue that cemented political bonds between men" and the objects of two-party exploitation, which meant that "women were welcomed into public political space" in order to "reinforce partisan principles," but were at the same time "criticized for their public activities when it served the political opposition to do so."

AHR 107: 538; *EAL* 38: 139-52; *FHQ* 82: 97-99; *JAH* 89: 1029-30; *JAS* 37: 313; *JER* 22: 126-29; *RAH* 29: 502-509; *WMQ* 58: 764-69.

241 Bryan, Helen. *Martha Washington: First Lady of Liberty*. New York: Wiley, 2002. xiii, 417 p. ISBN 0471158925; ISBN 9780471158929; OCLC 49350512; LC Call Number E312.19 .B79; Dewey 973.41092. Citations: 3.

Presents a full biography of Martha Washington, calling her "an extremely important figure in her own right." Discusses her finances and temper, as well as her relationship with her slaves, characterizing it as typical for the eighteenth century. Notes that she was dutiful and an ideal consort and that she influenced government by arranging social gatherings at which public officials could exchange ideas.

Booklist 95: 868; *JSH* 69: 874-75; *VMHB* 110: 265-66.

242 Carlisle, Elizabeth Pendergast. *Earthbound and Heavenbent: Elizabeth Porter Phelps and Life at Forty Acres, 1747–1817*. New York: Scribner, 2004. xvi, 368 p. ISBN 0743244400; ISBN 9780743244404; OCLC 52765962; LC Call Number CT275.P5885; Dewey 974.4/23. Citations: 0.

Presents a biography of Phelps, an avid diarist and correspondent from Hadley, Massachusetts. Discusses Phelps's routines, personal struggles, family life, farm management, reading habits, interests in education, and observations on politics, local and international events, and religion.

Booklist 100: 943.

243 Chávez-García, Miroslava. *Negotiating Conquest: Gender and Power in California, 1770s to 1880s*. Tucson: University of Arizona Press, 2004. xxvi, 240 p. ISBN 0816523789; ISBN 9780816523788; OCLC 54817175; LC Call Number F870.M5; Dewey 305.8/968/720794. Citations: 10.

Studies the changing roles of Mexican and Native women in the eighteenth and nineteenth centuries. Makes use of court records, county, state, and church records, census data, letters, memoirs, and novels, mostly from the Los Angeles region. Notes that, before the Mexican War, women used property ownership as a means to some independence, but that after the American conquest, which hurt California economically and destabilized families, new legal options for divorce

appeared, creating even greater opportunities for women to increase their power within families.
WHQ 37: 513-14.

244   Davies, Kate. *Catharine Macaulay and Mercy Otis Warren: The Revolutionary Atlantic and the Politics of Gender*. Oxford: Oxford University Press, 2005. xi, 319 p. ISBN 0199281106; ISBN 9780199281107; OCLC 61499865; LC Call Number DA3.M25; Dewey 941.07/3082. Citations: 15.
Describes the "epistolary friendship" between Macaulay and Warren. Argues that both Macaulay and Warren "saw themselves, as women and as writers, at the intellectual heart of Atlantic political culture" and denies the mutual exclusivity of eighteenth-century views of republicanism and feminism. Notes instead that the separation of private and public spheres was more fluid in the eighteenth century than in the classical eras. Stresses that the cultures of reading and writing in the eighteenth century were "social rather than private phenomena," meant partly for public consumption rather than merely domestic counters to the masculine realm. Suggests that Macaulay promoted herself as a leading republican figure, while Warren focused, as did contemporaries like Abigail Adams and Hannah Winthrop, on letter writing to record and to comment upon significant historical events. Finds that, when they met face-to-face in 1785, Macaulay and Warren quarreled over the value of social clubs, which Warren found unworthy and corruptive of the new republic. Concludes that both writers were staunch supporters of women's intellectual freedom and, because eighteenth-century understanding of republicanism   was intertwined with that of gender, both dealt with matters of sexual inequality in ways that likely were not "fully enunciated or wholly coherent" to later feminists, but still raise vital questions about the transatlantic politics of gender.
AHR 113: 460-61; *EAL* 43: 223-27; *JAH* 93: 1214-15; *NEQ* 79: 663-65; *WMQ* 64: 433-36.

245   Dillon, Elizabeth Maddock. *The Gender of Freedom: Fictions of Liberalism and the Literary Public Sphere*. Stanford, Calif.: Stanford University Press, 2004. x, 310 p. ISBN 0804729417; ISBN 9780804729413; OCLC 53824117; LC Call Number PS169.L5; Dewey 810.9/3552. Citations: 37.
Contends that liberalism depends heavily upon the concept of gender and that women's private status has informed liberalism from the beginning. Notes that, while some have argued that liberalism problematically excludes women, and "that the figure of the woman within liberalism often stands opposed to the autonomous, white male liberal subject," that "this opposition is itself crucial to liberal thought and culture." Claims that early liberalist rhetoric was employed in both Ann Hutchinson's trial and Winthrop's account of the trial to the Massachusetts Bay Colony's English sponsors. Argues, in fact, that the antinomian controversy represented not a straightforward repression of women, but actually involved a lengthy, sophisticated negotiation of women's political power. Draws a correlation between the development of marriage into an increasingly intensive relationship between individuals and the increasing decentralization of political culture, and explains that marriage strengthened liberalist structures by emphasizing sexual differences through heterosexual

desire. Explores four infanticide narratives that spurred nineteenth-century sentimental novelists' primary concern with the mother-child bond, arguing that the repeated image of the dead child in sentimental fiction produced "the freedom of the liberal subject through [the] affective abundance" that the child's death created.

EAL 40: 391-95; *WMQ* 63: 846-49.

246 Fischer, Kirsten. *Suspect Relations: Sex, Race, and Resistance in Colonial North Carolina*. Ithaca, N. Y.: Cornell University Press, 2002. xiv, 265 p. ISBN 0801486793; ISBN 9780801486791; ISBN 0801438225; ISBN 9780801438226; OCLC 47120306; LC Call Number F257 .F53; Dewey 306.7/09756/09033. Citations: 35.

Asserts that, over time, North Carolinians moved from a fluid and culturally determined understanding of race and gender to a biological view. Explores ideas of race and sex in seventeenth-century England, cross-cultural sex, the regulation of sexuality, particularly among servants, defamation suits, and sexual violence. Explains that Quaker and Native American women especially challenged English understanding of an orderly society. Explains that sexual misbehavior, including interracial sex, symbolized disorderliness to English elites, and became a focal point of regulation. Notes that women often sued for defamation based on sexual slurs because sexuality was associated with identity, while such suits became rarer among men. Finds that courts generally reserved physical punishments to white women and to black men and women, allowing white men to escape with, at most, a fine. Notes that only lower-class men, rarely, and men of color were punished for the rape of white women and that North Carolinians saw white men as having a legal title to the bodies of women of color, both Native Americans and African Americans, so forcible sex was not deemed rape. Concludes that prohibitions of both marriage and sex with Native Americans and African Americans essentially created a permanent underclass, while stigmatizing white women who participated in either.

AHR 107: 1550; *HRNB* 30: 148; *JAH* 89: 1507-1508; *JSH* 69: 872-73; *NCHR* 79: 373-74; *RAH* 31: 342-48; *SCHM* 104: 287-89; *Soc Hist* 28: 416-18; *VQR* 78: 117; *WMQ* 60: 231-35.

247 Gillespie, Joanna Bowen. *The Life and Times of Martha Laurens Ramsay, 1759–1811*. Columbia: University of South Carolina Press, 2001. xxviii, 315 p. ISBN 1570033730; ISBN 9781570033735; OCLC 46343444; LC Call Number F279.C453; Dewey 975.7/91503/092. Citations: 8.

Describes Ramsay's family and upbringing as a member of the South Carolina gentry and the impact of her mother's death. Argues that Ramsay's significance comes from her "conscious determination to shape her life around a formal religious covenant." Describes Martha's travels to Europe, her marriage to David Ramsay, her religious commitment, and her children and the encouragement of the children to pursue civic virtue and individual accomplishment. Finds that Martha viewed her life's crises through a religious lens, taking solace in faith and moving beyond the strictures of the sphere of womanhood. Points out that Ramsay mentioned slavery rarely and that her "own

few words acknowledging the existence of slavery reveal nothing of her true feelings, either about the institution itself or individual personal slaves."
AHR 107: 1224-25; *GHQ* 86: 119-21; *JAH* 89: 1028-29; *JER* 22: 307-309; *JSH* 69: 154-55; *SCHM* 106: 170-72; *WMQ* 59: 522-26.

248   Hambleton, Else L. *Daughters of Eve: Pregnant Brides and Unwed Mothers in Seventeenth-Century Massachusetts.* New York: Routledge, 2004. xix, 192 p. ISBN 0415948606; ISBN 9780415948609; OCLC 54694519; LC Call Number HQ999.U6; Dewey 306.874/32/ 09744509032. Citations: 0.
Analyzes 255 fornication cases prosecuted in Essex County, Massachusetts, between 1640 and 1685, including the cases of 151 couples prosecuted for fornication when their first children arrived too soon after their wedding days and 104 cases of single women prosecuted after giving birth out of wedlock. Concludes that Puritans were "sexually repressive and repressed," that women who engaged in extramarital sex were punished more severely than men, that rape or other forms of coercion played an important role in fornication cases, that Puritan New England's record of sex crime prosecutions was unique in the British Atlantic world, and that Puritan sexual attitudes and behaviors changed over time, as more persons engaged in extramarital sex and as the treatment of these sex crimes became more lenient. Claims that the historiography on Puritan sexuality largely overstates "Puritan liberality on sexual issues" and the "numbers of couples engaging in extramarital and premarital sexual intercourse."
AJLH 49: 495-97.

249   Harris, Sharon M. *Executing Race: Early American Women's Narratives of Race, Society, and the Law.* Columbus: Ohio State University Press, 2005. x, 240 p. ISBN 0814209750 (hbk.); ISBN 9780814209752 (hbk.); ISBN 0814251315 (pbk.); ISBN 9780814251317 (pbk.); OCLC 56371671; LC Call Number PS149 .H37; Dewey 818/.108099287 22. Citations: 8.
Views race and gender together ideologically, noting that women used racial hierarchies to argue for white female freedoms at the expense of women of color. Discusses narratives of infanticide, pointing out that legal, religious, and journalistic views of infanticide cases made them a form of cultural capital. Sees a connection between infanticide and witchcraft during the colonial period, examines unequal sentences given to white, mixed-race, and Native American women convicted of infanticide, and traces the changing legal discourse concerning infanticide from the seventeenth-century to the early national period. Discusses the work of Ann Eliza Bleeker and Margaretta Bleeker Faugeres and Tenney's *Female Quixotism*, as well as African American poet Lucy Terry.
Am Lit 78: 185-87; *EAL* 41: 555-67.

250   Hucho, Christine. *Weiblich und Fremd: Deutschsprachige Einwandererinnen im Pennsylvania des 18. Jahrhunderts.* Frankfurt: Peter Lang, 2005. 585 p. ISBN 3631504217; ISBN 9783631504215; OCLC 60561715; LC Call Number F160.G3; Dewey 305.48831074809033. Citations: 0.

Studies the experiences of German female immigrants, from their leaving various German territories and migrating to America to their settlement in Pennsylvania and their role in preserving ethnic culture. Concludes that German immigrant women reacted to the pressures to assimilate in various ways, from rejection to resignation to enthusiastic support. Notes that German men expected women to preserve traditional culture through language, clothing, and cuisine. Compares three religious groups, Lutheran, Moravian, and Schwenkfelder, highlighting the diversity of experience among German-speaking women in the colonies. Finds that Lutheran women were excluded from formal church government, but that some, such as pastors' wives, maintained high profiles in religious communities, while Schwenkfelder women pursued modesty and humility, had relatively little contact with outsiders, maintained distinctive dress, and strictly sought to preserve their religious and ethnic cultural identity in America. Explains that Moravian women lived and governed themselves separately and worked extensively in missions among the pastorless Reformed and Lutheran communities.
WMQ 65: 378-84.

251 Kennedy, Cynthia M. *Braided Relations, Entwined Lives: The Women of Charleston's Urban Slave Society*. Bloomington: Indiana University Press, 2005. xiv, 311 p. ISBN 0253346150; ISBN 9780253346155; OCLC 59879609; LC Call Number HQ1439.C42; LC Call Number E185.93.S7; Dewey 305.4/09757/915. Citations: 8.
Presents a social history of women in Charleston between the American Revolution and the Civil War. Covers the political, social, and economic environment of the city and the impact of race, class, and gender, emphasizing the subordination of women as an "imperative to slave society." Discusses work, leisure, and intimacy, noting the real and imagined roles that women played. Focuses on the lives of and relationships among enslaved women, free laboring white women, free black and brown women, and slaveholding women. Finds that free women of color likely outnumbered their male counterparts in the city in the four decades preceding the Civil War and that women of color adopted prevailing elite ideals in social relations and in the valuing of lighter colored skin.
AHR 112: 196; *HRNB* 34: 83; *JAH* 93: 862-63; *JSH* 73: 881-82; *SCHM* 108: 259-61.

252 Lacey, Barbara E., ed. *The World of Hannah Heaton: The Diary of an Eighteenth-Century New England Farm Woman*. DeKalb: Northern Illinois University Press, 2003. xxxii, 343 p. ISBN 0875803121; ISBN 9780875803128; OCLC 51264532; LC Call Number BR1720.H38; Dewey 974.6/702/092. Citations: 2.
Presents Heaton's complete journal, which chronicles the life of an eighteenth-century Connecticut farm woman. Covers the importance of family and church in Heaton's life, recording spiritual trials, concerns about impending childbirths, and the extreme difficulties of farm labor. Reveals the overwhelming sense of sin that alienated Heaton from God and community and a household of virtually continual conflict and resentment, one tainted by Heaton's belief that she

wrongly married an unconverted man. Shows that Heaton sympathized with the revolutionary cause, but saw the war as a suffering visited on New England for its sins and that she worried about her two grown sons, who were in military service.
WMQ 61: 152-55.

253 Lindenauer, Leslie J. *Piety and Power: Gender and Religious Culture in the American Colonies, 1630–1700*. New York: Routledge, 2001. xxviii, 181 p. ISBN 0415933927; ISBN 9780415933926; OCLC 49403566; LC Call Number BR520 .L56; Dewey 277.3/06/082. Citations: 4.
Focuses on the sources, development, and impact of feminine piety in early America, examining in particular its realization in Puritan New England, Dutch Reformed New York, and Anglican Virginia. Explains similarities and demographic and social disparities in terms of common religious values and behaviors, noting that women in all three regions drew upon similar sources of Protestant piety and made similar contributions to Protestant culture in each colony. Considers the self, the family, the church, and the community "as a series of ever-expanding spheres—from the intensely private to the most public—where women exercised the voice of authority," which grew out of literacy and a sense of "soul equality." Notes that women's private practice of Protestant spirituality often bled into public spaces, particularly in the New World, which had the effect of feminizing the churches and highlighting disparity between religious ideals and practice. Concludes that, contrary to the view that females lost power to men as the colonial period progressed, women were in fact "active participants in American political culture."
AHR 108: 514-15; *CH* 75: 444-46; *JAH* 90: 988-89.

254 Lombard, Anne S. *Making Manhood: Growing Up Male in Colonial New England*. Cambridge, Mass.: Harvard University Press, 2003. x, 299 p. ISBN 0674010582; ISBN 9780674010581; OCLC 51342477; LC Call Number HQ1090.5.N36; Dewey 305.31/0974. Citations: 12.
Considers "what did it mean to be a man" in colonial New England in the century after the end of King Philip's War. Characterizes farmers as family-centered heads of households who strove to secure sufficient land in their lifetimes to settle their sons close to home. Describes seventeenth-century rural New England society, the stages of male development, marriages and divorces, male-on-male violence, and the impact of manhood on politics, as demonstrated in the controversy over paper money, notions of good government revealed in annual election sermons, and pamphlet literature on British taxation of the colonies. Finds that older men accused of assault sought to justify use of force as moderate and reasonable, as those who failed to control passions were considered effeminate and were censured or harshly punished. Explains that reason was largely overthrown in the eighteenth century, resulting in more uncontrolled violence inflicted by young men who sought to demonstrate aggressive masculinity in confrontations with other young males. Suggests that gendered language used in conflicts, including the lead-up to the Revolution, reaffirmed long-standing ideals about responsible fatherhood.
AHR 109: 514-15; *JAH* 91: 604-605; *NEQ* 78: 314-16; *WMQ* 61: 132-35.

255 MacMullen, Ramsay, ed. *Sarah's Choice, 1828–1832*. By Sarah Dwight Woolsey. New Haven, Conn.: PastTimes Press, 2001. xii, 205 p. ISBN 0965878015; ISBN 9780965878012; OCLC 48871565; LC Call Number F123 .W66; Dewey 974.7/03. Citations: 3.
Presents Woolsey's correspondence, which reveals a stressful courtship and the complications of intergenerational relationships. Includes fifty-seven letters from Woolsey to Hunn Carrington Beach of Utica, New York. Notes that the relationship between the two was largely clandestine, which was necessitated by family opposition and the resultant tension between Sarah and her parents, which ultimately caused Sarah to end the relationship with Carrington. Finds that Sarah dutifully found a husband.
JER 21: 724-26; *NEQ* 75: 338-40; *WMQ* 59: 996-1000.

256 Mattern, David B. and Holly C. Shulman, eds. *The Selected Letters of Dolley Payne Madison*. Charlottesville: University of Virginia Press, 2003. xviii, 442 p. ISBN 081392152X; ISBN9780813921525; OCLC 50291125; LC Call Number E342.1.M18; Dewey 973.5/1/092. Citations: 4.
Publishes about 300 letters to and from Dolley Payne Madison, organizing the letters according to the major periods of Madison's adult life, from her experiences in Philadelphia during the epidemic of 1793 to her death in Washington in 1849. Includes an index and a biographical guide.
JER 24: 136-38; *PMHB* 128: 408-409; *VMHB* 111: 192-93; *WMQ* 61: 191-94.

257 Mays, Dorothy A., ed. *Women in Early America: Struggle, Survival, and Freedom in a New World*. Santa Barbara, Calif.: ABC-Clio, 2004. xxi, 495 p. ISBN 1851094296 (hbk.); ISBN 9781851094295 (hbk.); ISBN 1851094342 (electronic); ISBN 9781851094349 (electronic); OCLC 56493967; LC Call Number HQ1416 .M395; Dewey 305.4/0973/09032 22. Citations: 1.
Presents an encyclopedia on American women from 1607 to 1812 intended "for pre-collegiate as well as college-level researchers." Includes about 175 entries on various groups, activities, persons, and other topics. Emphasizes eastern North America and women of European descent, but includes entries on African American and Native American women. Provides entries ranging one to seven pages in length, which include a list of further readings. Supplies an appendix on common household chores and one that presents ten primary documents. Includes an annotated bibliography.
Booklist 101: 1237.

258 Meyers, Debra. *Common Whores, Vertuous Women, and Loveing Wives: Free Will Christian Women in Colonial Maryland*. Bloomington: Indiana University Press, 2003. xiv, 249 p. ISBN 0253341930; ISBN 9780253341938; OCLC 50184818; LC Call Number HQ1438.M3; Dewey 305.4/09752. Citations: 6.
Argues that Maryland women from "free will" theological traditions (e.g., Catholic, "Arminian Anglican," and Quaker) possessed more legal rights than women in predestinarian churches. Explains that the theologies of such churches tended to exalt women, while predestinarian theology characterized women as morally vulnerable. Finds from a review of seventeenth- and early-eighteenth-

century wills, court records, and popular devotional and theological works that many Maryland women retained remarkable authority in inheritance rights, and enjoyed "more egalitarian familial structures that resulted in a more equitable social, political, and economic world."
AHR 108: 1440-41; *HRNB* 32: 12-13; *JAH* 91: 212-13; *JSH* 70: 894-95; *WMQ* 61: 565-68.

259   Moitt, Bernard. *Women and Slavery in the French Antilles, 1635–1848.* Bloomington: Indiana University Press, 2001. xx, 217 p. ISBN 0253339138 (hbk.); ISBN 9780253339133 (hbk.); ISBN 0253214521 (pbk.); ISBN 9780253214522 (pbk.); OCLC 45700675; LC Call Number HT1079 .W48; Dewey 305.48/9625/09729. Citations: 18.
Examines black women's labor and resistance, arguing that "the fortunes of the slave plantations were accumulated largely on the backs of enslaved black women who performed a disproportionate amount of hard labor" and that "women's roles often permitted them to engage in specific forms of resistance." Describes work in the field, the household, and within the family unit and larger community, as well as connections of other labor systems and slavery, the process of manumission, and the use of legal instruments for resistance. Asserts that, in the development of slavery, "the African alternative was cheaper, but not inevitable." Concludes that gender was more in balance on large plantations than previously noted, that men almost exclusively held industrial, agricultural, transportation, and skilled occupations, that female slaves undertook the heaviest field work, and that female slaves resisted slavery much more than previously believed, through insolence, running away, violence, and even poisoning.
JAH 89: 1499-1500; *J Interdis Hist* 33: 675-76; *WMQ* 61: 568-70.

260   Morgan, Jennifer L. *Laboring Women: Reproduction and Gender in New World Slavery.* Philadelphia: University of Pennsylvania Press, 2004. 279 p. ISBN 0812237781 (hbk.); ISBN 9780812237788 (hbk.); ISBN 0812218736 (pbk.); ISBN 9780812218732 (pbk.); OCLC 53485319; LC Call Number HT1048 .M67; Dewey 306.3/62/082097 22. Citations: 46.
Examines women's lives "across time and space" to find "ways in which ideologies of race and gender contributed to a set of common experiences for enslaved women." Discusses the transition that slaves endured from Africa to the Americas, "the gendering of racial ideology," and the characterization of African women in travel narratives. Analyzes West African gender roles, the gendered experiences of the middle passage, and the demographics of the slave trade and slave production. Finds that Europeans used the notion of African women's sexuality and reproductive behavior to justify enslavement. Notes that reproduction shaped women's encounters with work, community, and culture and that reproduction, not the specific type of labor, was the key influence on slave women's identities. Explains that slaveholders encouraged sexual relationships, willed a woman's future children to the slaveholder's heirs, and placed a high monetary value on women who had demonstrated an ability to bear children.
AHR 110: 442-43; *JAH* 92: 195; *RAH* 33: 41-46; *WMQ* 62: 536-39.

261 Ousterhout, Anne M. *The Most Learned Woman in America: A Life of Elizabeth Graeme Fergusson.* University Park: Pennsylvania State University Press, 2004. xx, 391 p. ISBN 0271023112; ISBN 9780271023113; OCLC 53284888; LC Call Number F158.4.F47; Dewey 811/.1. Citations: 9.

Portrays Fergusson as a highly educated master of classical and modern languages, and as a poet, correspondent, commonplace book compiler, and ground-breaking hostess of a literary salon. Notes that Fergusson suffered through a miserable private life, which included a failed marriage, humiliation, and poverty. Places Fergusson in the context of Revolutionary Pennsylvania, noting the challenges that her loyalism brought, including property confiscation and occupation and eventual destruction of her home by soldiers. Details her poverty after the war and death in 1801, her poetry, and women's roles in literary culture generally.
EAL 41: 555-67; *JAH* 91: 1441-42; *PMHB* 129: 349-51; *WMQ* 61: 770-73.

262 Powers, Karen Vieira. *Women in the Crucible of Conquest: The Gendered Genesis of Spanish American Society, 1500–1600.* Albuquerque: University of New Mexico Press, 2005. ix, 230 p. ISBN 0826335187 (hbk.); ISBN 9780826335180 (hbk.); ISBN 0826335195 (pbk.); ISBN 9780826335197 (pbk.); OCLC 56840703; LC Call Number HQ1460.5 .P68; Dewey 305.4/098/09034. Citations: 11.

Surveys the role of women in Spanish American society during the sixteenth century. Contends that in this period the status of these women declined, particularly native women who were negatively affected by European conquest and colonization. Describes diminution of native women's legal status and property rights, abuse and sexual victimization, and the material losses that they suffered due to changes in labor conditions and demands for tribute.
WMQ 64: 183-94.

263 Roberts, Cokie. *Founding Mothers: The Women Who Raised Our Nation.* New York: William Morrow, 2004. xx, 359 p. ISBN 0060090251; ISBN 9780060090258; OCLC 54365478; LC Call Number E176 .R63; Dewey 973.3/092/2. Citations: 6.

Studies the mothers, wives, and daughters of Founders, such as Mercy Otis Warren, Deborah Sampson, Peggy Shippen, Martha Washington, and Abigail Adams. Describes the anxieties about and material and security challenges of the Revolutionary era.
Booklist 100: 1242; *LJ* 129n12: 99; *LJ* 129n20: 183.

264 Saxton, Martha. *Being Good: Women's Moral Values in Early America.* New York: Hill and Wang, 2003. x, 388 p. ISBN 0374110115 (hbk.); ISBN 9780374110116 (hbk.); ISBN 0809016338 (pbk.); ISBN 9780809016334 (pbk.); OCLC 50645380; LC Call Number BJ1610 .S39; Dewey 170/.82/0973. Citations: 9.

Explores culturally prescribed moral values for women in seventeenth-century Boston, eighteenth-century Virginia, and nineteenth-century St. Louis. Finds that white Bostonians emphasized feminine ideals of chastity, obedience, piety, humility, modesty, and self-control, and denigrated non-white women as incapable of maintaining the same standards. Explains that women in Virginia were likewise expected to be deferential, chaste, and self-controlled, but were also ideally to be empathetic, refined, romantic, and flirtatious, without being—as slaves were thought to be—promiscuous and immoral. Finds that in St. Louis, similarly, the white Anglo-American cultural values centered on chastity, modesty, obedience, and sexual restraint, while French sensibilities were more focused on pleasure and physical and emotional expressiveness. Asserts that notions of "being good" changed over time and were affected by race, ethnicity, and class, but that the ultimate goal of each moral system was to control women. *AHR* 109: 185-86; *HRNB* 31: 148; *JAH* 90: 1430-31; *J Soc Hist* 38: 550-53; *LJ* 128: 107-108; *PMHB* 128: 90-92.

265 Schloesser, Pauline. *The Fair Sex: White Women and Racial Patriarchy in the Early American Republic.* New York: New York University Press, 2002. xii, 243 p. ISBN 0814797628; ISBN 9780814797624; ISBN 0814797636; ISBN 9780814797631; OCLC 47690826; LC Call Number HQ1075.5.U6; Dewey 305.42/0973/09033. Citations: 9.
Applies a theory of racial patriarchy to the explanation of the roots of white and male supremacy in the early United States. Focuses on the lives and work of Mercy Otis Warren, Abigail Smith Adams, and Judith Sargent Murray, noting that each consented to racial hierarchy over gender hierarchy and in so doing condoned racial patriarchy. Argues that white women held a unique place in this racial and gender hierarchy, that they maintained a high status from their whiteness and a low position due to their sex. Finds that early American institutions like schools, slavery, and churches, helped to reinforce racial patriarchy.
JAH 89: 1513-14; *WMQ* 59: 1037-40.

266 Schmidt, Gary D. *A Passionate Usefulness: The Life and Literary Labors of Hannah Adams.* Charlottesville: University of Virginia Press, 2004. x, 454 p. ISBN 0813922720; ISBN 9780813922720; OCLC 53839821; LC Call Number PS1004.A37; Dewey: 808/.0092. Citations: 3.
Explores the life of Adams (1755-1831) and her rise from lowly beginnings to literary prominence. Explains that Adams lived in near poverty, took a number of menial jobs, and then took advantage of the bourgeoning book market in late-eighteenth-century New England to compile useful information on religion and regional history. Notes that she gained acceptance among intellectuals, was the first woman admitted to the Boston Athenaeum's private library, and was "the first American writer to craft a full history of the Jews." Characterizes Adams as a compiler, Federalist, Christian, and patriot, who rejected enthusiasm and anarchy.
Am Lit 77: 657-63; *JER* 25: 307-310; *NEQ* 79: 322-24.

267 Snyder, Terri L. *Brabbling Women: Disorderly Speech and the Law in Early Virginia.* Ithaca, N.Y.: Cornell University Press, 2003. xiv, 182 p. ISBN 0801440521; ISBN 9780801440526; OCLC 50809147; LC Call Number HQ1438.V5; Dewey 305.4/09755. Citations: 10.

Explores legal cases involving seventeenth- and eighteenth-century Virginia women who challenged social conventions and patriarchal power, particularly through "disorderly speech." Focuses on York County court cases, including those of rape, slander, adultery, and other domestic matters and notes that women played key roles in Bacon's Rebellion and the Tobacco Cutting Riots of 1682. Finds that such women came from all social strata, but most were of poor to middling status and that in the eighteenth century cases of disorderly women became less public as domestic relations increasingly became privatized.
AHR 109: 515-16; *18c Stds* 39: 130-34; *JAH* 91: 991; *JSH* 70: 891-92; *VMHB* 111: 301-302; *WMQ* 61: 359-61.

268 Sturtz, Linda L. *Within Her Power: Propertied Women in Colonial Virginia.* New York: Routledge, 2002. xvi, 278 p. ISBN 0415928559 (hbk.); ISBN 9780415928557 (hbk.); ISBN 0415928826 (pbk.); ISBN 9780415928823 (pbk.); OCLC 48098431; LC Call Number HQ1438.V5; Dewey 305.4/09755. Citations: 12.
Refutes the notion that demography was the main factor that allowed women in early Virginia to amass property, noting that initiative also played a significant part, along with access to capital, markets, and the legal system. Discusses land and slave inheritance among women and business activities, including the ways in which women used personal relationships for economic advantage, and the methods that slaveowners used to protect their daughters' interests in family slaves. Explains that women were also at a disadvantage compared to men in the control of slaves and the operation of businesses, and frequently had to rely upon the courts to assert authority. Concludes that, despite examples of autonomy, largely a woman still served as "more the means of transfer of property, rather than an individual with control over property."
AHR 108: 1139-40; *JAH* 90: 616-17; *J Econ Hist* 63: 894-95; *VMHB* 112: 304-306; *WMQ* 60: 225-29.

269 Turner, David M. *Fashioning Adultery: Gender, Sex, and Civility in England, 1660–1740.* Cambridge: Cambridge University Press, 2002. xii, 236 p. ISBN 0521792444; ISBN 9780521792448; OCLC 49248519; LC Call Number HQ806 .T87; Dewey 306.73/6/0942. Citations: 25.
Traces changes in views on marital infidelity in English literature between the mid-seventeenth and mid-eighteenth centuries. Finds that church prosecutions for adultery, the rise in print culture, and increased concerns with politeness and "gentlemanly" behavior made adultery more of a private matter between concerned parties and less of a public issue. Explains that material culture and emphasis on private space helped to create norms of polite behavior and to shape attitudes about adultery, including those related to cuckoldry, which by the mid-eighteenth century largely involved personal, internal shame.
AHR 108: 1522-23; *CJH* 34: 132-34; *J Brit Stds* 44: 178-86; *J Interdis Hist* 34: 633-34; *16c J* 35: 855-56; *Soc Hist* 29: 514-67; *WMQ* 61: 368-71.

270 Vietto, Angela. *Women and Authorship in Revolutionary America.* Burlington, Vt.: Ashgate, 2005. ix, 147 p. ISBN 0754653382; ISBN

Explores gender ideology through notions of "literary sorority, narrative authority of the republican mother, historical examples of female warriors, and the claiming of citizenship through written political analyses. Traces changing writing strategies of Judith Sargent Murray, Mercy Otis Warren, Hannah Adams, Hannah Mather Crocker, Elizabeth Graeme Fergusson, Annis Boudinot Stockton, Sarah Pogson, and Sarah Wentworth Morton. Contends that "the relationship between authorship and gender is far from static" since at each instance of writing the author "entered a cultural context that, in regard to both her gender identity and her vocation as an author, was constantly changing."
Am Lit 80: 170-72.

9 Frontier

271 Achenbach, Joel. *The Grand Idea: George Washington's Potomac and the Race to the West*. New York: Simon and Schuster, 2004. 367 p. ISBN 0684848570; ISBN 9780684848570; OCLC 54543937; LC Call Number F187.P8 A23; Dewey 975.2/03. Citations: 5.

Describes Washington's 1784 journey into the backcountry of Virginia and of Pennsylvania in search of commercial transportation routes from the Potomac westward. Discusses Washington's observations of frontier life, of the region's natural features, and of various peoples living in the backcountry. Contends that Washington saw westward expansion as the key to an independent, prosperous United States and that his trip set in stark relief disputes over land ownership and the power that it brought. Notes that Washington viewed the west as important for Virginians in particular, as they were in direct competition with the more entrepreneurial residents of New York City and Philadelphia. Concludes that, because Virginians did not have "a sufficient spirit of commerce," the Potomac as a major navigation artery never came to pass.
Booklist 100n18: 1592; *JAH* 92: 591-92; *LJ* 129n13: 92.

272 Buchanan, John. *Jackson's Way: Andrew Jackson and the People of the Western Waters*. New York: Wiley, 2001. xiii, 434 p. ISBN 0471282537; ISBN 9780471282532; OCLC 44266136; LC Call Number E382 .B89; Dewey 976 21. Citations: 5.

Examines the settlement of the west and Jackson's role in it. Describes initial explorations of the Old Southwest and Tennessee in the seventeenth century, including interactions among Native American groups in the region and struggles between Indians and early European settlers. Focuses on the Cumberland region, the area around present-day Nashville, and Jackson's military and political careers. Sees the displacement of Native Americans as inevitable, as were the Creek wars.

Booklist 97: 1036; *GHQ* 85: 486-88; *HRNB* 29: 109; *IMH* 98: 322-24; *J Mil Hist* 65: 792-93; *JSH* 68: 690-91; *NCHR* 79: 274-75; *SCHM* 103: 85-87.

273 Carstens, Kenneth Charles and Nancy Son Carstens, eds. *The Life of George Rogers Clark, 1752–1818: Triumphs and Tragedies.* Westport, Conn.: Praeger, 2004. xviii, 348 p. ISBN 0313322171; ISBN 9780313322174; OCLC 55518018; LC Call Number E207.C5 L54; Dewey 973.3/3/092. Citations: 1.
Presents papers on Clark's early life, the Kaskaskia expedition, the French influence on Clark, Clark and Native Americans, the Clark-Teresa "De Leyba" myth, the victory at Vincennes, the importance of Detroit to Clark, Fort Jefferson (1780 – 81), the Illinois Battalion and the slave trade, Clark's supply lines, the 1780 Shawnee campaign, Clark's ambush at Hood's Point, the Virginia campaign (1781), Clark on the Kentucky frontier between 1783 and 1809, the "French conspiracies," Clark's time at Locust Grove (1809–1818), the Clark portraits and legacy, and research materials on Clark.
IMH 101: 393-97; *JER* 25: 502-504.

274 Cerami, Charles A. *Jefferson's Great Gamble: The Remarkable Story of Jefferson, Napoleon and the Men Behind the Louisiana Purchase.* Naperville, Ill.: Sourcebooks, 2003. 309 p. ISBN 1570719454; ISBN 9781570719455; ISBN 1402202407; ISBN 9781402202407; OCLC 50960773; LC Call Number E333 .C465; Dewey 973.4/6 21. Citations: 7.
Discusses the roles in the Louisiana Purchase of Jefferson, Napoleon, Madison, Talleyrand, Livingston, and Monroe. Claims "that intelligent persons who understood the big picture were able to make wise decisions beyond their normal level," which led to a successful result for the United States. Intended for a general readership.
Booklist 99: 1137; *LJ* 128n8: 134; *PMHB* 128: 317-19.

275 Daniels, Christine and Michael V. Kennedy, eds. *Negotiated Empires: Centers and Peripheries in the Americas, 1500–1820.* New York: Routledge, 2002. viii, 328 p. ISBN 041592538X (hbk.); ISBN 9780415925389 (hbk.); ISBN 0415925398 (pbk.); ISBN 9780415925396 (pbk.); OCLC 47136486; LC Call Number E18.82 .N44; Dewey 970 21. Citations: 45.
Presents essays on colonial Spanish America and frontier Latin America, Puebla and Mexico City from the mid-sixteenth to the mid-seventeenth centuries, the economic agency of the Spanish state, the development of Spanish Indian policy, the Luso-Brazilian world from 1500 to 1808, Vila Boa de Goiás, the core and periphery of seventeenth- and eighteenth-century Dutch America and French North America, the idea of frontier in the seventeenth-century French Caribbean, Britain and its overseas "peripheries" from 1550 to 1780, as well as changing Anglo-American definitions of empire, the colonial American impressions of the late eighteenth-century British Asiatic empire, and the postcolonial American concepts of center and periphery.
AHR 108: 480; *HAHR* 85: 125-27; *JAH* 90: 1420-21; *J Econ Hist* 63: 882-83; *J Interdis Hist* 35: 139-40.

276 Finger, John R. *Tennessee Frontiers: Three Regions in Transition.* Bloomington: Indiana University Press, 2001. xxiii, 382 p. ISBN 0253339855; ISBN 9780253339850; OCLC 46420254; LC Call Number F436 .F56; Dewey 976.8. Citations: 5.

Takes into account both the "early interaction of Native American and Euro-Americans" and the emergence of the market economy in the development of the Tennessee frontier through the 1830s. Contends that the Euro-American desire for land was the vehicle of historical change and, of course, necessitated treaty negotiations with the Cherokees and political coercion of all Native American groups. Explains that this land hunger led to speculation and, ultimately, economic exploitation and that land shaped the development of early Tennessee political institutions, parties, and culture and determined both loyalties in the American Revolution and positions taken on debates on the federal Constitution. Shows that by 1840 the Nashville basin and counties along the Mississippi River were the most populous, had the most slaves, and were the most agriculturally productive. Finds that, though settled first, the Appalachian region of east Tennessee developed more slowly and remained on the economic margins through the mid-nineteenth century. Attributes Tennessee's regional development in the 1830s to enhanced internal improvements and increased access to markets. Refutes the idea of frontier individualism, noting that settlers often relied on state and national governments to help in acquisition of land from Native Americans, safety and security, and better transportation.
AHR 108: 185-86; *GHQ* 86: 457-60; *HRNB* 30: 103; *IMH* 99: 63-64.

277 Hallock, Thomas. *From the Fallen Tree: Frontier Narratives, Environmental Politics, and the Roots of a National Pastoral, 1749–1826.* Chapel Hill: University of North Carolina Press, 2003. xix, 289 p. ISBN 0807828203 (hbk.); ISBN 9780807828205 (hbk.); ISBN 0807854913 (pbk.); ISBN 9780807854914 (pbk.); OCLC 52091287; LC Call Number E179.5 .H186; Dewey 973/.07/2. Citations: 14.

Examines the trans-Appalachian West using literary criticism, the new western history, environmental history, and ecological criticism, focusing on "spatialized accounts" or "cartographic texts" and the ways in which "writings about place also negotiated cross-cultural relations." Explains that, like frontier settlers, early American authors like cartographer Lewis Evans and explorers Lewis and Clark had to engage with native peoples and generally maintained cultural boundaries in doing so. Treats the writings of John and William Bartram, Jane Colden, James Fenimore Cooper, Timothy Dwight, John Filson, Anne Grant, Thomas Jefferson, and J. Hector St. John de Crevecoeur, with a focus on the impact on narrative forms of claiming the West and on recognition of the "Other" within these texts. Analyzes the texts' acknowledgement of the Native presence even as their authors sought to erase that presence.
AHR 110: 476-77; *Am Lit* 77: 200-202; *EAL* 40: 163-71; *18c Stds* 39: 120-30; *JAH* 91: 1008-1009; *JER* 24: 684-86; *WMQ* 62: 126-29.

278 Hinderaker, Eric and Peter C. Mancall. *At the Edge of Empire: The Backcountry in British North America.* Baltimore, Md.: Johns Hopkins University Press, 2003. ix, 210 p. ISBN 0801871360 (hbk.); ISBN

9780801871368 (hbk.); ISBN 0801871379 (pbk.); ISBN 9780801871375 (pbk.); OCLC 49680056; LC Call Number E188 .H56; Dewey 973.2. Citations: 12.
Surveys relations between Indians and British colonists from early English exploration to the American Revolution. Focuses on the "edge of empire" east of the Mississippi River, placing backcountry struggles in the contexts of empire and intertribal relations. Examines the problems of trade, diplomacy, warfare, and ideologies of racism. Calls the backcountry a "realm in which the ordinary rules of English governance and behavior did not apply" and an area in which imperial authority "collapsed under the weight of a backcountry grown too large and complicated to administer or control." Views the region as "an ambiguous zone, neither Indian country nor yet fully incorporated into the ambit of British governance and Anglo-American control." Concludes that the British established a pattern of frontier and backcountry settlement, whereby contact and conflict eventually became accommodation and gradual incorporation.
CJH 39: 631; *18c Stds* 39: 120-30; *HRNB* 32: 59; *IMH* 101: 84-85; *NEQ* 78: 140-42; *NCHR* 83: 270-71; *PMHB* 128: 399-400; *WMQ* 62: 788-91.

279 Hoffman, Paul E. *Florida's Frontiers*. Bloomington: Indiana University Press, 2002. xx, 470 p. ISBN 0253340195; ISBN 9780253340191; OCLC 47013080; LC Call Number F314 .H75; Dewey 975.9. Citations: 14.
Traces Florida history from the coming of Europeans in the early 1500s to the closing of the frontier in 1860. Outlines five frontiers, beginning with the establishment of St. Augustine in 1565, the inland frontier between the Spanish and the Indians (1609–50), the territorial struggle between the English and the Spanish after the 1680s, the English occupation of Florida (1763–84), the reversion to Spain, and the eventual takeover of Florida (1821) by U.S. forces and the subsequent clashes with remaining Native Americans. Examines Spanish exploration and conquest of native villages, the establishment of Franciscan missions among the Indians in the interior, and English encroachments in these areas. Describes the effects of the British takeover of Florida (1763–84), the Spanish re-acquisition, and the U.S. invasion in the early nineteenth century. Notes that poor soil and a sparse population hampered Indian resistance.
AHR 108: 183-84; *Ethnohistory* 54: 778-79; *FHQ* 83: 329-31; *GHQ* 86: 286-88; *HAHR* 84: 134-35; *JAH* 89: 1522-23; *JSH* 69: 862-63; *WMQ* 60: 643-53.

280 Lightfoot, Kent G. *Indians, Missionaries, and Merchants: The Legacy of Colonial Encounters on the California Frontiers*. Berkeley: University of California Press, 2005. xviii, 338 p. ISBN 0520208242; ISBN 9780520208247; OCLC 54974329; LC Call Number E78.C15; Dewey 979.4/02. Citations: 49.
Explores the relative dearth of land holdings and the federal recognition of coastal California Indian groups between Santa Rosa and San Juan Capistrano. Compares effects of Franciscan missions and Russian commercial colonies of coastal California vis-à-vis enculturation, relocation, demographic change, social mobility, labor, and interethnic unions involving natives. Asserts that succeeding generations of natives lost traditional identification with geographic areas and lost their cultural identities. Notes continuity of various pre-contact social, dietetic, and manufacturing traditions, which reveal an underground

indigenous culture. Explains that Russian companies were narrowly interested in acquiring sea otter pelts and developing agriculture to supply permanent colonial holdings in Alaska, and therefore enculturation did not exist and relocation did not occur. Contends that, instead, and due to Spanish competition, Russian colonists gave natives many options, and did not push proselytization aggressively. Concludes that, therefore, the Russian presence had little documented impact on demography, while the Spanish missions had disastrous impacts, as California Indian populations were dispersed, forced off lands by the growth of ranches and the pressure of the Gold Rush, and later U.S. land grants depended upon groups between Santa Rosa and San Juan Capistrano being forced off their occupied lands.
JAEH 26: 81-83; *JAH* 92: 955; *PHR* 74: 622-24; *WHQ* 37: 373-74.

281 Oatis, Steven J. *A Colonial Complex: South Carolina's Frontiers in the Era of the Yamasee War, 1680–1730.* Lincoln: University of Nebraska Press, 2004. ix, 399 p. ISBN 0803235755; ISBN 9780803235755; OCLC 55124635; LC Call Number F272 .O18; Dewey 975.7/02. Citations: 11.
Views Native American groups surrounding Charles Town as a defensive perimeter, arguing that there was no monolithic "southern frontier," but rather a "southeastern frontier complex." Discusses the Yamasee War, connecting it to the Creek-Cherokee War of the 1720s and to continuing Indian resistance to European infiltration. Concludes that the War rearranged "the physical and human geography of the Southeast," influenced "the mercantile and military competition" among the various colonial powers, and demonstrated that Indians "remained far more than mere auxiliaries in this three-way imperial struggle." Denies that the Yamasee War was any sort of historical turning point, and was not "a confrontation between champions of a dynamic and expansive 'English' way of life on one side, and defenders of a timeless, traditional, and utterly doomed 'Indian' way of life, on the other."
AHR 111: 152-53; *Ethnohistory* 54: 205-206; *FHQ* 84: 264-66; *GHQ* 89: 253-56; *JAEH* 26: 81-83; *J Mil Hist* 70: 496-97; *JSH* 72: 157-58; *SCHM* 107: 156-58; *WMQ* 62: 543-45.

282 Pace, Robert F. and Donald S. Frazier. *Frontier Texas: History of a Borderland to 1880.* Abilene, Tex.: State House Press, 2004. 272 p. ISBN 1880510839; ISBN 9781880510834; OCLC 54349627; LC Call Number F386 .P215; Dewey 976.4/02. Citations: 6.
Covers the area around Abilene, all the way up to the panhandle and south to the San Saba River, surveying the region's history. Discusses ranching, cattle drives, buffalo hunting, and frontier forts. Characterizes west Texas as "a crossroads for humanity ... a climatic, geographical, political, and cultural borderland." Emphasizes the "perseverance, toughness, and determination" of the region's settlers. Intended for general readership.
Ag Hist 80: 262-63; *Hist Teach* 38: 558-59; *JSH* 72: 647-48; *SHQ* 109: 151-52.

283 Philyaw, Leslie Scott. *Virginia's Western Visions: Political and Cultural Expansion on an Early American Frontier.* Knoxville: University of Tennessee

Press, 2004. xxvii, 180 p. ISBN 1572333073; ISBN 9781572333079; OCLC 53485400; LC Call Number F229 .P56; Dewey 975.5/01. Citations: 6.

Asserts that Virginia's settlers immediately looked west, that after 1676 they were successful in recreating colonial institutions on the frontier, and that after the Revolution gave up the westward vision in favor of a more limited view of Virginia. Stresses the work of elite planters in forming a westward orientation, influence that continued until the 1750s, when imperial administrators exerted authority over western settlement (e.g., the Proclamation of 1763) and lower-order squatters poured into the frontier. Explains that the Revolution-era disputes over western lands caused Virginians to scale back their ambitions and that the state's leaders completely abandoned western claims after the Revolution.

AHR 111: 165-66; *GHQ* 89: 412-14; *JAH* 93: 198-99; *JER* 25: 482-85; *JSH* 72: 160-61; *NCHR* 82: 510-11; *VMHB* 114: 402-403; *WMQ* 66: 640-52.

284 Rachels, David and Edward Watts, eds. *The First West: Writing from the American Frontier, 1776–1860*. New York: Oxford University Press, 2002. xvi, 944 p. ISBN 0195141334; ISBN 9780195141337; OCLC 45804950; LC Call Number PS561 .F57; Dewey 810.9/3278. Citations: 4.

Presents pieces related to the region from the Appalachians to the Mississippi between the American Revolution to the Civil War. Includes articles from John Filson, Daniel Boone, James Kirke Paulding, Timothy Flint, Thomas Bang Thorpe, Johnson Jones Hooper, Black Hawk, Benjamin Drake, John Tanner, William Warren, Zadok Cramer, Charles Ball, James Williams, Alice Cary, Margaret Fuller, Eliza Farnham, Rebecca Burlend, Hugh Henry, Henry Marie Brackenridge, James Hall, William Gallagher, William Coggeshall, Gilbert Imlay, Manasseh Cutler, Henry Rowe Schoolcraft, George Copway, Lyman Beecher, Thomas Jefferson, Lewis and Clark, Thomas Ford, and U.S. treaties with various Native American tribes.

EAL 38: 536-39.

10 Migration

285 Carpin, Gervais. *Le Réseau du Canada: Étude du Mode Migratoire de la France vers la Nouvelle-France, 1628–1662*. Sillery, Que.: Septentrion, 2001. vi, 552 p. ISBN 2894481977; ISBN 9782894481974; ISBN 2840502070; OCLC 48117711; LC Call Number JV7212 .C376; Dewey 971.01/62. Citations: 6.
Describes migration from France to New France between 1627 and 1662, the activities of the Company of New France, the role of Richelieu in organizing the Compagnie des Cent-Associés, settler recruitment, particularly in and around La Rochelle, Dieppe, and Percheron Tourouvre, political and economic factors influencing settlement, and work contracts under which migrants labored.
CHR 85: 585-86.

286 Dorman, John Frederick, ed. *Adventurers of Purse and Person, Virginia, 1607-1624/5*. Baltimore, Md.: Genealogical Publishing, 2004–2007. 3 vols. ISBN 0806317442 (v. 1); ISBN 9780806317441 (v. 1); ISBN 0806317639 (v. 2); ISBN 9780806317632 (v. 2); ISBN 9780806317755 (v. 3); ISBN 0806317752 (v. 3); OCLC 54456619; LC Call Number F225 .A7; Dewey 929/.3755. Citations: 1.
Represents a fourth edition. Provides a muster list of 1624/25 (first volume) and tracks the descendants of the "Adventurers of Purse," the stockholders in the Virginia Company, and the "Adventurers of Person," common immigrants, who arrived in Virginia between 1607 and 1625, totaling 149 families. Includes new research that traces the descendants from the fourth to the sixth generations.
JSH 74: 1040-41.

287 Grabbe, Hans-Jürgen. *Vor der großen Flut: Die europäische Migration in die Vereinigten Staaten von Amerika, 1783–1820*. Stuttgart: Steiner, 2001. 458

p. ISBN 3515078142; ISBN 9783515078146; OCLC 50859368; LC Call Number E184.E95 G73; Dewey 304.8/7304/09033. Citations: 6.

Measures the annual numbers of immigrants from Europe, their origins, and their increases and decreases in the late eighteenth and early nineteenth centuries. Uses data from emigrant aid organizations, passenger ship estimates, press reports, and consulate observations, among others. Estimates that 366,400 European immigrants arrived in the United States during the period 1783–1820. Finds that migration dropped during periods of depression and international wars and rebounded during the Peace of Amiens and after the end of the Napoleonic wars. Notes that peak years were 1784 (20,330), 1801 (27,600) and 1818 (32,310) and that the largest numbers for the period were from Ireland (200,000), Great Britain (88,000), and Germany (32,000). Discovers patterns related to transatlantic trade routes (e.g., ships carrying flax to Irish linen factories returned with Irish immigrants, tobacco ships from Baltimore to ports in Germany and the Netherlands brought back immigrants from central Europe, etc.). Finds that fares fell, especially after 1815, which attracted travelers from Britain to New York.

AHR 108: 158-59; *JAH* 90: 216-17; *J Econ Hist* 65: 1181-83.

288 Miller, Kerby A., Arnold Schrier, Bruce D. Boling, and David N. Doyle, eds. *Irish Immigrants in the Land of Canaan: Letters and Memoirs from Colonial and Revolutionary America, 1675–1815*. New York: Oxford University Press, 2003. xxvii, 788 p. ISBN 0195045130 (hbk.); ISBN 9780195045130 (hbk.); ISBN 0195154894 (pbk.); ISBN 9780195154894 (pbk.); OCLC 50477195; LC Call Number E184.I6; Dewey 973/.049162. Citations: 37.

Explores early Irish immigration to the United States through essays and primary documents. Presents "historically representative and inherently interesting" documents organized around the themes of the background and causes of emigration, the process of Irish emigration to the New World, the nature of work (farming, skilled and unskilled labor, commerce, and the professions), and immigrants' relationships to the American Revolution and national politics and ideals. Provides annotations, bibliographic essays, and appendices that explain editorial conventions and linguistic variations.

JAEH 23: 161-62; *JAH* 98: 828; *J Brit Stds* 45: 159-61; *J Soc Hist* 40: 525-26; *PMHB* 130: 239-40; *RAH* 32: 305-16.

11 Labor and Class

289 Hessinger, Rodney. *Seduced, Abandoned, and Reborn: Visions of Youth in Middle-Class America, 1780–1850*. Philadelphia: University of Pennsylvania Press, 2005. 255 p. ISBN 0812238796; ISBN 9780812238792; OCLC 57965846; LC Call Number HQ796 .H465; Dewey 305.235/086/220973. Citations: 10.

Argues that early nineteenth-century northeastern urban moralists created middle-class identity through novels, advice literature, Sunday schools, and higher education, all of which were designed to restrain the young. Emphasizes the tensions between youth and the elders who sought to curb youthful impulses, which resulted from loosened patriarchal controls, greater choices and temptations, and increased competition in the cultural marketplace. Studies Philadelphia prostitution, student unrest at the University of Pennsylvania, and conservative Presbyterians' adoption of the Sunday School Movement as a counterpoint to revivalism and to limit youthful rebellion. Views advice manuals as seeking to blunt the dangerous expansion of market freedoms available to young men while showing these men that moral behavior would result in material wealth and the satisfaction of self-interest. Studies anti-masturbation literature, arguing that it illustrated reformers' fears that the urban market society offered too many opportunities for youthful self-indulgence. Notes that this literature provided a gender wedge by associating indulgence with femaleness, thereby promoting bourgeois ideals of gender difference and chastity and abandoning the notion of male self-control in favor of coercive, intrusive approaches by the mid-nineteenth century.

AHR 111: 1168-69; *CH* 75: 932-34; *HRNB* 34: 11; *JAH* 93: 209-210; *JER* 26: 331-32; *NEQ* 79: 494-95; *Penn Hist* 73: 364-66; *PMHB* 131: 113-14; *RAH* 34:162-68; *WMQ* 63: 421-24.

290 Hood, Adrienne D. *The Weaver's Craft: Cloth, Commerce, and Industry in Early Pennsylvania.* Philadelphia: University of Pennsylvania Press, 2003. 230 p. ISBN 0812237358; ISBN 9780812237351; OCLC 51848544; LC Call Number TS1324.P4; Dewey 338.4/7677/09748. Citations: 14.

Studies cloth manufacturing in eighteenth-century Chester County, Pennsylvania with the aim to explain regional differences in textile production and industrialization. Examines probate and tax records, local account books and newspapers, and diaries and correspondence to demonstrate the importance of cloth in British North America, the integration of home production, and the colonial acquisition of fabric for clothes, household linens, and farming. Reviews the role of English and Continental immigrants to Pennsylvania in establishing traditional gendered practices that combined agriculture and skilled craft production within the same household economy. Argues that southeastern Pennsylvania represents an alternate model of American industrialization, one that retained traditional male-dominated weaving, whereas in New England young women gradually brought weaving into the home and then moved into the new commercial mills. Finds that in the Philadelphia region, textile production developed in the city, focused on more complex cloths, and relied on hand production through much of the nineteenth century. Challenges widely accepted wisdom on the pervasiveness of colonial barter economies, the ability of colonists to produce fine fabrics, and assumptions about self-sufficiency.

AHR 109: 895-96; *Am Stds* 44: 156-57; *JAH* 91: 613; *JER* 25: 113-15; *PMHB* 129: 228-29.

291 Humphrey, Thomas J. *Land and Liberty: Hudson Valley Riots in the Age of Revolution.* Dekalb: Northern Illinois University Press, 2004. x, 191 p. ISBN 0875803296; ISBN 9780875803296; OCLC 54096736; LC Call Number F127.H8; Dewey 974.7/302. Citations: 8.

Describes the formation of the colony's landholding system and the significance of the Hudson River and access to international markets from the 1740s onward, a process that led to higher rents, formal contracts, and elimination of commons land. Points out that the region was characterized by large leasehold estates and exploitative tenancy arrangements, a proprietor class that insisted on the deference of the working poor, and a group of tenants that resented lease arrangements and demanded land and independence. Explains that tenants viewed freeholds, political democracy, and liberty as inseparable. Finds that tenant legal remedies failed because of proprietor power, both formal and informal. Explains that various title challenges led to landlords' tolerating chronic indebtedness and evicting only the most difficult tenants and that tenant riots, which were treated harshly by landlords, erupted periodically in the 1750s and 1760s. Argues that the Revolution changed the relationship between landlord and tenant, as the latter acquired a new vocabulary and framework of resistance. Contends that Hudson Valley tenants generally tried to avoid taking sides in the Revolution, and usually did so only to find a direct path to land ownership, and this sometimes meant supporting the Revolution and sometimes meant supporting the Crown. Concludes that the landlords were seeking to preserve their property holdings and quashed unrest through the machinery of

state, but that they had to accede to wider political participation in order to maintain title to the land.
AHR 111: 163-64; *JAH* 92: 590-91; *WMQ* 62: 557-61.

292 Lewis, Charlene M. Boyer. *Ladies and Gentlemen on Display: Planter Society at the Virginia Springs, 1790–1860*. Charlottesville: University Press of Virginia, 2001. x, 293 p. ISBN 0813920795 (hbk.); ISBN 9780813920795 (hbk.); ISBN 0813920809 (pbk.); ISBN 9780813920801 (pbk.); OCLC 47050181; LC Call Number F230 .L67; Dewey 306/.09755/09034. Citations: 13.
Demonstrates that when elite southerners relaxed at the Virginia Springs, they were really reinforcing the power relations of southern society and southern identity. Discusses the serene, natural setting, including the classical architecture and English gardens, nineteenth-century notions of nature and health, and the "community and competition" and exclusiveness of the springs. Explains that southerners valued hierarchy and most visitors to the springs came to see and to be seen or to regain health. Concludes that "Through display, contest, and scrutiny, southern ladies and gentlemen defined themselves and consolidated their claims to status."
AHR 108: 518-19; *GHQ* 86: 298-99; *IMH* 98: 320-21; *JAH* 89: 1521-22; *JER* 22: 704-706; *JSH* 70: 417-18; *RAH* 30: 555-63; *VMHB* 110: 269-70.

293 Milford, T.A. *The Gardiners of Massachusetts: Provincial Ambition and the British-American Career*. Durham: University of New Hampshire Press, 2005. xiv, 306 p. ISBN 1584655038 (hbk.); ISBN 9781584655039 (hbk.); ISBN 1584655046 (pbk.); ISBN 9781584655046 (pbk.); OCLC 59712236; LC Call Number F73.9.B7; Dewey 974.4/03/0922. Citations: 3.
Studies three male members of the Gardiners, a prominent Boston family that retained and cultivated transatlantic ties and cosmopolitan worldviews. Contends that the male family members maintained a classical liberal spirit that both encouraged the Revolution and helped to shape the new nation. Emphasizes the professions as a way to advance "middling men" and join the ranks of "the most learned and articulate of Americans . . . familiar and comfortable with the progressive literature of political economy generated within the British Empire." Finds that such "merchants, lawyers, doctors, master craftsmen, and their literary sons and brothers became important molders of opinion and taste."
AHR 111: 1501-1502; *JAH* 93: 841-42; *JER* 27: 368-75; *NEQ* 79: 665-68.

294 Newman, Simon P. *Embodied History: The Lives of the Poor in Early Philadelphia*. Philadelphia: University of Pennsylvania Press, 2003. xii, 211 p. ISBN 0812237315 (hbk.); ISBN 9780812237313 (hbk.); ISBN 0812218485 (pbk.); ISBN 9780812218480 (pbk.); OCLC 51613993; LC Call Number HV4046.P5; Dewey 305.569097481109033. Citations: 18.
Focuses on the experiences of the poor and the ways in which they gave their lives meaning, seeking insight into "their experiences, beliefs, values and culture." Describes the efforts of members of middling and elite groups to control the bodies of the poor, efforts that were brought on by increased poverty and apparent declines in deferential behavior. Explains that the upper orders

classified, regulated, and restrained the poor in newly created institutions, whose missions were to "recondition" impoverished bodies. Examines the records of the Philadelphia Almshouse, the Pennsylvania Hospital for the Sick Poor, and the Walnut Street Jail, finding that administrators evaluated bodily manifestations of impoverishment and thereby reached conclusions about the morality and treatment of inmates. Explains that many poor resisted these reform efforts by controlling their own appearances and the names by which they called themselves. Finds that many inmates in fact exploited the new system and formed communities of their own within the institutions.
AHR 109: 176-77; *HRNB* 32: 58; *JAH* 91: 613-14; *JAS* 38: 154-55; *JER* 23: 615-17; *J Soc Hist* 38: 782-84; *Penn Hist* 71: 233-35; *PMHB* 128: 314-15; *WMQ* 61: 182-84.

295 Smith, Billy G., ed. *Down and Out in Early America*. University Park: Pennsylvania State University Press, 2004. xx, 327 p. ISBN 0271023163 (hbk.); ISBN 9780271023168 (hbk.); ISBN 0271023171 (pbk.); ISBN 9780271023175 (pbk.); OCLC 53223579; LC Call Number HC110.P6; Dewey 362.5/0973/09033. Citations: 12.
Presents articles on poverty and politics in early America and in the Hudson River valley specifically, the relationship between poverty and death in early Philadelphia, gender and infant mortality among the working poor in late eighteenth and early nineteenth centuries, slaves and poverty, poor relief in eighteenth-century Rhode Island and in colonial Philadelphia, almshouse administration around Philadelphia between 1790 and 1860, abandoned children in late eighteenth-century Charleston, religious explanations of poverty in colonial Massachusetts, and the Delaware Indians and poverty in colonial New Jersey.
JAH 91: 1439-40.

296 Tarule, Robert. *The Artisan of Ipswich: Craftsmanship and Community in Colonial New England*. Baltimore, Md.: Johns Hopkins University Press, 2004. xi, 155 p. ISBN 0801878691 (hbk.); ISBN 9780801878695 (hbk.); ISBN 0801887526 (pbk.); ISBN 9780801887529 (pbk.); OCLC 53483547; LC Call Number TT25.I67; Dewey 745.4/0974/09032. Citations: 5.
Describes the work of Ipswich joiner Thomas Dennis, arguing that he was "a fine artisan, and his carving, many say, was the best done in the seventeenth-century New World." Discusses Dennis's apprenticeship in England and his removal to and work in Massachusetts and emphasizes the importance of white oak to the development of material culture in America.
NEQ 78: 662-64.

12 Economics and Business

297 Baucom, Ian. *Specters of the Atlantic: Finance Capital, Slavery, and the Philosophy of History*. Durham, N.C.: Duke University Press, 2005. x, 387 p. ISBN 0822335581 (hbk.); ISBN 9780822335580 (hbk.); ISBN 0822335964 (pbk.); ISBN 9780822335962 (pbk.); OCLC 60455015; LC Call Number HT1162 .B38; Dewey 306.3/62. Citations: 46.

Recounts the September 1781 incident in which the captain of the *Zong*, a British slave ship, ordered 133 slaves thrown into the sea so that the ship owners could file an insurance claim for lost cargo. Traces the reactions to the event, the legal actions that followed, and the social and economic contexts in which the Liverpool owners of the ship operated. Argues that violence has been essential to the development of modern capitalism and of the Atlantic world. Connects the *Zong* tragedy to modern speculation and finance and human rights discourse. *AHR* 114: 148-49; *BHR* 80: 778-80; *JER* 27: 342-46; *J Econ Hist* 67: 1078-79; *WMQ* 66: 1007-1010.

298 Bezís-Selfa, John. *Forging America: Ironworkers, Adventurers, and the Industrious Revolution*. Ithaca, N.Y.: Cornell University Press, 2003. xi, 279 p. ISBN 0801439930; ISBN 9780801439933; OCLC 52418120; LC Call Number HD9515 .B478; Dewey 338.4/76691/09730903 21. Citations: 16.

Explains that iron production in early America provided a nexus between capital and labor and between industrial and political revolutions. Finds that unfree and female labor was vital to early industrial development and that slaves performed both routine and skilled work, doing so alongside both indentured and free workers. Concludes that the United States relied directly on slave labor to launch its industrial revolution and that the iron industry "provided the foundation upon which the United States could develop a vibrant economy." *AHR* 110: 141-42; *JAH* 91: 1014; *JER* 24: 673-75; *J Econ Hist* 65: 266-68; *JSH* 71: 869-70; *Penn Hist* 71: 522-24; *PMHB* 129: 235-36; *WMQ* 62: 349-54.

299   Breen, T.H. *The Marketplace of Revolution: How Consumer Politics Shaped American Independence.* New York: Oxford University Press, 2004. xviii, 380 p. ISBN 0195063953; ISBN 9780195063950; OCLC 53324960; LC Call Number E209 .B77; Dewey 973.3/1. Citations: 93.

Identifies the Stamp Act as the central event leading to the American Revolution in that it provided a mercantile and consumer impetus for rebellion. Traces the "creation of a new consumer society" in America prior to the 1760s, whereby colonists became part of an "Empire of Goods." Argues that imports initially brought North Americans closer to the mother country, but that, when taxed, imports became convenient targets of resistance. Contends that the consumer marketplace transcended regionalism and allowed Americans to conceive of a nation. Notes that non-importation and non-consumption served to energize and demonstrate political concerns through a "strikingly new commercial language" that involved discussions of luxury and indebtedness. Concludes that "Choice in the consumer marketplace gradually merged with a discourse of rights, so that efforts by British Parliament that seemed to curtail participation were interpreted not only as an annoyance, but also as an attack on basic human rights."

AHR 110: 129-30; *Booklist* 100: 813; *BHR* 79: 353-63; *HRNB* 33: 16; *JAH* 91: 1416-17; *JER* 26: 498-502; *JSH* 71: 426-29; *NEQ* 78: 467-69; *Penn Hist* 72: 390-92; *PMHB* 129: 231-32; *RAH* 32: 329-40; *VMHB* 112: 69-70; *WMQ* 61: 765-69.

300   Bruegel, Martin. *Farm, Shop, Landing: The Rise of a Market Society in the Hudson Valley, 1780–1860.* Durham, N.C.: Duke University Press, 2002. xiv, 305 p. ISBN 0822328356 (hbk.); ISBN 0822328496 (pbk.); OCLC 47989988; LC Call Number HC107.N72 C693; Dewey 330.9747/3703 21. Citations: 21.

Examines the capitalist transformation of the Hudson River valley between 1780 and 1860, emphasizing the roles that both rich and poor men and women played. Argues that, by the 1850s, valley residents had internalized market principles in all aspects of interaction, including labor, religion, politics, and economics. Explains that this happened through a combination of state intervention in the economy, individual entrepreneurship, and increasing contact with external markets, factors that helped to overcome traditional ways of life. Argues that late in the eighteenth century Greene and Columbia counties were on the margins of the international market economy due to the New York feudal manor system, the use of barter and labor exchanges rather than cash, the mismatch of local market prices and commodity prices in New York City, and social dependence upon honor, mutual support, and deference. Explains that entrepreneurs opened industries, creating new markets for farmers and others.

Ag Hist 76: 726-28; *AHR* 108: 829-30; *CJH* 38: 352-53; *HRNB* 30: 146; *JAH* 90: 218-19; *JER* 22: 700-703; *J Econ Hist* 62: 890-91; *J Interdis Hist* 34: 470-71; *J Soc Hist* 37: 247-49; *RAH* 31: 389-96.

301   Clarke, John. *Land, Power, and Economics on the Frontier of Upper Canada.* Montreal: McGill-Queen's University Press. 2001. xxxvii, 747 p. ISBN 0773520627; ISBN 9780773520622; ISBN 0773521941; ISBN 9780773521940; OCLC 44674148; LC Call Number HD319.O5; Dewey 333.3/09713/3109034. Citations: 12.

Explains that "Upper Canada, from the time of its formation until the mid-nineteenth century was a preindustrial, agrarian community in which access to land was of primary importance to settlers and residents because it was the basis [both] of life and of economic and social prestige." Contends that both British land policy and its implementation reflected the rejection of unruly democratic impulses of the United States and the confirmation of the traditional English relationship between landed wealth and power. Discusses the operation of colonial land boards, noting that policy recognized two classes of land owners: (1) ordinary settlers, who could obtain conditional grants to land that would be confirmed once settlement duties were paid and (2) office holders and magistrates, who often received land in return for loyal service. Notes that land prices increased over time due to local factors, such as location near markets and relative development. Finds that speculation was widespread and that men of the upper orders used political, social, and personal influence to affect land prices and sales.
AHR 108: 505-506; *J Econ Hist* 62: 264-65; *J Soc Hist* 36: 779-81; *WHQ* 33: 503-504.

302 Coclanis, Peter A., ed. *The Atlantic Economy during the Seventeenth and Eighteenth Centuries: Organization, Operation, Practice, and Personnel.* Columbia: University of South Carolina Press, 2005. xix, 377 p. ISBN 1570035547; ISBN 9781570035548; OCLC 56066429; LC Call Number HF4045 .C66; Dewey 330.9182/1/09032 22. Citations: 15.
Presents essays on the Dutch Atlantic economy, the market economy of Madeira from the seventeenth through the early nineteenth centuries, the role of the cloth trade in the Atlantic economy, finance and trade in the British Atlantic economy between 1600 and 1830, Spain's Atlantic empire in the early seventeenth century, the relationship among Atlantic commerce, political opposition, and colonial regionalism, Dutch and New Netherland merchants in the seventeenth-century Chesapeake, the illicit slave trade in eighteenth-century Martinique, seventeenth- and eighteenth-century Cuban tobacco, the role of Cape Coast Castle in the slave trade from 1750 to 1790, the importance of Indians to the economy of eighteenth-century Carolina, exchange patterns of Colonial Chesapeake planters, and the trade of South Carolina rice and indigo in the Atlantic world.
AHR 111: 792-93; *BHR* 80: 780-83; *Econ Hist Rev* 58: 862-63; *18c Stds* 41: 110-13; *FHQ* 84: 449-51; *GHQ* 90: 449-51; *JAH* 93: 182-83; *J Econ Hist* 67: 1076-77; *JSH* 72: 642-43; *SCHM* 107: 353-55; *WMQ* 63: 385-92.

303 Dunn, Walter S. *The New Imperial Economy: The British Army and the American Frontier, 1764–1768.* Westport, Conn.: Praeger Publishers, 2001. viii, 208 p. ISBN 0275971805; ISBN 9780275971809; OCLC 44517897; LC Call Number HF485 .D86; Dewey 973.3/11 21. Citations: 2.
Describes the importance of the frontier immediately after the French and Indian War. Discusses the British economy, the transatlantic trade, and the mainland colonial economies, summarizing North American products and exports, and describing transportation networks. Concludes that "not the fur trade, but the intercourse among the people to satisfy the needs of the Indians, led to the

development of the frontier and the emergence of a new nation." Suggests that frontier consumption on the part of Indians, European settlers, and army members spurred colonial growth and led to structural economic changes that helped to cause the Revolution.
J Econ Hist 61: 574-75; *WMQ* 59: 746-66.

304 Dunn, Walter S. *Opening New Markets: The British Army and the Old Northwest.* Westport, Conn.: Praeger, 2002. x, 200 p. ISBN 0275973298; ISBN 9780275973292; OCLC 48467063; LC Call Number F482 .D87; Dewey 977/.01 21. Citations: 2.
Claims that after the Seven Years' War the economic consequences of British policies along the trans-Appalachian frontier benefited British merchants and French traders in Canada while harming the interests of American merchants, specifically those doing business in Canada, the lower Great Lakes region, Pennsylvania, the Ohio Valley, and the Mississippi Valley, who had become wealthy in their wartime supply of the British army. Finds that after 1768 these merchants suffered greatly due to the drastic reduction of British forces in North America and the redeployment of many western regiments to the East Coast. Contends that the post-1765 British restriction of fur trade transactions to army posts harmed colonial traders who could no longer travel freely among western Indian villages, which were then served almost exclusively by French traders. Notes that American businessmen in the West who attempted to recoup their losses through speculation in lands north of the Ohio River were rebuffed by British policies seeking to limit European expansion beyond the Appalachians. Concludes that disgruntled colonial merchants, "hemmed in on all sides and facing increasing deficits," turned against the British government and became Revolutionary leaders.
JAH 90: 621-22; *J Mil Hist* 67: 558-59.

305 Earle, Carville. *The American Way: A Geographical History of Crisis and Recovery.* Lanham, Md.: Rowman and Littlefield, 2003. xviii, 449 p. ISBN 0847687120; ISBN 9780847687121; OCLC 51677694; LC Call Number E179.5 .E36; Dewey 911./73 21. Citations: 12.
Identifies completed American historical cycles, each encompassing both good and bad economic periods, and two opposing approaches to political economy that have dominated in alternate cycles (1630 – 1680s, 1740s – 1780s, 1830s – 1880s, and 1930s – 1970s). Calls these alternate cycle approaches "republican" in the colonial period and "democratic" afterwards and notes that they were characterized by relative egalitarianism and nationalism. Finds that the second approach is associated with "salutary neglect," Hamiltonian Federalism, the Gilded Age, and Reaganomics. Emphasizes that there have been variations in each of the iterations of these two approaches, but that both have strong biases toward liberty. Concludes, though, that "Liberty's price, one might say, is an enduring inequality—a price that Americans, when judged by their histories of income and wealth, are more than willing to pay."
AHR 109: 1219-20; *J Econ Hist* 63: 1163-65; *JHG* 31: 183; *WMQ* 61: 556-59.

306 Foster, A. Kristen. *Moral Visions and Material Ambitions: Philadelphia Struggles to Define the Republic, 1776–1836.* Lanham, Md.: Lexington Books, 2004. 216 p. ISBN 0739107585; ISBN 9780739107584; OCLC 53284880; LC Call Number F158.44 .F67; Dewey 974.8/1103. Citations: 4.

Studies the political and social ideas of those who sought material betterment in early industrial Philadelphia, particularly the ways in which white males' ambitions influenced their views of political economy and community responsibility. Argues that the post-Revolution free market economy fostered individualism among ambitious citizens, rather than community-minded behavior and relegated "middle-class radicalism" to "the city's political periphery," thereby ensuring the establishment of "the moderate republic." Finds that laborers demanded "economic justice, or guaranteed incomes," and a moral economy, while elites and the middle class sought a strictly market economy based on individual ambition, believing that such an arrangement "would make the commonwealth stronger." Examines the conflict regarding the 1776 state constitution, political arguments advanced in the U.S. Constitution and ratification debates, important labor conspiracy trials, and the struggles of free blacks and women. Suggests that defenders of the moral economy "fought for the heart and soul of the [Jeffersonian] party" and the Revolution, but were defeated by entrepreneurs who abandoned "any link to a plan that sought the retooling of the city's and the nation's economic structure."
AHR 111: 155-56; *JAH* 92: 200-201; *JER* 25: 498-500; *WMQ* 62: 121-22.

307 Gruenwald, Kim M. *River of Enterprise: The Commercial Origins of Regional Identity in the Ohio Valley, 1790–1850.* Bloomington: Indiana University Press, 2002. xvi, 214 p. ISBN 0253341329; ISBN 9780253341327; OCLC 48871720; LC Call Number F518 .G78; Dewey 977/.02 21. Citations: 15.

Argues that during the early national period merchants from river towns played a vital role in making the Ohio River a symbol of regional unity. Contends that the early nineteenth-century river was not merely a north-south boundary and that the idea of the "West" was not merely the story of frontier farmers and squatters. Tells the story of the Dudley Woodbridge family of Marietta, which originally migrated from New England to the river settlement in 1788 and, like other such families, gradually extended their influence and linked the west and east through extensive trading networks. Explains that, prior to the widespread use of canals and railroads, settlers conceived of the region as a unified whole, but that transportation advances eventually bound the area to large cities and other regions, reducing the significance of river towns. Points out that these changes caused settlers living north of the river to view themselves as Ohioans and resulted in greater alienation of those living to the south, particularly as the abolitionist influence expanded in the north.
AHR 109: 187-88; *BHR* 77: 300-302; *IMH* 101: 375-78; *JAH* 90: 1010-1011; *J Econ Hist* 64: 262-63; *JER* 23: 123-25; *J Interdis Hist* 35: 653-54; *JSH* 70: 132-33; *PMHB* 127: 113-114; *WHQ* 35: 79-80.

308 Higman, B.W. *Plantation Jamaica, 1750 –1850: Capital and Control in a Colonial Economy.* Kingston, Jamaica: University of the West Indies Press,

2005. xiv, 386 p. ISBN 9766401659; ISBN 9789766401658; OCLC 62868347; LC Call Number HD1471.J25; Dewey 306.349097292. Citations: 16.

Suggests that Jamaican attorneys were managers and not lawyers and were often also proprietors, which makes unclear the division between owners and employees. Stresses that the role of the attorney in running an estate required the performance of a remarkable range of activities and a diverse skill set. Notes that attorneys were not mere stand-ins for absentees, but rather became professional managers who were responsible for creating and maintaining managerial hierarchies and task specialization schemes. Presents case studies of Simon Taylor at Golden Grove between 1765 and 1775 and Isaac Jackson at Montpelier from 1839 to 1843, noting that both successfully managed a number of estates and advanced their own landed interests. Describes the various tasks of these attorneys, including the settlement of disputes with overseers and their employers and managing the complex geographical and environmental challenges involved in producing sugar. Emphasizes the key role of slaves, whom Taylor viewed exclusively in economic terms. Characterizes both Taylor and Jackson as successful in terms of sugar production and land acquisition.

Ag Hist 82: 103-105; *AHR* 111: 1230-31; *BHR* 80: 796-99; *Econ Hist Rev* 60: 639-40; *J Soc Hist* 42: 503-505.

309 Hunter, Phyllis Whitman. *Purchasing Identity in the Atlantic World: Massachusetts Merchants, 1670–1780*. Ithaca, N. Y.: Cornell University Press, 2001. xiv, 224 p. ISBN 0801438551; ISBN 9780801438554; OCLC 45558985; LC Call Number HC107.M4; Dewey 381/.09744/09032. Citations: 15.

Argues that the seventeenth-century mercantile elite was essentially a closed group, but that by 1730 was open to all with sufficient means and "credit" who dressed and acted like educated British gentlemen. Explains that the Revolution fractured the transatlantic community, leading to the replacement of polite refinement with homespun clothing and republican virtue. Presents biographical sketches of merchants and describes their houses, clothes, and personal possessions.

AHR 107: 1549-50; *JAH* 89: 606-607; *VQR* 78: 10; *WMQ* 59: 511-14.

310 Madsen, Axel. *John Jacob Astor: America's First Multimillionaire*. New York: John Wiley, 2001. vii, 312 p. ISBN 0471385034; ISBN 9780471385035; OCLC 44172996; LC Call Number HC102.5.A76; Dewey 380.1/092. Citations: 7.

Presents a biography of Astor. Discusses Astor's key role in the opening of the American West through the establishment of permanent outposts in the Oregon territory, which also helped to facilitate trade with China. Emphasizes Astor's unusual business acumen, which led him to diversify his interests and brought him fortunes in trade and Manhattan real estate. Places Astor's accomplishments in context, noting that independence allowed American merchants to enter the Pacific maritime, that competition for furs depleted the beaver supply, and that changing fashion tastes put an end to the active trade.

BHR 75: 596-98; *LJ* 126n3: 176-77; *PMHB* 126: 141-42.

311 Mann, Bruce H. *Republic of Debtors: Bankruptcy in the Age of American Independence.* Cambridge, Mass.: Harvard University Press, 2002. viii, 344 p. ISBN 0674009029; ISBN 9780674009028; ISBN 9780674032415; ISBN 0674032411; OCLC 49750941; LC Call Number HG3766 .M29; Dewey 332.7/5/0973 21. Citations: 52.

Examines bankruptcy law in the colonies, noting that inability to pay debts led to larger cultural and political debates over the meaning of failure. Explains that the growth of Atlantic commercial networks caused the American view of insolvency to shift "from sin to risk, from moral failure to economic failure." Describes the relationship between eighteenth-century debtors and creditors, the instruments of commercial credit available to merchants, and the effect of war on economic change. Comments that the Seven Years' War "demonstrated to all how far tremors in foreign markets rippled through colonial economies" and explains that the American Revolution and the opening of the trans-Appalachian frontier led to increased speculation in securities, bank stock, and land. Highlights insolvency's pairing with dependence and slavery, particularly in Jeffersonian thought. Suggests that the Bankruptcy Act of 1800 represented "a declaration that the new nation was, emphatically, a commercial republic." Notes that, as the meaning of bankruptcy changed, poor debtors received fewer protections than the wealthy, and that most laws were designed to protect creditors with large outstanding debts, while creditors lending less money had fewer options for recovery.

AHR 109: 898-99; *BHR* 78: 285-87; *CJH* 34: 181-82; *HRNB* 31: 149; *JAH* 90: 1426-27; *JER* 23: 474-77; *J Econ Hist* 63: 895-97; *LJ* 128n1: 129; *NEQ* 77: 655-59; *PMHB* 128: 204-205; *RAH* 34: 315-23; *WMQ* 60: 693-96.

312 Martin, Scott C., ed. *Cultural Change and the Market Revolution in America, 1789–1860.* Lanham, Md.: Rowman and Littlefield, 2005. vi, 298 p. ISBN 0742527700 (hbk.); ISBN 9780742527706 (hbk.); ISBN 0742527719 (pbk.); ISBN 9780742527713 (pbk.); OCLC 55518638; LC Call Number HC110.C3; Dewey 306.3/42. Citations: 7.

Presents articles on early nineteenth-century cultural history, focusing on "the values, practices, and institutions created by every social group," especially women, African Americans, and Native Americans. Includes pieces on the market revolution, market values in antebellum black protest thought, ethnicity and the marketplace in Charlotte, Vermont between 1845 and 1860, the Choctaw cattle economy from 1690 to 1830, Yankee peddlers, Southern consumers, the market revolution, sociability, social networks, and the creation of a provincial middle class between 1820 and 1860, education, manual labor, and the market revolution, animals, their exhibitors, and market culture in the early Republic, temperance nostalgia, market anxiety, and the reintegration of community in T.S. Arthur's *Ten Nights in a Bar-Room*, and nationalism, theater, and Jacksonian Indian policy.

AHR 110: 1168-69; *JAH* 92: 969-70; *JER* 26: 498-502.

313 Mustafa, Sam A. *Merchants and Migrations: Germans and Americans in Connection, 1776–1835.* Burlington, Vt.: Ashgate, 2001. xvii, 284 p. ISBN

0754605906 9780754605904; OCLC 46731143; LC Call Number HF3099 .M87; Dewey 382/.0943073. Citations: 6.

Examines the developing relationship between German and American merchants from the American Revolution to 1835. Contends that U.S.-German relations during this period were determined by the significance of the Hanseatic cities of Hamburg and Bremen, the lack of state intervention in the establishment of commercial relations, and the slow evolution of diplomatic relations resulting from commercial connections. Explores the common "merchant culture" of Hamburg, Bremen, Baltimore, and Philadelphia, the commitment to free trade among independent merchants, the impact of the Protestant ethic and of political republicanism, and the general mercantile cosmopolitan worldview. Finds that, despite official treaties between the United States and Prussia, American merchants were attracted to "the free-trading capitalist republics of the Hanse," whose citizens seemed to share American merchant values. Describes trade networks based on kinship, friendship, and personal initiative, and the role of diplomacy, particularly as carried out by counsels, "agents of commerce [and] transmitters of information." Explains that the United States and the Hanseatic cities established a reciprocal trade treaty in 1827 and that commercial arrangements with other states, including Prussia, laid the groundwork for German-American relations for the remainder of the nineteenth century.
AHR 108: 158; *J Econ Hist* 63: 919-21.

314 Netzloff, Mark. *England's Internal Colonies: Class, Capital, and the Literature of Early Modern English Colonialism.* New York: Palgrave Macmillan, 2003. xii, 280 p. ISBN 1403961832; ISBN 9781403961839; OCLC 52178211; LC Call Number PR428.I54; Dewey 820.9/358. Citations: 5.

Explores the relationship between the internal and external in England, noting that protocapitalism both provided the context for English expansion and created problems at home. Focuses on the roles of commerce, capital, and travel, arguing that tensions between mercantilism and capitalism are evident in early modern literature. Discusses boundaries and borders in the union of Scotland and England and efforts to erase the overt evidence of colonization in Ulster.
EHR 121: 934-35; *16c J* 39: 578-80.

315 Noll, Mark A., ed. *God and Mammon: Protestants, Money, and the Market, 1790–1860.* New York: Oxford University Press, 2002. xii, 313 p. ISBN 0195148002 (hbk.); ISBN 9780195148008 (hbk.); ISBN 0195148010 (pbk.); ISBN 9780195148015 (pbk.); OCLC 46240340; LC Call Number BR525 .G63; Dewey 261.8/5/0973. Citations: 18.

Presents thirteen essays on Protestantism and the market revolution and economics. Provides statistics on the economic power of the denominations and voluntary societies in comparison to leading industries, educational institutions, and the federal government. Explains that publishing, one of the nation's largest industries, benefited greatly from Protestant interests. Discusses marketing and the "businessmen's revival" of 1857–1858, in which the secular media exploited religion. Suggests that by the 1850s evangelicals had become comfortable with market values.
BHR 76: 583-85; *CH* 73: 226-28; *JAAR* 71: 708-711; *JAH* 90: 219-20.

316   Ormrod, David. *The Rise of Commercial Empires: England and the Netherlands in the Age of Mercantilism, 1650–1770*. New York: Cambridge University Press, 2003. xvii, 400 p. ISBN 0521819261; ISBN 9780521819268; OCLC 50271585; LC Call Number   HF3505 .O76; Dewey 382/.09410492; Dewey 330.94207. Citations: 43.

Compares British and Dutch international trade, examining patterns and competition, the main commodities of wool, linen, grain, and coal, and shipping, war, and protection. Finds that the British supplanted Dutch commercial supremacy after about 1690 as a result of aggressive policy, protectionism, strict control of colonial trade through the Navigation Acts, and military action. Attributes British success to British fiscal soundness, coherent policy, and strong navy, and contends that the United Provinces' failures were due to decentralization, overtaxation, and lack of a coherent trade policy.

AHR 109: 1304-1305; *BHR* 77: 552-55; *CJH* 40: 92-94; *Econ Hist Rev* 58: 860-61; *EHR* 118: 1333-35; *J Econ Hist* 63: 1154-55; *J Interdis Hist* 35: 125-27; *JSH* 70: 491-95; *16c J* 36: 860-62.

317   Peskin, Lawrence A. *Manufacturing Revolution: The Intellectual Origins of Early American Industry*. Baltimore, Md.: Johns Hopkins University Press, 2003. x, 294 p. ISBN 080187324X; ISBN 9780801873249; OCLC 51087976; LC Call Number HD9725 .P47; Dewey 338.0973/09/033. Citations: 20.

Traces the development of American industry from the British mercantile system of the 1760s, revolutionary non-importation, post-revolutionary economic crises, and Federalist manufacturing programs, to mechanic and agricultural voluntary societies, and the "ruralization of manufacturing." Emphasizes the roles of tariffs and of individuals such as Tench Coxe, Mathew Carey, and David Humphreys in early national industrial development. Concludes that the vision of large-scale American industry was in place by 1800 and that "The emerging American system was the culmination of the discourse colonial mechanics began during the unrest of the 1760s."

AHR 110: 788-90; *BHR* 78: 512-14; *Econ Hist Rev* 58: 217-18; *HRNB* 33: 16; *JAH* 91: 1437-38; *JER* 25: 488-90; *J Econ Hist* 64: 1141-42; *Penn Hist* 72: 260-63; *PMHB* 130: 119-21; *WMQ* 62: 349-54.

318   Pope, Peter Edward. *Fish into Wine: The Newfoundland Plantation in the Seventeenth Century*. Chapel Hill: University of North Carolina Press, published for the Omohundro Institute of Early American History and Culture, Williamsburg, Virginia, 2004. xxvi, 463 p. ISBN 0807829102 (hbk.); ISBN 9780807829103 (hbk.); ISBN 0807855766 (pbk.); ISBN 9780807855768 (pbk.); OCLC 54374678; LC Call Number F1123 .P66; Dewey 971.8/01. Citations: 28.

Discusses the importance of fish to Newfoundland trade, noting that "European commercial activity in Atlantic Canada exceeded, in volume and value, European trade with the Gulf of Mexico." Explains that during the seventeenth century cod was a primary English export to the Mediterranean, resulting in the importation of Spanish wine and the tremendous influx of fishers and settlers to Newfoundland. Argues that permanent settlers and temporary fishermen worked well together to construct a strikingly modern, prosperous, and cosmopolitan economy. Concludes that the island was sensitive to market fluctuations and imperial politics and regulation.

AHR 111: 1496; *JAH* 92: 580-81; *J Interdis Hist* 37: 653-55; *NEQ* 78: 493-95; *16c J* 36: 1228-29.

319 Rilling, Donna J. *Making Houses, Crafting Capitalism: Builders in Philadelphia, 1790–1850.* Philadelphia: University of Pennsylvania Press, 2001. xii, 261 p. ISBN 0812235800; ISBN 9780812235807; OCLC 44775069; LC Call Number TH24.P4; Dewey 338.4/76908/0974811. Citations: 23.

Studies the careers of Philadelphia builders John Munday (1790s), Moses Lancaster (1800s and 1810s), and Warnet Myers (1820s and 1830s), noting that each went from artisan to entrepreneur and then became overextended and the victims of recession. Examines the effects of capital and credit, materials diversification, economic and building cycles, and cultural and labor networks. Finds that laws and customs on land and credit directly affected builders, that the sources of building finance were diverse, but also volatile, and that small capital requirements in Philadelphia benefited low-scale builders and encouraged the production of row houses.

AHR 107: 194; *BHR* 75: 822-24; *Econ Hist Rev* 55: 378-79; *JAH* 89: 206; *J Econ Hist* 62: 248-50; *Penn Hist* 68: 541-44; *PMHB* 126: 508-510.

320 Siskind, Janet. *Rum and Axes: The Rise of a Connecticut Merchant Family, 1795–1850.* Ithaca: Cornell University Press, 2002. xii, 191 p. ISBN 0801439329; ISBN 9780801439322; OCLC 46937430; LC Call Number HF3161.C7; Dewey 381/.09746. Citations: 5.

Studies the business activities of three generations of the Watkinson family, particularly the ways in which its members amassed and used capital and approached work. Discusses shifts in interest from trade to manufacturing and the creation of networks through marriage. Explains that such networks of trade obscured the realities of slavery and other tragedies involved in commercial life and that industrialists avoided unpleasantness by intentionally setting their houses and churches at a distance from their sites of production.

JAH 89: 1030-31; *NEQ* 75: 682-84.

321 Truxes, Thomas M., ed. *Letterbook of Greg & Cunningham, 1756–57: Merchants of New York and Belfast.* New York: Oxford University Press, 2001. xxxi, 430 p. ISBN 0197262198; ISBN 9780197262191; OCLC 44154027; LC Call Number HC251 .B7; HF3095.5 .N7; Dewey 382.0941670747109033. Citations: 7.

Discusses the activities of a transatlantic, Irish-American merchant firm in the early years of the Seven Years' War. Focuses on the various partners, the correspondence that they produced, goods traded, use of bills of exchange and maritime insurance, and ship management. Presents in chronological order 338 letters sent by Waddell Cunningham between May 1756 and January 1757, the partnership agreements between Cunningham and Thomas Gregg, newspaper advertisements published between 1752 and 1757, and the wills of the two partners, along with a glossary of contemporary maritime and mercantile terms. Provides information on "individual persons, business enterprises, places, ships,

commodities, business practices and other features of Greg & Cunningham's economic, political and social environment."
J Econ Hist 62: 1170-71.

322 Wright, Robert E. *The First Wall Street: Chestnut Street, Philadelphia, and the Birth of American Finance*. Chicago: University of Chicago Press, 2005. viii, 210 p. ISBN 0226910261; ISBN 9780226910260; OCLC 58985935; LC Call Number HG5131.P5; Dewey 332.64/273/09034. Citations: 17.
Examines the first American financial center: Chestnut Street in Philadelphia, on which were located the nation's first stock exchange, the U.S. Mint, the Bank of the United States, and several insurance companies. Explains that the concentration of such interests came from a confluence of political power, information, capital, and entrepreneurship. Traces the decline of Philadelphia as a financial center to the Jacksonian period, as the city's early innovators passed away and the Bank of the U.S. charter expired, and as the position of New York was enhanced by the development of the Erie Canal.
AHR 112: 192-93; *JAH* 93: 511-12; *JER* 31: 170-77; *J Econ Hist* 66: 837-39; *PMHB* 131: 111-113; *RAH* 34: 315-23.

323 Wright, Robert E. *Hamilton Unbound: Finance and the Creation of the American Republic*. Westport, Conn.: Greenwood Press, 2002. xii, 230 p. ISBN 0313323976; ISBN 9780313323973; ISBN 0275978168; ISBN 9780275978167; OCLC 49226430; LC Call Number HG181 .W746; Dewey 332/.0973/09033. Citations: 15.
Surveys early American economic history, asserting that colonists' desire to gain control of monetary policy was a primary cause of the American Revolution, that federal and state constitutions sought to solve the "principal-agent" problem, that financial development, economic growth, and political stability were inextricably linked, that New York City legislative elections were influenced by Aaron Burr's Manhattan Company's extending credit to local artisans, who in turn voted Republican, that better credit rating practices in the early nineteenth century led to a decline in dueling in the North, and that the economic activity of women moved from active involvement in businesses in the late eighteenth century to more passive investment in securities in the mid-nineteenth century.
AHR 109: 899-900; *JAH* 91: 608-609; *JER* 23: 280-82; *J Econ Hist* 63:897-98.

324 Wright, Robert E. *Origins of Commercial Banking in America, 1750–1800*. Lanham: Rowman & Littlefield, 2001. xii, 219 p. ISBN 0742520862 (hbk.); ISBN 9780742520868 (hbk.); ISBN 0742520870 (pbk.); ISBN 9780742520875 (pbk.); OCLC 46580168; LC Call Number HG2466 .W75; Dewey 332.1/2/097309033. Citations: 14.
Focuses on the problems with liquidity that plagued the colonial and post-Revolution American economies. Explains that prior to the Revolution public and private bills of credit were notoriously difficult to convert to cash and that money was both varied (many coin denominations and foreign currencies in circulation) and relatively scarce. Finds that liquidity issues slowed debt repayments, fostered a grey economy in which most goods and services were

created and traded outside of commercial markets, restricted the volume and speed of trade, and encouraged rampant bartering. Argues that after the Revolution the demand for marketable commodities grew, markets expanded, and money was more readily available. Considers the development of the banking sector, particularly in New York and Pennsylvania, and contends that early banks protected monied interests, but were vital in transforming American society.

AHR 108: 192; *BHR* 76: 580-82; *JAH* 90: 208-209; *J Econ Hist* 62: 615-16.

325 Wright, Robert E. *The Wealth of Nations Rediscovered: Integration and Expansion in American Financial Markets, 1780–1850.* Cambridge: Cambridge University Press, 2002. xi, 240 p. ISBN 0521812372; ISBN 9780521812375; OCLC 48390769; LC Call Number HG181 .W75; Dewey 332.63/2/0973. Citations: 30.

Notes the problem of information asymmetry in early America, finding that it created inefficiencies in capital markets, markets that were already limited by kinship networks and geography. Explains that, starting in the 1790s, financial intermediaries (e.g., banks, brokers, objective credit rating services) began reducing the asymmetry and thus correcting inefficiencies. Contends that Hamilton's program was vital to American development and that, surprisingly, many Americans of nearly all social strata participated in the financial services sector as shareholders or borrowers. Concludes that the development of financial institutions and markets were more important to early American economic development than were productivity gains, bourgeoning manufacturing, or transportation and communications improvements.

AHR 109: 900-901; *BHR* 77: 500-501; *JAH* 91: 999-1000; *JAS* 37: 523-24; *J Interdis Hist* 35: 308-309.

13 Society

326 Aronson, Marc. *Witch-Hunt: Mysteries of the Salem Witch Trials.* New York: Simon and Schuster, 2005. xvi, 272 p. ISBN 1416903151 (pbk.); ISBN 9781416903154 (pbk.); OCLC 61323618; LC Call Number KFM2478.8 .W5; Dewey 133.43. Citations: 1.

Surveys the belief systems in effect at the time of the Salem episodes, the various roles of participants, the tests of persons suspected of being witches, and various trials, confessions, and recantations. Discusses recent historiography on Salem witchcraft and provides questions for students regarding the motives of accusers, witnesses, judges, and skeptics. Reprints portions of documents related to the controversy, noting that the "truth of the crowd versus that of the individual was a recurring issue in the Salem trials." Concludes that group accusations only dissipated when "skeptics, martyrs and ministers" challenged the persecutions.
Hist Teach 37: 401-402.

327 Baumgarten, Linda. *What Clothes Reveal: The Language of Clothing in Colonial and Federal America.* Williamsburg, Va. and New Haven, Conn.: The Colonial Williamsburg Foundation in Association with Yale University Press, 2002. xii, 265 p. ISBN 0879352167; ISBN 9780879352165; ISBN 0300095805; ISBN 9780300095807; OCLC 49959172; LC Call Number GT607 .B38; Dewey 391/.00973 21. Citations: 13.

Describes the collection of eighteenth- and nineteenth-century costumes at colonial Williamsburg, including clothing for the upper orders and those for work, everyday wear, nursing, and maternity, and those clothes worn by slaves. Reviews the process and history of collecting garments and includes more than 350 color photographs. Draws upon contemporary descriptions of fashions, noting their myths and meanings and the ways in which they delineated social class and segments of a person's life cycle. Makes use of modern scientific techniques to determine methods and places of manufacture. Identifies the ideas of homespun and self-sufficiency as mythic constructions, undermined by widespread purchase and importation of clothing, even among the likes of Thomas Jefferson. Finds that clothes signaled "the wearer's gender, country of origin, occupation, economic level, activity and attitude" and concludes that "Nowhere was social inequality more evident than in the clothes people wore." *JAH* 90: 1429-30; *NEQ* 76: 657-59; *WMQ* 60: 697-99.

328 Berland, Kevin, Jan Kirsten Gilliam, and Kenneth A. Lockridge, eds. *The Commonplace Book of William Byrd II of Westover*. Chapel Hill: University of North Carolina Press, published for the Omohundro Institute of Early American History and Culture, 2001. xviii, 319 p. ISBN 080782612X; ISBN 9780807826126; OCLC 44493324; LC Call Number F229 .B94; Dewey 975.5/02/092. Citations: 11.
Presents Byrd's commonplace book, which is made up of almost six hundred entries on a wide range of subjects, including science, medicine, religion, women, love, education, reading, and conversation. Provides an introduction that touches upon Byrd's background, education, written work, and creation of the commonplace book. Argues that the commonplace book represents Byrd's attempts to deal with failed efforts while in England to secure social acceptance and a wealthy bride and that the book helped him to come to grips with his role as a Virginia gentleman. Notes that the commonplace book lacks "any apparent scheme of organization or topical coherence," which demonstrates crisis in Byrd's life more clearly than do his formulaic diaries. Distinguishes among entries that deal with serious issues and those that Byrd found merely entertaining, but makes clear that the purpose of the book was to create an ordered self to resolve worldly tensions and contradictions. Finds that the "most remarkable array of entries in Byrd's commonplace book concerns the nature of women and the disadvantages of marriage," which reveal Byrd's "contempt for women."
EAL 39: 188-95; *JSH* 68: 923-24; *VMHB* 109: 220-21; *VQR* 77: 131-32; *WMQ* 59: 292-96.

329 Buckridge, Steeve O. *The Language of Dress: Resistance and Accommodation in Jamaica, 1760–1890*. Kingston, Jamaica: University of the West Indies Press, 2004. xvii, 270 p. ISBN 9766401438; ISBN 9789766401436; OCLC 55141684; LC Call Number GT667 .B83; Dewey 391.009/7292. Citations: 3.
Examines slave clothing in Jamaica, noting that male slaves received a larger allotment than did women, which reinforces the notion of female subordination. Finds that occupation and status dictated the clothing that slaves wore and that runaways dressed differently, mimicking the styles of free women. Contends that clothing became a form of resistance, that the adoption of African styles (e.g., headwraps and necklaces) was a way for slaves to maintain identity and deny their masters power over them. Notes that slaves sometimes appropriated European symbols and participated in the Christmas tradition of dressing like their masters in order to subvert temporarily the plantation power structure. Explains that the creole style of dress represented "a conscious effort to

maintain, preserve and support the African elements in dress brought to the Caribbean." Finds that after slavery's abolition freed women modified European styles of dress "to receive some validation for themselves and their race," an effort that ultimately failed.
AHR 110: 1222-23.

330 Burnard, Trevor. *Creole Gentlemen: The Maryland Elite, 1691–1776*. New York: Routledge, 2002. x, 278 p. ISBN 0415931738 (hbk.); ISBN 9780415931731 (hbk.); ISBN 0415931746 (pbk.); ISBN 9780415931748 (pbk.); OCLC 47183445; LC Call Number F184 .B89; Dewey 975.2/02 21. Citations: 7.
Studies Maryland's eighteenth-century elite, focusing on the wealthy from Anne Arundel, Baltimore, Talbot, and Somerset counties. Examines 461 probate records covering the period from 1691 to 1776 for men leaving personal estates of greater than £650. Finds that Maryland's elite were less wealthy than those to the south, that few held fifty or more slaves, and that they were more similar to wealthy farmers in Delaware and Pennsylvania than to planters in Virginia and the Carolinas. Notes that the Maryland elites were generally not entrepreneurial and sought to avoid risk and to manage assets efficiently. Characterizes the Maryland elite as a relatively fluid group, open to all who could demonstrate gentility through wealth, status, and behavior. Notes that, through the early eighteenth century, members of the elite engaged in commerce and planting, but gradually dropped the former in favor of tobacco and grain production in the belief that planting promoted virtue. Explains that, unlike their counterparts from Virginia, members of the Maryland elite did not build up high indebtedness to British merchants.
AHR 108: 185; *JAH* 90: 205-206; *J Soc Hist* 38: 823-25; *VMHB* 110: 493-94; *WMQ* 60: 219-22.

331 Carr, Jacqueline Barbara. *After the Siege: A Social History of Boston, 1775–1800*. Boston, Mass.: Northeastern University Press, 2005. xv, 318 p. ISBN 1555536298; ISBN 9781555536299; OCLC 54822894; LC Call Number F73.44 .C37; Dewey 974.4/6102 22. Citations: 3.
Provides "a social portrait of Boston" that focuses "on the lives of lower- and middle-income groups" in the last quarter of the eighteenth century. Uses tax assessments and records of the Overseers of the Poor to gain insight into differences of real property, migrations, the impact of smallpox outbreaks, and changes in business patterns. Notes that after the Revolution "Poor relief, public education, the just market, and the presence of the theater in Boston" became "central concerns."
AHR 110: 1527-28; *JAH* 92: 957-58; *JER* 25: 665-68; *NEQ* 78: 508-510; *WMQ* 62: 554-56.

332 Demos, John. *Circles and Lines: The Shape of Life in Early America*. Cambridge, Mass.: Harvard University Press, 2004. xi, 98 p. ISBN 0674013247; ISBN 9780674013247; OCLC 53374896; LC Call Number E162 .D46; Dewey 973. Citations: 9.

Publishes the 2002 William E. Massey, Sr. Lectures in the History of American Civilization, which were presented at Harvard. Presents an overview of the patterns of life among ordinary people from early Anglo-American colonial settlement to the mid-nineteenth century. Points out that the earliest colonists experienced the world in the predominantly circular patterns of diurnal, lunar and annual cycles (e.g., marriages peaked following harvests, laws limited laborers' wages during short winter days, etc.). Demonstrates that witchcraft accusations had a diurnal rhythm (e.g., suspicious "accidents" occurred in the daytime, while more spectral horrors happened at night). Explains that increased use of clocks and the rise of the "new nation" in the eighteenth century challenged the cyclical view and that by the early nineteenth century linear ideas of progress and even a cult of "the new" were displacing old patterns. Claims that linearity of the railroad and westward expansion compared culturally to the rise of autobiography, which emphasized "incidents" rather than "providences," and to the stressing of self-improvement and personal progress.
Ag Hist 80: 371-73; *AHR* 110: 1163-64; *CJH* 40: 557-59; *HRNB* 33: 17; *JAS* 39: 552-53; *J Soc Hist* 39: 289-90; *LJ* 129n6: 106; *PMHB* 129: 483-84.

333 Ekirch, A. Roger. *At Day's Close: Night in Times Past.* New York: W.W. Norton & Company, 2005. xxxii, 447 p. ISBN 0393050890; ISBN 9780393050899; OCLC 57564726; LC Call Number HN8 .E48; Dewey 306.4 22. Citations: 28.
Presents a social history of night in pre-industrial Europe and America. Views nighttime as full of "opportunity and promise" for disenfranchised persons, but also characterized by fear of the unknown and of the treacherous, including wolves, demons, spirits, thieves, and arsonists. Provides insights on pre-industrial sleep patterns, noting that prior to the introduction of artificial light, sleep came in two parts, "first sleep," followed by a period of an hour or so when individuals experienced restful meditation ("quiet wakefulness"), and then a second sleep until the morning. Suggests that nighttime activities among the "lower orders" enhanced their sense of autonomy and safeguarded against social disorder by acting as a safety valve. Surmises that the poor must have suffered from chronic sleep deprivation and argues that the night was a time of tremendous danger and exploitation for women. Finds that European concerns about increased social disorder led to increased efforts to regulate nighttime activities. Notes that the introduction of artificial lighting at the end of the eighteenth century led to an expansion of working hours at night.
AHR 110: 1480-81; *Booklist* 101: 1621; *18c Stds* 41: 599-600; *EHR* 122: 1084-85; *J Brit Stds* 48: 780-81; *J Soc Hist* 40: 745-46; *WMQ* 64: 230-32.

334 Fowler, Damon Lee, ed. *Dining at Monticello: In Good Taste and Abundance.* Charlottesville, Va.: Thomas Jefferson Foundation, 2005. v, 202 p. ISBN 1882886259; ISBN 9781882886258; OCLC 57392636; LC Call Number TX715 .D58422; Dewey 641.5973 D615. Citations: 3.
Includes essays on the production, distribution, preparation, consumption, and disposal of food in Thomas Jefferson's household, Jefferson's place in American food history, presidential hospitality, the influence of French cooking, women and housekeeping, African Americans, vegetable gardening, wine, and

Jefferson's dietary philosophy, as well as shorter pieces on Jefferson's possible vegetarianism, *à la française* service, "tongues and sounds," differences in nineteenth century and twentieth-century flour, and the training of the Monticello cooks. Includes a collection of recipes and seeks to explain why Jefferson family papers included so many dessert recipes.
JSH 72: 659-60; *VMHB* 113: 418-19.

335 Francis, Richard. *Judge Sewall's Apology: The Salem Witch Trials and the Forming of an American Conscience.* New York: Fourth Estate, 2005. xvii, 412 p. ISBN 0007163622; ISBN 9780007163625; OCLC 57550291; LC Call Number F67 .S525; Dewey 974.4/02/092. Citations: 5.
Examines the rise of secular thought in Massachusetts in the seventeenth century through the lens of Samuel Sewall's life. Reviews Sewall's life, noting that he rejected a religious vocation in favor of public offices and was one of nine judges who condemned the alleged witches of Salem in 1692, which was a turning point for Sewall. Describes Sewall's public 1697 apology for his role in the trials, noting that he was the only one of the three judges to do so and that he was rebuffed by his social circle as a result. Characterizes Sewall as courageous for taking difficult positions, not only on the conviction of witchcraft suspects, but also on the colonists' treatment of Indians and slaves.
Booklist 101: 1986; *NEQ* 79: 173-76.

336 Friend, Craig Thompson. *Along the Maysville Road: The Early American Republic in the Trans-Appalachian West.* Knoxville: University of Tennessee Press, 2005. xii, 378 p. ISBN 1572333154; ISBN 9781572333154; OCLC 55124616; LC Call Number F459.M47; Dewey 976.4/545. Citations: 4.
Traces evolving society, culture, and economy along the Maysville Road from the late eighteenth century to the 1830s, focusing on the aspirations of Kentucky settlers. Describes the frontier population as increasingly multicultural and multiethnic, as the New Jersey Welsh, New Englanders, generally poor settlers from the Mid-Atlantic and lower South, and African Americans from the Southeast mingled together. Explains that the arrival of elites helped to make clearer the lines of social hierarchy and the goals of collective interest, which gradually replaced the individualism of pioneer culture. Finds that the Kentucky Constitution of 1792 essentially granted elites political power and that the elites changed the landscape by building estates that included brick homes, imported glass, slave quarters, and ornamental gardens. Shows that the middling artisans and merchants who served the needs of the elites began settling towns along the Maysville Road and themselves began to accumulate wealth, social status, and political power in their local communities. Asserts that credit ties with the east and rapid growth had deleterious effects on communities and the environment, as fields were clear cut and natural resources strained.
AHR 112: 1162-63; *IMH* 102: 159-60; *JAH* 92: 1423; *JER* 27: 349-52; *JSH* 72: 457-58; *VMHB* 114: 508-509; *WMQ* 62: 815-18.

337 Godbeer, Richard. *Escaping Salem: The Other Witch Hunt of 1692.* New York: Oxford University Press, 2004. xiv, 177 p. ISBN 0195161297 (hbk.); ISBN 9780195161298 (hbk.); ISBN 0195161300 (pbk.); ISBN 9780195161304 (pbk.); OCLC 55625521; LC Call Number KFC3678.8.W5; Dewey 133.4/3/097469. Citations: 3.

Examines the 1692 witchcraft scare in Stamford, Connecticut involving Katherine Branch, a seventeen-year-old maidservant of Daniel and Abigail Wescot. Explains that in April 1692 Branch began weeping, convulsing, moaning, claiming paralysis, and reporting that a cat spoke to her and that the Devil manifested himself as a black calf and white dog. Describes the indictments and trials of Elizabeth Clawson and Mercy Disborough and notes the insistence of Connecticut Deputy Governor William Jones that unless the court got a confession from the accused or had at least two witnesses to confirm that the defendants had "entered a compact with Satan," both would go free, an opinion confirmed by Connecticut ministers. Finds that Stamford officials and many residents responded to witchcraft with a complex, nuanced combination of hysteria and caution. Describes the methodological and interpretive issues regarding use of documents, such as court transcripts and legal commentaries.
Hist Teach 39: 121-23; *JAS* 40: 663; *WMQ* 63: 604-607.

338 Godbeer, Richard. *Sexual Revolution in Early America*. Baltimore, Md.: Johns Hopkins University Press, 2002. xiv, 430 p. ISBN 0801868009; ISBN 9780801868009; OCLC 46866189; LC Call Number HQ18.U5; Dewey 306.70973. Citations: 40.

Explores the relationship between sex and the shifting Anglo-American social order from 1600 to 1800. Sees a conflict during the seventeenth century between traditional, informal marriages and ongoing political efforts to regulate sexual behavior. Finds that in the mid-eighteenth century Americans opted for "a more individualistic marketplace of sexual desire and fulfillment." Discusses the efforts of New England magistrates to eliminate premarital sex and informal marriages, efforts frustrated by migration and by community tolerance for folk traditions. Claims that ministers' writings indicate that "the most remarkable aspect of Puritan sexuality" was "its eroticization of the spiritual." Finds that congregations, not courts, regulated sex in New England and that enforcement varied widely. Discovers that sexual regulations differed between the Chesapeake and Carolina, including divorce customs and the Chesapeake gentry's concern about enforcement for the sake of public order and image as opposed to the regulation-free Carolinas, which tolerated English marriages with Indians and more open sexual relations with slaves. Examines the "sexual revolution" of the mid-eighteenth century, noting that New England courts stopped trying to regulate sex, privacy became a virtue, parents used bundling, and premarital pregnancies increased. Explores the increase of moral tales that made women guardians of republican virtue and gave them full responsibility for proper sexual relations.
AHR 108: 826-27; *EAL* 38: 521-26; *JAH* 90: 614-15; *J Interdis Hist* 34: 98-100; *LJ* 127n9: 108; *NEQ* 77: 170-73; *PMHB* 128: 77-78; *RAH* 31: 495-502; *WMQ* 61: 177-81.

339 Hamilton, Phillip. *The Making and Unmaking of a Revolutionary Family: The Tuckers of Virginia, 1752–1830*. Charlottesville: University of Virginia

Press, 2003. xiv, 250 p. ISBN 0813921643; ISBN 9780813921648; OCLC 50982346; LC Call Number F225 .H215; Dewey 975.5/0086/21. Citations: 7.

Explores the Tucker family over three generations, focusing on its activities in Virginia, Bermuda, England, South Carolina, Missouri, and New York City and on gender issues and economic and political activities. Argues that the Tuckers illustrated a critical cultural shift from the values of land ownership, personal independence, and close kin connections to emphasis on personal education and abilities over patronage relationships, liquid assets, such as bank stock, over real estate as a foundation for wealth, and professional accomplishments as more significant than genteel appearances. Finds that the commercialization, individualism, and democratization of the Revolution generally triggered a shift in family life and gender relations, undermined the power of the gentry, and spurred hardened sectionalism.

Ag Hist 78: 377-79; *AHR* 109: 896-97; *JAH* 91: 612-13; *JER* 24: 494-97; *JSH* 70: 899-900; *NCHR* 81: 342-43; *VMHB* 111: 304-305; *WMQ* 61: 571-73.

340 Harbury, Katharine E. *Colonial Virginia's Cooking Dynasty*. Columbia: University of South Carolina Press, 2004. xviii, 479 p. ISBN 157003513X; ISBN 9781570035135; OCLC 52566879; LC Call Number TX715 .H258; Dewey 394.1/09755 22. Citations: 3.

Studies the evolution of foodways across three generations of Virginia women by examining the cookbooks of the Randolph family, including an anonymous collection (circa 1700), one produced by Jane Boiling Randolph (1739-1743), and the 1824 work of Mary Randolph, *The Virginia Housewife*. Describes the social and cultural background of Virginia colonial elites, underscoring contrasts between the male public world and the private sphere of women. Analyzes the socioeconomic and medicinal importance to Virginia households of meats, dairy foods, vegetables, fruits, sauces, condiments, sugar, and tobacco products. Lists recipes from the unidentified collection and from Jane Randolph's cookbook and compares them with other contemporary works. Provides notes on seventeenth- and eighteenth-century cooking terms. Explains that for women personal hospitality enhanced their own reputations and that cookbooks became a vehicle to express individualism. Argues that education and the American Revolution influenced the role of women and their use of food.

JSH 72: 159-60; *VMHB* 112: 190-91.

341 Herndon, Ruth Wallis. *Unwelcome Americans: Living on the Margin in Early New England*. Philadelphia: University of Pennsylvania Press, 2001. xvi, 243 p. ISBN 0812235924 (hbk.); ISBN 9780812235920 (hbk.); ISBN 0812217659 (pbk.); ISBN 9780812217650 (pbk.); OCLC 45087322; LC Call Number HN79.A11; Dewey 305.5/6/0974. Citations: 21.

Analyzes the use of the warning out system between 1751 and 1800 in fourteen of Rhode Island's twenty-seven towns. Seeks to "take us inside the lives of the eighteenth-century poor" in order to "put a human face on poverty" and "hear the voices of the poor." Finds that the fourteen town councils issued 1,924 warning out orders and conducted 772 examinations of transients in the latter half of the eighteenth century. Examines those who were ordered to leave individual towns, noting "the essentially discretionary nature of warning out," as

the socially undesirable, the destitute, and potentially destitute faced town councils. Shows that the warning out system could be used as a "way of protecting" a wife from an abusive husband. Underscores that the era was not a time of opportunity for persons of color and the poor and explains that alcohol and having children out of wedlock often led to one's being warned out.
AHR 107: 188-89; *Ethnohistory* 52: 437-48; *FHQ* 81: 354-56; *HRNB* 29: 156; *JAH* 89: 199-200; *NEQ* 75: 678-81; *WMQ* 59: 289-92.

342 Isenberg, Nancy, and Andrew Burstein, eds. *Mortal Remains: Death in Early America*. Philadelphia: University of Pennsylvania Press, 2003. viii, 253 p. ISBN 0812236785 (hbk.); ISBN 9780812236781 (hbk.); ISBN 081221823X (pbk.); ISBN 9780812218237 (pbk.); OCLC 49901887; LC Call Number HQ1073.5.U6; Dewey 306.9. Citations: 22.
Contains twelve essays covering the narrative use Indian deaths by Christian missionaries, the disinterment of executed British Revolutionary War officer John André and James Fenimore Cooper's fictionalized account of André's execution, European and American attitudes toward Indian burial mounds compared to attitudes toward the remains of Revolutionary War prisoners, the gendered descriptions of angels from the seventeenth to the nineteenth centuries, southern white dismemberment of the corpses of executed slaves, and African beliefs about the afterlife.
AHR 109: 901-902; *Am Lit* 75: 684; *EAL* 39: 137-45; *JAAR* 72: 261-63; *JAH* 90: 990-91; *JER* 23: 267-69; *NEQ* 77: 165-68; *PMHB* 128: 211-13; *WMQ* 60: 889-92.

343 Johnson, Claudia Durst. *Daily Life in Colonial New England*. Westport, Conn.: Greenwood Press, 2002. xxvii, 215 p. ISBN 0313314586; ISBN 9780313314582; OCLC 44812143; LC Call Number F7 .J59; Dewey 974/.02. Citations: 1.
Presents a topically organized account of New England before the Revolution. Discusses Puritan doctrine, family life, social institutions, labor, Native Americans, slavery, and the persecution of religious dissenters. Intended for secondary students and general audiences.
Hist Teach 39: 532-33.

344 Johnston, A.J.B. *Control and Order in French Colonial Louisbourg, 1713–1758*. East Lansing: Michigan State University Press, 2001. xlvi, 346 p. ISBN 0870135708 (hbk.); ISBN 9780870135705 (hbk.); ISBN 0870135716 (pbk.); ISBN 9780870135712 (pbk.); OCLC 45830071; LC Call Number F1039.5.L8; Dewey 971.6/955. Citations: 9.
Asks how much of Louisbourg society was "a repetition of known ways of doing things in France or in New France" and how much of it derived from "local conditions at Ile Royale." Studies the foundation and growth of Louisbourg, civilian society and the role of the military, and the settlement's sense of order, as demonstrated in town planning, operation of criminal courts, and the behaviors of various persons and groups. Concludes that Louisbourg was "an obvious overseas extension of France" and very similar to Canada proper. Finds that, at the same time, the fishing economy, ethnically diverse

population, lack of local family traditions, imbalance of sexes, large military presence, and limited role of the Roman Catholic Church, made it "a distinctive place."
AHR 106: 1786; *JAH* 89: 605.

345 Kierner, Cynthia A. *Scandal at Bizarre: Rumor and Reputation in Jefferson's America*. New York: Palgrave Macmillan, 2004. x, 246 p. ISBN 1403961158; ISBN 9781403961150; OCLC 54959871; LC Call Number F234.F18; LC Call Number CS71.R193; Dewey 975.5/63202. Citations: 5.
Explores a 1792 scandal involving Mary Harrison and Judith, Richard, and Nancy Randolph in which Richard was accused of adultery and infanticide. Argues that the sensationalism of the episode was made possible by the uncertainties of 1790s post-Revolutionary Virginia in which "political values, class identities, gender conventions and attitudes toward slavery, work, and family life" were being reconsidered. Includes the Randolphs among the "decayed gentry," which was struggling in the early republic to maintain its dominant position. Finds that the loss of power and influence made such persons more vulnerable to the rumors and gossip of those in lower social orders. Stresses the role of slaves in the origins of the scandal, noting that, through gossip, this otherwise powerless group gained a measure of power over the masters, and goaded Randolph Harrison "into taking more seriously his responsibility to act benevolently and protectively toward both his black and white dependents." Finds that slave gossip focused on Nancy, while white gossip centered on Richard, who was viewed as a "failed patriarch." Stresses that the episode illustrates the social limitations of gender, as neither Nancy nor Judith could limit the damage of the scandal.
Booklist 101: 809; *JAH* 93: 508-509; *JSH* 73: 436-38; *LJ* 130n2: 97-98; *VMHB* 113: 420-21; *VQR* 81: 256; *WMQ* 62: 569-73.

346 McCarthy, Kathleen D. *American Creed: Philanthropy and the Rise of Civil Society, 1700–1865*. Chicago, Ill.: University of Chicago Press, 2003. xi, 319 p. ISBN 0226561984; ISBN 9780226561981; OCLC 50143953; LC Call Number HV91 .M375; Dewey 361.7/63/097309034 21. Citations: 23.
Finds that from the eighteenth century to the 1830s a "geography of generosity" emerged, which was centered in Boston, New York, and Philadelphia, but was not common in the South. Explores patterns of giving for public ends, the social significance of non-profit organizations through the 1820s, and government efforts to limit the activities of certain groups during the Jacksonian era in order to bring them in line with the expectations of white, male, typically non-inclusive society. Notes that women and African Americans were active in voluntary benevolent and reform societies. Asserts that such activities were largely non-political and involved options for social and economic action specific to the northern capitalist marketplace. Notes that, throughout U.S. history, "philanthropy, governance, and the economy were inherently linked." Claims that the ideals of such philanthropic groups (egalitarianism, religious liberty, civic responsibility, freedom of speech and the press, and the freedom to assemble) became essential elements of the national creed.

AHR 109: 1556-57; *JAH* 91: 982-84; *JER* 23: 617-20; *JSH* 70: 893-94; *NEQ* 77: 323-25; *RAH* 32: 506-511.

347 McWilliams, James E. *A Revolution in Eating: How the Quest for Food Shaped America.* New York: Columbia University Press, 2005. 386 p. ISBN 0231129920; ISBN 9780231129923; OCLC 56942105; LC Call Number TX633 .M3; Dewey 394.1/2/0973. Citations: 19.
Studies the foodways of English colonists in America, which brings together economic, political, cultural, and environmental aspects of settlement. Places foodways on a continuum, from the Caribbean, where British colonists had diets least like those living in England, and the New England colonies, where the foodways were recreated from the British template. Finds that other regions were somewhere in between these extremes and that lack of interest in permanent settlement, the tropical climate, and the emphasis on cash crops caused English settlers of the Caribbean to follow local foodways. Shows that diet indicated status (e.g., the parts of the pig that one ate) and the relative importance of tradition and local conditions (e.g., New Englanders' acceptance of corn, but refusal to allow it to replace wheat). Asserts that the Revolution was, in part, influenced by foodways because colonists fought to preserve an agrarian way that was different from that of England and that after the Revolution, Americans further simplified cuisine as a reaction to British food culture. Concludes that the simplicity of English cuisine made it particularly well-suited to adaptation in a new environment.
AHR 111: 823-24; *EAL* 41: 587-92; *JAH* 93: 178-79; *JSH* 72: 919-20; *LJ* 130n9: 139; *NEQ* 81: 733-35; *RAH* 34: 393-98.

348 Norton, Mary Beth. *In the Devil's Snare: The Salem Witchcraft Crisis of 1692.* New York: Alfred A. Knopf, 2002. viii, 436 p. ISBN 037540709X; ISBN 9780375407093; ISBN 0965460975; ISBN 9780965460972; OCLC 48449691; LC Call Number BF1575 .N67; Dewey 133.4/3/097445. Citations: 43.
Stresses the role of military and political crises in the origins of the Salem witchcraft episode. Notes that Essex County was situated "near the front lines of an armed conflict that today is little known but which at the time commanded [settlers'] lives and thoughts" and that repeated Indian attacks along New England's northeastern frontier beginning in 1688 resulted in physical and psychological devastation and conjured memories of King Philip's War and created widespread panic. Points out that a significant number of the accusers in Salem were orphaned refugees from Maine, that anxiety about Indian assaults appears frequently in the trial depositions, and that colonists' accounts of Indians' mutilation of their enemies mirrored common images of witches who threatened to tear their victims to pieces. Explains that male suspects who did not fit the usual witch stereotype became vulnerable to accusation because of their association with the frontier. Argues that Massachusetts leaders' support for the Salem court masked a lack of success in repelling the Indian attacks.
Booklist 98: 1820; *JAH* 91: 201-202; *LJ* 127n14: 193; *NEQ* 76: 484-87; *RAH* 31: 485-94; *WMQ* 60: 427-30.

349   Rath, Richard Cullen. *How Early America Sounded*. Ithaca, N.Y.: Cornell University Press, 2003. xi, 227 p. ISBN 0801441269; ISBN 9780801441264; OCLC 53013074; LC Call Number E162 .R38; Dewey 973.2. Citations: 35.
Describes early North American and Caribbean "soundways," defined as "the paths, trajectories, transformations, mediations, practices, and techniques—in short, the ways—that people employ to interpret and express their attitudes and beliefs about sound." Studies the significance of thunder and lightning, music, vocal tonalities and rhythms, gendered voices, and the acoustics of meetinghouses and churches, treaty circles, horns, and churchbells. Claims that sound was more important to early Americans than to nineteenth- and twentieth-century Americans, who rely more on visual cues.
AHR 110: 126-27; *JAH* 91: 1427; *J Soc Hist* 38: 1109-11; *JSH* 73: 150; *LJ* 128n20: 139; *NEQ* 78: 495-98; *RAH* 32: 144-50; *VMHB* 112: 71-72; *WMQ* 61: 745-47.

350   Roach, Marilynne K. *The Salem Witch Trials: A Day-by-Day Chronicle of a Community Under Siege*. New York: Cooper Square Press, 2002. xlvii, 688 p. ISBN 0815412215; ISBN 9780815412212; OCLC 49553507; LC Call Number BF1575 .R63; Dewey 133.4/3/097445. Citations: 7.
Presents a day-by-day chronology from January 1, 1692 to January 14, 1697. Includes an introduction and biographical appendices.
LJ 127n18: 108.

351   Salinger, Sharon V. *Taverns and Drinking in Early America*. Baltimore, Md.: Johns Hopkins University Press, 2002. xi, 309 p. ISBN 0801868785; ISBN 9780801868788; OCLC 49551853; LC Call Number   E162 .S23; Dewey 394.130973. Citations: 15.
Describes colonial public houses, their keepers and regulators, and their patrons. Notes that ministers and government officials often raised concerns about the number of taverns in America and the activities that occurred in and around them and therefore pushed for laws that limited the number of taverns. Explains that some leaders frequented the taverns and neglected to enforce regulations of public houses. Argues that taverns and drinking in early America "provide a guide to the nature of public culture, to the articulation of classes, and to the locus of political action." Finds that urban taverns were more likely to attract female patrons and customers from a single class or occupational group than were rural houses. Concludes that "Despite periodic attacks on the public houses and drinking behavior by both religious and secular leaders, the tavern maintained its privileged place within the colonies and thrived everywhere."
AHR 109: 513-14; *BHR* 78: 106-109; *JAH* 90: 1426; *J Soc Hist* 38: 774-76; *JSH* 70: 644-45; *NEQ* 76: 654-57; *NCHR* 80: 247-48; *PMHB* 127: 437-38; *Soc Hist* 29: 132-33; *SCHM* 104: 205-207; *VMHB* 110: 492-93; *WMQ* 61: 378-80.

352   Teja, Jesús F. de la and Ross Frank, eds. *Choice, Persuasion, and Coercion: Social Control on Spain's North American Frontiers*. Albuquerque: University of New Mexico Press, 2005. xxi, 338 p. ISBN 0826336469; ISBN 9780826336460; OCLC 59360140; LC Call Number E49.2.S7; LC Call Number F1410; Dewey 303.3/3/0970903. Citations: 10.

Presents eleven essays covering social control on the Florida frontier, in multiethnic Louisiana (1763–1803), in late colonial New Mexico, in northeastern New Spain, in native Texas, in colonial Sonora, in Saltillo, Mexico, and in Alta California (1769–1821). Includes pieces on gender, power, and magic in Nueva Vizcaya and the case of Nuevo Santander.
AHR 111: 785-87; *HAHR* 87: 586-87; *JAEH* 25: 174-77; *JAH* 93: 494-95; *J Interdis Hist* 37: 621-22; *SHQ* 110: 293-94; *WHQ* 38: 401-402 .

353 Wermuth, Thomas S. *Rip Van Winkle's Neighbors: The Transformation of Rural Society in the Hudson River Valley, 1720–1850.* Albany: State University of New York Press, 2001. viii, 186 p. ISBN 079145083X (hbk.); ISBN 9780791450833 (hbk.); ISBN 0791450848 (pbk.); ISBN 9780791450840 (pbk.); OCLC 45699068; LC Call Number HC107.N72; Dewey 303.4/09747/3. Citations: 8.
Focuses on Ulster County and the town of Kingston. Examines late-seventeenth-century Dutch settlement of the area, its economy and political culture, the economic impact of the Revolution, and the region's "market revolution" in the early nineteenth century. Finds that Ulster farmers were well-integrated into the market economy through downriver sales of grain and barrel staves, but that local governments also attempted to regulate faraway commerce through the establishment of restrictions on land use and of limits on prices and interest rates. Explores risk taking among farmers and merchants, noting that risk takers were generally more prosperous and more likely to use cash than those who relied on safer, more local trade. Explains that provision purchases during the Revolution had a significant impact on local economies, but that the post-Revolution economy was marked more by continuity than by transformation in markets and consumption. Concludes that the more major changes occurred in government and public policy, as elected town governments replaced eighteenth-century local corporations and private concerns overcame public economic regulation.
Ag Hist 76: 62-64; *BHR* 76: 373-75; *Hist Teach* 35: 426-27; *JER* 22: 700-703; *J Econ Hist* 62: 250-51; *Penn Hist* 70: 227-29; *WMQ* 59: 533-36.

354 Williams, Ian. *Rum: A Social and Sociable History of the Real Spirit of 1776.* New York: Nation Books, 2005. xvii, 340 p. ISBN 1560256516; ISBN 9781560256519; OCLC 61117854; LC Call Number TP607.R9; Dewey 641.2/59/0973; Dewey 641.2/59097090333333. Citations: 1.
Explores the importance of rum to colonial North America and the Caribbean, noting the liquor's inextricable tie to slavery, its origins as a by-product of Barbadian sugar refining and molasses production, and its role in the coming of the American Revolution.
Booklist 102: 17.

14 Families and Children

355 Buckley, Thomas E. *The Great Catastrophe of My Life: Divorce in the Old Dominion.* Chapel Hill: University of North Carolina Press, 2002. xiv, 346 p. ISBN 0807827126 (hbk.); ISBN 9780807827123 (hbk.); ISBN 0807853801 (pbk.); ISBN 9780807853801 (pbk.); OCLC 48871203; LC Call Number HQ835.V8 B83; Dewey 306.89/09755 21. Citations: 7.
Discusses the political, religious, and social contexts of legislative divorce in Virginia from the aftermath of the American Revolution through 1851, as well as the main causes of divorce, including interracial sex, physical abuse, adultery, and desertion. Describes the legal process of divorce and the social consequences of divorce, particularly for women. Analyzes 471 divorce petitions submitted between 1786 and 1851, noting that they came from men, women, and couples and from both rich and poor, but that men were more successful in their petitions than were women. Finds that legislators, seeking to preserve marriage, approved only petitions reflecting the most egregious cases of abuse and abandonment and had to be persuaded that "continuing a particular marriage after one party had flagrantly violated normative societal values might damage the common good more than the dissolution of the union." Finds that only about one-third of the petitions were approved, but that the mounting case load prompted the legislators to move some cases to the courts in 1827. Explains that, in the 1840s, conservatives sought to move additional petitions to the courts in order to make the process even stricter and that, by 1851, all divorces went through the courts, reflecting "the commanding influence of nineteenth-century evangelical Christianity in southern legal culture and its outlook on marriage and divorce."

AHR 108: 1450-51; *AJLH* 46: 96-97; *JAH* 90: 1017; *J Interdis Hist* 34: 471-72; *J Soc Hist* 39: 284-87; *JSH* 70: 914-15; *NCHR* 80: 246-47; *VMHB* 110: 489-90; *WMQ* 60: 687-89.

356 Main, Gloria L. *Peoples of a Spacious Land: Families and Cultures in Colonial New England.* Cambridge, Mass.: Harvard University Press, 2001. xiv, 316 p. ISBN 0674006283; ISBN 9780674006287; OCLC 46240244; LC Call Number HQ535 .M347; Dewey 306.85/0974 21. Citations: 23.

Describes New England family culture, drawing a contrast between Narragansett children, who were socialized for independence (interaction with peers that encouraged self-discipline), and their New England counterparts, who were raised to be obedient, submissive, and dependent (coercion by elders through corporal punishment). Emphasizes that early New England settlements were not intentional and that settlers often lived among and interacted with strangers, that males had little or no identity prior to marriage, and that elderly persons garnered little respect in the "traditional" society of the seventeenth century, but secured greater independence and honor in the more "modern" society of the eighteenth century. Concludes that the aggressive pursuit of property "turned hitherto ethnocentric English into confirmed racists," that gossip acted as "the guardian of propriety," and that communities hesitated to punish domestic violence, noting reluctance "to threaten the rights of all husbands by taking action against one."

AHR 107: 1221; *Econ Hist Rev* 55: 587; *JAH* 89: 610-11; *JAS* 39: 330-31; *J Econ Hist* 62: 613-15; *LJ* 126n13: 132; *NEQ* 75: 688-93; *Soc Hist* 28: 418-20; *WMQ* 59: 725-28.

357 Noël, Françoise. *Family Life and Sociability in Upper and Lower Canada, 1780–1870: A View from Diaries and Family Correspondence.* Ithaca, N.Y.: McGill-Queen's University Press, 2003. xii, 372 p. ISBN 0773524452; ISBN 9780773524453; OCLC 50109431; LC Call Number HQ559 .N64; Dewey 306.8/09713/09034. Citations: 16.

Covers courtship and engagement, marriage and married life, childbirth and infancy, and childhood among families in late-eighteenth- and early nineteenth-century Canada, and discusses aspects of kinship, gender, and community. Includes information on the Duvernay and Papineau families, and finds that the values and relationships among French-Canadian families were not much different from those of conservative English-speaking families. Concludes that "young people had considerable latitude in choosing a mate and expected love to be the basis of marriage," though "parents were concerned with the choices their children made." Finds that parents expressed "mutual concern and love of their children" and that "family sociability was seldom restricted to the domestic circle."

AHR 109: 891-92; *CHR* 85: 126-29; *J Interdis Hist* 35: 168-69.

358 Premo, Bianca. *Children of the Father King: Youth, Authority, and Legal Minority in Colonial Lima.* Chapel Hill: University of North Carolina Press, 2005. xiii, 350 p. ISBN 0807829544 (hbk.); ISBN 9780807829547 (hbk.); ISBN 0807856193 (pbk.); ISBN 9780807856192 (pbk.); OCLC 57465752; LC Call Number HQ792.P4; Dewey 305.23/0985/09032. Citations: 33.

Studies laws and criminal, inheritance, and ecclesiastical records to provide an account of elite and political and judicial attitudes towards children and a survey of children's lives in Lima. Discusses legal minority and adult authority, child-adult relations, convents, schools for Indian boys, foundling homes, roles of race, class, and gender, Enlightenment views on education and economics, Bourbon social reforms, and the interplay of patriarchy and slavery. Finds that, despite significant change over the course of two centuries, hierarchy and social order was preserved.

AHR 111: 1570-71; *HAHR* 87: 591-92; *J Interdis Hist* 38: 321-23; *J Soc Hist* 41: 447-49; *J Soc Hist* 41: 1060-62; *WMQ* 63: 587-96.

359   Shammas, Carole. *A History of Household Government in America.* Charlottesville: University of Virginia Press, 2002. xvi, 232 p. ISBN 0813921252 (hbk.); ISBN 9780813921259 (hbk.); ISBN 0813921260 (pbk.); ISBN 9780813921266 (pbk.); OCLC 49683569; LC Call Number HQ536 .S4814; Dewey 306.85/0973. Citations: 21.

Surveys household government in America from the colonial era through the twentieth century. Finds that heads of households in colonial America had more power than those in Europe and that the American Revolution did not effectively change that condition. Notes that the situation began to change in the nineteenth century when American fathers became less and less able to influence their children's marriage choices, slavery and servitude became less common in the north, divorce laws and child custody arrangements became more favorable to women, and public institutions developed. Concludes that between 1840 and 1880 the authority of household heads collapsed, a change that was "Much more central to the definition of a modern United States" than was "industrialization or urbanization."

AHR 109: 186-87; *HRNB* 31: 146-47; *JAH* 91: 242-43; *J Econ Hist* 63: 602-604; *J Soc Hist* 40: 516-18; *JSH* 70: 916-17; *WMQ* 60: 684-86.

360   Sievens, Mary Beth. *Stray Wives: Marital Conflict in Early National New England.* New York: New York University Press, 2005. xii, 171 p. ISBN 081474009X; ISBN 9780814740095; OCLC 59279868; LC Call Number HQ537 .S54; Dewey 306.872/0974/09034. Citations: 6.

Looks at elopement notices (i.e., public allegations that one's spouse had abandoned the household) published in Vermont and Connecticut between 1790 and 1830, as well as at census data, court, birth, and death records, legal treatises, sermons, and advice literature from across New England. Notes charges of infidelity, wifely disobedience, failure to manage the household properly, and of husbands' abusing their wives or failing to support their families. Finds that only about one-third of cases revealed in elopement notices resulted in divorce court filings, largely because culture and coverture law significantly limited the bargaining power of women. Explains that more than ninety-five percent of newspaper notices were placed by men, often as warnings to local merchants not to let the estranged wives rely on their husbands' credit. Notes that women, on the other hand, placed notices in order to bargain with their husbands or to solicit public sympathy. Discovers that women exerted power by seeking divorce, living apart from their husbands without formal approval, controlling their own assets, and relying upon family support networks. Finds that most divorced women did not remarry, but that cases of estrangement usually resulted in nominal reconciliation, and that some such cases were published as notices in newspapers. Concludes that marital relationships were embedded in and dependent upon larger social, family, and community networks.

AHR 112: 1160-61; *AJLH* 47: 455-56; *JAH* 93: 197-98; *JER* 27: 188-92; *J Soc Hist* 40: 779-82; *NEQ* 79: 320-22; *WMQ* 63: 638-40.

361 Steenburg, Nancy Hathaway. *Children and the Criminal Law in Connecticut, 1635–1855: Changing Perceptions of Childhood.* New York: Routledge, 2005. vii, 262 p. ISBN 0415971802; ISBN 9780415971805; OCLC 56192212; LC Call Number KFC4195.S74; Dewey 345.746/08. Citations: 3.

Examines court records produced between 1639 and 1855 in New London County, Connecticut involving persons under age twenty-one, as well as the late-eighteenth-century work of Zephaniah Swift, and laws related to children passed in the Connecticut General Assembly. Covers various crimes, including physical and sexual abuse of children, and notes nineteenth-century social movements, illustrated by the opening of a state reform school. Explains that colonial Connecticut law recognized different ages of consent and eligibility for various activities, such as sex, use of tobacco, and militia service. Traces shifts in treatment of children, from restitution to retribution to rehabilitation, but notes that movements were inconsistent and involved variables of class, ethnicity, and race. Contends that law went from the purpose of protecting orderly relationships irrespective of age to that of enforcing age-specific cultural norms. Concludes that middle-class children were typically sheltered, while transient, black, Native American, and Irish minors were more likely to be prosecuted, convicted, and sentenced harshly.

AJLH 48: 99-100; *JAH* 92: 1424; *WMQ* 63: 587-96.

15 Rural Life and Agriculture

362 Adams, Stephen. *The Best and Worst Country in the World: Perspectives on the Early Virginia Landscape*. Charlottesville: University Press of Virginia, 2001. xii, 305 p. ISBN 081392037X (hbk.); ISBN 9780813920375 (hbk.); ISBN 0813920388 (pbk.); ISBN 9780813920382 (pbk.); OCLC 45661613; LC Call Number F229 .A3; Dewey 975.5/01. Citations: 4.

Presents an environmental history of the Virginia colony up to 1700, outlining and assessing the geologic, political, and economic forces that shaped the area. Gathers views of Virginia from letters, broadsides, and images, noting modification of the physical environment and of individuals' notions of place. Explains that ideas of landscape are subjective and specific to the eras in which they are developed. Emphasizes that explorers, settlers, traders, planters, and government officials gradually forged a colony based upon acquisitiveness and an increasing lack of appreciation of the beauty of the wilderness. Expresses disappointment that seventeenth-century Virginians did not value the natural aesthetic more.
Am Lit 75: 467-70; *VMHB* 110: 400-401.

363 Anderson, Virginia DeJohn. *Creatures of Empire: How Domestic Animals Transformed Early America*. New York: Oxford University Press, 2004. xi, 322 p. ISBN 0195158601 (hbk.); ISBN 9780195158601 (hbk.); ISBN 0195304462 (pbk.); ISBN 9780195304466 (pbk.); OCLC 54669883; LC Call Number SF51 .A655; Dewey 636/.0973 22. Citations: 33.

Describes the role of domestic animals in seventeenth-century New England and the Chesapeake region. Notes that Indians respected animals and did not understand English settlers' keeping livestock as property. Explains that in the New World the English required more and more land for their animals and their crops, and that their feral animals destroyed Indian food sources and provided an additional source of tension between natives and Europeans. Contends that New Englanders were more advanced than were Chesapeake settlers in creating a mixed-husbandry system.

Ag Hist 81: 152-53; *AHR* 110: 1158-59; *JAH* 92: 953-54; *J Brit Stds* 44: 826-28; *J Soc Hist* 40: 510-13; *JSH* 72: 443-44; *LJ* 129n15: 67; *NEQ* 78: 643-46; *RAH* 33: 481-92; *Soc Hist* 31: 248-50; *VMHB* 113: 82-83; *WMQ* 65: 818-20.

364 Carney, Judith A. *Black Rice: The African Origins of Rice Cultivation in the Americas*. Cambridge, Mass.: Harvard University Press, 2001. xiv, 240 p. ISBN 0674004523 (hbk.); ISBN 9780674004528 (hbk.); ISBN 0674008340 (pbk.); ISBN 9780674008342 (pbk.); OCLC 45270253; LC Call Number SB191.R5; Dewey 633.1/8/0975. Citations: 100.

Tells the story of the transferal to the coastal lower South of west African "indigenous knowledge systems" regarding the cultivation of rice. Discusses European descriptions of rice cultivation along the west African coast and in the Niger River Delta. Claims that the English used experience in channeling water, derived from milling and irrigation, to create the conditions for rice growth in South Carolina and Georgia, but that African expertise with the crop in the form of enslaved farmers was critical to the success of the rice crop in the New World. Explains that "rice culture" relied heavily upon the labor and knowledge of African women and that the crop's success in America provided slaves some power to negotiate labor terms.

Ag Hist 76: 120-22; *AHR* 108: 157-58; *Am Stds* 43: 145-46; *FHQ* 81: 200-202; *GHQ* 86: 635-36; *HAHR* 83: 206-208; *JAH* 89: 196-97; *JAS* 37: 463-64; *J Econ Hist* 62: 247-48; *J Interdis Hist* 33: 307-308; *JSH* 69: 140-41; *NCHR* 79: 380-81; *WMQ* 59: 739-42.

365 Donahue, Brian. *The Great Meadow: Farmers and the Land in Colonial Concord*. New Haven, Conn.: Yale University Press, 2004. xix, 311 p. ISBN 0300097514 (hbk.); ISBN 9780300097511 (hbk.); ISBN 9780300123692 (pbk.); ISBN 0300123698 (pbk.); OCLC 53903867; LC Call Number S451.M4; Dewey 630/.9744/4. Citations: 33.

Challenges the predominant view that colonial New England farmers engaged in wasteful and unsustainable practices, whereby land was worn out, causing migration to new land. Focuses on Concord and argues that early New England farming practices were actually ecologically viable. Explains "how colonial husbandry actually worked." Notes that both Indian subsistence practices and English agricultural ways changed over time based on environmental limits and that Concord's early settlers balanced grain and livestock production, clearing only as many acres as could be replenished with manure. Explains that farmers adapted lands for various uses, retaining sandy soils for crops, pastures for summer grazing, meadows for cutting winter fodder, and woodlands primarily for fuel. Contends that Concord's settlers engaged in this sort of ecologically sustainable farming through the Revolution, but that demographic pressures and market production gradually led to increased emphasis on dairying, which caused widespread clearing of woodlands and their conversion to arable meadows.

Ag Hist 81: 133-35; *AHR* 111: 473-74; *JAH* 92: 184-85; *JHG* 31: 364-65; *NEQ* 78: 312-14; *WMQ* 62: 123-25.

366 Keber, Martha L. *Seas of Gold, Seas of Cotton: Christophe Poulain DuBignon of Jekyll Island*. Athens: University of Georgia Press, 2002. xiii, 312 p. ISBN 0820323608; ISBN 9780820323602; OCLC 48767566; LC Call Number F292.G58; Dewey 975.8/742. Citations: 2.
Describes the life of Christophe Poulain DuBignon (1739-1825), French mariner and nobleman who spent the last thirty years of his life as a cotton planter on Jekyll Island, Georgia. Places the life of DuBignon in the context of the Seven Years War, the eras of the American and French Revolutions, and the early and antebellum years of the American republic, noting the ups and downs of cotton prices, which often followed political and weather events. Recounts British raids on DuBignon's plantation, which involved loss of slaves, burning of the cotton house and gin, and theft or destruction of private possessions.
Ag Hist 78: 239-41; *HRNB* 31: 29; *JSH* 69: 877-78.

367 Kennedy, Roger G. *Mr. Jefferson's Lost Cause: Land, Farmers, Slavery, and the Louisiana Purchase*. Oxford: Oxford University Press, 2003. xviii, 350 p. ISBN 0195153472; ISBN 9780195153477; ISBN 9780195176070; ISBN 0195176073; OCLC 50477081; LC Call Number E333 .K46; Dewey 973.4/6/092. Citations: 27.
Describes Jefferson's views on land and agriculture, his reactions to trans-Appalachian settlement and expansion into the lower Mississippi valley, the business arrangements that undergirded the cotton kingdom, which emphasized debt accumulation, land exhaustion, and westward movement, contemporary resistance to the plantation system, negotiations for the Louisiana Purchase and American covert actions in Florida, and the legacy of early American agrarian policy. Argues that prior to 1784 Thomas Jefferson "expressed in radical language his aversion to slavery and his preference for a republic of free and independent farmers" and presented proposals for a virtuous republic that made wise use of public lands and "a benign labor system." Asserts that, "Had different outcomes been achieved in a score of narrow contests between 1802 and 1820," especially with regard to the Louisiana Purchase, the Civil War "might have been prevented." Explains that Jefferson failed "to tip the balance" when various public policy options facilitated "the spread of slavery."
AHR 109: 1561-62; *HRNB* 32: 11; *IMH* 100: 346-63; *JAH* 91: 223-25; *JER* 23: 283-85; *JSH* 70: 420-21; *LJ* 128n1: 133; *Penn Hist* 72: 263-65; *PMHB* 128: 89-90; *VMHB* 111: 411-13; *WMQ* 61: 588-92.

368 Loewer, H. Peter. *Jefferson's Garden*. Mechanicsburg, Penn.: Stackpole Books, 2004. xii, 260 p. ISBN 0811700763; ISBN 9780811700764; OCLC 52133050; LC Call Number SB451.34.V8; Dewey 635.9/09755/482. Citations: 2.

Recounts Jefferson's records and letters to friends and colleagues on the subject of gardening. Studies the plants that Jefferson cultivated, including fifty-five annuals and perennials, six shrubs, eight trees, and five vines and the origins of each.
LJ 128n19: 90.

369 Schwartz, Stuart B., ed. *Tropical Babylons: Sugar and the Making of the Atlantic World, 1450–1680*. Chapel Hill: University of North Carolina Press, 2004. xvi, 347 p. ISBN 0807828750 (hbk.); ISBN 9780807828755 (hbk.); ISBN 0807855383 (pbk.); ISBN 9780807855386 (pbk.); OCLC 54206797; LC Call Number HD9100.5 .T76; Dewey 338.4/76641/0918210903. Citations: 37.
Presents articles on sugar in Iberia, the sugar economy of Madeira and the Canaries between the mid-fifteenth and mid-seventeenth centuries, the sugar economy of Española in the sixteenth century, sugar and slavery in early colonial Cuba, the early Brazilian sugar industry from 1550 to 1670, the Atlantic slave trade to 1650, the expansion of the sugar market in Western Europe, and a new perspective on the Barbadian "sugar revolution" of the seventeenth century.
Ag Hist 81: 270-72; *AHR* 110: 1128-29; *BHR* 79: 407-409; *Econ Hist Rev* 58: 859-60; *JAH* 92: 579-80; *JAS* 40: 199; *J Econ Hist* 64: 1159-60; *J Interdis Hist* 37: 489-91.

16 Religion

370 Atwood, Craig D. *Community of the Cross: Moravian Piety in Colonial Bethlehem*. University Park: Pennsylvania State University Press, 2004. xi, 283 p. ISBN 0271023678; ISBN 9780271023670; OCLC 54935375; LC Call Number BX8565 .A84; Dewey 284/.674822 22. Citations: 15.

Examines the Moravians in the context of transatlantic German Pietism, the settlement of Bethlehem, Pennsylvania, Moravian liturgy, and the theology of Nicholas Ludwig von Zinzendorf, particularly as it relates to meditation on the wounds and the body of Christ. Contends that piety was the "heart and soul" of Bethlehem, which was "the embodiment of Zinzendorf's vision," but that Zinzendorf rejected any "system of rational propositions about God" and that his ideas about bloody wounds embarrassed later Moravian leaders as overzealous. Contends that Bethlehem's decline after 1761 "is related to a rejection of Zinzendorf's theology in favor of a moderate form of American evangelicalism during this same period." Concludes that Bethlehem was nonetheless "one of the most significant, successful, and unusual religious communities in colonial North America."

AHR 111: 154-55; *JAH* 92: 193; *J Religion* 85: 500-501; *PMHB* 130: 113-14; *WMQ* 61: 762-65.

371 Bach, Jeff. *Voices of the Turtledoves: The Sacred World of Ephrata*. University Park: Pennsylvania State University Press and the Pennsylvania German Society, 2003. xx, 282 p. ISBN 0271022507; ISBN 9780271022505; ISBN 3525558279; ISBN 9783525558270; OCLC 50982350; LC Call Number BX7817.P4 B33; LC Call Number GR110.P4 A37; Dewey 286/.3/097481 21. Citations: 10.

Discusses the religious groundings of the Ephrata community, the visions of Conrad Beissel, rituals, gender roles, and the uses of mystical language,

manuscript art, and esoteric knowledge of the community. Focuses on "the unique religious language and ritual of this distinctive community, virtually unknown beyond the circle of regional interest." Argues that Beissel drew upon Pietism and Anabaptism to fashion "a unique synthesis of religious thought and practice from the Old World embodied in a singular religious community in the New World." Explains that Ephrata "departed radically from traditional gender constructions" and that its large buildings expressed "awareness of God's presence," mysticism, and pilgrimage.
AHR 109: 1222; *CH* 73: 442-44; *JAH* 91: 216-17; *Penn Hist* 72: 251-53; *PMHB* 129: 106-107; *WMQ* 61: 158-61.

372 Bell, James B. *The Imperial Origins of the King's Church in Early America, 1607–1783*. New York: Palgrave, 2004. xxv, 298 p. ISBN 1403932190; ISBN 9781403932198; OCLC 53223696; LC Call Number BX5881.B45. Citations: 7.
Describes the founding of the Church of England in the American colonies in the early seventeenth century, administrative difficulties that the Church experienced in the absence of an American bishop, and powers over the colonial Church that were granted to royal governors, to the SPG, and to local vestries. Explains that post-1675 imperial policy of the English government directly affected the fate of the Church of England in early America. Notes that struggles with New England Congregationalists prior to the Revolution "irreparably restrained the development of the colonial church." Contends that, by 1775, "the King's church was one of the smallest religious groups in the colonies" and that after the Revolution the numbers of active American clergy had dropped by greater than half.
CH 77: 1060-61; *EHR* 123: 211-12; *WMQ* 64: 859-61.

373 Bozeman, Theodore Dwight. *The Precisianist Strain: Disciplinary Religion and Antinomian Backlash in Puritanism to 1638*. Chapel Hill: University of North Carolina Press, published for the Omohundro Institute of Early American History and Culture, 2004. xv, 349 p. ISBN 0807828505; ISBN 9780807828502; OCLC 52471294; LC Call Number BX9334.3 .B69; Dewey 285/.9. Citations: 23.
Studies the efforts of sixteenth-century English Presbyterians to establish a system that would ensure godliness among the people—regardless of spiritual status—and thereby avoid divine punishment. Explains that, after the collapse of the Presbyterian movement in the 1590s, Puritans "redirected an unabated appetite for discipline into the first great pietist venture in Protestant history," the focus on individual conversion through grace that would result in a change in behavior. Traces this late sixteenth-century shift to Presbyterian Thomas Cartwright and especially his follower Richard Greenham. Notes that this self-examination elevated levels of anxiety among the faithful such that some Puritan clerics in the 1610s "defected from the practice of piety" in order to give members of their flocks some psychological relief in the form of antinomianism. Identifies John Cotton as the originator of the antinomian movement in Massachusetts, thought Cotton remained an advocate of a "semi-antinomian, protospiritualist gospel that still claimed a place in the disciplinary Puritan

world." Concludes that Hutchinson took Cotton's position to its theological extreme and that "religious faith antinomian-style was Puritanism's ideal 'other.'"

AHR 109: 1196; *J Brit Stds* 44: 604-606; *J Religion* 85: 663-64; *J Relig Hist* 32: 118-20; *NEQ* 78: 669-71; *WMQ* 62: 325-30.

374 Breen, Louise A. *Transgressing the Bounds: Subversive Enterprises among the Puritan Elite in Massachusetts, 1630–1692.* New York: Oxford University Press, 2001. viii, 292 p. ISBN 0195138007; ISBN 9780195138009; OCLC 43615468; LC Call Number F67 .B82; Dewey 974.4/02/08825. Citations: 15.

Examines dissent within Massachusetts Puritanism from the antinomian crisis through arguments over covenant, toleration, economics, the place of natives in society, and the Salem witchcraft trials. Argues that throughout the seventeenth century dissenters tended to be more cosmopolitan, internationalist, more likely to be engaged in commerce, and more inclusive of natives (in other words, more sophisticated and more receptive to new thought and accepting of other people). Denies that dissenters were marginalized, arguing that they were, instead, often more elite than their opponents. Finds that orthodox New Englanders were generally more oppressive and intolerant and concludes that the tragedies involving Indian military encounters could have been avoided had the dissenters won out in the antinomian crisis.

AHR 107: 185-86; *HRNB* 30: 54-55; *JAH* 90: 207-208; *J Religion* 83: 438-39; *NEQ* 75: 151-54.

375 Bressler, Ann Lee. *The Universalist Movement in America, 1770–1880.* New York: Oxford University Press, 2001. x, 204 p. ISBN 0195129865; ISBN 9780195129861; OCLC 42863212; LC Call Number BX9933 .B74; Dewey 289.1/73. Citations: 13.

Traces the early history of American Universalism, noting the influence of theologian Hosea Ballou, the importance of the teachings of Jonathan Edwards, and the view that the movement represented the "improvement" of Calvinism. Claims that Universalism was a popular movement that drew from both urban and rural areas, largely from persons of Calvinist Baptist backgrounds. Examines the connections of Universalism to more extreme movements and practices, such as phrenology, mesmerism, hypnotism, and spiritualism. Contends that through the nineteenth century, though, Universalists became increasingly caught up in the culture of individualism and moralism—that they "were shifting their attention from divine power to human potential and were thus becoming ever more typical representatives of the moderate, liberal reformism of the age"—and that, by 1870, the early ideals of the movement had faded.

CH 71: 910-12; *JAH* 89: 613-14; *WMQ* 59: 527-30.

376 Brock, Peter, ed. *Liberty and Conscience: A Documentary History of the Experiences of Conscientious Objectors in America through the Civil War.* New York: Oxford University Press, 2002. xi, 194 p. ISBN 0195151216 (hbk.); ISBN 9780195151213 (hbk.); ISBN 0195151224 (pbk.); ISBN 9780195151220 (pbk.);

OCLC 47667232; LC Call Number UB342.U5; Dewey 355.2/24/09730903. Citations: 2.

Collects documents on American pacifism and conscientious objection from 1658 through the Civil War. Includes pieces colonial Quaker testimony, pacifism in the seventeenth-century English West Indies, conscientious objectors in the French and Indian War and American Revolution, militia service, payment of taxes, conscription, the hiring of substitutes, and the testimonies of Moravians, Methodists, and members of German peace sects, conscientious objection in Upper Canada in the early nineteenth century, anti-war witnessing and "pacific exemption" in the early republic and antebellum America, and the Civil War draft, taxation, and substitutions.
JAAR 72: 238-40.

377 Brodeur, Raymond, ed. *Femme, Mystique et Missionnaire: Marie Guyart de l'Incarnation: Tours, 1599-Québec, 1672: Actes du Colloque Organisé par le Centre d'Études Marie-de-l'Incarnation sous les Auspices du Centre Interuniversitaire d'Études Québécoises qui s'est Tenu à Loretteville, Québec, du 22 au 25 Septembre 1999.* Sainte-Foy, Québec: Presses de l'Université Laval, 2001. xiii, 387 p. ISBN 2763778135; ISBN 9782763778136; OCLC 48242642; LC Call Number BX4705.M36; Dewey 271/.97402. Citations: 6.

Presents thirty papers from a September 1999 symposium on Marie-de-l'Incarnation. Emphasizes transatlantic missionary work of Marie Guyart and others among Native Americans, particularly the Iroquois, the idea of the "other," the use of violence and crusade imagery, the role of the Ursulines in Quebec and the surrounding regions, the feminine mysticism of Marie-de-l'Incarnation and the application of psychoanalysis to mystical experiences, the Relation of 1654, and the idea of maternity.
CHR 85: 371-75.

378 Brown, Candy Gunther. *The Word in the World: Evangelical Writing, Publishing, and Reading in America, 1789–1880.* Chapel Hill: University of North Carolina Press, 2004. xiv, 336 p. ISBN 0807828386 (hbk.); ISBN 9780807828380 (hbk.); ISBN 0807855111 (pbk.); ISBN 9780807855119 (pbk.); OCLC 52775142; LC Call Number Z480.R4; Dewey 070.5/0973/09034. Citations: 20.

Contends that, from the late eighteenth century to the late nineteenth century evangelicals sought "to enact a set of sometimes competing core narrative structures that envisioned the Christian life as contending for the faith, exemplifying the priesthood of all believers, sanctifying the world," and "creating a universal church" and that these story lines "balanced the goals of maintaining the Word's purity and creating a transformative presence in the world." Explains that evangelicals strived for these objectives through the refinement of a printed and well-marketed collection of bibles, tracts, hymnals, sermons, children's books, periodicals, advice manuals, theological works, and religious fiction. Notes that though the literature and its marketing contained secular elements, the enterprise remained at its core evangelical. Concludes that this print culture successfully "contained and reconciled a multiplicity of strains

in dialectical tension: individual and community, local and universal, temporal and timeless, presence and purity, and Word and world."
AHR 110: 139-40; *Am Lit* 77: 850-52; *BHR* 78: 532-35; *CH* 74: 638-40; *IMH* 101: 301-302; *JAH* 91: 1456; *JER* 25: 310-12; *J Interdis Hist* 37: 302-303; *JSH* 71: 432-33.

379 Brown, Robert E. *Jonathan Edwards and the Bible*. Bloomington: Indiana University Press, 2002. xxii, 292 p. ISBN 0253340934; ISBN 9780253340931; OCLC 48163037; LC Call Number BS500 .B75; Dewey 220.6/092 21. Citations: 20.
Points out that the Bible was at the center of much of Edwards's writing and that biblical criticism was crucial to his theology, epistemology, typology, eschatology, psychology, and philosophy of religion. Contends that Edwards's intellectual work after the 1720s focused on defending Christian belief against religious rationalism espoused by deists. Notes that Edwards focused on the Bible's divine authority, supernatural revelation, and historical authenticity to counter the critical history and rationalistic natural religion of his opponents. Shows that, at the same time, Edwards was immersed in transatlantic intellectual culture and was able to use deists' methods (particularly those found in science and history) to defend his view of the Bible. Explains that Edwards's tactics caused him to modernize his theology and adjust his biblical interpretation to follow critical modes of discourse, planting the seeds of nineteenth-century American critical hermeneutics.
Am Stds 44: 286-87; *CH* 72: 416-18; *JAH* 90: 993-94; *J Interdis Hist* 16: 185-86; *J Religion* 83: 462-64; *NEQ* 77: 333-34; *RAH* 34: 131-49; *WMQ* 61: 135-51.

380 Bush, Sargent, ed. *The Correspondence of John Cotton*. Chapel Hill: University of North Carolina Press, published for the Omohundro Institute of Early American History and Culture, 2001. xviii, 548 p. ISBN 0807826359; ISBN 9780807826355; OCLC 45317132; LC Call Number BX7260.C79; Dewey 285.8/092. Citations: 4.
Prints 125 letters from and to Cotton, including 54 not previously published. Divides the correspondence into periods covering his years as vicar in England, the time prior to his emigration to New England, the Antinomian Controversy, and the last part of his life. Provides annotations and retains the original orthography, syntax, and punctuation in the manuscript versions, seeking "to bring the reader as close to the letter and its moment of composition as possible." Suggests that Cotton viewed the pen "as God's chosen instrument."
EAL 39: 182-88; *NEQ* 75: 323-25; *WMQ* 59: 503-508.

381 Byrd, James P., Jr. *The Challenges of Roger Williams: Religious Liberty, Violent Persecution, and the Bible*. Macon, Ga.: Mercer University Press, 2002. xii, 286 p. ISBN 0865547718; ISBN 9780865547711; OCLC 49531496; LC Call Number BR1608.U6; Dewey 261.7/2/092. Citations: 4.
Examines the practice and "important biblical dimensions" of Williams, calling him a "pivotal radical" and connecting Williams's views to those of John Winthrop, John Cotton, and Thomas Hooker. Studies Williams's use of the Bible through Williams's interpretation of various themes and passages,

including God's national Old Testament covenants, Jesus's parable of the wheat and the weeds, Paul's teachings on obedience to civil magistrates (Romans 13), and the image of the whore and the beast (Revelations 17). Argues that Williams used the Bible as the basis for every one of his practices and intellectual positions.
JAH 90: 618-19; *WMQ* 62: 530-32.

382 Cashin, Edward J. *Beloved Bethesda: A History of George Whitefield's Home for Boys, 1740–2000*. Macon, Ga.: Mercer University Press, 2001. x, 278 p. ISBN 086554722X; ISBN 9780865547223; OCLC 45714720; LC Call Number HV995.S45 C37; Dewey 362.73/2/09758724 21. Citations: 2.
Traces the founding and development of the orphan home established by George Whitefield near Savannah, Georgia in 1740. Discusses the Spanish influence in the region, Whitefield's role in the origins of slavery in Georgia, his troubled marriage, and his relationship with the Countess of Huntingdon. Explains that Whitefield's fund-raising tour in support of the home launched the Great Awakening and that the survival of Bethesda to the twentieth century can be tied directly to Whitefield's commitment.
GHQ 85: 620-22; *JSH* 69: 405-406; *WMQ* 59: 1008-1011.

383 Como, David R. *Blown by the Spirit: Puritanism and the Emergence of an Antinomian Underground in Pre-Civil War England*. Stanford, Calif.: Stanford University Press, 2004. xii, 513 p. ISBN 0804744432; ISBN 9780804744430; OCLC 53231193; LC Call Number BR757 .C68; Dewey 273/.6/0942 22. Citations: 38.
Surveys sectarian groups—mystics, Familists, Grindletonians, and general Antinomians—and their relationships to mainstream Puritanism in the two decades prior to the English Civil War. Places these groups along the continuum of English Calvinism, noting internal tensions and disagreements among them. Sees Puritanism as a "fractured landscape" unified only by opposition to moral and theological compromises of the Church of England, but splintered by divergent doctrinal, social, political, and cultural interests. Traces Antinomianism from the beginning of the seventeenth century, noting that Antinomians were generally critics of William Perkins' "practical divinity." Discusses the views of John Traske, Robert Towne, John Eaton, John Everarde, and Roger Brearley, head of the "Grindletonians," noting that these theologians made up a "puritan underground" of "perfectionists" or "antilegalists." Identifies the theological sources of antilegalism as the Pauline epistles, Luther's writings, and the medieval *Theologica Germanica*, which also influenced perfectionists, as did the works of the Family of Love founder Hendrik Niclaes. Suggests that the anti-radicalism of the late 1620s was politically driven by loyalists intent on embarrassing all groups that could be termed "puritan" and by moderate Puritans who sought to disavow those on their theological and social left. Finds that some radicals functioned for long periods of time as Anglican clergy or as moderate Puritans.
AHR 110: 214-15;*CJH* 40: 102-104; *CH* 75: 428-31; *EHR* 122: 760-61; *J Brit Stds* 44: 593-94; *J Brit Stds* 44: 604-606; *J Interdis Hist* 36: 251-52; *J Religion* 85: 307-308; *J Relig Hist* 32: 118-20; *16c J* 37: 600-602; *WMQ* 62: 325-30.

384 Connors, Richard and Andrew Colin Gow, eds. *Anglo-American Millennialism, from Milton to the Millerites*. Boston, Mass.: Brill, 2004. xviii, 210 p. ISBN 9004138218; ISBN 9789004138216; OCLC 54035065; LC Call Number BR757 .A74; Dewey 236/.9 22. Citations: 4.

Presents essays that examine the notion of innovation and historical progress in the writings of Foxe and Milton, Anglican millennialism in early seventeenth-century Virginia, eighteenth-century millennialism and apocalypticism in America, the connection of millennialism to Revolutionary American political theology, and Millerism in the eastern townships of Lower Canada.

AHR 110: 1131-32; *CH* 74: 859-60; *16c J* 37: 779-80.

385 DeRogatis, Amy. *Moral Geography: Maps, Missionaries, and the American Frontier*. New York: Columbia University Press, 2003. xiv, 242 p. ISBN 0231127898 (pbk.); ISBN 9780231127899 (pbk.); ISBN 023112788X (hbk.); ISBN 9780231127882 (hbk.); OCLC 50479279; LC Call Number BV2803.O3; Dewey 277.71/3081. Citations: 17.

Studies settlement in the Western Reserve between 1780 and 1820. Notes that New Englanders were drawn to the wilderness by the notion that the new territory was part of Connecticut, including its religious culture. Contends that exploring the "moral geography" of the territory helps to tease out "the moral implications of power struggles on a religiously constructed landscape." Finds that surveyors and land speculators, United Plan missionaries and ministers, and exploratory travelers influenced decisions to settle and that the lack of a commons and untended fields created concern about disorder and immorality. Argues that surveyors and missionaries tacitly cooperated to impose New England values on geography and persons. Finds that missionaries disapproved of the exercises of revivalism, which muted religious pluralism and manipulated settlers' habits.

JAH 91: 227-28; *JHG* 30: 803-805; *J Religion* 84: 617-18; *J Relig Hist* 32: 124-25; *PHR* 74: 128-29.

386 Dreisbach, Daniel L. and Mark David Hall, eds. *The Founders on God and Government*. Lanham, Md.: Rowman and Littlefield, 2004. xx, 314 p. ISBN 0742522784 (hbk.); ISBN 9780742522787 (hbk.); ISBN 0742522792 (pbk.); ISBN 9780742522794 (pbk.); OCLC 55055141; LC Call Number BR520 .F68; Dewey 322/.1/097309033 22. Citations: 12.

Claims that George Washington, John Adams, Thomas Jefferson, James Madison, Benjamin Franklin, John Witherspoon, James Wilson, and George Mason actively encouraged the communitarian values of Protestant Christianity and were essentially impervious to Enlightenment ideas.

JER 26: 333-38; *VMHB* 113: 187-88.

387 Duncan, Jason K. *Citizens or Papists? The Politics of Anti-Catholicism in New York, 1685–1821*. New York: Fordham University Press, 2005. xviii, 253 p. ISBN 0823225127; ISBN 9780823225125; OCLC 60697070; LC Call Number BR520 .D86; LC Call Number BX1766; Dewey 305.6/82747. Citations: 6.

Traces political activities of New York Roman Catholics from the colonial period through the beginning of the Jacksonian era. Notes that colonial anti-Catholicism manifested itself in laws directed against Catholics and rumors of Catholic plots and conspiracies. Contends that views began to shift in the Revolution, when Catholics contributed to the cause and the French alliance assuaged Protestant bigotry. Argues that Catholic defense of political interests played a major role in the formation of the state's party system. Points out that Catholics and Federalists formed a temporary alliance based on opposition to the radicalization and excesses of the French Revolution, but eventually found their ways to the Democrats. Notes that the early nineteenth-century wave of Catholic immigrants was generally made up of poor persons, which strained relationships with Protestants and led to a surge in anti-Catholic and anti-Irish sentiment.
AHR 113: 168; *HRNB* 34: 111; *JAH* 93: 500-501; *JER* 26: 661-65.

388 Edwards, Jonathan. *Works of Jonathan Edwards*. Volume 19: *Sermons and Discourses, 1734–1738*. Edited by M. X. Lesser. New Haven, Conn.: Yale University Press, 2001. xiv, 849 p. ISBN 0300087144; ISBN 9780300087147; OCLC 45446381; LC Call Number BX7117 .E3; Dewey 285.8 s; Dewey 252/.058. Citations: 13.
Includes important Edwards theological writings and sermons such as "Justification by Faith Alone," "The Excellency of Christ," and "A City on a Hill." Presents detailed instructions to Northampton parishioners on how to cope with the notoriety that the Great Awakening had brought to the community. Provides sermons that address the suicide of Edwards's uncle, Joseph Hawley, and the seating controversy that came about as the result of the construction of a new meetinghouse. Includes pieces on speculative theological issues, pastoral life, conversion, and declension. Presents Edwards's full account of the Northampton revival, *A Faithful Narrative of the Surprising Work of God*, which was published in 1737 in London and Edinburgh and later issued in Boston. Includes also *Discourses on Various Important Subjects*, five sermons about the Awakening, and the only collection of sermons that he published.
EAL 39: 147-66; *WMQ* 61: 135-51.

389 Edwards, Jonathan. *Works of Jonathan Edwards*. Volume 20: *The "Miscellanies" (Entry Nos. 833–1152)*. Edited by Amy Plantinga Pauw. New Haven, Conn.: Yale University Press, 2002. xii, 569 p. ISBN 0300091745; ISBN 9780300091748; OCLC 50347945; LC Call Number BX7117 .E3; Dewey 285.8 s; Dewey 252/.058. Citations: 5.
Publishes the personal theological notebooks kept by Edwards on miscellaneous subjects and written between 1740 and 1751, when Edwards was engaged in controversy and disputes with his Northampton congregation that culminated in his dismissal. Provides Edwards's accounts of and reflections on the revivals of the Great Awakening, and their surprising abatements.
EAL 39: 147-66; *WMQ* 61: 135-51.

390 Edwards, Jonathan. *Works of Jonathan Edwards*. Volume 21: *Writings on the Trinity, Grace, and Faith*. Edited by Sang Hyun Lee. New Haven, Conn.: Yale University Press, 2003. xiv, 582 p. ISBN 0300095058; ISBN

9780300095050; OCLC 49355920; LC Call Number BX7117 .E3; Dewey 285.8 s; Dewey 230/.58. Citations: 9.

Draws from Edwards's essays and topical notebooks to provide reflections on the doctrines of grace and faith and the nature of the Trinity. Includes well-known and previously published pieces, items newly re-edited from the original manuscripts, and documents that have never before been published.
EAL 39: 147-66; *WMQ* 61: 135-51.

391 Edwards, Jonathan. *Works of Jonathan Edwards*. Volume 22: *Sermons and Discourses, 1739–1742*. Edited by Harry S. Stout and Nathan O. Hatch with Kyle P. Farley. New Haven, Conn.: Yale University Press, 2003. xii, 566 p. ISBN 0300095724; ISBN 9780300095722; OCLC 49853232; LC Call Number BX7117 .E3; Dewey 285.8 s; Dewey 252/.058. Citations: 8.

Presents sermons and discourses dealing largely with the Great Awakening in Northampton, Massachusetts and elsewhere. Transcribes the original manuscript of *Sinners in the Hands of an Angry God*, along with the text of its first printed edition. Provides "Christ the Spiritual Sun," an account of the excommunication of "Mrs. Bridgman," and "Keeping the Presence of the Lord," in which Edwards weighs in on "false experiences" and revival excesses. Includes the sermon "The Blowing of the Great Trumpet," in which "Edwards reminded hearers of salvation's joys and the sweetness of God's love."
EAL 39: 147-66; *WMQ* 61: 135-51.

392 Foster, William Henry. *The Captor's Narrative: Catholic Women and Their Puritan Men on the Early American Frontier*. Ithaca, N.Y.: Cornell University Press, 2003. ix, 205 p. ISBN 0801440599; ISBN 9780801440595; OCLC 50859310; LC Call Number HQ1075.5.C2; Dewey 971.01/8. Citations: 10.

Examines how French Canadian Catholic women purchased and used Anglo-American captives from the late seventeenth- and mid-eighteenth-century colonial wars. Considers the lives of Marguerite Bourgeoys, founder of the lay women's community the Congregation Notre-Dame de Montreal, and Agathe de Saint-Pere, supposed founder of the Canadian textile industry, among others, who had a need for captive labor. Explores the various motives of women who made use of the labor of captives, finding that nuns like Marguerite Bourgeoys likely used religious justification, while Agathe de Saint-Pere, a high-status Catholic laywoman, felt no such need to defend her actions. Reconstructs the stories of captives Matthew Pauling, Jean Andresse, and Edward Barlow, patients at the Hotel-Dieu de Montreal, and others retained to work in the home or workshop of Agathe de Saint-Pere. Covers the lives and work of female captives, particularly those who joined Catholic religious orders, and describes the early captivity experience of Lydia Longley, taken at age twenty in a 1694 Abenaki raid and purchased by a wealthy French Canadian businessman.
AHR 109: 506-507; *JAH* 91: 215-16; *WMQ* 61: 356-58.

393 Gaustad, Edwin S. *Roger Williams*. New York: Oxford University Press, 2005. x, 150 p. ISBN 019518369X; ISBN 9780195183696; OCLC 56894490; LC Call Number F82.W7; Dewey 974.5/02/092. Citations: 6.

Traces the career of Williams from colonial outsider to founder and leader of Providence Plantations. Analyzes Williams's ideas on religion and government, placing them in historical and philosophical context and connecting them to the origins of the First Amendment to the U.S. Constitution. Claims that Williams never intended to remove religion entirely from the public sphere, but rather that Williams rejected the exercise of political power by a single religious group. *Booklist* 101: 1562; *JAS* 42: 156; *JAS* 43: 387.

394 Gerona, Carla. *Night Journeys: The Power of Dreams in Transatlantic Quaker Culture*. Charlottesville: University of Virginia Press, 2004. x, 290 p. ISBN 0813923107; ISBN 9780813923109; OCLC 55044749; LC Call Number BX7748.D73; Dewey 289.6/09/033. Citations: 5.
Examines the social and political dimensions of so-called "night journeys" and their importance in shaping the culture of American Quakerism from revolutionary England to post-revolutionary America. Asserts that dreams are models for culture, reflections of internal psychological states that were, in Quakerism, a "collective endeavor" that illuminated tensions between individual agency and social control. Outlines the seventeenth-century origins of the Society of Friends in a context of upheaval in which belief in the prophetic potential of dreams was normal and was used to critique the state and established church. Explains that Quakers developed a practice of recording, circulating, sharing, discussing, and interpreting prophetic dreams, which shaped a common Quaker identity in the process. Notes that, especially among women, dreams became "increasingly moralistic" and concerned with the regulation of behavior and discipline. Contends that dreams retained their radical potential throughout the Revolution and continued to "help make private thoughts into public statements, reconfigure relations between males and females, and allow the disenfranchised a powerful pulpit to express distinctive beliefs."
AHR 110: 1489; *J Brit Stds* 45: 643-44; *JER* 25: 677-80; *J Religion* 86: 310-12; *NEQ* 78: 667-69.

395 Gordis, Lisa M. *Opening Scripture: Bible Reading and Interpretive Authority in Puritan New England*. Chicago: University of Chicago Press, 2003. xii, 309 p. ISBN 0226304124; ISBN 9780226304120; OCLC 49773672; LC Call Number BS500 .G67; Dewey 220.6/09744/09032 21. Citations: 18.
Finds that the first generation of New England Puritans included able literary critics, that clerics like John Cotton, Thomas Shepard, Thomas Hooker, and Roger Williams believed themselves to be "interpreting in the Spirit" and "could not accept the possibility that competing doctrines might be derived by legitimate and Spirit-guided exegesis." Asserts that, at the same time, ministers "nevertheless upheld the importance of lay reading and interpretation," modeled a reading practice, believed that "each text had a single, clear, and literal meaning," and "encouraged their congregants to feel empowered as readers." Demonstrates the importance of Massachusetts' early culture of biblical literacy. Asserts "a more fluid view of Puritan interpretative practices, and thus of Puritan interpretive authority." Finds that Williams's assertion that humans could never escape the worldly made unified interpretations impossible: "For Williams, misreading was a necessary consequence of the human reader's

position in the corrupt earthly realm." Takes up the role of lay reading in Antinomian Controversy, noting that in the "debates about the indwelling of the Spirit and the nature of revelation, participants spent a good deal of time sorting out the relationship among God's word as revealed in the Bible, God's word as preached, the legitimate assistance of the Holy Spirit to a Christian reader of the Bible, and the possibility of genuine revelations separate from the biblical text." *CH* 75: 681-82; *EAL* 39: 208-12; *JAAR* 73: 922-24; *JAH* 90: 1422-23; *J Religion* 84: 460-62; *NEQ* 78: 301-303.

396 Greer, Allan and Jodi Bilinkoff, ed. *Colonial Saints: Discovering the Holy in the Americas.* New York: Routledge, 2003. xxii, 317 p. ISBN 0415934958 (hbk.); ISBN 9780415934954 (hbk.); ISBN 0415934966 (pbk.); ISBN 9780415934961 (pbk.); OCLC 50695328; LC Call Number BX4659.A45; Dewey 235/.2/097. Citations: 28.
Presents articles on St. Anne imagery and maternal archetypes in Spain and Mexico, the Haitian Lwa, Diego de Ocaña's hagiography, shamans versus Jesuits in Guaraní missions, St. Anthony in Portuguese America, Francisco Losa and Gregorio López on the New Spain frontier, representations of female holiness in New France, the martyrdom of Isaac Jogues, Quaker executions in seventeenth-century Massachusetts, uses of hagiography in New France, Catherine Tekakwitha in New France and New Spain, Rosa de Lima (1586-1617), and Mexico's virgin of Guadalupe in the seventeenth century.
AHR 109: 1194-96; *CH* 74: 637-38; *JAAR* 72: 534-36; *16c J* 35: 609-10; *WMQ* 60: 911-14.

397 Greer, Allan. *Mohawk Saint: Catherine Tekakwitha and the Jesuits.* Oxford: Oxford University Press, 2005. xiv, 249 p. ISBN 0195174879; ISBN 9780195174878; OCLC 54022617; LC Call Number E99.M8; Dewey 282/.092. Citations: 20.
Describes Tekakwitha's concept of Christianity, her mysticism, and her relationship to Jesuit missionary Claude Chauchetiere. Discusses the very different childhoods of Tekakwitha and Chauchetiere to show the unlikelihood that the two could come to share mystical experiences and find unique meanings and purposes within Christianity. Examines how in Tekakwitha's brief time at the Christian Indian community known as Kahnawake, Chauchetiere and his Jesuit colleague Pierre Cholenec singled her out as a serious, humble, Indian virgin. Notes the memory and continuing significance of Tekakwitha among Catholic devotees in the nineteenth and twentieth centuries. Points out that Jesuits' ideals of celibacy and purity conflicted with their sense of the wild, hellish Canada and that Tekakwitha became a symbol of the struggle between the Jesuit sense of the ideal self and the perceived horrors of a savage land.
CHR 86: 704-706; *CH* 77: 730-31; *EHR* 121: 937-39; *J Interdis Hist* 37: 655-56; *16c J* 38: 232-34; *WMQ* 65: 378-84.

398 Guenther, Karen. *"Rememb'ring Our Time and Work is the Lords": The Experiences of Quakers on the Eighteenth-Century Pennsylvania Frontier.* Selinsgrove, Penn.: Susquehanna University Press, 2005. 251 p. ISBN

1575910934; ISBN 9781575910932; OCLC 59401769; LC Call Number F157.B3; Dewey 974.8/1602. Citations: 2.

Focuses on the Quakers of the Exeter Monthly Meeting, who lived on the Pennsylvania frontier. Explains that these Friends were a small minority among German-speakers, had a limited role in county government, and were pacifists living under constant threat of attack by Native Americans. Discusses office holding, the impact of wars and revolution, wealth accumulation, wills and inheritance patterns, geographical mobility, ecclesiastical discipline, education, and slavery. Finds that a small group of families exerted significant influence and that marriages affected migration into and out of the monthly meeting. Notes that Quakers were well-represented among the top economic strata, but that rich Quakers did not dominate the leadership of the meeting, as piety was more important. Shows that during the Seven Years' War and the American Revolution, many Friends turned their backs on pacifism. Indicates that Exeter Quakers were likely influenced by non-Quakers vis-à-vis slavery and thus were relatively late among Friends in manumitting slaves.
JAH 93: 837-38; *Penn Hist* 75: 296-98; *PMHB* 131: 210-211.

399 Gura, Philip F. *Jonathan Edwards: America's Evangelical*. New York: Hill and Wang, 2005. xv, 284 p. ISBN 0809030314 (hbk.); ISBN 9780809030316 (hbk.); ISBN 0809061961 (pbk.); ISBN 9780809061969 (pbk.); OCLC 55000330; LC Call Number BX7260.E3; Dewey 285.8/092. Citations: 13.

Stresses the events that shaped Edwards's thinking, including revivals and conflicts within the Northampton church, and transatlantic discussions of free will, election, and the sovereignty of God. Views Edwards's life and career in the context of the geography and economy of the Connecticut Valley, life at Yale College, the work of ministers Solomon Stoddard and William Williams, political conditions in Stockbridge, and the beginnings of Princeton College. Summarizes Edwards's arguments in *Freedom of the Will, End in Creation, Nature of True Virtue*, and *Original Sin*.
AHR 111: 1164-65; *Booklist* 101: 1038-39; *EAL* 44: 423-32; *18c Stds* 41: 113-16; *HRNB* 34: 46; *LJ* 130n4: 90; *NEQ* 78: 304-306; *RAH* 34: 131-49.

400 Holifield, E. Brooks. *Theology in America: Christian Thought from the Age of the Puritans to the Civil War*. New Haven, Conn.: Yale University Press, 2003. ix, 617 p. ISBN 0300095740 (hbk.); ISBN 9780300095746 (hbk.); ISBN 030010765X (pbk.); ISBN 9780300107654 (pbk.); OCLC 51768938; LC Call Number BT30.U6; Dewey 230/.0973. Citations: 30.

Describes the varieties of ideas forwarded by American theologians, particularly those within the dominant Reformed tradition. Focuses on the understanding of reason in religion, arguing that most theologians had a "preoccupation" with establishing, advancing, and defending the reasonableness of Christianity. Explains that New England theologians in the eighteenth century adopted evidentialism—the notion that rational evidence confirmed the truth of biblical revelation—in response to challenges from both European and domestic deists. Finds that up to the middle of the nineteenth century Christian evidentialism was enthusiastically accepted among all American Christian theologians except among some Catholics, Lutherans, and a few dissenters like the

transcendentalists, Horace Bushnell, and the Mercersburg theologians who supported more intuitive modes of rationality. Concludes that continuing theological engagement with Europeans was vital to religious inquiry among nearly all theologians in the early republic, professionals and populists alike, and also critical to intensifying denominational loyalties and class tensions among Americans.
AHR 109: 1265-66; *CH* 73: 666-81; *EAL* 44: 179-94; *JAAR* 73: 932-34; *JAH* 91: 607-608; *JER* 25: 479-82; *J Religion* 85: 293-300; *LJ* 128n15: 63; *RAH* 32: 1-6; *WMQ* 62: 767-70.

401 Holmes, David L. *The Religion of the Founding Fathers*. Charlottesville, Va.: Ash Lawn-Highland, 2003. 156 p. ISBN 0976097907; ISBN 9780976097907; OCLC 52937773; LC Call Number BL2747.4 .H65; Dewey 200/.92/273. Citations: 1.
Examines the culture and religion of six of the Founding Fathers (Franklin, Washington, Adams, Jefferson, Madison, and Monroe), noting that many subscribed to various forms of deism and that all six were either deists or Unitarians. Argues that the Founders were not radical, anti-Christians, but rather generally held to standard Christian religious convictions of the time, admired the ethics of Christ, and believed that religion could be benevolent. Explains that many attended Baptist, Presbyterian, or Episcopal churches depending on their locations, valuing adherence to simple virtue and morality more than adherence to any particular doctrines. Asserts that the connection to church exhibited by recent presidents is very different from the practices of the Founders.
LJ 131n6: 99-100; *VMHB* 112: 192-93.

402 Holmes, Stephen R. *God of Grace and God of Glory: An Account of the Theology of Jonathan Edwards*. Grand Rapids, Mich.: William B. Eerdmans Publishing, 2001. xiv, 289 p. ISBN 0802839142; ISBN 9780802839145; OCLC 46916583; LC Call Number BX7260.E3; Dewey 230/.58/092. Citations: 12.
Compares Edwards's thought to that of other Reformed theologians, especially John Calvin and Karl Barth. Explores Edwards's thinking on the glory of God as the purpose of creation, the glory of the created order, the glory of God in the work of redemption, the community of God's glory, God's self-glorification in the damnation of sinners, and divine election.
J Religion 83: 467-69.

403 Hutson, James H. *Forgotten Features of the Founding: The Recovery of Religious Themes in the Early American Republic*. Lanham, Md.: Lexington Books, 2003. xi, 197 p. ISBN 0739105701 (hbk.); ISBN 9780739105702 (hbk.); ISBN 073910571X (pbk.); ISBN 9780739105719 (pbk.); OCLC 51613924; LC Call Number BR516 .H783; Dewey 322/.1/097309033. Citations: 0.
Asserts that religion was a major factor in American politics, that elected officials have been seen as having a sacred calling to ensure a virtuous nation, that the late eighteenth-century resurgence of belief in future rewards and punishments was vital to good citizenship, and that most Americans believed that their rights were rooted in religion.
JAH 91: 609-610.

404 Juster, Susan. *Doomsayers: Anglo-American Prophecy in the Age of Revolution.* Philadelphia: University of Pennsylvania Press, 2003. x, 276 p. ISBN 0812237323; ISBN 9780812237320; OCLC 51460537; LC Call Number BR520 .J87; Dewey 231.7/45/097309033. Citations: 22.

Studies more than 300 Anglo-American prophets active between 1765 and 1815, such as David Austin, Richard Brothers, Nimrod Hughes, James Bicheno, Jemima Wilkinson, and Joanna Southcott, finding significant differences among male and females. Underscores methods by which prophets reached the public, including publication of tracts and conducting street performances. Places such activities in the contexts of capitalism and the opening of the public square. Explains that men were typically seen as demagogues who espoused republican ideologies and women as "mystagogues" who "rejected entirely the linguistic and epistemological precepts of Painite republicanism while insisting that they, too, spoke for the common people."

AHR 109: 1197-98; *EAL* 41: 347-64; *JAH* 91: 607; *JAS* 38: 147-48; *J Brit Stds* 45: 173-74; *JER* 24: 132-36; *WMQ* 61: 155-58.

405 Kamil, Neil. Fortress of the Soul: Violence, Metaphysics, and Material Life in the Huguenots' New World, 1517–1751. Baltimore, Md.: Johns Hopkins University Press, 2005. xxiv, 1058 p. ISBN 0801873908; ISBN 9780801873904; OCLC 58754925; LC Call Number F128.9.H9; Dewey 974.7/00441/0088242. Citations: 18.

Studies the relationships among Huguenot artisans, the things they made, and their religious views. Argues that radical "heterodox" Protestants, threatened with violent suppression, developed a secret world of meaning for the sake of security and self-preservation. Claims that Huguenots expressed this secret spirituality in writing and material culture that was out in the open, yet hidden from Catholic oppressors. Discusses the pottery of Huguenot polemicist Bernard Palissy and the philosophy of Paracelsus, Giordano Bruno, and Menocchio, noting that Palissy combined virtuous artisanal industry with the Neoplatonic ideal of unity of soul and matter. Examines the life of Huguenot refugee Elias Neau, John Winthrop Jr.'s efforts to build a Neoplatonic refuge in Connecticut, Huguenot communities in London, and Huguenot craft shops of Long Island, New York City, and the Hudson. Contends that the Neoplatonic "material-holiness synthesis" borne of the Huguenot culture of resistance aided the forging of cross-ethnic connections, which were manifested in furniture.

AHR 112: 162; *CH* 75: 673-75; *18c Stds* 41: 262-65; *JAH* 92: 1410-11; *J Interdis Hist* 38: 279-80; *16c J* 38: 548-50; *WMQ* 64: 220-29.

406 Kapitzke, Robert L. *Religion, Power, and Politics in Colonial St. Augustine.* Gainesville: University Press of Florida, 2001. xii, 219 p. ISBN 081302076X; ISBN 9780813020761; OCLC 45263898; LC Call Number BX1418.S18; Dewey 282/.75918. Citations: 8.

Examines religious life in St. Augustine and its influence in colonial government between 1680 and 1763. Describes disagreements between governors and parish priests, legal disputes on ecclesiastical asylum, squabbles between secular and regular clerics, and the general decline of religion during the eighteenth century. Stresses the primary role Catholicism played in shaping the colony's social

order and notes that the clergy had the same social and political influence in Florida as in the rest of Spanish America. Argues that the "jurisdictional conflicts that erupted between secular and ecclesiastical forces in St. Augustine differed only in scale, not in type, from the conflicts fought in Mexico, Peru, Cuba, Guatemala, and other Spanish colonies." Argues that English raids and changes in imperial government in the eighteenth century led to uncertainty about Florida's future, which undermined the church's ability to attract qualified secular priests, decreased Franciscan influence, promoted intra-church conflict over jurisdiction, and caused the rise of secular governmental authority at church expense. Finds that these conditions led to "more languid Catholicism, supervised by a professionally static and morally undisciplined clergy."
FHQ 81: 350-52; *GHQ* 85: 610-612; *JSH* 69: 141-42; *WMQ* 60: 643-53.

407 Kidd, Thomas S. *The Protestant Interest: New England After Puritanism.* New Haven, Conn.: Yale University Press, 2004. xi, 212 p. ISBN 0300104219; ISBN 9780300104219; OCLC 55067722; LC Call Number BR530 .K53; Dewey 280/.4/097409033. Citations: 10.
Discusses the "Protestant interest," a relatively broad ideology that supplanted the more narrowly focused Puritanism and included a more latitudinarian theology, which allowed low-church Anglicans and Presbyterians to come together in celebration of the British Empire and its Protestant monarchs, particularly George I and the later Hanovers, and in more virulent denigration of Roman Catholicism. Explains that descriptions of "Popish" conspiracies became a mainstay of New England's print culture and that one of the most notable led to the killing of Jesuit missionary Father Sebastien Rale and the scalping of many of his followers. Notes that this ideological shift laid the groundwork for the millennialism of the Great Awakening.
AHR 110: 1161-62; *CH* 74: 875-76; *HRNB* 33: 95; *JAH* 92: 1420; *J Religion* 86: 126-27; *VQR* 81: 254.

408 Kling, David W. and Douglas A. Sweeney, eds. *Jonathan Edwards at Home and Abroad: Historical Memories, Cultural Movements, Global Horizons.* Columbia: University of South Carolina Press, 2003. xxiv, 330 p. ISBN 1570035199; ISBN 9781570035197; OCLC 52750172; LC Call Number BX7260.E3; Dewey 285.8/092. Citations: 2.
Includes papers on the challenges of writing Edwards's biography, Edwards's later notebooks and the history of the work of redemption, Edwards's ministry to children, gender in eighteenth-century Northampton, Massachusetts, Edwards's views of depravity, Edwardsian piety, the new divinity, and race, Edwards and nineteenth-century women's fiction, Edwardsian thought in popular American culture, the international scope of Edwards's legacy, the reception of Edwards by early evangelicals in England, Edwards's Scottish connection, Edwards and David Brainerd, Edwards's influence on missionary thinking and promotion, and Edwards in print abroad.
AHR 110: 123-24; *JAH* 91: 1426; *RAH* 34: 131-49.

409 Knoppers, Laura Lunger, ed. *Puritanism and Its Discontents.* Newark: University of Delaware Press, 2003. 264 p. ISBN 0874138175; ISBN

9780874138177; OCLC 50604821; LC Call Number BX9334.3 .P87; Dewey 285/.9. Citations: 12.

Presents articles on Puritanism in the English revolution, uses of the word "Puritan" between 1625 and 1640, Matthew Arnold's construction of Puritanism, Anti-Calvinists and the Republican threat in early Stuart Cambridge, the Emmanuel College election of 1622, Mary Chudleigh's *The Song of the Three Children Paraphras'd*, Puritan-Indian discourse in early New England, images of the Turk in anti-Puritan polemic, assurance, community, and the Puritan self in the antinomian controversy in Massachusetts, and Cotton Mather's *Magnalia Christi Americana*.

AHR 109: 1196-97; *CH* 72: 896-97; *EAL* 39: 399-405; *16c J* 35: 1237-39.

410   Krugler, John D. *English and Catholic: The Lords Baltimore in the Seventeenth Century*. Baltimore, Md.: Johns Hopkins University Press, 2004. xii, 319 p. ISBN 0801879639; ISBN 9780801879630; OCLC 53967315; LC Call Number JA2 .J65; LC Call Number F184 .K78; Dewey 975.2/02/0922. Citations: 13.

Examines the ways in which the Catholic Lords Baltimore conceived of and implemented a unique vision of religious freedom and economic adventure in their activities in Ireland, Newfoundland, and eventually Maryland. Refutes the notion that the Lords Baltimore were Catholic refugees fleeing Protestant England, arguing instead that they were loyal English colonial adventurers whose primary aim was to make a return on their investments and secondarily to live peacefully with fellow subjects who were Protestants. Characterizes the Lords Baltimore's views on church and state as being in the vanguard of Enlightenment thought on toleration and human freedom. Stresses that the Lords Baltimore were more secular than colonists in New England and their views were much more in line with English colonists in the rest of the Atlantic. Rejects the idea that the Calverts' manorial system was feudalistic, contending instead that it represented a forward-looking arrangement that helped to ensure religious freedom and economic stability. Details the struggles of the Calverts with the Jesuits and, eventually, Anglicans, both of whom demanded privilege and preference from the proprietors.

AHR 110: 1525-26; *CH* 75: 208-210; *EHR* 121: 306-307; *JAH* 93: 180; *J Brit Stds* 44: 829-31; *WMQ* 63: 192-95.

411   Lambert, Frank. *The Founding Fathers and the Place of Religion in America*. Princeton, N.J.: Princeton University Press, 2003. xiv, 328 p. ISBN 0691088292; ISBN 9780691088297; OCLC 49576755; LC Call Number BR516 .L29; Dewey 322/.1/0973. Citations: 31.

Examines "religious regulation," "religious competition," and "religious liberty," which represents the progression in America from the colonial to the founding eras. Explains that religious regulation characterized the dominant early Puritan and Anglican settlements, in which prevalent groups sought religious liberty only for themselves and closely proscribed religious activities of competing groups. Finds that such regulation ended in New England in the late seventeenth century, but continued in the Anglican colonies until the American Revolution. Notes that early eighteenth-century population growth,

immigration, geographic expansion, and Enlightenment-inspired calls for freedom of conscience led to strained religious institutions and increased religious competition. Contends that the Founders advanced the cause of religious liberty, "believing that a free, competitive, religious market would both ensure religious vitality and prevent religious wars" and that "Religious liberty, not religious regulation, was the more effective bond in a pluralistic society." Contends that Jefferson's election in 1800 and re-election in 1804 proves that the American people supported religious freedom over formal, historic Christianity. Concludes that the "central paradox of religion in America" pits the Puritans' "belief in the superiority of one faith as the foundation of a moral nation" against "unfettered religious liberty" espoused by the Founding Fathers.
AHR 109: 178-79; *Am Stds* 45: 144-45; *CH* 74: 178-80; *HRNB* 32: 12; *JAH* 90: 1427-28; *JER* 23: 480-82; *J Religion* 84: 274-75; *PMHB* 129: 107-109; *RAH* 31: 528-37.

412 LaPlante, Eve. *American Jezebel: The Uncommon Life of Anne Hutchinson, the Woman Who Defied the Puritans*. San Francisco, Calif.: Harper San Francisco, 2004. xxi, 312 p. ISBN 0060562331; ISBN 9780060562335; OCLC 53435383; LC Call Number F67.H92; Dewey 973.2/2/092. Citations: 8.
Portrays Hutchinson as a feminist and a fighter for religious freedom. Attributes Hutchinson's religious views to the radicalism of her father, who had been convicted of heresy when Anne was a young child. Distinguishes between her beliefs and those of her Puritan opponents and claims that the Antinomian controversy "set the stage for our modern concepts of religious freedom, gender equality, and civil rights."
Booklist 100: 1129; *LJ* 129n2: 102.

413 Little, J.I. *Borderland Religion: The Emergence of an English-Canadian Identity, 1792–1852*. Buffalo, N.Y.: University of Toronto Press, 2004. xv, 386 p. ISBN 080208916X (hbk.); ISBN 9780802089168 (hbk.); ISBN 0802086713 (pbk.); ISBN 9780802086716 (pbk.); OCLC 54692264; LC Call Number BR575.Q3; LC Call Number F1055.E53; Dewey 280/.4/097146. Citations: 14.
Studies Protestant churches and the emergence of an English-Canadian identity in the eastern townships of Quebec, particularly "how a common culture became differentiated on either side of an international boundary line." Notes that effective missionary support, strong financial assistance from Britain, and a loyalist political culture in Canada was more effective than New England radical revival preachers, denominational missionaries, and cultural and familial ties. Contends that "English Canadians from coast to coast arguably share more common values with each other than they do with the Americans who live a few miles to the south of their communities" and that "even among Protestants, the Canadian orientation has tended to be less radical and fundamentalist than that of Americans." Concludes that strains of radical religion and politics existed in the region between 1792 and 1852, but that conservative religious and political cultures predominated.
AHR 111: 460-61; *CH* 75: 452-53; *CHR* 86: 706-707; *J Interdis Hist* 37: 163-65.

414 Longenecker, Stephen L. *Shenandoah Religion: Outsiders and the Mainstream, 1716–1865.* Waco, Tex.: Baylor University Press, 2002. xiv, 247 p. ISBN 0918954835 (pbk.); ISBN 9780918954831 (pbk.); OCLC 49922364; LC Call Number BR555.V8; Dewey 277.55/907. Citations: 4.
Explores four eras of extraordinary social, political, or economic upheaval between 1716 and 1865—the American, Methodist, market, and southern "revolutions"—in order to explain why "some outsiders drift back into the mainstream while others retain their non-conformity." Finds that the groups that actively separated themselves from the world (Dunkers, Mennonites, Quakers, and United Brethren) resisted movement to the mainstream, while those groups defined as outsiders on the basis of a single characteristic moved quickly into the mainstream if that characteristic lost its boundary-marking function.
JAH 90: 1007-1008; *J Religion* 83: 614-15; *JSH* 70: 127-28; *VMHB* 110: 401-402.

415 Mapp, Alf J. *The Faiths of Our Fathers: What America's Founders Really Believed.* Lanham, Md.: Rowman and Littefield, 2003. viii, 183 p. ISBN 0742531147; ISBN 9780742531147; ISBN 0742531155; ISBN 9780742531154; ISBN 0742532526; ISBN 9780742532526; OCLC 52109227; LC Call Number E302.5 .M26; Dewey 270.7/092/273 21. Citations: 1.
Discusses the religious beliefs of eleven of the Founders, including George Washington, John Adams, Benjamin Franklin, Thomas Jefferson, Alexander Hamilton, John Marshall, George Mason, Charles Carroll of Carrollton, and James Madison. Describes the ways in which religion influenced their values, actions, and politics. Concludes that religion was vital to shaping the characters of all eleven.
HRNB 32: 57.

416 Marsden, George M. *Jonathan Edwards: A Life.* New Haven, Conn.: Yale University Press, 2003. xx, 615 p. ISBN 0300096933; ISBN 9780300096934; OCLC 50479216; LC Call Number BX7260.E3; Dewey 285.8/092. Citations: 43.
Surveys Edwards' thought and theology in their historical and intellectual contexts. Characterizes Edwards as studious and not particularly social, noting that he preferred to prepare sermons, write, and offer spiritual counsel. Compares Edwards's cultural influence to that of Benjamin Franklin, explaining that Edwards is largely responsible for the evangelical, revivalist thread of American life to the present day. Reminds the reader that Edwards's own family produced "scores of clergymen, thirteen presidents of institutions of higher learning, sixty-five professors, and many other persons of notable achievements."
AHR 109: 177-78; *CH* 76: 207-210; *EAL* 39: 195-201; *EAL* 39: 405-407; *JAAR* 72: 269-72; *JAH* 90: 1423-24; *RAH* 34: 131-49; *WMQ* 61: 135-51.

417 Mulder, Philip N. *A Controversial Spirit: Evangelical Awakenings in the South.* New York: Oxford University Press, 2002. x, 233 p. ISBN 0195131630; ISBN 9780195131635; OCLC 47126752; LC Call Number BR515 .M82; Dewey 280/.4/0975. Citations: 6.

Explores the relationship among Presbyterians, Baptists, and Methodists in Virginia and North Carolina in the late colonial, revolutionary, and early national periods. Argues that, while awakening presented the opportunity for transcendent spirituality and diminished rivalry, the leaders of the various denominations fostered instead adversarial relationships and competition for converts. Contends that this competition intensified as a result of the Revolution, as each group made use of revivalist tactics to bring in new members. Concludes that denominational particularity and exclusivity have exerted significant ideological and institutional influence on American evangelicalism.

AHR 108: 187-88; *CH* 72: 905-907; *JAH* 89: 1516-17; *JER* 23: 113-15; *JSH* 69: 878-79; *NCHR* 80: 240-41; *VMHB* 111: 302-303.

418 Muldoon, James, ed. *The Spiritual Conversion of the Americas.* Gainesville: University Press of Florida, 2004. viii, 273 p. ISBN 0813027713; ISBN 9780813027715; OCLC 55939471; LC Call Number BV2755 .S65; Dewey 266/.0230407. Citations: 9.

Presents pieces conversion practices on the New Mexico frontier, "medieval" and "modern" conversion among the Hurons of New France, John Eliot's mission to the Indians, the seventeenth-century conversion debate among Lutherans, the Mohawks in central New York (1690-1710), missions and mobility on the Spanish-American frontier, guilt discourse and acculturation in early Spanish America, conversion in Portuguese America, new English conversions in New France, and the trope of trade in English missionary writings.

CH 75: 443-44; *HAHR* 86: 352-53; *JAH* 92: 959-60.

419 Murphy, Andrew R. *Conscience and Community: Revisiting Toleration and Religious Dissent in Early Modern England and America.* University Park: Pennsylvania State University Press, 2001. xxii, 337 p. ISBN 0271021055 (hbk.); ISBN 9780271021058 (hbk.); ISBN 0271021063 (pbk.); ISBN 9780271021065 (pbk.); OCLC 44885387; LC Call Number BR757 .M87; Dewey 323.44209032. Citations: 31.

Challenges the notions (1) that religious toleration is self-evident and that antitolerationists were narrow minded, self-interested, or seeking to preserve their own power, (2) that religious toleration is a product of skepticism or unbelief, and (3) that the modern debate concerning the natural extension of religious liberty is related to issues of gender, race, and ethnicity. Critiques modern liberal theory and discusses religious dissent in Massachusetts Bay Colony and Rhode Island, the thought and practice of Anne Hutchinson, the Quakers, and Roger Williams, social and political theory among Puritan clerics and magistrates, antitolerationist views informed by covenant theology and contractarian thinking, concerns about order and the security of life and property in a religiously pluralistic world, the overwhelmingly Protestant arguments in favor of toleration, the relative lack of originality in arguments for and against toleration in the 1670s and 1680s, pragmatic compromises arising from the Glorious Revolution, and the schism of George Keith in Pennsylvania and its resultant limited claims for religious freedom.

CH 72: 669-71; *J Mod Hist* 81: 607-36; *J Religion* 82: 638-39; *Penn Hist* 71: 102-104; *PMHB* 127: 344-45; *WMQ* 59: 515-18.

420 Nelson, John K. *A Blessed Company: Parishes, Parsons, and Parishioners in Anglican Virginia, 1690–1776*. Chapel Hill: University of North Carolina Press, 2001. xiv, 477 p. ISBN 0807826634; ISBN 9780807826638; OCLC 46685207; LC Call Number BX5917.V8; Dewey 283/.755/09032. Citations: 16. Studies the Church of England in eighteenth-century Virginia, noting that the church shaped the lives of the settlers, cooperated closely with county courts to maintain order, and served to regulate behavior, provide rituals, and care for colonists. Contends that practices of worship in Virginia mirrored those in England and that parishes benefited from parsons who were well-educated, bright, capable, moral, well-integrated into their communities, and maintained high social standing, and who throughout the eighteenth century came increasingly from within the colony. Suggests that more than half of Virginians participated in church activities regularly and that clergy were well-paid and church buildings well-maintained. Finds that, despite the effects of the Great Awakening, Anglicanism continued to be strong, efficient, and in growth mode, even to the time of the American Revolution.
AHR 107: 1222-23; *CH* 72: 219-20; *JAH* 89: 1021-22; *J Relig Hist* 29: 94-96; *JSH* 69: 672-74; *NCHR* 79: 467-68; *VMHB* 110: 262-64; *WMQ* 60: 449-53.

421 Noll, Mark A. *America's God: From Jonathan Edwards to Abraham Lincoln*. New York: Oxford University Press, 2002. xiv, 622 p. ISBN 0195151119; ISBN 9780195151114; ISBN 0195182995; ISBN 9780195182996; OCLC 47892625; LC Call Number BT30.U6; Dewey 230/.0973. Citations: 90.
Asserts that only seventeen percent of Americans were churched in 1790, and that evangelical groups grew because republicanism encouraged religious agency, resulting in evangelicals making up "the vast majority of American congregations (at least 85%)" and 40% of the population by 1860. Contends that the interplay between religious and civic versions of freedom allowed evangelical Protestantism to play a major role in the creation of American nationalism. Finds that evangelical Protestants largely agreed on common sense epistemology and moral theory. Notes that many Whigs were Presbyterians, Unitarians, and Congregationalists, while Baptists, Methodists, and Universalists held Democratic sympathies. Concludes that the main feature of American Protestantism was its willingness to embrace disestablishment and the "voluntary" style of ministry and churches.
AHR 108: 1144-45; *CH* 72: 630-33; *EAL* 44: 179-94; *JAAR* 73: 264-67; *JAH* 91: 595-97; *J Interdis Hist* 35: 651-52; *J Religion* 85: 293-300; *LJ* 127n18: 96; *RAH* 32: 7-13; *WMQ* 61: 539-44.

422 Noll, Mark A. *The Rise of Evangelicalism: The Age of Edwards, Whitefield, and the Wesleys*. Nottingham: Inter-Varsity, 2004. 320 p. ISBN 1844740013; ISBN 9781844740017; OCLC 53710450; LC Call Number BR1640 .N65; Dewey 280.409033; Dewey 270/.7. Citations: 19.

Discusses Baptist John Bunyan, Lutheran Philip Jakob Spener, and numerous Anglicans, as well as Jonathan Edwards, George Whitefield, John Wesley, and Charles Wesley, Moravian August Gottlieb Spangenberg, Welsh Methodist Howell Harris, Church of Scotland minister John Erskine, the American Presbyterians William Tennent, Gilbert Tennent, and Samuel Davies, American Baptist Isaac Backus, British Anglicans John Newton and Hannah More, Canadian minister Henry Alline, black Baptist preacher David George, and many American leaders who came to prominence in the years after the American Revolution. Points out that evangelicalism was both a cross-denominational and cross-national phenomenon, and that, while generally politically conservative, leaders presaged the modern era, looking to Lockean psychology for interpretations of experimental Christianity and opposing tradition in the same way as Enlightenment thinkers did. Argues that "the shaping of early evangelicalism was very much a male affair" and that evangelicals were particularly prominent in missionary endeavors.
JAH 92: 191-92; *J Religion* 85: 660-62.

423 Novak, Michael. *On Two Wings: Humble Faith and Common Sense at the American Founding*. San Francisco, Calif.: Encounter Books, 2002. 235 p. ISBN 1893554341; ISBN 9781893554344; OCLC 47893081; LC Call Number BL2525 .N68; Dewey 200/.973/09033. Citations: 9.
Contends that religion exerted significant influence on the Founders. Claims that the Founders understood their world in terms of a "Hebrew metaphysics," an Old Testament view that stressed God's purposeful, creative design, a notion that Adams and others used to justify the Revolution. Explains that Founders turned to prayer often during and after the war. Finds that members of the founding generation were concerned that church-state separation would cause popular alienation from "the great religious principles on which the natural right to religious liberty is based."
JER 22: 521-23; *LJ* 126n19: 72.

424 Pauw, Amy Plantinga. *The Supreme Harmony of All: The Trinitarian Theology of Jonathan Edwards*. Grand Rapids, Mich.: William B. Eerdmans Publishing Company, 2002. x, 196 p. ISBN 0802849849 (pbk.); ISBN 9780802849847 (pbk.); OCLC 49530126; LC Call Number BT111.3.P38; Dewey 231/.044/092. Citations: 14.
Examines Edwards's doctrine of the trinity, arguing that Edwards's Trinitarian theology expressed in his "Miscellanies" serves to clarify philosophical, theological, and pastoral themes in the wider body of his work. Contends that the doctrine of the trinity provides "a strong link between two aspects of his thought that often have seemed disconnected: his profound metaphysical musings and his zeal for the church and the Christian life." Describes Edwards's common models of God, one that unified Christ and the Spirit and another that emphasized "that society of the three persons of the Godhead," each of which used different theological vocabularies and presuppositions, thereby resulting in an "experimental, ad hoc quality" in Edwards's writings. Notes that Edwards's ponderings, however, had a direct effect on his envisioning harmonious consent among the persons of the trinity as the perfect analogy of Christian community

and therefore became both "an unrealizable blueprint for Edwards's church in Northampton" and resulted in "harsh pastoral moralism" that ultimately led to his dismissal as the congregation's minister.
18c Stds 41: 113-16; *JAH* 90: 619; *J Religion* 84: 122-23; *WMQ* 61: 135-51.

425 Reff, Daniel T. *Plagues, Priests, and Demons: Sacred Narratives and the Rise of Christianity in the Old World and the New.* New York: Cambridge University Press, 2005. xiii, 290 p. ISBN 0521840783 (hbk.); ISBN 9780521840781 (hbk.); ISBN 0521600502 (pbk.); ISBN 9780521600507 (pbk.); OCLC 54778554; LC Call Number BV2110 .R44; Dewey 270. Citations: 18.
Compares the "rise of Christianity" in ancient and early medieval Europe to that in colonial Latin America. Sees parallels between the Aztec and Roman empires and between epidemic disease in the Mediterranean in the first century after Jesus's death and in the early period of Spanish conquest in the New World, arguing that the demographic crisis in both cases aided the expansion of Christianity. Contends that Jesuit missionaries in sixteenth- and seventeenth-century America deliberately mimicked ancient Christian texts in order to enhance the legitimacy of their missions.
AHR 111: 1133-34; *CH* 75: 472-74; *Ethnohistory* 54: 569-70; *HAHR* 86: 639-40.

426 Reid-Maroney, Nina. *Philadelphia's Enlightenment, 1740–1800: Kingdom of Christ, Empire of Reason.* Westport, Conn.: Greenwood Press, 2001. xvi, 199 p. ISBN 0313314721; ISBN 9780313314728; OCLC 44026171; LC Call Number BR520 .R43; Dewey 277.3/07. Citations: 13.
Examines the "Philadelphia Circle," a mixture of Old Side and New Side leaders in the aftermath of the Great Awakening. Emphasizes the roles of Old Sider Francis Alison, who defended reason in higher education and tended toward deism, of Benjamin Rush, who favored the ideas of Jonathan Edwards, while maintaining the scientific sensibility of the Scottish Enlightenment, and of John Redman, Samuel Stanhope Smith, and Ebenezer Kinnersley, among others. Discusses the Circle members' prominent places in the American Philosophical Society, the College of Philadelphia, and the Pennsylvania Hospital and concludes that the more Calvinist Christian Enlightenment that informed the views of the Circle's members allowed for accommodation of both faith and reason.
AHR 107: 1221-22; *JAH* 89: 612-13; *Penn Hist* 69: 474-76; *PMHB* 127: 232-34; *WMQ* 59: 518-21.

427 Rohrer, S. Scott. *Hope's Promise: Religion and Acculturation in the Southern Backcountry.* Tuscaloosa: University of Alabama Press, 2005. xxxvi, 266 p. ISBN 0817314350; ISBN 9780817314354; OCLC 54989163; LC Call Number F262.F7; Dewey 975.6/6700882846. Citations: 7.
Details the founding and development of the Moravian colony of Wachovia in the North Carolina backcountry. Notes that the settlement was ethnically diverse, home to English- and German-speaking colonists, and that it sought to bring faith to bear as a unifier. Finds that colonists from different backgrounds

intermarried and that they remained engaged with the outside world, which allowed Wachovians to become more culturally southern and American.
AHR 111: 153-54; *CH* 75: 450-52; *GHQ* 89: 416-17; *HRNB* 33: 103; *JAH* 92: 1428-29; *JSH* 72: 453-54; *NCHR* 82: 390-91.

428 Saillant, John. *Black Puritan, Black Republican: The Life and Thought of Lemuel Haynes, 1753–1833.* New York: Oxford University Press, 2003. xii, 232 p. ISBN 0195157176; ISBN 9780195157178; OCLC 50080288; LC Call Number BX7260.H315; Dewey 285.8/092. Citations: 11.
Describes the life of Haynes, who served in the militia during the Revolution, essentially educated himself, and became a part of the Calvinist New Divinity movement, an abolitionist, and a Congregationalist minister and controversialist. Focuses on his theological and political ideas, noting connections between New Divinity beliefs and New England Federalism and between Haynes's theology and his critiques of slavery. Claims that Haynes's goals mirrored those of other eighteenth-century black abolitionists and views the "black republicanism of Lemuel Haynes as counterpoint to the beliefs of Jefferson and Madison."
EAL 42: 385-92; *WMQ* 61: 383-86.

429 Sassi, Jonathan D. *A Republic of Righteousness: The Public Christianity of the Post-Revolutionary New England Clergy.* New York: Oxford University Press, 2001. viii, 298 p. ISBN 019512989X; ISBN 9780195129892; OCLC 45320437; LC Call Number BR530 .S27; Dewey 277.4/081. Citations: 16.
Examines the civic preaching of New England Congregational clergy from 1783 to 1833. Defines public Christianity as the clergy's "utterances on the relationship of faith to life in society" and focuses on election sermons and fast, thanksgiving, Fourth of July, and Forefathers' Day addresses. Finds that patriotic, providential, and covenantal language helped to construct a continuous body of civic thought that extended from the Revolution to the evangelical era, but that clergy used the providential more than the covenantal and did not uncritically hold out America as a chosen nation, but rather saw that God rewarded or punished all nations on the basis of behavior. Concludes that church and state worked together to enforce moral law.
AHR 107: 1555-56; *JAH* 89: 1515-16; *JER* 22: 523-25; *RAH* 31: 356-62; *WMQ* 59: 1022-25.

430 Sparks, John. *The Roots of Appalachian Christianity: The Life and Legacy of Elder Shubal Stearns.* Lexington: University Press of Kentucky, 2001. xx, 327 p. ISBN 0813122236; ISBN 9780813122236; ISBN 0201746131; ISBN 9780201746136; OCLC 47136399; LC Call Number BX6495.S77; Dewey 286/.1/092. Citations: 5.
Explores the idea that Appalachian Baptists practice a faith brought to the region by the "Old Brethren," an eighteenth-century group of Separate Baptists, led by Stearns, who migrated from New England to the North Carolina Piedmont. Contends that "In the historical record of their activities can be found not only the origins of each of the distinctively 'Appalachian worship practices," but also "very nearly an entire history of the Appalachian people in capsule form."
CH 71: 434; *IMH* 99: 186-87; *JSH* 69: 679-80; *NCHR* 79: 278; *VQR* 78:106.

431   Sweeney, Douglas A. *Nathaniel Taylor, New Haven Theology, and the Legacy of Jonathan Edwards*. New York: Oxford University Press, 2003. xi, 255 p. ISBN 0195154282; ISBN 9780195154283; OCLC 48957885; LC Call Number BX7260.T32; Dewey 230/.58/092. Citations: 16.

Examines the theology of Taylor, who claimed to be an heir to Edwards. Confirms that Taylor used Edwardsian language to extend the "Edwardsian theological culture" that "flourished during the first four decades of the nineteenth century." Acknowledges that Taylor strayed slightly from Edwards on key concepts like original sin and atonement, but overall represents continuity. Rejects the notion that Taylor's positions represented a decline in New England theology, asserting instead that Taylor "set loose the forces of Edwardsian spirituality to empower the religious life of American culture at large."

AHR 109: 178; *CH* 74: 389-91; *JAH* 90: 1441-42; *JER* 24: 699-701; *WMQ* 61: 562-64.

432   Van Ruymbeke, Bertrand and Randy J. Sparks, eds. *Memory and Identity: The Huguenots in France and the Atlantic Diaspora*. Columbia: University of South Carolina Press, 2003. xvi, 335 p. ISBN 1570034842; ISBN 9781570034848; OCLC 51799090; LC Call Number BX9454.3 .M46; Dewey 284.509. Citations: 22.

Presents articles on the Huguenot diaspora, Huguenot identity and law in early modern France, mediation and reconciliation in the sixteenth-century Huguenot community, cultural boundaries in seventeenth-century French communities, French Protestant acceptance in Emden, acculturation in the French Church of London in the early seventeenth century, "strangers" in Norwich and Canterbury in the late sixteenth and early seventeenth centuries, Huguenots in the Dutch republic, Huguenot families and American immigration, Huguenot merchants in the Atlantic trade and the development of South Carolina's slave system, demography of Protestants in colonial New York City, Protestants of New France in the seventeenth and eighteenth centuries, Protestants in the colonization of the French West Indies, Cape Huguenots in South African apartheid, and Huguenot myths.

AHR 109: 863-64; *EHR* 120: 1445-46; *JSH* 71: 421-22; *16c J* 38: 289-90; *SCHM* 105: 306-308; *WMQ* 63: 188-91.

433   Vaudry, Richard W. *Anglicans and the Atlantic World: High Churchmen, Evangelicals, and the Quebec Connection*. Ithaca, N.Y.: McGill-Queen's University Press, 2003. xiii, 315 p. ISBN 0773525416; ISBN 9780773525412; OCLC 50940185; LC Call Number BX5612.Q3; Dewey 283/.714/09034. Citations: 3.

Examines the Anglican diocese of Quebec from the 1790s to the 1860s, focusing on the cultural, intellectual, and religious influences on the colonial church. Stresses the importance of the Anglican polity over the larger political context and concludes that fragmentation and dissension characterized the church more accurately than did unifying conservatism.

AHR 110: 1154-55.

434 Wagner, Walter H. *The Zinzendorf-Muhlenberg Encounter: A Controversy in Search of Understanding.* Nazareth, Penn.: Moravian Historical Society, 2002. v, 174 p. ISBN 0971906009; ISBN 9780971906006; OCLC 50008301; LC Call Number BX8593.Z6 W34; Dewey 284/.6/092. Citations: 2.

Studies the split between Lutherans and Moravians through an examination of a 1742 meeting of Moravian founder Count Ludwig von Zinzendorf and Lutheran pastor Heinrich Melchior Muhlenberg. Contends that the essential differences between the groups were minimal, but that fissures were rooted in European controversies and based on attitudes toward authority.

CH 72: 902-903; *PMHB* 127: 109-110.

435 Weddle, Meredith Baldwin. *Walking in the Way of Peace: Quaker Pacifism in the Seventeenth Century.* New York: Oxford University Press, 2001. xvi, 348 p. ISBN 019513138X; ISBN 9780195131383; OCLC 42708122; LC Call Number BX7639 .W43; Dewey 261.8/73/088286. Citations: 14.

Seeks "to identify issues relating to the peace testimony, to discern motivations, and [to] discover actual practice" among seventeenth-century Quakers. Uses Rhode Island as a case study, noting that the colony was particularly vulnerable to attacks from Native Americans because of its geographic position, economic limitations, small settlements, and alienation from other English colonies. Explains that Rhode Island colonists did not rely upon peace testimony during King Philip's War and that Quaker responses were remarkably varied, ranging from disengagement to indirect participation to direct military action. Finds that none of these behaviors was criticized by other Friends and concludes that this silence "is persuasive evidence that New England Quakers were not sufficiently in accord on the peace testimony to standardize its practical meaning."

AHR 107: 1528-39; *CH* 71: 431-33; *JAH* 89: 612; *J Brit Stds* 43: 266-71; *J Religion* 83: 282-84; *NEQ* 75: 325-28; *PMHB* 126: 651-52; *RAH* 30: 198-203.

436 Weir, David A. *Early New England: A Covenanted Society.* Grand Rapids, Mich.: William B. Eerdmans Publishing Company, 2005. xviii, 460 p. ISBN 0802813526 (pbk.); ISBN 9780802813527 (pbk.); OCLC 55124602; LC Call Number BR530.W45; Dewey 322/.1/097409032. Citations: 16.

Surveys Puritan church and civil covenants from 1620 to 1708 in New England and in parts of New York and New Jersey. Examines the form and language of charters and patents, observing that "there was no singular 'New England Mind' concerning the civil magistracy or its specific foundational conceptualization." Explains that instead there was tremendous diversity among the civil covenants, including those of Rhode Island and Gorges's colony in Maine. Finds that church covenants were somewhat formulaic and emphasized "unity of thought," but that even they exhibited local differences.

AHR 111: 1500-1501; *CH* 75: 679-81; *JAH* 93: 176-77; *J Brit Stds* 45: 641-42; *J Relig Hist* 32: 504-505; *NEQ* 79: 485-87; *WMQ* 63: 600-604.

437 Wellenreuther, Hermann and Carola Wessel, eds. *The Moravian Mission Diaries of David Zeisberger, 1771–1781.* University Park: Pennsylvania State University Press, 2005. x, 666 p. ISBN 0271025220; ISBN 9780271025223;

OCLC 56068718; LC Call Number E98.M6; Dewey 305.897/345/009033. Citations: 5.

Translates Zeisberger's diaries, which cover attitudes toward and distinctions among Indians, particularly the Iroquois, Delawares, and Shawnees, and mission work in the upper Ohio valley during the Revolution. Includes notes on persons and places and congregation membership lists.

JER 26: 170-72; *Penn Hist* 72: 388-90; *PMHB* 130: 333-34.

438 Winship, Michael P. *Making Heretics: Militant Protestantism and Free Grace in Massachusetts, 1636¬1641*. Princeton, N.J.: Princeton University Press, 2002. xv, 322 p. ISBN 0691089434; ISBN 9780691089430; OCLC 47825194; LC Call Number F67 .W7; Dewey 277.44/06. Citations: 36.

Renames the antinomian controversy the "free grace controversy," arguing that the episode focused not on antinomianism narrowly, but rather "how best to magnify the free grace of God." Deemphasizes the role of Anne Hutchinson and stresses the influence of Henry Vane, John Wheelwright, and Thomas Shepard. Criticizes previous historical interpretations as overly deterministic and dualistic ("radical / orthodox; conservative / innovative; free market / agrarian; patriarch / proto-feminist") and makes the case that the event was not as crucial to early American development as is often thought, yet was still "the worst domestic political crisis Massachusetts's government faced until the American Revolution."

AHR 108: 184-85; *CH* 75: 206-208; *EAL* 39: 167-70; *EHR* 120: 835-37; *JAH* 89: 1501-1502; *J Religion* 85: 127-28; *J Relig Hist* 29: 357; *NEQ* 76: 634-39; *RAH* 31: 24-31.

439 Winship, Michael P. *The Times and Trials of Anne Hutchinson: Puritans Divided*. Lawrence: University Press of Kansas, 2005. xi, 168 p. ISBN 070061379X (hbk.); ISBN 9780700613793 (hbk.); ISBN 0700613803 (pbk.); ISBN 9780700613809 (pbk.); OCLC 56880090; LC Call Number BX7148.M4; Dewey 273/.6/09744. Citations: 9.

Explains that Hutchinson has become "the most famous, or infamous, Englishwoman in colonial American history." Reviews her life and trial, noting that Hutchinson's role in the antinomian controversy was less significant but more complex than generally thought. Points out that Winthrop sought to put the spotlight on Hutchinson in order to deflect attention from other prominent men involved in the episode. Emphasizes the conflicts between Cotton and Shepard and contends that Wheelwright's trial was far more significant than Hutchinson's.

J Interdis Hist 37: 459-60; *NEQ* 79: 314-16; *WMQ* 63: 604-607.

17 American Revolution

440 Bodle, Wayne. *The Valley Forge Winter: Civilians and Soldiers in War.* University Park: Pennsylvania State University Press, 2002. xiv, 335 p. ISBN 0271022302; ISBN 9780271022307; OCLC 50292530; LC Call Number E234 .B63; Dewey 973.3/341 21. Citations: 7.
Sets the Valley Forge story in the context of Sir William Howe's 1777–78 campaign and the battles at Brandywine and Germantown. Indicates that the Continental Army was not on the verge of collapse at the end of 1777, but that Washington sought to cultivate that image in order to convince Congress and the states to supply more provisions and to institute reforms. Finds little evidence that Baron von Steuben had a significant impact on the effectiveness of the American force.
JAH 91: 219-20; *J Mil Hist* 67: 1279-80; *WMQ* 60: 914-17.

441 Brodsky, Alyn. *Benjamin Rush: Patriot and Physician.* New York: Truman Talley Books, 2004. viii, 404 p. ISBN 0312309112; ISBN 9780312309114; OCLC 54006701; LC Call Number E302.6.R85; Dewey 973.3/092. Citations: 3.
Presents a biography for general readership that covers Rush's ancestry, education in Scotland, work as a physician in Philadelphia, time in Europe, role in the Revolution (particularly as a pamphleteer, instigator of Thomas Paine, and signer of the Declaration of Independence), friend to the other Founders, and leader in movements for mental health reform and the education of women.
Booklist 100: 1692; *Penn Hist* 72: 254-55; *PMHB* 129: 485-86.

442 Buchanan, John. *The Road to Valley Forge: How Washington Built the Army that Won the Revolution.* Hoboken, N.J.: John Wiley and Sons, 2004. xvi, 368 p. ISBN 0471441562; ISBN 9780471441564; OCLC 54372030; LC Call Number E259 .B83; Dewey 973.3/3/092. Citations: 2.

Recounts Washington's leadership between August 1776 and the winter of 1777–78, describing battles and leaders and analyzing Washington's decisions. Argues that Washington gained confidence and experience as time wore on, profitably listened to his advisors, dealt well with politicians, understood and acknowledged his own shortcomings, and developed remarkable rapport with his men.
Booklist 101: 296; *HRNB* 33: 105-106; *J Mil Hist* 69: 549-51.

443 Buker, George E. *The Penobscot Expedition: Commodore Saltonstall and the Massachusetts Conspiracy of 1779*. Annapolis, Md.: Naval Institute Press, 2002. xii, 204 p. ISBN 1557502129; ISBN 9781557502124; OCLC 47869426; LC Call Number E235 .B85; Dewey 973.3/35 21. Citations: 4.
Tells the story of a failed American military expedition, mounted by General Solomon Lovell and Captain Dudley Saltonstall against a fortified British position near Penobscot Bay in Maine. Explains that Saltonstall was court-martialed, Lovell escaped blame, and Paul Revere was reprimanded for cowardice and disobeying an order.
JAH 90: 210.

444 Burg, David F., ed. *The American Revolution: An Eyewitness History*. New York: Facts on File, 2001. xvi, 432 p. ISBN 0816041350; ISBN 9780816041350; OCLC 45532471; LC Call Number E275.A2 B87; Dewey 973.3/092/2. Citations: 0.
Presents chronologies, commentary, and documents designed to give students a sense of the Revolution through the eyes of participants. Includes excerpts from letters, diaries, speeches, and newspaper articles, as well as drawings and maps.
Booklist 98: 1175.

445 Chadwick, Bruce. *The First American Army: The Untold Story of George Washington and the Men Behind America's First Fight for Freedom*. Naperville, Ill.: Sourcebooks, 2005. 399 p. ISBN 1402205066; ISBN 9781402205064; OCLC 60931428; LC Call Number E259 .C43; Dewey 973.3/4 22. Citations: 1.
Uses diaries and journals to tell the story of the Revolution from the perspective of eight men, including four enlisted soldiers (Elijah Fisher, John Greenwood, Ebenezer Wild, and Jeremiah Greenman), two officers (James McMichael and Sylvanus Seely), a chaplain (Ammi Robbins), and a physician (Lewis Beebe). Covers Benedict Arnold's march to Quebec, soldiers' family lives, Washington's views of the common soldier, treatment of prisoners of war, and the positions of women and African Americans.
Booklist 102: 15-16; *JSH* 73: 155-57.

446 Chadwick, Bruce. *George Washington's War: The Forging of a Revolutionary Leader and the American Presidency*. Naperville, Ill.: Sourcebooks, 2004. 569 p. ISBN 1402202229 (hbk.); ISBN 9781402202223 (hbk.); ISBN 140220406X (pbk.); ISBN 9781402204067 (pbk.); OCLC 54487503; LC Call Number E312.25 .C48; Dewey 973.3/3/092 22. Citations: 1.
Outlines the challenges that Washington faced in developing a reliable, professional fighting force, such as short-term enlistments, provisioning, and

wages. Suggests that Washington understood the value of inspiration and of keeping his force together in order to outlast the British.
Booklist 100: 1418; *LJ* 129n7: 99.

447 Chávez, Thomas E. *Spain and the Independence of the United States: An Intrinsic Gift.* Albuquerque: University of New Mexico Press, 2002. xii, 286 p. ISBN 0826327931; ISBN 9780826327932; ISBN 9780826327949; ISBN 082632794X; OCLC 48265526; LC Call Number E269.S63; Dewey 973.3/46. Citations: 11.
Reviews Spanish involvement in the American Revolutionary War, suggesting that the government of Charles III was able to balance Spain's numerous interests and commitments in South America, the Caribbean, and the Gulf Coast of North America, while seeking to reclaim Minorca and Gibraltar in Europe. Notes that the siege of Gibraltar was the primary objective for Madrid, followed in importance by the war in the Caribbean and the American Revolution. Concludes that "United States independence, as we know it today, probably would not have happened without Spain" and that "The overall Spanish strategy is what finally resulted in the defeat of Great Britain."
18c Stds 38: 539-45; *FHQ* 82: 223-25; *HAHR* 85: 730-31; *HRNB* 31: 12-13; *JAH* 90: 209; *J Mil Hist* 67: 561-63; *JSH* 69: 881-82; *SCHM* 104: 139-41; *SHQ* 106: 476-77.

448 Cogliano, Francis D. *American Maritime Prisoners in the Revolutionary War: The Captivity of William Russell.* Annapolis, Md.: Naval Institute Press, 2001. xv, 218 p. ISBN 1557501947; ISBN 9781557501943; OCLC 45668882; LC Call Number E281.R87; Dewey 973.3/71. Citations: 3.
Describes the experiences of several thousand American seamen who were captured during the Revolutionary War, focusing on the plight of William Russell, a Massachusetts schoolmaster who had participated in the Boston Tea Party and in the Rhode Island campaign of 1778, became a privateer, and was captured in September 1779 and held at Mill Prison, just outside of Plymouth, England. Discusses Russell's detention there from December 1779 until his release in a prisoner exchange in June 1782. Examines British prison administration and discipline, food, sanitary conditions, and medical facilities and describes illnesses among jailed Americans, ways in which prisoners governed themselves, resistance to authority, escape attempts, and efforts to obtain news from America.
J Mil Hist 66: 552-53.

449 Cohen, Sheldon S. *British Supporters of the American Revolution, 1775-1783: The Role of the "Middling-Level" Activists.* Woodbridge, Suffolk, U.K.: Boydell Press, 2004. xvi, 181 p. ISBN 1843830116; ISBN 9781843830115; OCLC 55616128; LC Call Number E249.3 .C64; Dewey 973.3. Citations: 6.
Studies five "middling-level" persons—two merchants, two nonconformist religious leaders, and one apothecary—who assisted in some way American seaman prisoners of war held in England and Ireland. Explains that the American sailors were treated as traitors and pirates, and thus were denied the status of prisoners of war. Traces poor treatment of prisoners, including mental

abuse, to their being charged with treason and describes the terrible physical conditions of all three prisons. Highlights the work of Griffith Williams, a London apothecary who helped to hide escapees and to ferry them from London to the safety of the Continent.
AHR 111: 562-63; *JAH* 92: 1417-18.

450 Cox, Caroline. *A Proper Sense of Honor: Service and Sacrifice in George Washington's Army*. Chapel Hill: University of North Carolina Press, 2004. xxii, 338 p. ISBN 080782884X; ISBN 9780807828847; OCLC 54529087; LC Call Number E259 .C695; Dewey 973.3/4 22. Citations: 14.
Describes the make-up and values of the common soldiery and officer corps, military justice and punishment, diseases and military medicine, soldier death and burial, and rules and actual treatment of prisoners of war. Explains that the Continental Army reflected colonial views of class and the social composition of European forces, due to "the unthinking decision to divide the army into officers who were gentlemen and soldiers who were not." Notes that, as a result of this social division, officers focused on personal honor, while common soldiers concerned themselves with mere survival. Finds significant differences in punishments assigned to soldiers (e.g., floggings, running the gauntlet, execution) and to officers (public or private reprimands, dismissal from the army). Discovers that officers received better health care than did soldiers, that officers who died in service warranted public mention, while soldiers suffering the same fate remained unnamed, and that higher-status prisoners received better treatment than common soldiers. Concludes that captured enlisted soldiers were forced to consider whether "the honorable thing to do was to choose death rather than serve with the British" and that many opted for the former "to protect and defend a more refined sense of dignity and honor than the world would allow them."
AHR 110: 1165-66; *GHQ* 89: 414-16; *JAH* 92: 590; *JER* 26: 122-25; *J Mil Hist* 69: 230-31; *NCHR* 82: 101-102; *WMQ* 63: 203-205.

451 Dallison, Robert L. *Hope Restored: The American Revolution and the Founding of New Brunswick*. Fredericton, N.B.: Goose Lane Editions and New Brunswick Military Heritage Project, 2003. 120 p. ISBN 0864923716; ISBN 9780864923714; OCLC 52837502; LC Call Number E 263 .N9 D34; LC Call Number F1043 .D28; Dewey 971.5/101. Citations: 2.
Relates the experiences of Loyalist regiment members who settled in New Brunswick after the American Revolution. Provides details on the specific regiments, including the various engagements in which they were involved. Describes the difficulties Loyalists experienced in their relocation to New Brunswick. Stresses that severe weather added to the privations of early settlement life and concludes that some of the settlers were unable to "make the necessary adjustment or face another challenge."
CHR 85: 816-18.

452 Dorigny, Marcel and Marie-Jeanne Rossignol, eds. *La France et les Amériques au temps de Jefferson et de Miranda*. Paris: Société des Études

Robespierristes, 2001. 173 p. ISBN 2908327430; ISBN 9782908327434; OCLC 301675741; LC Call Number E183.8 F8F7; Dewey 970.3. Citations: 4.

Collects essays on French, North American, and South American revolutions, particularly the diplomatic, political, economic, social, and military aspects. Includes essays on political biography and elite adaptation to shifting economic and political environments in Louisiana and Cuba.

HAHR 83: 777-78.

453 Dunn, Walter S. *People of the American Frontier: The Coming of the American Revolution*. Westport, Conn.: Praeger, 2005. xi, 235 p. ISBN 0275981819; ISBN 9780275981815; OCLC 56685251; LC Call Number E179.5 .D95; Dewey 973.2. Citations: 0.

Claims that settlers rarely fought with Indians from the 1750s to the 1770s. Notes that one exception, Pontiac's Uprising, can be attributed to the influence of French traders, and that another, the American Revolution, came about when the British hired Indians to raid colonial settlements. Suggests that continuing relationships between French traders and Indians allowed the interior French fur trade to remain during this period, despite the best efforts of British merchants to capture this business. Contends that western colonial merchants were moved to Revolution in part because of British policy prohibiting trans-Appalachian land speculation and because of the movement of important British army customers to new posts along the east coast. Finds that British merchants had relatively few interactions with frontier farmers and that there were fewer such farmers than historians have claimed.

Booklist 101: 1744; *HRNB* 33: 144.

454 Fingerhut, Eugene R. and Joseph S. Tiedemann, eds. *The Other New York: The American Revolution beyond New York City, 1763–1787*. Albany: State University of New York Press, 2005. xi, 246 p. ISBN 0791463710; ISBN 9780791463710; OCLC 54852888; LC Call Number E263.N6 O87; Dewey 974.7/03 22. Citations: 3.

Includes articles on Kings, Queens, Suffolk, Richmond, Staten Island, Westchester, Dutchess, Orange, Ulster, Albany, Tryon, and Charlotte counties in the Revolutionary era. Essays discuss each region and outlines the geography of the county, political alliances, and the racial, religious, and social diversity of each area. Describes how rural New Yorkers reacted to British attempts to exercise greater control over the colonists. Notes that British action affected every New Yorker, but that some reacted more violently to the Townsend duties or the Coercive Act than to the Stamp Act. Explains that freehold and tenant farmers found colonial boycotts more burdensome and damaging than the Stamp Act and thus that boycotts of British goods encouraged loyalism among some farmers.

AHR 111: 829-30; *JAS* 41: 243-44.

455 Fischer, David Hackett. Washington's Crossing. New York: Oxford University Press, 2004. x, 564 p. ISBN 0195170342 (hbk.); ISBN 9780195170344 (hbk.); ISBN 019518159X (pbk.); ISBN 9780195181593 (pbk.); OCLC 53075605; LC Call Number E263.P4 F575; Dewey 973.3/32. Citations: 28.

Places Washington's crossing of the Delaware River in the context of the 1776 campaign, which was disastrous for the Continental Army. Discusses the British and Hessian armies involved, including their cultures and leadership and asserts that the Continentals, despite repeated defeats, displayed "an extraordinary optimism, even an optimistic fatalism" prior to the attack on Trenton. Explains that American commanders were disorganized, the troops undisciplined, and most enlistments expiring. Claims, then, that Washington's offensive in December perhaps saved the American cause, as victories at Trenton and then at Princeton buoyed American hopes and preserved Washington's command. Includes illustrations, maps, and appendices on troop strength, casualties, and weather.

AHR 110: 784; *Booklist* 100: 946; *JAH* 92: 589; *LJ* 129n2: 106; *Penn Hist* 73: 366-69; *PMHB* 129: 353-54; *RAH* 32: 159-65; *VMHB* 113: 179-80; *VQR* 80: 280.

456 Fleming, Thomas J. *Washington's Secret War: The Hidden History of Valley Forge*. New York: Smithsonian Books/Collins, 2005. xiii, 384 p. ISBN 0060829621; ISBN 9780060829629; OCLC 61529854; LC Call Number E234 .F43; Dewey 973.3/341 22. Citations: 0.

Describes Washington's leadership of the Continental Army during the Valley Forge encampment in winter of 1777–78, calling his successful preservation of the army a "secret war." Stresses that Washington not only had to deal with the military movements and activities of the British, but also had to work with the Continental Congress and fellow army officers who sought a change in leadership. Discusses the "Conway Cabal," and Congress's open interference in military affairs. Portrays Washington as a master politician, who was able to appear steady and above the fray. Intended for a general readership.

Booklist 102: 22; *LJ* 130n14: 157-59.

457 Gabriel, Michael P. *Major General Richard Montgomery: The Making of an American Hero*. Cranbury, N.J.: Fairleigh Dickinson University Press, 2002. 277 p. ISBN 0838639313; ISBN 9780838639313; OCLC 48163369; LC Call Number E207.M7 G33; Dewey 973.3/092. Citations: 2.

Discusses the life and career of Montgomery, characterizing him as dutiful, somewhat fatalistic, and very capable. Describes his northern campaign, the siege of St. Johns, negotiations with Canadians and the English, and the march to Montreal. Defends Montgomery's decision to attack Montreal as calculated, but too optimistic.

JAH 90: 623-24; *J Mil Hist* 67: 560-61; *Penn Hist* 71: 239-41.

458 Gabriel, Michael P., ed. *Québec During the American Invasion, 1775–1776: The Journal of François Baby, Gabriel Taschereau, and Jenkin Williams*. East Lansing: Michigan State University Press, 2005. 141 p. ISBN 0870137409 (pbk.); ISBN 9780870137402 (pbk.); OCLC 57069273; LC Call Number E231 .B125; Dewey 971.4/45102 22. Citations: 3.

Presents an annotated English version of the "Rapport Baby," an official report describing rural Quebec during its occupation by the Continental Army in 1775 and 1776. Details the reactions of the Quebec peasantry to the invaders at the onset of the American Revolutionary War, ranging from resisting orders to taking up arms, supporting "rebellion" against the Americans, pledging allegiance to Congress or the king, holding local elections, spreading propaganda and rumors, and informing against opponents.
CHR 88: 524-25; *J Mil Hist* 70: 500-501.

459 Golway, Terry. *Washington's General: Nathanael Greene and the Triumph of the American Revolution.* New York: Henry Holt, 2005. x, 355 p. ISBN 0805070664; ISBN 9780805070668; OCLC 55220273; LC Call Number E207.G9; Dewey 973.3/3/092. Citations: 2.
Contends that Greene, a revolutionary hero, has been largely overlooked, due to his death soon after the end of the Revolutionary War. Traces the life of Greene, including military and business ambitions, characterizing him as a hard worker who rose from the Continental Army's quartermaster to the victorious commander of the American Southern army.
Booklist 101n8: 702; *LJ* 130n2: 97.

460 Gordon, John W. *South Carolina and the American Revolution: A Battlefield History.* Columbia: University of South Carolina Press, 2003. xix, 238 p. ISBN 157003480X; ISBN 9781570034800; OCLC 50333997; LC Call Number E230.5.S6; Dewey 973.3/3/09757. Citations: 4.
Reviews chronologically the Revolution's engagements in South Carolina. Explains the 1780 Charleston campaign, later efforts to retake the city during 1781 and 1782, frontier fighting early in the war, colonial society and politics, lowcountry-backcountry divisions, and the long-term effects of the Regulator movement.
FHQ 82: 490-92; *GHQ* 88: 98-99; *J Mil Hist* 68: 246-48; *JSH* 70: 649-51; *NCHR* 81: 233-34; *SCHM* 104: 130-32.

461 Gould, Eliga H. and Peter S. Onuf, eds. *Empire and Nation: The American Revolution in the Atlantic World.* Baltimore, Md.: Johns Hopkins University Press, 2005. viii, 381 p. ISBN 0801879124; ISBN 9780801879128; OCLC 55149281; LC Call Number E209 .E45; Dewey 973.3/1 22. Citations: 33.
Presents articles on British policies prior to the Revolution, nationalism and internationalism, war and state formation, the constitutional thought of John Adams, the republicanization of the common law, society in the tobacco South, Irish immigration to Philadelphia in the last decade of the eighteenth century, the development of federalism, civil society, religion, and politics in post-Revolutionary America, the Loyalist diaspora, early slave narratives, the British Caribbean in the Revolutionary era, and concepts of freedom and migration.
AHR 111: 435-36; *EHR* 121: 861-63; *HRNB* 34: 5; *JAH* 92: 1416-17; *JAS* 40: 664; *J Brit Stds* 45: 413-14; *JER* 26: 668-70; *JSH* 73: 683-85; *NCHR* 83: 271-72; *16c J* 39: 1177-78; *SCHM* 108: 280-82; *VMHB* 113: 416-18; *WMQ* 64: 203-20.

462   Grainger, John D. *The Battle of Yorktown, 1781: A Reassessment.* Rochester, N.Y.: Boydell Press, 2005. 203 p. ISBN 1843831376; ISBN 9781843831372; OCLC 57311901; LC Call Number E241.Y6; Dewey 973.3/37. Citations: 4.

Places the Yorktown engagement in the context of the larger military campaign and political environment. Explains that the battle resulted in a new stalemate, not the end of the conflict, as the British still held New York. Finds instead that the battle decisively undermined parliamentary support for the North ministry. Views Yorktown as "one of those relatively minor events which have disproportionate effects, because it brought the participants' minds to the point of the larger decision of whether to continue the war."

EHR 121: 358-59; *J Mil Hist* 70: 502-504.

463   Hall, Leslie. *Land & Allegiance in Revolutionary Georgia.* Athens: University of Georgia Press, 2001. xvi, 231 p. ISBN 0820322628; ISBN 9780820322629; OCLC 44172950; LC Call Number E263.G3; Dewey 975.8/03. Citations: 4.

Suggests that revolutionary ideology, resentment of parliamentary taxation, and suspicion of standing armies was relatively unimportant in Georgia, and that the colony benefited greatly from imperial economic concessions and the stationing of British regulars near large populations of Creeks and Cherokees. Explains that, as a result, revolution came late and tepidly to Georgia and that, throughout the 1770s and 1780s, changes in colonial governments brought the use formulaic pledges of allegiance as a means of retaining property. Notes that, for most Georgians, the main aim was protection of economic interests, specifically land and slaves, so pledges were seen more as a sort of currency than as a sound commitment. Points out that, typically, Georgians were more concerned with land acquisition, Indian attacks, and slave rebellions, than about reports on the progress of the revolution in other colonies. Concludes that the final straw in favor of revolution in Georgia was rumors in 1775 of British agents arming Indians and seeking to incite slave uprisings. Contends that, even so, Georgians remained willing to offer loyalty in exchange for effective civil government and material security.

AHR 107: 1225-26; *GHQ* 86: 620-34; *JAH* 89: 204-205; *JSH* 68: 680-81; *NCHR* 78: 389-90; *WMQ* 60: 243-46.

464   Hallahan, William H. *The Day the Revolution Ended, 19 October 1781.* New York: Wiley, 2004. ix, 292 p. ISBN 0471262404; ISBN 9780471262404; OCLC 51855501; LC Call Number E230 .H35; Dewey 973.3/37. Citations: 1.

Presents a narrative of the final year of the Revolutionary War for a general audience. Describes British and American military actions in Virginia, which led to Cornwallis's surrender at Yorktown. Begins with Benedict Arnold's raid on Virginia in late 1780, which highlighted the state's vulnerabilities and encouraged greater preparation among patriot leaders. Describes the clashes between Cornwallis and Greene during the Carolina campaign, including the battle of Guilford Courthouse.

Booklist 100: 476; *J Mil Hist* 68: 594-95; *VMHB* 113: 87-88.

465 Hammon, Neal O. and Richard Taylor. *Virginia's Western War: 1775–1786*. Mechanicsburg, Penn.: Stackpole Books, 2002. xl, 279 p. ISBN 081171389X; ISBN 9780811713894; OCLC 48951408; LC Call Number E263.V8; Dewey 973.3/3. Citations: 1.
Traces the development of frontier Virginia during an intense period of Indian and revolutionary violence, from land speculation after the French and Indian War through Anthony Wayne's 1795 expedition against Native Americans in the upper Ohio River Valley. Claims that the economic and military value of frontier Virginia played a critical role in the movement for American independence.
J Mil Hist 67: 935-36; *VMHB* 110: 406-407.

466 Harvey, Robert. *"A Few Bloody Noses"*: *The Realities and Mythologies of the American Revolution*. Woodstock, N.Y.: Overlook Press, 2002. xii, 478 p. ISBN 1585672734; ISBN 9781585672738; OCLC 48965189; LC Call Number E208 .H376; Dewey 973.3. Citations: 2.
Seeks to refute myths about the American Revolution. Notes that many British thought that the colonies were "of little importance and certainly not worth the waste of young men's lives or large amounts of money," and that the British army struggled to counter "a continual guerilla war of attrition." Suggests that Americans were more concerned about restrictions on westward expansion than about taxation without representation. Intended for general readership.
Booklist 98: 1672.

467 Higginbotham, Don, ed. *Revolution in America: Considerations and Comparisons*. Charlottesville: University of Virginia Press, 2005. xi, 230 p. ISBN 0813923832 (hbk.); ISBN 9780813923833 (hbk.); ISBN 0813923840 (pbk.); ISBN 9780813923840 (pbk.); OCLC 58043470; LC Call Number E208 .H58; Dewey 973.3. Citations: 1.
Contains eight essays covering George Washington and the generation of Virginians who took a leading role in the American Revolution, the ways in which the experience of war influenced the development of national institutions and nationalism, particularly in the context of European patterns of state formation, the influence of European military training on military education in the United States, and comparisons of the American South on the eve of the Civil War to the British colonies on the eve of the American Revolution.
FHQ 85: 342-45; *HRNB* 35: 62; *JER* 28: 517-22; *JSH* 73: 428-30; *NCHR* 84: 100-101; *VMHB* 114: 517-19.

468 Huff, Randall. *The Revolutionary War Era*. Westport, Conn.: Greenwood Press, 2004. xxi, 241 p. ISBN 0313322627; ISBN 9780313322624; OCLC 54529427; LC Call Number E163 .H84; Dewey 973.3. Citations: 0.
Presents a reference work focusing on ordinary life and covering chronologically the period from 1763 to 1783. Intended for high school and college students.
Hist Teach 39: 267-68.

469 Isaac, Rhys. *Landon Carter's Uneasy Kingdom: Revolution and Rebellion on a Virginia Plantation.* New York: Oxford University Press, 2004. xxii, 423 p. ISBN 0195159268; ISBN 9780195159264; OCLC 53284882; LC Call Number F229.C32; Dewey: 975.5/2302/092. Citations: 14.

Explores the tensions between tradition and change during the American Revolution in Virginia, focusing on interactions between the local and the Atlantic, between the personal and the political, and between common narratives of members of different classes. Uses Landon Carter's diaries to examine in detail the Revolution-era attack on patriarchal authority in Virginia. Provides a brief biography of Carter, describes the various texts that became Carter's Diary, and argues that the Diary "deserves a prominent place in American literature" as a mainstay of "gentrylore," stories told by agricultural elites about those underlings who have worked the land. Presents "Landon Carter as a storyteller," the "scriptwriter and theater director of a major historical stage show." Explains the ways in which Carter wrote himself, his slaves, his family, and his neighbors into various narrative structures and envisions the alternate stories that Carter's objects would have told. Contends that Carter had a "split personality," one divided between his devotion to the patriarchal order and his desire for self-conscious, rational order.

AHR 111: 830-31; *18c Stds* 39: 130-34; *J Soc Hist* 39: 1240-44; *JSH* 72: 429-42; *LJ* 129n11: 82; *NCHR* 82: 260-61; *RAH* 33: 493-500; *VMHB* 113: 182-85; *WMQ* 62: 295-98.

470 Ketchum, Richard M. *Divided Loyalties: How the American Revolution Came to New York.* New York: Henry Holt, 2002. xiv, 447 p. ISBN 0805061193; ISBN 9780805061192; OCLC 49225983; LC Call Number E263.N6; Dewey 974.7/03. Citations: 6.

Uses correspondence and diaries, among other sources, to highlight the conflicts among colonists in Revolutionary New York. Points out that the colony factionalized relatively quickly and reflected larger imperial, political, and economic divisions. Tells stories of friends and families torn apart by the Revolution, featuring in particular the Livingstons and DeLanceys. Includes descriptions of noteworthy locations and revolutionary fortifications in New York City and an appendix of the main actors of the era.

Booklist 99: 50; *LJ* 127n14: 192.

471 Knouff, Gregory T. *The Soldiers' Revolution: Pennsylvanians in Arms and the Forging of Early American Identity.* University Park: Pennsylvania State University Press, 2004. xxiv, 312 p. ISBN 027102335X; ISBN 9780271023359; OCLC 53284890; LC Call Number E263.P4; Dewey 973.3/448. Citations: 11.

Examines soldiers' motivations and their ties to communities, arguing that local conditions largely determined one's armed participation in the Revolution. Finds that, among Pennsylvanians, taking up arms was directly related to the closeness of the war to one's home and to the region's concept of man-as-warrior, which was particularly operative along the western frontier. Points out that the masculine ideal and the notion of "women's work" sometimes proved fatal in camps where soldiers refused to keep living quarters sanitary. Examines pension records for what they indicate about veterans' memories of the Revolution,

arguing that those who served made the United States a "localist white male nation," based "on racism, male dominance, and the obfuscation of class conflict." Contends that localism "yielded a new, popular world view in which identities were simply polarized: whites and nonwhites," yet was also compatible with support for the federal constitution. Concludes that "Various imagined communities were, then, the bedrock of the national republic."
JAH 91: 1429-30; *JER* 25: 115-18; *J Mil Hist* 69: 551-52; *Penn Hist* 71: 512-14; *PMHB* 129: 351-52; *WMQ* 61: 773-76.

472 Krawczynski, Keith. *William Henry Drayton: South Carolina Revolutionary Patriot*. Baton Rouge: Louisiana State University Press, 2001. xii, 358 p. ISBN 0807126616; ISBN 9780807126615; OCLC 45668917; LC Call Number E302.6.D7; Dewey 975.7/03/092. Citations: 4.
Aims to rescue Drayton "from the ash heap of history." Studies his political career in the context of Revolutionary South Carolina, rejecting the idea that Drayton's support of the Revolution was an effort to avoid debt repayment, an opportunity to take revenge on British officials who blocked his attempts to gain Catawba Indian lands, or a move to regain popularity. Attributes Drayton's adoption of the patriot cause to constitutional and ideological concerns. Contends that Drayton's opposition to non-importation (1768–70) was not in support of royal policy, but rather his rejection of an extra-legal assembly. Notes that Drayton had changed positions by 1775 due to increased harshness of British policy. Describes Drayton's efforts to neutralize backcountry loyalism and his pro-independence radicalism of 1775 and 1776. Examines Drayton's service in the Continental Congress from March 1778 until his death in September 1779, including his role in factionalism and his dispute with Henry Laurens.
FHQ 82: 225-27; *GHQ* 86: 121-23; *JAH* 89: 1027-28; *JSH* 69: 410-12; *NCHR* 79: 272-73; *SCHM* 105: 234-37; *WMQ* 60: 248-50.

473 Lee, Wayne E. *Crowds and Soldiers in Revolutionary North Carolina: The Culture of Violence in Riot and War*. Gainesville: University Press of Florida, 2001. xvi, 380 p. ISBN 0813020956; ISBN 9780813020952; OCLC 45202020; LC Call Number E263.N8; Dewey 975.6/03. Citations: 11.
Describes the culture of violence in Revolution-era North Carolina, focusing on riots and military engagements, particularly their shared cultural meanings. Finds that, even while rioting or war making, persons held to behaviors rooted in apparent legitimacy. Explains how colonists adapted European norms on aggression after their encounters with Native Americans and how Revolutionary militiamen interpreted the same norms differently from Continental soldiers. Studies the Stamp Act and Enfield land riots, and the early phases of the Regulator movement. Finds that in each instance the rioters started by petitioning government and, when that failed, took limited but forceful action against specific targets, while attempting to maintain an air of legitimacy. Argues that the same process of "adherence to form, demonization, and retaliatory escalation" led to increasing violence during the Revolutionary War in North Carolina in 1780 and 1781, violence that was informed both by knowledge of European military practices (e.g., standing professional armies,

the fighting of decisive battles, civil treatment of prisoners of war, protection of the civilian population) and the experiences of colonial militias (wars against Indians that were based on revenge, ambush, and surprise attacks, involved enslaved or killed captives, depended on the destruction of Native food resources, and made little distinction among men, women, and children).
AHR 107: 1225; *GHQ* 86: 124; *HRNB* 30: 101-102; *JAH* 89: 1024; *J Mil Hist* 66: 197-98; *JSH* 69: 409-410; *NCHR* 81: 104; *WMQ* 59: 767-70.

474 McCullough, David G. *1776: America and Britain at War*. London: Allen Lane, 2005. 386 p. ISBN 0743226712; ISBN 9780743226714; OCLC 57557578; LC Call Number E208 .M396; Dewey 973.3. Citations: 14.
Tells the story of the year 1776, noting that it was a difficult year for the American struggle against Great Britain, as New York was lost and the Continental Army lost battle after battle. Notes Washington's many strategic mistakes and attributes the immediate survival of the American cause to the escape of the Continental force from New York. Concludes that the nation's movement into the following year was due to Washington's leadership and persistence.
Booklist 101: 1100; *Booklist* 102: 87; *GHQ* 89: 544-46; *LJ* 130n6: 109; *LJ* 130n7: 102; *LJ* 130n19: 106.

475 Messer, Peter C. *Stories of Independence: Identity, Ideology, and History in Eighteenth-Century America*. DeKalb: Northern Illinois University Press, 2005. x, 258 p. ISBN 0875803504; ISBN 9780875803500; OCLC 61204306; LC Call Number E188 .M47; Dewey 973.3/1 22. Citations: 9.
Examines the ways in which historians of the Revolutionary era shaped their attitudes about the past. Divides historians into the provincial school, whose historians gave credit for colonial success to the colonists themselves, and imperial school, whose historians criticized colonists for mistreating Indians and owning slaves, while crediting the imperial structure for providing order. Notes that the generation after the Revolution saw an intellectual shift from republicanism to liberalism, which was heavily influenced by the writers of the Scottish Enlightenment. Views Commonwealth writers as influential on colonial historians who favored continued ties with Britain.
AHR 112: 500-501; *JAH* 93: 844-45; *JER* 28: 517-22; *JSH* 73: 425-26; *NEQ* 80: 329-31; *PMHB* 131: 110-111; *RAH* 35: 18-24; *VMHB* 114: 405-406; *WMQ* 63: 625-28.

476 Morley, Vincent. *Irish Opinion and the American Revolution, 1760–1783*. New York: Cambridge University Press, 2002. x, 366 p. ISBN 0521813867; ISBN 9780521813860; OCLC 50056191; LC Call Number E249.3 .M67; LC Call Number DK465.A4; Dewey 941.507. Citations: 15.
Studies Irish opinions about and the impact in Ireland of the American Revolution. Finds that the Irish were largely interested in the Revolution as a crisis within the empire and not as a cause for Ireland's separation from Britain. Argues that Irish public opinion shifted a great deal between 1775 and 1783, that the attitudes of Anglicans were heavily influenced by changing diplomatic and military circumstances, and that the Catholic community was significantly

divided in its response to the American Revolution. Confirms that the Catholic clerical and landed elites were staunchly pro-British throughout the period, but contends that the majority of Irish Catholics maintained an anti-British stance. Finds that after 1773 heightened tensions between the military and the civilian population led to attacks on and mutilations of soldiers. Notes that the American war allowed some Irish politicians to take significant economic and constitutional concessions from the weakened British government, that the political culture in Ireland changed during the period, and that debates on free trade and legislative independence sparked the emergence of a politically conscious and active middle class.

AHR 108: 1217-18; *EHR* 119: 995-96; *JAH* 90: 997-98; *J Mod Hist* 77: 771-73.

477 Morton, Joseph C. *The American Revolution*. Westport, Conn.: Greenwood Press, 2003. xviii, 218 p. ISBN 0313317925; ISBN 9780313317927; OCLC 51518291; LC Call Number E208 .M9; Dewey 973.3. Citations: 1.

Presents a narrative of the events leading up to, during, and directly after the American Revolution. Includes illustrations and biographical profiles of nineteen major figures, eleven primary documents, and an extensive annotated bibliography.

Hist Teach 38: 129-30.

478 Murray, Aaron R., ed. *American Revolution: Battles and Leaders*. New York: DK, 2004. 95 p. ISBN 078949888X (hbk.); ISBN 9780789498885 (hbk.); ISBN 0789498898 (pbk.); ISBN 9780789498892 (pbk.); OCLC 53973851; LC Call Number E208 .M8; Dewey 973.3/3. Citations: 0.

Presents information and statistics on leaders and battles of the American Revolution, including chronologically organized summaries of battles. Provides portraits, battle maps, photos, and other illustrations.

LJ 100n15: 1371.

479 Nash, Gary B. *The Unknown American Revolution: The Unruly Birth of Democracy and the Struggle to Create America*. New York: Viking, 2005. xxix, 512 p. ISBN 0670034207; ISBN 9780670034208; OCLC 58807699; LC Call Number E208 .N33; Dewey 973.3. Citations: 23.

Extends the American Revolution back to the mid-eighteenth century, when an increasing number of discontented African Americans, Indians, women, urban workers, and rural farmers began to demand better treatment in colonial society and thereby made possible the movement for American independence. Presents vignettes on Thomas Peters, Dragging Canoe, Venture Smith, Herman Husband, Boston King, Thomas Paine, Anthony Benezet, Joseph Brant, Ethan Allen, Mum Bett, Ebenezer McIntosh, and mutinous troops in the Continental Army. Discusses black participation in the Revolutionary War, the work of Quaker abolitionists, and how America missed its best opportunity to end slavery in the immediate aftermath of independence.

AHR 111: 827; *HRNB* 33: 143; *Hist Teach* 40: 283-84; *JAH* 93: 189-90; *JER* 26: 338-41; *LJ* 130n12: 98; *RAH* 34: 291-306.

480 Nester, William R. *The Frontier War for American Independence.* Mechanicsburg, Penn.: Stackpole Books, 2004. 423 p. ISBN 0811700771; ISBN 9780811700771; OCLC 52963301; LC Call Number E230 .N47; Dewey 973.3. Citations: 3.

Presents a military and diplomatic history of the American Revolutionary War. Examines British frontier policies and colonial responses, and describes, chronologically, western engagements of the War, including Spanish, British, and Native American campaigns in Florida and the Mississippi valley. Notes two types of campaigns, large-scale efforts undertaken by regulars or volunteers with assistance from Indian guides, scouts, and flankers, and small-scale raids by Indians with the occasional participation of white officers and volunteers. Asserts that the frontier war was "at once genocidal and decisive" in favor of the Americans, but that American military failures on the frontier might also have prolonged the Revolution. Explains that the frontier conflicts "diverted huge amounts of men, money, supplies, and energies from the East Coast." Concludes that the frontier war "accelerated the development of American nationalism" and that American "identity was forged in part by consciously contrasting it with 'savages,' who impeded the nation's destiny."
JAH 92: 197-98; *J Mil Hist* 69: 228-30.

481 Newman, Paul Douglas. *Fries's Rebellion: The Enduring Struggle for the American Revolution.* Philadelphia: University of Pennsylvania Press, 2004. xii, 259 p. ISBN 081223815X (hbk.); ISBN 9780812238150 (hbk.); ISBN 0812219201 (pbk.); ISBN 9780812219203 (pbk.); OCLC 55019128; LC Call Number E326 .N49; Dewey 973.4/4. Citations: 10.

Identifies 211 people who were involved in Fries's Rebellion (1798–99). Finds that many had fought in the American Revolution or were related to a veteran, most were German-American property owners from the middling economic and social orders. Notes that the Federalists' so-called "House Tax" and "Direct Tax," as well as the Sedition Act led to organized, largely peaceful resistance in which many of the revolutionary protest practices (e.g., raising liberty poles, forming associations to warn off assessors, and petitioning) were used. Contends that the rebels sought to participate in the determination of the constitutionality of taxation measures, a power that they believed had been earned from the American Revolution, but which even Jeffersonians believed went too far. Notes that the Rebellion "peacefully concluded without gunfire, fisticuffs, or bloodshed," and that President John Adams pardoned the rebels, causing the Hamiltonians to begin working against Adams's reelection.
AHR 111: 156-57; *JAH* 92: 963; *JER* 26: 341-43; *Penn Hist* 72: 255-59; *PMHB* 130: 336-37; *WMQ* 62: 557-61.

482 Nicolson, Colin. *The "Infamas Govener": Francis Bernard and the Origins of the American Revolution.* Boston, Mass.: Northeastern University Press, 2001. xiv, 326 p. ISBN 1555534635; ISBN 9781555534639; OCLC 44019484; LC Call Number F137.B47; Dewey 974.4/02/092. Citations: 1.

Reviews the life and career of Bernard, characterizing him as well-educated, but ill-prepared for the governorship of Massachusetts. Discusses the decline in British-colonial relations, leading to Bernard's call for troops in 1768 and the

sensational publication of his letters to British ministers. Contends that had Bernard condemned the Stamp Act publically and concentrated on winning over those who feared and opposed mob action, he would have been able to uphold royal authority in the colony through the early 1770s. Demonstrates that opposition to the leaders of the Boston crowd was significant in the legislature and in the towns. Blames Bernard for poor policy decisions that solidified colonial resistance. Finds that the British patronage system confirmed the notion of interests among royal servants, while in Massachusetts the concept of a disinterested officeholder had become more fully formed, though unintentionally and by necessity.
JAH 89: 203-204; *WMQ* 58: 1013-16.

483   Raphael, Ray. *The First American Revolution: Before Lexington and Concord.* New York: New Press, 2002. xiv, 273 p. ISBN 156584730X; ISBN 9781565847309; OCLC 47623909; LC Call Number E216 .R25; Dewey 973.3. Citations: 4.
Focuses on western Massachusetts prior to the Revolutionary War, noting that imperial policy affected the region in the 1760s and early 1770s and that area patriots reacted through intimidation of judges, councilors, and Crown servants. Emphasizes that citizen action was truly revolutionary and that "the revolutionaries of 1774 pioneered the concept of participatory democracy, with all the decisions made by popular consent." Concludes that this shift of power represented the "real" revolution and "far outreached the intentions of the so-called 'Founding Fathers.'"
JAH 89: 1509-10.

484   Raphael, Ray. *A People's History of the American Revolution: How Common People Shaped the Fight for Independence.* New York: New Press, 2001. xii, 386 p. ISBN 1565846532; ISBN 9781565846531; OCLC 44769144; LC Call Number E275.A2; Dewey 973.3/092/2. Citations: 12.
Presents a narrative of the American Revolution that emphasizes the roles of common people like Joseph Plumb Martin, Temperance Smith, and David George. Asserts that "By uncovering the stories of farmers, artisans, and laborers, we discern how plain folk helped create a revolution strong enough to evict the British Empire from the thirteen colonies" and that "by digging deeper still, we learn how people with no political standing—women, Native Americans, African Americans—altered the shape of a war conceived by others." Concludes that "The story of our nation's founding, told so often from the perspective of the founding fathers,' will never ring true unless it can take some account of the Massachusetts farmers who closed the courts, the poor men and boys who fought the battles, the women who followed the troops, the loyalists who viewed themselves as rebels, the pacifists who refused to sign oaths of allegiance, the Native Americans who struggled for their own independence, the southern slaves who fled to the British, [and] the northern slaves who negotiated their freedom by joining the Continental Army."
Booklist 97: 1223-24; *EHR* 118: 450-51;*18c Stds* 35: 326-32; *LJ* 126n1: 132; *PMHB* 126: 130-32; *RAH* 29: 502-510; *VMHB* 109: 330-31; *WMQ* 59: 326-30.

485 Rhodehamel, John, ed. *The American Revolution: Writings from the War of Independence.* New York: Literary Classics of the United States, distributed by Penguin Books, 2001. xviii, 878 p. ISBN 1883011914; ISBN 9781883011918; OCLC 45024354; LC Call Number E203.A579; Dewey 973.3. Citations: 4.
Presents more than 120 excerpts from the writings of about seventy persons who had first-hand knowledge of Revolutionary War campaigns and battles.
Booklist 97: 1528; *EAL* 38: 161-70; *LJ* 126n9: 138.

486 Schecter, Barnet. *The Battle for New York: The City at the Heart of the American Revolution.* New York: Walker, 2002. viii, 454 p. ISBN 0802713742; ISBN 9780802713742; OCLC 50658296; LC Call Number E230.5.N4; Dewey 973.3/32. Citations: 8.
Surveys the role of New York in the Revolution, contending that the British obsession with holding the city was ultimately a liability. Suggests that Washington nearly lost the Revolutionary War at the Battle of Long Island, but that British commander William Howe failed to press his advantage.
Booklist 99: 51; *LJ* 127n14: 192.

487 Stockdale, Eric. *'Tis Treason, My Good Man!: Four Revolutionary Presidents and a Piccadilly Bookshop.* New Castle, Del.: Oak Knoll Press, 2005. xii, 421 p. ISBN 1584561580; ISBN 9781584561583; ISBN 0712306994; ISBN 9780712306997; OCLC 57069359; LC Call Number Z330.6.L6; Dewey 381/.45002/09421. Citations: 4.
Considers American propaganda produced in England before and during the Revolutionary War, particularly the case of London bookseller John Stockdale, who dealt with authors in the colonies, with Benjamin Franklin, and with four future U.S. presidents.
EHR 122: 836-37.

488 Unger, Harlow Giles. *Lafayette.* Hoboken, N.J.: Wiley, 2002. xxiii, 452 p. ISBN 0471394327 (hbk.); ISBN 9780471394327 (hbk.); ISBN 9780471468851 (pbk.); ISBN 0471468851 (pbk.); OCLC 49775469; LC Call Number E207.L2; Dewey 944.04/092. Citations: 6.
Presents a biography of Lafayette for a general readership. Emphasizes Lafayette's personal relationship with Washington, his diplomatic and economic importance to Revolution-era Americans, and his fear of misuse of military and political power. Portrays Lafayette positively, but casts French radical republicans in a negative light.
J Mil Hist 67: 1287-88; *LJ* 127n13: 111; *VMHB* 110: 495-96; *WMQ* 62: 745-64.

489 Van Buskirk, Judith L. *Generous Enemies: Patriots and Loyalists in Revolutionary New York.* Philadelphia: University of Pennsylvania Press, 2002. x, 260 p. ISBN 0812236750 (hbk.); ISBN 9780812236750 (hbk.); ISBN 0812218221 (pbk.); ISBN 9780812218220 (pbk.); OCLC 49530268; LC Call Number E263.N6; Dewey 973.3/4471. Citations: 11.
Surveys relations among persons in revolutionary New York, maintaining that interactions remained largely civil and that adversarial conduct was limited by well-established cultural codes. Discusses business interactions, social visits,

family relationships, the political status of free and enslaved Africans, and the position of loyalists, particularly after the British surrender at Yorktown. Finds that few supported war, that many changed sides during the conflict, and that loyalist support for British troops was not ironclad. Concludes that patriot and loyalist communities in New York operated "in close, sustained proximity, each testing the limits of military and political authority" and "learned to survive on their own terms and in so doing became generous enemies."
AHR 109: 182-83; *JAH* 90: 998-99; *JAS* 37: 521-22; *JAS* 38: 172; *Penn Hist* 71: 237-39; *WMQ* 60: 453-56.

490 Walsh, John Evangelist. *The Execution of Major Andre*. New York: Palgrave, 2001. 239 p. ISBN 0312238894; ISBN 9780312238896; OCLC 46474098; LC Call Number E280.A5; Dewey 973.38/6/092. Citations: 5.
Discusses the trial and execution of Major John Andre after his capture by American troops in September 1780. Notes the significance of Andre to the plot with Benedict Arnold to surrender West Point and Washington's unusually stern refusal of clemency. Portrays Andre as ambitious and arrogant.
LJ 126n19: 81.

491 Ward, Harry M. *Between the Lines: Banditti of the American Revolution*. Westport, Conn.: Praeger, 2002. xiv, 329 p. ISBN 0275976335; ISBN 9780275976330; OCLC 48544193; LC Call Number E209 .W36 ; Dewey 973.3. Citations: 4.
Focuses on the space "between the lines" of the regular armies in the Revolution, where irregular and not strictly military activity occurred. Describes plundering, the movement of refugees, and action in various regions. Contends that "the banditti phenomenon" largely applied to loyalists who were provoked by patriot excesses. Explains that patriots generally controlled the countryside and that loyalists, "confronted with dire threats to their lives, families, and property," became refugees who "returned to wreak vengeance."
FHQ 82: 372-73; *GHQ* 87: 457-59; *JAH* 90: 999; *JSH* 72: 162-63; *NCHR* 80: 241-42; *SCHM* 104: 214-15; *VMHB* 110: 494-95.

492 Warner, Jessica. *John the Painter: Terrorist of the American Revolution*. New York: Thunder's Mouth Press, 2004. xiii, 298 p. ISBN 156858315X; ISBN 9781568583150; OCLC 57226329; LC Call Number E280.A49; Dewey 973.3/85. Citations: 4.
Examines the life of John Aitken, a Scotsman who apprenticed as a house painter, came to America as an indentured servant, and returned to Britain, where he burned the Portsmouth naval dockyard and was hanged for his crime in 1777. Notes Aitken's relationships with Silas Deane and with English spy Edward Bancroft and the complexities of class and ethnicity that shaped Aitken's life and activities.
Booklist 101: 298; *WMQ* 62: 745-64.

493 Weintraub, Stanley. *Iron Tears: America's Battle for Freedom, Britain's Quagmire, 1775–1783*. New York: Free Press, 2005. xviii, 375 p. ISBN:

0743226879; ISBN 9780743226875; OCLC 56592341; LC Call Number E249.3 .W45; Dewey 973.3. Citations: 9.

Examines "the war from three divergent and distinct vantage points," that of the battlefields, of the leadership of Washington, and of English politics and public opinion. Asserts that the chances that the British could put down the American uprising were small, even at the outset, given the length of supply lines, the government's bleak financial position, popular support for the Revolution in the colonies, mediocre leadership, and limited support in Parliament for continuing military action.

Booklist 101: 703; *HRNB* 33: 149; *JSH* 73: 155-57; *LJ* 130n1: 130.

494   Wilson, David K. *The Southern Strategy: Britain's Conquest of South Carolina and Georgia, 1775–1780.* Columbia: University of South Carolina Press, 2005. xvi, 341 p. ISBN 1570035733; ISBN 9781570035739; OCLC 56951286; LC Call Number E230.5.S7; Dewey 973.3/3/0975. Citations: 3.

Describes British efforts to subdue Virginia and the Carolinas prior to the southern campaign of 1780–81, from the battle at Great Bridge, Briar Creek, and Stono Ferry to the battles at Savannah and Waxhaws, just after the fall of Charleston. Argues that the failure of the later strategy was directly related to the British inability to activate southern loyalist support earlier in the war.

GHQ 90: 451-53; *J Mil Hist* 70: 828-29; *JSH* 73: 430-32; *NCHR* 83: 107-108; *SCHM* 107: 339-40.

495   York, Neil Longley. *Turning the World Upside Down: The War of American Independence and the Problem of Empire.* xiii, 193 p. ISBN 0275976939; ISBN 9780275976934; OCLC 52001228; LC Call Number E210 .Y67; Dewey 973.3/11. Citations: 3.

Surveys American history from exploration and colonization to the early nineteenth century, with particular emphasis on imperial and diplomatic contexts. Explains that the struggle among European powers for dominance in the New World was directly related for the desire for increased power in the Old World. Notes that the British ultimately accepted American independence in order to discourage a stronger Franco-American alliance and that the U.S. Constitution was created and the federal government constructed in response to external threats.

JAH 91: 994-95.

496   Young, Alfred F. *Masquerade: The Life and Times of Deborah Sampson, Continental Soldier.* New York: Alfred A. Knopf, 2004. x, 417 p. ISBN 0679441654; ISBN 9780679441656; OCLC 52079888; LC Call Number E276.G36; Dewey 973.3/092. Citations: 17.

Describes the life of Sampson, with emphasis on the eighteen months that she served in Continental Army in disguise, her later life (including marriage to Benjamin Gannett), the stories told about her, and her public efforts to secure a pension. Concludes that "Sampson defied convention, yet she repeatedly sought shelter by attempting to conform to convention."

AHR 112: 190; *Booklist* 100: 947; *JAH* 93: 502; *LJ* 129n2: 102-103; *LJ* 129n3: 143; *RAH* 32: 493-98; *WMQ* 63: 629-31.

18 War of 1812

497 Buel, Richard. *America on the Brink: How the Political Struggle over the War of 1812 Almost Destroyed the Young Republic.* New York: Palgrave, 2005. xiv, 302 p. ISBN 1403962383; ISBN 9781403962386; OCLC 55510543; LC Call Number E310 .B83; Dewey 320.973/09/034. Citations: 9.
Examines the political implications of the War of 1812. Suggests that the Federalists bear responsibility for the conflict with Britain because they provoked the Republican leadership into taking an extreme position in order to maintain credibility. Explains that the Federalists were thereby guilty of "orchestrating the extremism they pretended to restrain," largely through the rhetorical excesses that were required to deliver a unified message to the populace. Singles out Josiah Quincy for evoking "national honor" in the assault on the political opposition, particularly the Republican position on the embargo. Points out the irony of the Federalist dissolution after the Hartford Convention, which was assembled in an effort to retain public credibility.
AHR 111: 477; *JAH* 92: 968-69; *LJ* 130n5: 95.

498 Cusick, James G. *The Other War of 1812: The Patriot War and the American Invasion of Spanish East Florida.* Gainesville: University Press of Florida, 2003. xvi, 370 p. ISBN 0813026482; ISBN 9780813026480; OCLC 51810891; LC Call Number E359.5.F6; Dewey 973.5/23/09759. Citations: 9.
Describes the Patriot War, including its effect on the local population, as scorched-earth tactics and long-standing personal vendettas took their tolls. Contends that Madison did not openly encourage the involvement of the United States via the work of General George Mathews, but rather wanted Mathews to delay. Argues that Mathews instead actively sought to bring East Florida into the United States, regardless of risk or cost. Reveals that John Houstoun McIntosh, after meeting with Mathews in July 1811 to discuss the overthrow of the Spanish, immediately alerted those same authorities to Mathews's plans.

Concludes that the Patriot War should be better integrated into the historiography of the War of 1812.

AHR 110: 135-36; *FHQ* 83: 199-202; *GHQ* 88: 435-36; *JAH* 91: 1001; *JER* 25: 135-38; *J Mil Hist* 68: 599-601; *JSH* 71: 147-49; *SCHM* 107: 59-62.

499 Gough, Barry. *Fighting Sail on Lake Huron and Georgian Bay: The War of 1812 and Its Aftermath.* Annapolis: Naval Institute Press, 2002. xxiv, 215 p. ISBN 1557503141; ISBN 9781557503145; OCLC 48661322; LC Call Number E360 .G68; Dewey 973.5/25 21. Citations: 8.

Tells the story of the War of 1812 on the far northwestern frontier between the United States and Canada, focusing on Fort Mackinac, Michigan and British supply lines from York (present-day Toronto) to Lake Simcoe. Examines the region's geography, military and naval engagements, difficulties of supply and communication, relationships among military forces, the involvement of Native Americans, and Canadian trappers and merchants, and the aftermath of the War, which saw the abandonment of several naval establishments. Expresses surprise at "How a small party of armed men accomplished the negation of American advantages" in this region, especially given the challenges of naval warfare on Lake Huron and the surrounding areas. Explains that success required the possession of "local knowledge" to maintain Indian alliances and secure the fur trade until the end of the war.

JAH 90: 631-32; *J Mil Hist* 67: 566-67.

19 Constitution

500 Amar, Akhil Reed. *America's Constitution: A Biography*. New York: Random House, 2005. xii, 657 p. ISBN 1400062624; ISBN 9781400062621; OCLC 57170135; LC Call Number KF4541 .A87; Dewey 342.7302/9. Citations: 116.

Provides a "comprehensive account of America's Constitution, introducing the reader both to the legal text (and its consequences) and to the political deeds that gave rise to that text." Reviews each article and amendment, describing the historical and political context for each. Presents arguments forwarded by Federalists and Antifederalists on various matters, including the nature of the presidency and the power of the government to end slavery. Calls the genius of the Constitution its capability to embrace both the will of the state and that of the people. Describes the sources for the document, such as English government and practices, existing state constitutions, and philosophical models. Contends that the document was remarkably populist and republican for its day. Argues that the Founders never meant constitutional review to be done only by judges, but to be undertaken by the executive and by Congress, and even by the people in their service as jurors and their duties as citizens.

Booklist 102n1: 27; *LJ* 130n13: 104.

501 Berkin, Carol. *A Brilliant Solution: Inventing the American Constitution*. New York: Harcourt, 2002. 310 p. ISBN 0151009481; ISBN 9780151009480; OCLC 49663906; LC Call Number E303 .B47; Dewey 973.3/18. Citations: 7.

Discusses the Framers of the Constitution, noting that most were wealthy lawyers who never "questioned the class, gender or racial bases of their privileged status" and who "spoke of 'equality' or 'unalienable' rights as if these were universal in a society that sustained slavery and female subordination." Traces delegates' debates over a central government, representation, the executive and its veto power, elections, and amendments. Views the Convention

delegates as "men who recognized the idea of compromise, [and] who knew concessions had to be made for the greater good."
Booklist 98: 1914; *LJ* 127n13: 114-15; *NEQ* 77: 152-55; *PMHB* 127: 111-12.

502 Bogus, Carl T., ed. *The Second Amendment in Law and History: Historians and Constitutional Scholars on the Right to Bear Arms.* New York: New Press, 2002. x, 358 p. ISBN 1565846990; ISBN 9781565846999; OCLC 49315724; LC Call Number KF3941.S43; Dewey 344.73/0533. Citations: 8.
Surveys the Second Amendment debate from the point of view of collective rights theorists. Presents essays that argue that legal scholarship does not reflect a universal embrace of the individual rights view, that the standard model work is not solidly grounded in archival research, that the legislative history of the Amendment does not support the standard model's account, and that individual rights scholars rely too much on the ideas of the Antifederalists who, as a result of ratification defeat, were not well represented in the First Congress, which framed the Bill of Rights.
HRNB 30: 100; *JAH* 90: 212-13; *LJ* 127n1: 126-27.

503 Cerami, Charles A. *Young Patriots: The Remarkable Story of Two Men, Their Impossible Plan, and the Revolution that Created the Constitution.* Naperville, Ill.: Sourcebooks, 2005. xii, 354 p. ISBN 1402202350; ISBN 9781402202353; ISBN 1402202369; ISBN 9781402202360; OCLC 57693419; LC Call Number E303 .C38; Dewey 973.4/092/2. Citations: 0.
Focuses on the work of James Madison and Alexander Hamilton in crafting the Constitution and on the social and political contexts that led to the Convention. Attributes success in framing and ratification to the "rare personalities" of Madison and Hamilton and their willingness to work together at vital moments, despite personal differences. Intended for general readership.
Booklist 101: 1893; *HRNB* 34: 38.

504 Collier, Christopher. *All Politics Is Local: Family, Friends, and Provincial Interests in the Creation of the Constitution.* Hanover, N.H.: University Press of New England, 2003. xiv, 224 p. ISBN 158465290X; ISBN 9781584652908; OCLC 52838262; LC Call Number F99 .C65; Dewey 973.3/18 22. Citations: 5.
Attempts to explain resistance to the creation and ratification of the Constitution. Examines "dual localism": the specific concerns that each state's delegates brought to Philadelphia in 1787 and the considerations brought to bear in the various state ratifying conventions. Uses Connecticut as a case study, describing the geographical, political, social, and economic circumstances that influenced the state's decision-makers.
AHR 110: 132; *AJLH* 47: 331-32; *JAH* 91: 996-97; *JER* 25: 126-27; *NEQ* 78: 457-59; *WMQ* 61: 578-81.

505 Edling, Max M. *A Revolution in Favor of Government: Origins of the U.S. Constitution and the Making of the American State.* New York: Oxford University Press, 2003. xii, 333 p. ISBN 0195148703; ISBN 9780195148701; OCLC 50809975; LC Call Number KF4541 .E28; Dewey 342.73/029. Citations: 24.

Seeks to replace the two major approaches to understanding the origins of the U.S. Constitution—the Progressive view (themes of class and limitations of democracy) and the debate between classical republicanism and liberalism in the founding era—with a new paradigm. Claims that these interpretations follow too closely the vision of James Madison and thereby conclude that the Constitution is primarily concerned with limiting government power. Argues that the Constitution was, instead, an attempt to build a state and should be viewed in the context of Hamiltonian aspirations of establishing European-style economic and military power.

AHR 110: 132-33; *BHR* 78: 99-101; *HRNB* 32: 98-99; *JAH* 91: 1432-33; *J Econ Hist* 64: 1139-40; *JER* 25: 123-26.

506 Elkins, Stanley, Eric McKitrick, and Leo Weinstein, eds. *Men of Little Faith: Selected Writings of Cecelia Kenyon.* Amherst: University of Massachusetts Press, 2002. vi, 287 p. ISBN 1558493476; ISBN 9781558493476; OCLC 49512719; LC Call Number E210 .K46; Dewey 973.3 21. Citations: 2.

Provides a guide to Kenyon's work which, the editors argue, has been taken too much for granted. Emphasizes Kenyon's efforts to blunt the extraordinary influence of Charles Beard's theory of economic determinism and its application to the American founding era and to stress the role of ideas both in the Revolution and in the origins of the Constitution.

WMQ 61: 776-80.

507 Goldstone, Lawrence. *Dark Bargain: Slavery, Profits, and the Struggle for the Constitution.* New York: Walker and Company, 2005. vii, 230 p. ISBN 0802714609; ISBN 9780802714602; OCLC 59879537; LC Call Number KF4510 .G65; Dewey 342.7302/9 22. Citations: 3.

Explores the formation of the U.S. Constitution, attributing its compromises to a victory of men with regional economic interests over those with higher ideals.

Booklist 102: 9-10; *LJ* 130n16: 93.

508 Hendrickson, David C. *Peace Pact: The Lost World of the American Founding.* Lawrence: University Press of Kansas, 2003. xiv, 402 p. ISBN 0700612378; ISBN 9780700612376; OCLC 51059111; LC Call Number JK116 .H45; Dewey 320.973/09/033. Citations: 34.

Reinterprets the creation of the U.S. Constitution as a document inspired by "internationalist" precedents, a peace treaty that ended a war of revolution and became the basis of an alliance between the states. Compares the Philadelphia Convention to proceedings in Vienna (1815), Paris (1919), and San Francisco (1945), noting that the Framers likewise had as their goal a "society of states" similar to a European "grand alliance" that would occupy the middle ground between extremes of "international anarchy" and "universal empire."

AHR 109: 897-98; *HRNB* 32: 12; *JAH* 91: 220-21; *J Interdis His* 36: 274-75; *WMQ* 61: 184-87.

509 Johnson, Calvin H. *Righteous Anger at the Wicked States: The Meaning of the Founders' Constitution.* New York: Cambridge University Press, 2005. xv,

294 p. ISBN 9780521852326; ISBN 0521852323; OCLC 57068527; LC Call Number KF4541 .J64; Dewey 342.7302/9. Citations: 15.

Argues that popular anger at the states for failing to adopt the federal imposts of 1781 and 1783 and for refusing to pay their shares of Congress's annual requisitions led to the movement for the Constitution. Sees the Constitution primarily as a document that empowers Congress to levy and collect taxes, largely so that the national government may borrow money to wage wars.
AHR 111: 1508-1509; *JER* 28: 143-53; *J Interdis Hist* 37: 298-99.

510 Kaminski, John P. and Gaspare J. Saladino, eds. *The Documentary History of the Ratification of the Constitution, VII: Ratification of the Constitution by the States, Massachusetts.* Madison: State Historical Society of Wisconsin, 2001. 518 p. ISBN 0870203339; ISBN 9780870203336; ISBN 0870203266; ISBN 9780870203268; OCLC 63753851; LC Call Number KF4502 .D63; Dewey 342.73. Citations: 3.

Presents documents on the Constitutional ratification debates in Massachusetts. Provides public and private commentaries on the state convention, including excepts from journals, letters, minutes, reports, and newspaper articles.
WMQ 59: 776-86.

511 Larson, Edward J. and Michael P. Winship, eds. *The Constitutional Convention: A Narrative History from the Notes of James Madison.* New York: Modern Library, 2005. x, 229 p. ISBN 9780812975178 (hbk.); ISBN 0812975170 (pbk.); OCLC 58422567; LC Call Number KF4510 .M33; Dewey 342.7302/92. Citations: 7.

Edits and annotates Madison's text and the notes of other delegates in an effort to explain the main controversies of the Constitutional Convention.
Booklist 102: 9; *LJ* 130n97.

512 McGarvie, Mark D. *One Nation Under Law: America's Early National Struggles to Separate Church and State.* Dekalb: Northern Illinois University Press, 2004. xii, 256 p. ISBN 0875803334 (hbk.); ISBN 9780875803333 (hbk.); ISBN 0875806066 (pbk.); ISBN 9780875806068 (pbk.); OCLC 54500266; LC Call Number KF4865 .M35; Dewey 322/.1/0973 22. Citations: 10.

Argues that the separation of church and state resulted from the contract clause of the Constitution, not the First Amendment, and that the separation of church and state was part of the original intent of the Constitution's Framers. Contends that the Framers sought to replace colonial Christian communitarianism and classical republicanism with a radically new, liberal society. Asserts that "The process of disestablishment" represented America's "greatest ideological debate" prior to the Civil War. Finds that Jeffersonian Republicans were liberals who encouraged voluntary, self-harmonizing relations between free and equal citizens, while Christian and classical republican communitarians, largely Federalists, held to the belief that humans were lazy and sinful, making government and religion vital to the maintenance of social order. Contends that, in the Dartmouth College case, Americans accepted the institutional separation of religion from the state, even while continuing to disagree about the nature of humanity in civil society.

AHR 110: 1170-71; *AJLH* 47: 340-41; *CJH* 41: 589-91; *CH* 75: 683-84; *JAH* 92: 966-67; *JER* 26: 333-38; *JSH* 72: 657-59; *SCHM* 107: 64-65; *VMHB* 113: 318-19.

513 McGuire, Robert A. *To Form a More Perfect Union: A New Economic Interpretation of the United States Constitution.* New York: Oxford University Press, 2003. xii, 395 p. ISBN 0195139704; ISBN 9780195139709; OCLC 46837023; LC Call Number KF4520 .M393; Dewey 342.73/029. Citations: 13.
Undertakes econometric analyses of voting patterns in both the Philadelphia convention and the state ratifying conventions in order to test Beard's hypothesis statistically. Uses a multivariate statistical approach to roll call analysis in order to determine the marginal influence of specific independent variables (e.g., slaveholding, religious and educational backgrounds, age, military service, ethnicity, holdings of public and private securities and western lands, and credit or debtor status). Contends that the document's form is a direct result of the interests of writers and ratifiers of the Constitution and that the Constitution would have been much different had the composition of the Philadelphia convention and the state ratifying conventions included more debtors, more slaveholders, and more men from interior areas of the country.
JAH 91: 1431-32; *J Econ Hist* 66: 255-57.

514 Siemers, David J. *Ratifying the Republic: Antifederalists and Federalists in Constitutional Time.* Stanford, Calif.: Stanford University Press, 2002. xx, 292 p. ISBN 0804741069 (hbk.); ISBN 9780804741064 (hbk.); ISBN 9780804751032 (pbk.); ISBN 080475103X (pbk.); OCLC 49225420; LC Call Number JK116 .S54; Dewey 320.473/049/09033. Citations: 14.
Seeks to explain why questions about the Constitution's legitimacy seemed to cease after its ratification. Contends that Antifederalists helped to legitimize the Constitution, largely because Antifederalist leaders were committed to popular sovereignty (expressed through the ratification process) and the rule of law (demonstrated in the orderly debate of Hamilton's financial program). Notes that during the 1790s many Antifederalists joined with former Federalists ("Madisonians"). Concludes that Madison rejected the ideas contained in Federalist No.10 when the Federalists demonstrated that an interested minority could seize control of government, prompting Madison to seek a majority by means of a political party and the two-party system.
AHR 109: 180-81; *HRNB* 31: 12; *JAH* 90: 1002-1003; *JSH* 70: 900-901; *NEQ* 77: 152-55; *WMQ* 61: 776-80.

515 Slonim, Shlomo. *Framers' Construction/Beardian Deconstruction: Essays on the Constitutional Design of 1787.* New York: P. Lang, 2001. xii, 295 p. ISBN 0820448915; ISBN 9780820448916; OCLC 44860927; LC Call Number KF4541 .S57; Dewey 342.73/029. Citations: 0.
Publishes nine articles that trace the motivations of delegates, the development of specific clauses, the origins of the Electoral College, and the historiography of the Constitution. Rejects the Beardian interpretation as sloppy and wrong-headed.
HRNB 32: 99.

516   Uviller, H. Richard and William G. Merkel. *The Militia and the Right to Arms, or, How the Second Amendment Fell Silent*. Durham, N.C.: Duke University Press, 2002. xii, 338 p. ISBN 0822330318 (hbk.); ISBN 9780822330318 (hbk.); ISBN 0822330172 (pbk.); ISBN 9780822330172 (pbk.); OCLC 50782360; LC Call Number KF3941; LC Call Number UA42.U95; Dewey 323.430973. Citations: 18.

Contends that individuals hold the right to bear arms, which is not identical to the right of self-defense or the allowance of taking up arms against the government. Traces the evolution of the militia into the National Guard and concludes that the Second Amendment emerged from the eighteenth-century fear of standing armies and concern for civic virtue.

AHR 108: 1442-43; *HRNB* 31: 107; *JAH* 90: 1552-53; *JAS* 38: 174-75; *J Mil Hist* 68: 248-49; *JSH* 70: 970-71; *LJ* 128n6: 114-15; *NCHR* 81: 487-88; *RAH* 31: 519-27.

517   Vile, John R. *The Constitutional Convention of 1787: A Comprehensive Encyclopedia of America's Founding*. Santa Barbara, Calif.: ABC-CLIO, 2005. lxxv, 1009 p. ISBN 1851096698; ISBN 9781851096695; ISBN 1851096744 (electronic); ISBN 9781851096749 (electronic); OCLC 60814090; LC Call Number KF4510 .V55; Dewey 342.7302/92. Citations: 3.

Presents more than 400 entries on the persons involved in the framing of the Constitution, constitutional provisions, states and nations, committees, documents, plans and forms of government, ideological influences, and constituencies affected. Includes chronologies, documents, charts on committees, and lists of signers.

Booklist 102: 76.

518   Wakelyn, Jon L. *Birth of the Bill of Rights: Encyclopedia of the Antifederalists*. Westport, Conn.: Greenwood Press, 2004. 682 p. ISBN 0313317399 (set); ISBN 9780313317392 (set); ISBN 0313331944 (v. 1); ISBN 9780313331947 (v. 1); ISBN 0313331952 (v. 2); ISBN 9780313331954 (v. 2); OCLC 55018686; LC Call Number E302.5 .W35; LC Call Number KF4515; Dewey 973.4/092/2. Citations: 2.

Presents biographies of 140 Antifederalists, along with their major writings from state ratifying conventions.

Booklist 101: 1219; *LJ* 129n20: 172.

519   Wootton, David, ed. *The Essential Federalist and Anti-Federalist Papers*. Indianapolis, Ind.: Hackett Publishing, 2003. xliii, 343 p. ISBN 0872206556; ISBN 9780872206557; ISBN 0872206564; ISBN 9780872206564; OCLC 52387899; LC Call Number KF4515 .E85; Dewey 342.73/024. Citations: 6.

Discusses the historical sources of the Constitution and presents excerpts from the writings of Antifederalists and Federalists.

Hist Teach 38: 425-26.

20 Politics and Government

520 Ackerman, Bruce A. *The Failure of the Founding Fathers: Jefferson, Marshall, and the Rise of Presidential Democracy.* Cambridge, Mass.: Harvard University Press, 2005. 384 p. ISBN 0674018664; ISBN 9780674018662; OCLC 58919429; LC Call Number E331 .A15; Dewey 320.973/09/034. Citations: 38.

Provides a critique, from a legal perspective, of the Founders' as framers of the Constitution. Notes that the goal of law is to reduce legal uncertainties and that, where the selection of Presidents is concerned, the Founders did not establish an effective system. Explains that the Crisis of 1800 was a direct result of partisanship and of a faulty Electoral College system. Presents generally negative characterizations of Hamilton and of Marshall and views the Judiciary Act of 1801 as both beneficial to Supreme Court justices and as politically suspect for its facilitating the packing of the judiciary with Federalist judges. Finds that Republican repeal of the Act raised serious constitutional questions related to the formation and maintenance of a truly independent judiciary. Concludes that there will always be tension between "the will of the People, as expressed by the Constitution" and the "voice of the nation, as expressed by its living representatives." Fears that we continue to live with the "grotesque absurdities of the current system," which threaten the survival of the republic.
AHR 112: 841-42; *AJLH* 48: 227-31; *JAH* 93: 506-507; *JER* 26: 475-77; *JSH* 73: 687-90; *LJ* 130n15: 75; *Wilson Q* 29n4: 124.

521 Adams, William Howard. *Gouverneur Morris: An Independent Life.* New Haven, Conn.: Yale University Press, 2003. xvi, 345 p. ISBN 0300099800; ISBN 9780300099805; OCLC 52079678; LC Call Number E302.6 .M7; Dewey 973.4/092. Citations: 12.

Seeks to put Morris "at the top rank of international nation builders," characterizing him as one of the leading figures of his generation. Presents a full

biography of Morris, describing his early life and his careers as a lawyer, politician, statesman, diplomat, and businessman. Explains that Morris never really escaped his aristocratic upbringing and that he craved order and remained suspicious of democracy throughout and after the Revolution. Notes that he did, however, maintain more progressive positions in support of religious toleration and the abolition of slavery. Reconciles Morris's support of the Virginia Plan with his opposition to slavery interests, noting that he "did not hesitate to spell out what he perceived as an insurmountable cultural and political gap between the urban, commercial society of the progressive East and the agrarian Southwest built on human bondage." Notes that Morris played a vital role in the creation of the Senate and in the definition of independent executive and judicial branches. Argues that Morris exerted tremendous influence on the style of writing exhibited in the Constitution, which elevated the document "onto the moral plane of the Declaration."
AHR 110: 134-35; *Booklist* 100n4: 382; *JAH* 91: 996; *JER* 24: 486-89; *WMQ* 62: 745-64; *Wilson Q* 27: 111-14.

522 Alexander, John K. *Samuel Adams: America's Revolutionary Politician.* Lanham, Md.: Rowman and Littlefield Publishers, 2002. xii, 249 p. ISBN 0742521141 (hbk.); ISBN 9780742521148 (hbk.); ISBN 074252115X (pbk.); ISBN 9780742521155 (pbk.); OCLC 48014880; LC Call Number E302.6.A2; Dewey 973.3/092. Citations: 3.
Discusses Adams's career in Massachusetts politics and in the Continental Congress, and his role in the promotion of public education, discouragement of slave importation, and tepid support for the ratification of the Constitution. Contends that Adams possessed an extraordinary ability to express, manipulate, and channel popular grievances using the press and other communication networks. Characterizes Adams as devoted to liberty, highly principled, and sympathetic to common folk. Explains that Adams was a skillful communicator and the "first professional and first modern politician."
PMHB 128: 202-204; *WMQ* 60: 238-40.

523 Appleby, Joyce O. and Arthur M. Schlesinger. *Thomas Jefferson.* New York: Times Books, 2003. xviii, 173 p. ISBN 0805069240; ISBN 9780805069242; OCLC 50645573; LC Call Number E332 .A67; Dewey 973.4/6/092. Citations: 9.
Considers Jefferson's political philosophy and career, including Jefferson's victory in the election of 1800, interpretation of the Constitution, reelection, support for westward expansion, and foreign policy. Focuses on Jefferson's time as President and concludes that "Americans' most pressing history assignment is coming to terms with Thomas Jefferson."
Booklist 99n9/10: 838; *LJ* 128n2: 99.

524 Bailyn, Bernard. *To Begin the World Anew: The Genius and Ambiguities of the American Founders.* New York: Alfred A. Knopf, 2003. xiv, 185 p. ISBN 0375413774; ISBN 9780375413773; OCLC 48964980; LC Call Number E302.1 .B16; Dewey 973.3 21. Citations: 35.

Presents brief essays on the tensions between pragmatism and idealism in early American politics. Compares the Founders to provincial artists, noting that they were able to combine simplicity and common sense with extraordinary vision to create a new republic. Sketches the political lives of Thomas Jefferson (marked by his struggle to put the ideals of the Revolution into practice), Benjamin Franklin (illustrated by the blending of realism and idealism in a new American foreign policy), and the writers of the Federalist Papers (who sought balance between power and liberty). Points out that the Founders' creativity had significant influence throughout the Atlantic world, even to the present day, particularly in debates over constitutional principles. Concludes "that America's successes, its great historical moments, have occurred when idealism and realism were combined."

AHR 109: 179-80; *Booklist* 99n7: 643; *EAL* 39: 393-99; *JAH* 90: 999-1000; *NEQ* 77: 325-27; *PMHB* 128: 80-82; *VMHB* 111: 80-81; *WMQ* 61: 573-77.

525 Beeman, Richard R. *The Varieties of Political Experience in Eighteenth-Century America.* Philadelphia: University of Pennsylvania Press, 2004. viii, 366 p. ISBN 0812237706; ISBN 9780812237702; OCLC 53887523; LC Call Number E188 .B44; Dewey 320.973/09/033 22. Citations: 12.

Surveys the breadth of political belief and experience in the various regions of pre-Revolutionary, eighteenth-century North America, which represented "numerous, diverse political cultures, diffuse and fragmented, often speaking altogether different political languages." Contends that, though diverse, American political cultures were all moving "toward a mode of political discourse and action that gave freer rein and greater legitimacy to those libertarian and popular impulses that would eventually be articulated in the Declaration of Independence."

AHR 110: 1162-63; *JAH* 92: 594-95; *JSH* 71: 871-72; *NCHR* 82: 100-101; *RAH* 32: 478-85; *VMHB* 112: 422-23; *WMQ* 62: 551-53.

526 Bernstein, Richard B. *Thomas Jefferson.* New York: Oxford University Press, 2003. xviii, 253 p. ISBN 0195169115 (hbk.); ISBN 9780195169119 (hbk.); ISBN 0195181301 (pbk.); ISBN 9780195181302 (pbk.); OCLC 51854624; LC Call Number E332 .B47; Dewey 973.4/6/092. Citations: 9.

Provides an introduction to Jefferson for students and general readers, covering Jefferson's youth, intellectual development, role in the Revolution, time in Europe, positions in government, election and service as President, and life in retirement. Characterizes Jefferson as a man of contradictions, one who "was caught between past and future, between his origins and his aspirations for himself and the nation, between who he was and what he wanted to be" and who "showed himself to be a versatile, adaptable chief executive."

Booklist 100: 196; *Hist Teach* 38: 401-402; *JAH* 91: 1435-36; *JER* 27: 346-49; *JSH* 72: 871-908; *LJ* 128n14: 177; *PMHB* 129: 234-35; *PSQ* 119: 722-23; *VMHB* 112: 306-307; *WMQ* 62: 745-64.

527 Billings, Warren M. *A Little Parliament: The Virginia General Assembly in the Seventeenth Century.* Richmond: The Library of Virginia, 2004. xxi, 284 p. ISBN 0884902021; ISBN 9780884902027; OCLC 53427529; LC Call Number

F229 .B55; LC Call Number JK83 .V8 B55; Dewey 328.755/09/032 22. Citations: 6.

Examines the founding and development of the Virginia legislature between 1619 and 1700. Discusses the commercial rise of a ruling class in the colony and provides brief biographies of some of Virginia's early political leaders. Describes the evolution of the assembly into a bicameral legislature after 1642 and the erosion of its considerable powers after Bacon's Rebellion, when the government in London attempted to reassert control over the colony. Notes that the legislature borrowed as much as it could from its English counterpart, but had to deal with unique local matters, such as the treatment of Indians and enslaved Africans. Suggests that the practices formed in the colony became the basis of American representative government.

AHR 110: 467-68; *AJLH* 49: 493-94; *JAH* 92: 185-86; *NCHR* 82: 98-100; *VMHB* 112: 186-88; *WMQ* 62: 136-38.

528   Billings, Warren M. *Sir William Berkeley and the Forging of Colonial Virginia*. Baton Rouge: Louisiana State University Press, 2004. xvii, 290 p. ISBN 0807130125; ISBN 9780807130124; OCLC 55149481; LC Call Number F229.B53 B55; Dewey 975.5/02/092. Citations: 6.

Presents a full biography of Berkeley (1605-1677), Virginia planter and the colony's royal governor after 1641. Places Berkeley's career in transatlantic context, describing his time at the court of Charles I, his home in Virginia, his removal from and return to power in the colony, and his efforts to develop the colony's agriculture, commercial networks, government, and society. Discusses Berkeley's role in Bacon's Rebellion, particularly his policies that helped to encourage the uprising, and its aftermath. Contends that Berkeley both "uniquely marked Virginia" and was shaped deeply by his time in the New World, becoming more of a man of Virginia than of England.

AHR 111: 151-52; *JAH* 92: 949-50; *JSH* 72: 156-57; *NCHR* 82: 98-100; *VMHB* 112: 420-22.

529   Booraem, Hendrik. *Young Hickory: The Making of Andrew Jackson*. Dallas, Tex.: Taylor Trade Publishing, 2001. xvi, 318 p. ISBN 0878332634; ISBN 9780878332632; OCLC 45102954; LC Call Number E382 .B67; Dewey 973.5/6/092. Citations: 3.

Reconstructs Jackson's early life, including his time in North Carolina, study of law, and personal habits. Claims that the Revolutionary era, during which time his mother and brothers died, resulted in Jackson's "total fearlessness, a sort of fatalistic feeling that the worst had already happened and there was nothing left to be terrified of." Notes that the young Jackson was bold and intimidating, but also exhibited social skills and facility with language and horses. Argues that Jackson moved west to take advantage of social connections, particularly with those in the legal profession.

Booklist 97: 1828-29; *HRNB* 30: 11; *JSH* 69: 686-87; *LJ* 126n12: 100; *NCHR* 80: 95-96; *WMQ* 62: 745-64.

530   Bowling, Kenneth R. and Donald R. Kennon, eds. *Establishing Congress: The Removal to Washington, D.C. and the Election of 1800*. Athens: Ohio

University Press, published for the United States Capitol Historical Society, 2005. x, 225 p. ISBN 0821416197; ISBN 9780821416198; OCLC 60189625; LC Call Number E321.E83; Dewey 973.4. Citations: 4.

Includes articles on the election of 1800, the effect of the shift from Federalist to Jeffersonian control, Washington, D.C. at the end of the eighteenth century and the movement of the government to the city, the Republican concept of nationhood and the Capitol, patronage and women in early national Washington, congressional accommodations in the early nineteenth century, the Federalist Congresses, and the burial plans for George Washington.

AHR 111: 285; *HRNB* 34: 42-43; *JAH* 93: 509-510; *JER* 26: 478-80; *JSH* 73: 166-68.

531 Bowling, Kenneth R. and Donald R. Kennon, eds. *The House and Senate in the 1790s: Petitioning, Lobbying, and Institutional Development.* Athens: Ohio University Press, 2002. x, 348 p. ISBN 0821414194; ISBN 9780821414194; OCLC 48177287; LC Call Number JK 1041 .H68; Dewey 328.73/09/033. Citations: 5.

Contains ten articles on Congress of the 1790s, with a focus on traditional political history, including elections and legislation. Presents pieces on the structuring of Congress, the First Congress, early lobbying and petitioning, *Chisholm v. Georgia,* the political aftermath of the Constitutional ratification debates, the relationship of the Senate to the states, the function of the Senate in Philadelphia, and the early institutional development of the House of Representatives.

JAH 90: 211-12; *JSH* 69: 884-85; *PMHB* 129: 109-111; *WMQ* 59: 1028-33.

532 Brands, H.W. *The First American: The Life and Times of Benjamin Franklin.* New York: Anchor Books, 2002. 765 p. ISBN 0385495404 (pbk.); ISBN 9780385495400 (pbk.); OCLC 49400426; LC Call Number E302.6.F8; Dewey 973.3092. Citations: 24.

Presents a biography of Franklin for a general readership. Characterizes Franklin as extraordinarily curious and inventive and as almost single-handedly responsible for the 1778 French alliance.

EAL 41: 535-53; *JAH* 88: 1508; *Penn Hist* 68: 533-37; *PMHB* 126: 327-40.

533 Bremer, Francis J. *John Winthrop: America's Forgotten Founding Father.* New York: Oxford University Press, 2003. xviii, 478 p. ISBN 0195149130; ISBN 9780195149135; OCLC 50866816; LC Call Number F67.W79; Dewey 974.4/02/092. Citations: 27.

Places Winthrop in the political, economic, and religious contexts of early modern England, noting that the Puritan mission was defined and shaped in the Old World and that "throughout his career as Massachusetts governor, Winthrop was trying to replicate the forms of English life that made up the ancient constitution while at the same time maintaining that New England was a parallel but not subordinate form of England itself." Rejects stereotypical views of Winthrop, arguing that the real Winthrop deserves to be recognized as an American founder who favored order and unity, but was anti-authoritarian and remarkably tolerant of diverse views. Contends that Winthrop was the moderate

voice in the antinomian crisis and held a conciliatory view on Robert Child's *Remonstrants* petition (1646).
AHR 109: 1221; *Booklist* 99: 1733; *J Brit Stds* 47: 189-90; *LJ* 128: 80; *NEQ* 77: 320-22; *RAH* 32: 137-43; *WMQ* 61: 129-32.

534 Brookhiser, Richard. *America's First Dynasty: The Adamses, 1735-1918.* New York: Free Press, 2002. 244 p. ISBN 0684868814; ISBN 9780684868813; OCLC 48098481; LC Call Number E322.1 .B76; Dewey 973.4/4/0922. Citations: 7.
Traces the history and contributions of members of the Adams family, including John Adams, John Quincy Adams, Charles Francis Adams, and Henry Adams. Characterizes the group as "admirable, and frequently lovable," but "seldom likable."
Booklist 99: 438; *LJ* 126: 106-107; *Wilson Q* 26: 121-22.

535 Brookhiser, Richard. *Gentleman Revolutionary: Gouverneur Morris, the Rake Who Wrote the Constitution.* New York: Free Press, 2003. xvii, 251 p. ISBN 0743223799; ISBN 9780743223799; OCLC 51810636; LC Call Number E302.6.M7; Dewey 973.4/092. Citations: 12.
Presents a biography of Morris that lauds Morris for his opposition to slavery, his role in writing the Constitution, and his diplomatic efforts in France. Covers his accomplishments as a legislator, his personal foibles, and his retirement.
Booklist 99: 1733; *LJ* 128: 95; *PMHB* 128: 405-406; *Wilson Q* 27: 111-14.

536 Bukovansky, Mlada. *Legitimacy and Power Politics: The American and French Revolutions in International Political Culture.* Princeton, N.J.: Princeton University Press, 2002. viii, 255 p. ISBN 0691074348; ISBN 9780691074344; OCLC 48223504; LC Call Number JC327 .B764; Dewey 306.2/0944/09033 21. Citations: 37.
Studies the American and French revolutions in order to explain the worldwide movement "from dynastically legitimated monarchical sovereignty to popularly legitimated national sovereignty." Argues that the French Revolution "lent significant weight to the idea that international politics was a [Hobbesian] state of nature," one that essentially doomed the reestablishment of the "Concert of Europe."
AHR 108: 801-802.

537 Burns, James MacGregor and Susan Dunn. *George Washington.* New York: Times Books, 2004. xviii, 185 p. ISBN 0805069364; ISBN 9780805069365; OCLC 52878597; LC Call Number E312 .B983; Dewey 973.3/092. Citations: 5.
Focuses on Washington's shaping of the American presidency and his distinguishing the executive branch from the other branches of government. Explains that Washington took a very collaborative approach to governing, consulting frequently with cabinet members. Argues that Washington negotiated among factions and competing policies, while seeking to shape the institution of the presidency and ensure the fledgling government's survival and stability.

Contends that Washington's second term was somewhat less successful than his first because he seemed to act in a more partisan way.
Booklist 100: 813; *JAH* 91: 1433-34.

538 Burstein, Andrew. *Jefferson's Secrets: Death and Desire at Monticello.* New York: Basic Books, 2005. ix, 351 p. ISBN 0465008127; ISBN 9780465008124; OCLC 469908863; LC Call Number E332.2 .B85; Dewey 973.4/6. Citations: 9.
Explores Jefferson's physicality, including his interest in and knowledge of medical and biological literature, and its relationship to his personal and political lives, particularly as he aged. Portrays Jefferson as an essentially sentimental patriarch, an individual who used his knowledge of biology to conclude that African Americans were inferior and that sexual activity was beneficial for males, a politician concerned about the way in which history would be written, and a human being considering death and religion.
AHR 111: 476; *Booklist* 101: 805; *JSH* 72: 871-908; *RAH* 33: 333-40; *VQR* 81: 241-49; *Wilson Q* 29: 107-109; *WMQ* 62: 569-73.

539 Burstein, Andrew. *Letters from the Head and Heart: Writings of Thomas Jefferson.* Charlottesville, Va.: Thomas Jefferson Foundation, distributed by the University of North Carolina Press, 2002. 100 p. ISBN 1882886208; ISBN 9781882886203; OCLC 50519106; LC Call Number E332.2 .B86; Dewey 973.4/6/092 B 21. Citations: 0.
Presents an intellectual and emotional portrait of Jefferson, noting in particular his use of language and his relationships with women.
NCHR 80: 486-88.

540 Chernow, Ron. *Alexander Hamilton.* New York: Penguin Press, 2004. 818 p. ISBN 1594200092; ISBN 9781594200090; ISBN 0143034758; ISBN 9780143034759; OCLC 53083988; LC Call Number E302.6.H2; Dewey 973.4/092. Citations: 46.
Argues that Hamilton was among the most important Founding Fathers, noting that he established in America his vision of the modern economic state. Discusses his birth and relatively humble upbringing, his service on Washington's staff, his co-authorship of The Federalist Papers, his debates with Jefferson, his service as the first treasury secretary, and his death at the hands of Aaron Burr.
Booklist 101: 259; *HRNB* 33: 3-4; *JAH* 93: 192-93; *LJ* 129n3: 138; *RAH* 33: 8-14.

541 Coquillette, Daniel R. and Neil Longley York, eds. *Portrait of a Patriot: The Major Political and Legal Papers of Josiah Quincy Junior.* Boston, Mass.: Colonial Society of Massachusetts, distributed by the University of Virginia Press, 2005. 5 vols. ISBN 0962073792 (v. 1); ISBN 9780962073793 (v. 1); ISBN 0962073784 (v. 2); ISBN 9780962073786 (v. 2); ISBN 9780979466205 (v. 3); ISBN 0979466202 (v. 3); ISBN 9780979466243 (v. 4); ISBN 0979466245 (v. 4); ISBN 9780979466267 (v. 5); ISBN 0979466261 (v. 5);

OCLC 62391785; LC Call Number E263.M4 Q72; LC Call Number F61 .C65; Dewey 016.9732/7092 22. Citations: 1.

Presents the Revolution-era writings of Josiah Quincy and an introductory biographical essay. Includes in Volume 1 Quincy's *Political Commonplace Book*, a book of maxims that provides the background and intellectual traditions that helped form Quincy's revolutionary ideology, which clearly benefited from Quincy's knowledge of Cicero, Hume, Montagu, Bacon, Bolingbroke, and Rousseau. Includes *The London Journal*, Quincy's account of his failed effort to prevent war while working toward American independence. Includes in Volume 2 Quincy's *Law Commonplace Book* and the journal that Quincy kept on his "Grand Tour" of the South in 1773. Includes in Volumes 3 and 4 Quincy's law reports between 1742 and 1775.

AJLH 49: 461-62; *JSH* 76: 136-37; *NCHR* 85: 455-56; *NEQ* 82: 195-97.

542 Cunningham, Noble E. *Jefferson and Monroe: Constant Friendship and Respect*. Charlottesville, Va.: Thomas Jefferson Foundation, distributed by the University of North Carolina Press, 2003. 80 p. ISBN 1882886216 (pbk.); ISBN 9781882886210 (pbk.); OCLC 51810801; LC Call Number E332.2 .C86; Dewey 973.5/4/092. Citations: 1.

Focuses on the relationship between the third and fifth presidents in a work intended for a general audience. Finds that Jefferson's failure to support Monroe's treaty with Great Britain temporarily caused estrangement between the two men, but that Jefferson turned to Monroe for help in the founding of the University of Virginia. Notes that Jefferson served as a political mentor to Monroe, providing advice while indicating full confidence in his protégé. Demonstrates that even the differences between the two men were more academic and pragmatic than personal. Concludes that the two developed an equal partnership characterized by "constant friendship and respect."

IMH 101: 185-86; *NCHR* 80: 486-88.

543 Currie, David P. *The Constitution in Congress: The Jeffersonians, 1801-1829*. Chicago, Ill.: University of Chicago Press, 2001. xviii, 387 p. ISBN 0226131173; ISBN 9780226131177; OCLC 45080031; LC Call Number KF4541 .C835; Dewey 342.73/029 21. Citations: 39.

Identifies constitutional issues that arose from the controversies during Jefferson's administration and later disagreements among Henry Clay, John C. Calhoun, and Daniel Webster. Argues for a post-originalist approach that emphasizes past experience in the assessment of constitutional doctrines or mechanisms. Finds that the "acuity of constitutional debate in Congress and Cabinet during the first third of the nineteenth century was great" and that "there was a marked correspondence between constitutional views and partisan political goals." Concludes that, during the first decades of the nineteenth century, federal judges "began to contribute significantly to constitutional interpretation," but that " Even when they did, however, the groundwork for their decisions had commonly been laid in extensive legislative and executive discussion of the measures under review."

J Interdis Hist 37: 415-22.

544 Dale, Elizabeth. *Debating—and Creating—Authority: The Failure of a Constitutional Ideal in Massachusetts Bay, 1629–1649.* Aldershot, U.K.: Ashgate, 2001. vi, 167 p. ISBN 075462126X; ISBN 9780754621263; OCLC 45700803; LC Call Number JK99.M39; Dewey 320.9744/09/032. Citations: 1.
Examines changes in the bases of political authority in Massachusetts during its first two decades. Finds that the Bay Colony was "founded as a theocracy" in which "all human authority derived from God," but in which there was uncertainty regarding the devolution of power. Explains that John Winthrop "wanted authority placed in the hands of a few political leaders," while Thomas Hooker believed that magistrates ought to be "subject to the advice of the religious leaders" and John Cotton and Thomas Shepard maintained that God's will regarding political authority could never be perfectly known. Argues that these ambiguities regarding the interpretation of Bay Colony theocracy encouraged the expression of "an antiauthoritarian streak in Massachusetts Bay Puritanism" that reached "into the ranks of the colonial leadership." Claims that the crisis of authority manifested itself in the trials of Anne Hutchinson.
JAH 90: 989-90.

545 Diggins, John P. *John Adams.* New York: Times Books, 2003. xx, 200 p. ISBN 0805069372; ISBN 9780805069372; OCLC 51172445; LC Call Number E322 .D54; Dewey 973.4/4/092. Citations: 2.
Provides a biography of Adams for a general readership, with a major focus on political history and philosophy. Argues that Adams' primary significance was as a political moralist.
Booklist 99: 1444.

546 Dorland, Michael and Maurice René Charland. *Law, Rhetoric, and Irony in the Formation of Canadian Civic Culture.* Buffalo, N.Y.: University of Toronto Press, 2002. xiv, 359 p. ISBN 080204283X (hbk.); ISBN 9780802042835 (hbk.); ISBN 0802081193 (pbk.); ISBN 9780802081193 (pbk.); OCLC 49204493; LC Call Number KE394 .D67; LC Call Number JL186.5; Dewey 971; Dewey 306.20971. Citations: 10.
Identifies five main modes of performance: (1) the courtly style of French absolutism; (2) a "monarchial style" that associates the British Crown with law and liberty; (3) the paradoxical "monarchial republican style" that represents republican sentiments without republican institutions; (4) a legal-administrative style that takes up linguistic dualism; and (5) a sense of irony that negotiates contradictions and expands the public sphere. Contends that, problematically, Canada came "into the modern age without having recourse to the facilities revolutionary language provides. Explains that, instead, Canadians have come to identity and understanding of civic culture in other, primarily rhetorical and legal ways, which brings with it alienation and the recognition that, because law can never fit all circumstances, difference and exception will be the normal state.
AHR 109: 507-508.

547 Dougherty, Keith L. *Collective Action under the Articles of Confederation.* Cambridge: Cambridge University Press, 2001. xiv, 211 p. ISBN 0521782090;

ISBN 9780521782098; OCLC 44026382; LC Call Number JK316 .D68; Dewey 320.973/09/033 21. Citations: 24.

Argues that the Constitution replaced the Articles mainly due to concerns about efficiency, that is, "the ability to satisfy mutual interests or mutual demands." Contends that states responded when it was in their best interest to do so, when federal action served their local interests. Espouses the theory that contributions provided jointly public and private benefits, which predicts greater contributions from states with the most to gain from collective action (e.g., those requiring immediate defense against the British). Tests this "joint products" hypotheses by examining the relationships between the supply of soldiers and army location and between payments of requisition money and locally held public debt. Finds that this model allowed the nascent United States to raise sufficient resources to survive initial crises, but not to be sustainable in the long term.

AHR 107: 1551-52; *JAH* 89: 1025-26; *J Econ Hist* 61: 863; *PSQ* 117: 173-74; *WMQ* 61: 582-88.

548 Dreisbach, Daniel L. *Thomas Jefferson and the Wall of Separation between Church and State.* New York: New York University Press, 2002. x, 282 p. ISBN 081471935X (hbk.) ; ISBN 9780814719350 (hbk.); ISBN 9780814719367 (pbk.); ISBN 0814719368 (pbk.); OCLC 49284086; LC Call Number E332.2 .D74; Dewey 973.46. Citations: 40.

Emphasizes the historical context in which Jefferson wrote his letter to the Danbury Baptist Association of Connecticut in early 1802. Stresses the importance of the Federalist-Republican divide in the election of 1800, arguing that Jefferson penned the letter as a response to political opponents who called Jefferson irreligious for his refusal to declare days of national fasting and thanksgiving. Points out that Jefferson carefully crafted the letter to reflect his interpretation of the First Amendment: that the national government and its chief executive should not attempt to exert authority in matters of religion. Points out that use of the wall metaphor was not new, nor was the use of other images to promote religious liberty. Traces the ways in which courts have used Jefferson's image of the wall of separation and discusses the "promises and perils of metaphors in the law."

AHR 108: 1142; *CH* 72: 418-20; *JAAR* 73: 913-15; *JAH* 90: 1003-1004; *JER* 23: 285-87; *JSH* 70: 652-53; *LJ* 127n12: 99-100; *VMHB* 111: 189; *WMQ* 61: 776-80.

549 Dubber, Markus Dirk. *The Police Power: Patriarchy and the Foundations of American Government.* New York: Columbia University Press, 2005. xviii, 268 p. ISBN 0231132069 (hbk.); ISBN 9780231132060 (hbk.); ISBN 0231132077 (pbk.); ISBN 9780231132077 (pbk.); OCLC 56752097; LC Call Number KF4695 .D82; Dewey 342.73/0418. Citations: 28.

Examines the development of police powers (i.e., the right of governments to safeguard public welfare). Explains that, in contrast to legal power, the exercise of which depends upon society's composition of autonomous persons capable of self-government, the police power is analogous to a household, where the state is the master who seeks to maximize the welfare of the members of the household. Claims that the tensions between law and police power were brought to America and continue to the present, largely because the latter is "undefined, and indeed indefinable" and insulated "from serious constitutional scrutiny." *AHR* 111: 465-66; *JAH* 93: 196-97.

550 Dubé, Jean-Claude. *The Chevalier de Montmagny (1601-1657): First Governor of New France.* Ottawa: University of Ottawa Press, 2005. xxvi, 381 p. ISBN 0776630288 (hbk.); ISBN 9780776630281 (hbk.); ISBN 0776605593 (pbk.); ISBN 9780776605593 (pbk.); OCLC 57474336; LC Call Number F1030.M77; Dewey 971.01/6/092. Citations: 4.

Provides an assessment of Montmagny, noting that he sought to protect colonists from the Iroquois, negotiating where possible due to limited military resources. Finds that the export of furs to France was a primary concern, as was the development of Quebec. Suggests that his appointment to the governorship of the Caribbean island of Saint-Christophe indicates that he succeeded well in Canada. Characterizes Montmagny as a courageous, dutiful, wise, prudent, and pious leader who benefited from a Jesuit education and who served well the French king, the Roman Catholic Church, and the order of the Knights of Malta. *AHR* 111: 457-58.

551 Dubois, Laurent. *Avengers of the New World: The Story of the Haitian Revolution.* Cambridge, Mass.: Harvard University Press, 2004. viii, 357 p. ISBN 0674013042; ISBN 9780674013049; OCLC 53178675; LC Call Number F1923 .D83; Dewey 972.94/03. Citations: 74.

Analyzes the Haitian Revolution (1791–1803). Asserts that the Revolution indicated that the rights claimed in "France's 1789 Declaration of the Rights of Man and Citizen were indeed universal" and that the Revolution was a "uniquely transcultural movement" that involved whites, mulattos, and blacks, regional and social complexity, and a variety of political schemes. Concludes that the Revolution's causes and consequences had international implications. *CJH* 41: 410-11; *LJ* 129n3: 139; *WMQ* 63: 197-202.

552 Dunn, Susan. *Jefferson's Second Revolution: The Election Crisis of 1800 and the Triumph of Republicanism.* Boston, Mass.: Houghton Mifflin, 2004. 372 p. ISBN 0618131647; ISBN 9780618131648; OCLC 54974609; LC Call Number E330 .D86; Dewey 324.973/044 22. Citations: 7.

Studies the election of 1800, analyzing events of the 1790s, such as Hamilton's financial program, the Whiskey Rebellion, the Jay Treaty, the election of 1796, the Alien and Sedition Acts, and the Virginia and Kentucky Resolutions. Stresses that after the election of 1800 parties quickly became "part of the fabric of American politics" and "their power had to be harnessed and exploited to make government work," but that "notions of a permanent opposition and of two equally potent and legitimate political parties had not yet come of age." Discusses the effect of the election on American political history through Jackson's victory in 1828. Concludes that only with the emergence of the second party system in the 1820s and 1830s was a two-party system of government finally solidified. *AHR* 110: 473-74; *Booklist* 101: 182; *HRNB* 33: 65.

553 Ellis, Joseph J. *His Excellency: George Washington*. New York: Alfred A. Knopf, 2004. xiv, 320 p. ISBN 1400040310 (hbk.); ISBN 9781400040315 (hbk.); ISBN 0739451537 (pbk.); ISBN 9780739451533 (pbk.); OCLC 54817026; LC Call Number E312 .E245; Dewey 973.4/1/092. Citations: 34.

Provides for a general audience a biography that characterizes Washington as a leader with energy, stamina, integrity, and vision and as an occasionally insecure, controlling, and shortsighted person. Examines Washington's personal development over time, contending that he was shaped both by the British system of deference, patronage, and hierarchy, which encouraged connections with the Fairfax family and formed the context for his efforts toward military advancement, and by frontier experiences gained as a surveyor and soldier in campaigns against the French and Indians. Argues that Washington's greatest military action was the inoculation of his troops against smallpox and that his decisions on slavery were not largely based on morality, but rather driven more by economics. Concludes that Washington's choice of a military career instead of college had a deep impact on him and prevented him from becoming overly idealistic.

AHR 111: 158-59; *Booklist* 101: 178; *HRNB* 33: 100-101; *JAH* 92: 592-93; *LJ* 129n13: 90; *RAH* 33: 162-68; *VMHB* 113: 188-90.

554 Ferling, John. *Adams vs. Jefferson: The Tumultuous Election of 1800*. New York: Oxford University Press, 2004. xx, 260 p. ISBN 0195167716 (hbk.); ISBN 9780195167719 (hbk.); ISBN 9780195189063 (pbk.); ISBN 019518906X (pbk.); OCLC 54959849; LC Call Number E330 .F47; Dewey 324.973/044 22. Citations: 13.

Sketches the four major candidates of the election of 1800 (John Adams, Thomas Jefferson, Aaron Burr, and Charles Coatesworth Pinckney), following their careers from the American Revolution to their presidential nominations. Traces the rise of national partisanship and the expanding role of parties in determining the structure of the presidential campaign of 1800. Concludes with a description of Jefferson's inauguration and ponders the question about the application of the word "revolution" to the 1800 election.

AHR 111: 475-76; *JAS* 39: 119-20; *JER* 27: 162-65; *JSH* 72: 871-908; *LJ* 129n7: 72-73; *RAH* 33: 15-22.

555 Ferling, John. *A Leap in the Dark: The Struggle to Create the American Republic*. New York: Oxford University Press, 2003. xviii, 558 p. ISBN: 0195159241 (hbk.); ISBN 9780195159240 (hbk.); ISBN 0195176006 (pbk.); ISBN 9780195176001 (pbk.); OCLC 51511252; LC Call Number E195 .F47; Dewey 973.3. Citations: 17.

Surveys the founding of the American republic from the Seven Years' War to the election of 1800. Contends that "political behavior usually owes more to economic considerations" than to political ideology or abstract ideas and that Shays's Rebellion helped move many, including George Washington, from neutrality to action on a strong central government. Takes up matters of foreign policy, including the work of John Jay on Spanish interference of navigation on the Mississippi. Concludes that sectional tensions were first truly aggravated by this perceived "failed diplomatic initiative with Spain."

AHR 109: 516-17; *Booklist* 99: 1731; *HRNB* 32: 11; *JAH* 91: 221-22; *JAS* 40: 427-28; *J Mil Hist* 68: 244-46; *JSH* 71: 142-44; *LJ* 128n12: 103; *RAH* 32: 14-19; *WMQ* 61: 573-77.

556 Freeman, Joanne B. *Affairs of Honor: National Politics in the Early Republic*. New Haven, Conn.: Yale University Press, 2001. xxiv, 376 p. ISBN 0300088779; ISBN 9780300088779; OCLC 46353290; LC Call Number E310 .F85; Dewey 306.2/0973/09034. Citations: 66.

Underscores that, faced with weak institutions and lack of formal precedents in the early republic, "reputation was the glue that held the polity together" and the motivation of political actions. Explores the means of political "combat," including gossip, letter writing, and publication of pamphlets, newspaper essays, and broadsides. Maintains that the nation's leaders were "torn between an unstoppable wave of democratic mass empowerment and their own assumptions about their status and role in the political process," but nonetheless viewed their peers as their main audience. Notes that to these politicians "public opinion represented the response to strategic conversations orchestrated by political leaders," that pamphlets were "typically aimed at a small circle of 'men of influence'" or "at wider circles of elite readers" and thus "pamphlet writers who addressed themselves to 'the people' did so more for effect than for accuracy." Points out that in most states "the choice of electors could be decided by a few influential men" and that, with the rise of mass party politics, dueling diminished.

AHR 108: 190-91; *Booklist* 98: 167-70; *EAL* 37: 537-49; *HRNB* 30: 54; *IMH* 98: 245-46; *JAH* 89: 620-21; *JER* 22: 124-26; *J Interdis Hist* 33: 486-87; *JSH* 69: 885-87; *RAH* 30: 389-93; *VMHB* 110: 407-408; *VQR* 78: 44; *WMQ* 59: 795-99.

557 Freeman, Joanne B., ed. *Writings*. By Alexander Hamilton. New York: Literary Classics of the United States, distributed by Penguin Books, 2001. xix, 1108 p. ISBN 1931082049; ISBN 9781931082044; OCLC 45871146; LC Call Number E302 .H22; Dewey 973.4/092 21. Citations: 9.

Arranges Hamilton's writings in chronological order, providing more than 170 letters, speeches, essays, reports, and memoranda written between 1769 and 1804, including all of Hamilton's contributions to *The Federalist*. Includes several conflicting eyewitness accounts of Hamilton's duel with Aaron Burr.

LJ 126n17: 115.

558 Grant, James. *John Adams: Party of One*. New York: Farrar, Straus and Giroux, 2005. 530 p. ISBN 0374113149 (hbk.); ISBN 9780374113148 (hbk.); ISBN 0374530238 (pbk.); ISBN 9780374530235 (pbk.); OCLC 55220408; LC Call Number E322 .G73; Dewey 973.4/4/092. Citations: 5.

Presents a traditional biography of the Adams, drawing significantly on Adams's personal life. Intended for a general readership.

Booklist 101: 808-809; *LJ* 130n1: 123; *NEQ* 78: 503-505.

559 Grizzard, Frank E. *George Washington: A Biographical Companion*. Santa Barbara, Calif.: ABC-CLIO, 2002. xix, 437 p. ISBN 1576070824; ISBN

9781576070826; OCLC 48428902; LC Call Number E312 .G88; Dewey 973.4/1/092 21. Citations: 3.

Provides 200 entries on persons, places, events, and items related to George Washington. Includes in each item a short bibliography and background information that explains the relationship of the topic to Washington's life. Presents selected writings, a chronology, and lists of family members, the military officers with whom Washington served, and his presidential advisors.

Booklist 98: 1546; *Booklist* 99: 1832; *J Mil Hist* 67: 231-32; *LJ* 127n13: 79-80; *VQR* 79: 16.

560 Halliday, E.M. *Understanding Thomas Jefferson.* New York: HarperCollins, 2001. xiii, 284 p. ISBN 0060197935; ISBN 9780060197933; OCLC 44764180; LC Call Number E332 .H183; Dewey 973.4/6/092. Citations: 4.

Seeks to refute claims that Jefferson was characterized largely by contradictions and mysteries, maintaining instead that apparent inconsistencies are completely understandable, given the historical and social contexts. Acknowledges Jefferson's shortcomings vis-à-vis blacks and women, but contends that his advocacy of human liberty outweighs any flaws. Focuses on Jefferson's sexual habits and the controversy regarding Sally Hemmings.

LJ 126n4: 113.

561 Harvey, Louis-Georges. *Le Printemps de l'Amérique Française: Américanité, Anticolonialisme, et Républicanisme dans le Discours Politique Québécois, 1805-1837.* Montréal: Boréal, 2005. 296 p. ISBN 276460324X (pbk.); ISBN 9782764603246 (pbk.); OCLC 60742247; LC Call Number F1032 .H27; Dewey 320.9714/09/034. Citations: 7.

Views Lower Canada political struggles as similar to those of the American patriot movement and of the Creole nationalists of South America and the Caribbean. Attributes to Lower Canada the values of agrarian virtue, equality, and rejection of official corruption and commerce. Rejects the view of Lower Canada as a closed society with an economically and politically backward elite, arguing instead that the republican political elite had a clearly articulated, progressive *projet de societe*. Claims that Lower Canada was open to information and ideas from abroad, that the colony's French-speaking elite was educated in a classical humanist curriculum, and that American books, newspapers, and travelers' accounts circulated in the colony.

CHR 87: 319-23.

562 Harvey, Tamara and Greg O'Brien, ed. *George Washington's South.* Gainesville: University Press of Florida, 2004. x, 345 p. ISBN 081302689X; ISBN 9780813026893; ISBN 0813029171; ISBN 9780813029177; OCLC 52347482; LC Call Number F213 .G48; Dewey 975/.03 21. Citations: 7.

Presents papers from a 1999 University of Mississippi conference commemorating the bicentennial of Washington's death. Includes articles on the boundaries of the Old Southwest, regional identity, cultures on the southern colonial frontier, elite fashion in French colonial New Orleans, Washington and the national memory, slavery at Mount Vernon, power in South Carolina as

illustrated by the case of Thomas Jeremiah, and Creeks and Indian resistance in the South.
18c Stds 38: 361-67; *FHQ* 83: 337-39; *JAH* 92: 198-99; *JER* 25: 120-23; *JSH* 71: 430-31; *NCHR* 81: 466-67; *SCHM* 106: 70-72; *VMHB* 112: 308-309.

563   Heideking, Jürgen and James A. Henretta, eds. *Republicanism and Liberalism in America and the German States, 1750–1850.* New York: Cambridge University Press, 2002. x, 309 p. ISBN 0521800668; ISBN 9780521800662; OCLC 45466133; LC Call Number E302.1 .R46; Dewey 320.51/0943/09033 21. Citations: 13.
Presents essays comparing intellectual developments in the German states and the United States. Challenges American exceptionalism by demonstrating that contemporary German political debates contained similar liberal-republican themes.
AHR 108: 1109-1110; *JAH* 90: 629-30.

564   Higginbotham, Don, ed. *George Washington Reconsidered.* Charlottesville: University Press of Virginia, 2001. x, 336 p. ISBN 0813920051 (hbk.); ISBN 9780813920054 (hbk.); ISBN 081392006X (pbk.); ISBN 9780813920061 (pbk.); OCLC 44612979; LC Call Number E312 .G36; Dewey 973.4/1/092. Citations: 5.
Presents thirteen essays covering historians' treatments of Washington, Washington as a military professional, the influence of the British tobacco trade on pre-Revolutionary Virginia, the significance of Mount Vernon, Washington in the slavery debate, the effect of wartime experiences on the creation and development of American government, Washington's view of westward expansion, an appraisal of the Washington presidency, Washington's attitude toward death and afterlife, Washington's papers, Washington's aloofness and protection of his reputation, and Americans' image of Washington over time.
HRNB 29: 155-56; *JSH* 68: 929-31; *NCHR* 79: 469-70; *PMHB* 126: 341-42; *WMQ* 62: 337-39.

565   Higginbotham, Don. *George Washington: Uniting a Nation.* Lanham, Md.: Rowman & Littlefield Publishers, 2002. xii, 175 p. ISBN 0742522083; ISBN 9780742522084; OCLC 49566316; LC Call Number E312.17 .H636; Dewey 973.4/1/092. Citations: 8.
Asserts that the process of winning independence and creating a stable union required Washington to deal with diversity and fragmentation among the states. Explains that colonists generally saw themselves as British prior to 1774 and sought to emulate the British gentry, which allowed Washington, as the image of gentlemanly refinement and virtue, to become a new national icon. Observes that Washington was keenly aware of his symbolic importance and thus skillfully used his public image to unite the new nation, first by promoting among his soldiers devotion to the common cause and rejection of local loyalties and personal interests and ambitions and later by advancing the central government's prestige and power. Describes Washington's influential support for adoption of the Bill of Rights and attributes his failure to deal with slavery to his fear that the issue would destroy fragile national unity. Concludes that

Washington employed republican vocabulary to promote political centralization and an active national government and that the Union's indissolubility was the dominant theme of Washington's farewell address.
JAH 91: 1433-34; *JSH* 70: 651-52; *NCHR* 80: 376; *PMHB* 128: 82-83; *VMHB* 112: 66-67; *WMQ* 62: 337-39.

566 Hitchens, Christopher. *Thomas Jefferson: Author of America*. New York: Atlas Books/HarperCollins Publishers, 2005. xiv, 188 p. ISBN 0060598964; ISBN 9780060598969; OCLC 60525341; LC Call Number E332 .H66; Dewey 973.4/6092. Citations: 6.
Asserts that Jefferson, for all of his flaws and contradictions, is "one of the few figures in our history whose absence simply cannot be imagined." Claims that, on racism and slavery, Jefferson knew that he was wrong, and sees Jefferson's "capitulation to a slave power that he half-abominated" as tragic. Contends that Jefferson had a rocky relationship with his mother and a bad experience with his first love, Rebecca Burwell, which led to early insecurity and low self-esteem and motivated his hard study, his taking up the practice of law, and his securing a good marriage. Underscores Jefferson's uneasiness with religion and holds him up as the forerunner of contemporary American secularism.
Booklist 101: 1427.

567 Holmes, Jerry, ed. *Thomas Jefferson: A Chronology of His Thoughts*. Lanham, Md.: Rowman and Littlefield, 2002. vii, 333 p. ISBN 0742521168; ISBN 9780742521162; OCLC 48222796; LC Call Number E332.2 .J49; Dewey 973.4/6/092. Citations: 2.
Includes excerpts from letters Jefferson wrote to members of his family and to various other correspondents from 1760 until his death in 1826. Provides selections from *The Farm Book*, *The Garden Book*, and his account books. Contends that Jefferson "must be viewed by the standards of [his] time" and concludes that "In the pantheon of American heroes, perhaps no one stands so tall as Thomas Jefferson," and that none has "contributed as much to the progress and improvement of the American mindset and way of life."
JER 23: 288-91.

568 Horn, James, Jan Ellen Lewis, and Peter S. Onuf, eds. *The Revolution of 1800: Democracy, Race, and the New Republic*. Charlottesville: University of Virginia Press, 2002. xx, 431 p. ISBN 0813921406 (hbk.); ISBN 9780813921402 (hbk.); ISBN 0813921414 (pbk.) ; ISBN 9780813921419 (pbk.); OCLC 49760581; LC Call Number E330 .R48; Dewey 324.973/044. Citations: 30.
Includes articles on the revolutionary potential of the election of 1800, the development of the "political presidency," corruption and compromise in the election of 1800, newspapers, celebrations, voting, and democratization in the early republic, Thomas Jefferson and the psychology of democracy, religious aspects of the revolution of 1800, Thomas Jefferson in Gabriel's Virginia, defenses of slavery, Judith Sargent Murray and the revolution of 1800, rebellion and republicanism in the revolutionary French Caribbean, the empire of liberty reconsidered, Joseph Gales and the making of the Jeffersonian middle class, the

U.S. national state before and after the revolution of 1800, and Upper Canada and Thomas Jefferson.

AHR 109: 518-19; *JAH* 91: 222-23; *JER* 23: 623-25; *PMHB* 128: 208-210; *VMHB* 111: 417-18; *WMQ* 61: 187-90.

569 Houston, Alan Craig, ed. *Franklin: The Autobiography and Other Writings on Politics, Economics, and Virtue*. New York: Cambridge University Press, 2004. lii, 381 p. ISBN 0521834961 (hbk.); ISBN 9780521834964 (hbk.); ISBN 0521542650 (pbk.); ISBN 9780521542654 (pbk.); OCLC 54462029; LC Call Number E302.6.F7; Dewey 973.3/092. Citations: 0.

Presents forty-five documents written by Benjamin Franklin, which illustrate Franklin's views on politics, economics, and virtue.

Hist Teach 39: 266-67.

570 Howe, John R. *Language and Political Meaning in Revolutionary America*. Amherst: University of Massachusetts Press, 2004. xii, 281 p. ISBN 1558494227; ISBN 9781558494220; OCLC 52547586; LC Call Number PE2809 .H69; LC Call Number PS195.P65; Dewey 306.44/0973/09033. Citations: 6.

Examines what revolutionary participants thought about the style, structure, and use of language in political documents. Analyzes late seventeenth- and early eighteenth-century responses to the replacement of Latin with vernacular English in the administrative, religious, and learned discourse. Discusses conservative advocates' attempts to reform the legal codes and state constitutions, the usage of metaphors in the revolutionary period, the practice of anonymous and pseudonymous public writings, and the role that linguistic shifts played in the debate between the Federalists and Antifederalists over the Constitution and Bill of Rights. Contends that conceptual structures "do not exist apart from the gritty reality of everyday politics."

IMH 102: 168-69; *JAH* 91: 1428-29; *JSH* 71: 669-70; *RAH* 32: 486-92.

571 Isaacson, Walter. *Benjamin Franklin: An American Life*. New York: Simon and Schuster, 2003. x, 590 p. ISBN 0684807610; ISBN 9780684807614; ISBN 0965042634; ISBN 9780965042635; OCLC 52090968; LC Call Number E302.6.F8; Dewey 973.3/092. Citations: 42.

Presents "a chronological narrative biography" of Franklin for a general readership. Emphasizes Franklin's penchant for self-promotion and his ambitions, scientific pursuits, personal quirks, relationships, and political views.

Booklist 99: 1736; *Booklist* 101: 502; *JAH* 91: 606; *LJ* 128n11: 80-81; *LJ* 129n132; *PMHB* 128: 311-12; *PSQ* 119: 343-44.

572 Jaher, Frederic Cople. *The Jews and the Nation: Revolution, Emancipation, State Formation, and the Liberal Paradigm in America and France*. Princeton, N. J.: Princeton University Press, 2003. x, 312 p. ISBN 069109649X; ISBN 9780691096490; OCLC 50205697; LC Call Number DS135.F82; Dewey 944/.004924. Citations: 13.

Compares the civic integration of Jews in the United States and France from the period of the American and French revolutions through the beginnings of the

American republic and the Napoleonic era. Argues that French Jews gained civil rights from revolution, while American Jews acquired their civil and political rights through the evolution of American democratic principles. Discusses the responses of American and French Jewish communities to the acquisition of national citizenship, noting that French distrust of Jews as a "nation within a nation" affected the debates in the National Constituent Assembly and delayed somewhat the granting of rights to Jews.
AHR 109: 148-49; *EHR* 119: 239-40; *JAH* 90: 1004-1005; *JAEH* 24: 86-87; *J Mod Hist* 77: 345-56; *WMQ* 60: 908-11.

573 Jensen, Laura. *Patriots, Settlers, and the Origins of American Social Policy*. Cambridge: Cambridge University Press, 2003. xii, 244 p. ISBN 0521818834 (hbk.); ISBN 9780521818834 (hbk.); ISBN 0521524261 (pbk.); ISBN 9780521524261 (pbk.); OCLC 50590871; LC Call Number HN13 .J46; Dewey 361.6/1. Citations: 15.
Analyzes policies that led to long-term social benefits in America, including Revolutionary military land grants and other sponsored settlement in the western territories. Indicates that these policies were crucial to state building in the early United States and argues that Americans built a central state infrastructure long before the American Civil War. Suggests that programmatic benefits were always arbitrary, political, and divisive, but concludes that selective pensions and land bounties "helped to reconstruct a state engaged in acts of warfare as a benevolent, 'welfare'-oriented state that was justified in its efforts to conquer space."
AHR 109: 1557-58; *JAH* 91: 1002; *J Econ Hist* 63: 1166-67; *J Interdis Hist* 35: 306-307.

574 Johnson, Paul. *George Washington: The Founding Father*. New York: Atlas Books/Harper Collins, 2005. 126 p. ISBN 006075365X; ISBN 9780060753658; OCLC 56413248; LC Call Number E312 .J67; Dewey 973.4/1/092. Citations: 1.
Emphasizes Washington's contradictions, noting that he was an avid chronicler who was also very guarded about the sorts of things that he revealed about himself, that he was a competent soldier who made stunning mistakes in leadership, that he hated slavery but failed to use his considerable power to limit or destroy it, and that he was a deist who feared the destruction of traditional Christianity. Concludes that Washington was a "genius" and was "one of the most important figures in world history."
Booklist 101: 1562.

575 Kaplan, Lawrence S. *Alexander Hamilton: Ambivalent Anglophile*. Wilmington, Del.: Scholarly Resources, Inc., 2002. xvi, 196 p. ISBN 0842028773 (hbk.); ISBN 9780842028776 (hbk.); ISBN 0842028781 (pbk.); ISBN 9780842028783 (pbk.); OCLC 49225835; LC Call Number E302.6.H2; Dewey 973.4/092. Citations: 4.
Presents a generally favorable portrait of Hamilton. Focuses on Hamilton's role in foreign policy, arguing that his differences with Jeffersonians on matters of diplomacy have been overstated. Explains that Hamilton and Jefferson agreed

on matters of public credit, the Nootka Sound crisis of 1790, American neutrality in the Anglo-French conflict, the critique of the Jay Treaty, and the acquisition of Louisiana. Concludes that Hamilton's supposed Anglophilia was merely pragmatic and that he was acutely aware of potential conflict between the United States and Britain.
JER 24: 694-97; *WMQ* 60: 465-67.

576 Kars, Marjoleine. *Breaking Loose Together: The Regulator Rebellion in Pre-Revolutionary North Carolina*. Chapel Hill: University of North Carolina Press, 2002. x, 286 p. ISBN 0807826723 (hbk.); ISBN 9780807826720 (hbk.); ISBN 0807849995 (pbk.); ISBN 9780807849996 (pbk.); OCLC 47755765; LC Call Number F257 .K37; Dewey 975.6/02. Citations: 16.
Portrays the Regulators as reluctant rebels, noting that settlers had been drawn to North Carolina by abundant, inexpensive land, the absence of Anglican hierarchy, the promise of self-sufficiency, and the idea that they would be left alone to farm. Finds that their expectations ran afoul of eastern elites who sought to strengthen the Anglican establishment and to use legal machinery to take over vast swaths of land. Draws parallels to the uprisings of the Whiskey and Shays rebels and extends the intellectual influence of the Regulators to the Populists of the nineteenth century. Concludes that the Regulation movement represented "an instance of resistance to the slow and massive shift in social conscience that accompanied the transition to market economies."
AHR 108: 825-26; *GHQ* 86: 290-92; *JAH* 89: 1508-1509; *J Interdis Hist* 34: 97-98; *JSH* 69: 879-80; *NCHR* 79: 459-60; *WMQ* 59: 1011-14.

577 Kersh, Rogan. *Dreams of a More Perfect Union*. Ithaca, N.Y.: Cornell University Press, 2001. xi, 358 p. ISBN 0801438128 (hbk.); ISBN 9780801438127 (hbk.); ISBN 0801489806 (pbk.); ISBN 9780801489808 (pbk.); OCLC 44802858; LC Call Number JK31 .K47; Dewey 320.54/0973/09033. Citations: 10.
Analyzes the concept of "union" from the eighteenth through the twentieth centuries. Finds that "union" represented a powerful idea in the eighteenth and nineteenth centuries, but by the early twentieth century had virtually disappeared. Explains that union meant different things to different persons at different times and in different places. Notes that, in the first half of the nineteenth century, three aspects of union dominated the discourse: (1) sustainable and pragmatic, advanced by men like James Madison and Henry Clay; (2) ethnocultural, emphasizing the superiority of Anglo-Saxon culture; and (3) principled, forwarded by the likes of Frederick Douglass and Abraham Lincoln. Contends that Reconstruction's failure led abolitionists and African Americans to abandon the notion of principled union and ultimately led to union's displacement by "celebratory nationalism."
AHR 107: 532-33; *JAH* 89: 617-18; *JER* 21: 695-97; *WMQ* 61: 582-88.

578 Kirschke, James J. *Gouverneur Morris: Author, Statesman, and Man of the World*. New York: Thomas Dunne Books, 2005. xxvi, 370 p. ISBN 031224195X; ISBN 9780312241957; OCLC 61262455; LC Call Number E302.6.M7; Dewey 973.4/092. Citations: 2.

Examines Morris's life and career, noting that he had a unique talent for boiling down debates and capturing essential elements on paper. Characterizes Morris as a talented and charming elitist, who demonstrated very bad judgment on a number of occasions.
JAH 93: 1220.

579 Kromkowski, Charles A. *Recreating the American Republic: Rules of Apportionment, Constitutional Change, and American Political Development, 1700–1870*. New York: Cambridge University Press, 2002. xxxiv, 451 p. ISBN 0521808480; ISBN 9780521808484; OCLC 49495179; LC Call Number JK31 .K76; Dewey 320.973/09/033. Citations: 7.
Investigates major constitutional changes in the representation in Congress allocated to the states during three periods: Revolution and Confederation (1774-1781), Constitution (1781-1788), and Civil War (1860-1870). Applies a "game theoretic" cost-benefit analysis to the problem for each era, which marked "several creations, transformations, and breakdowns in the American political order." Views the framing and adoption of the Articles of Confederation as a contest among the large, medium, and small states over Congress's powers and over the basis of state voting.
AHR 109: 181-82; *JAH* 90: 1428-29; *J Econ Hist* 63: 898-99; *JSH* 70: 126-27.

580 Lambert, Frank. *James Habersham: Loyalty, Politics, and Commerce in Colonial Georgia*. Athens: University of Georgia Press, 2005. x, 197 p. ISBN 0820325392; ISBN 9780820325392; OCLC 55738725; LC Call Number F289.H14; Dewey 975.8/02/092. Citations: 3.
Examines Habersham's "places and times" and "the structures that defined his possibilities and limitations." Covers Habersham's interactions with the political, religious, and economic changes of the era and argues that Habersham was steadfastly loyal to his family, God, Georgia, and the British Empire. Contends that Habersham used his wealth to fashion himself as an English gentleman with the proper trappings of garments, portraits, a wine cellar, and a library. Finds that Habersham reluctantly concluded that Georgia could not compete with Carolina without the help of slave labor. Discusses Habersham's loyalty to the Crown and his contention that the Sons of Liberty had taken "the powers of Government out of its proper and legal channels and invested it in a Mob."
AHR 111: 1502-1503; *GHQ* 89: 410-11; *JAH* 92: 1411-12; *JSH* 72: 450-52.

581 Larson, John Lauritz. *Internal Improvement: National Public Works and the Promise of Popular Government in the Early United States*. Chapel Hill: University of North Carolina Press, 2001. xviii, 324 p. ISBN 0807825956 (hbk.); ISBN 9780807825952 (hbk.); ISBN 0807849111 (pbk.); ISBN 9780807849118 (pbk.); OCLC 44727813; LC Call Number HC105 .L26; Dewey 338.973. Citations: 53.
Explores the causes and consequences of the often overlapping early federal and state government attempts to implement transportation infrastructure. Discusses the debates over the constitutionality of internal improvements, concerns over national consolidation and favoritism in road routes, and the strident language

employed. Challenges the common view that shortage of capital and imperfect technical expertise doomed public works. Compares the extraordinary early success of the Erie Canal with failed state projects in Virginia, Maryland, Pennsylvania, and North Carolina, explaining that the successes were influenced as much by the political and ideological disposition to improvement as by resource scarcity. Finds that among the failures, clashing local interests, and the lack of an overall national design were to blame. Explains that the failure of national internal improvements between the 1780s and the 1830s represented the triumph of classical liberal economic thinking over pursuit of a "republican birthright," the victory of modern industrial capitalism over republicanism, the shift of essential American ideology from popular consent to the rights of private property, and the roots of Populism and progressive reform movements.
AHR 107: 192-93; *AJLH* 45: 105-107; *JAH* 88: 1513-14; *JER* 21: 531-34; *J Econ Hist* 61: 864-65; *NCHR* 79: 471-72; *RAH* 30: 549-54.

582 Lenner, Andrew C. *The Federal Principle in American Politics, 1790–1833*. Lanham, Md.: Rowman and Littlefield Publishers, 2001. xiv, 223 p. ISBN 0945612761 (hbk.); ISBN 9780945612766 (hbk.); ISBN 0945612834 (pbk.); ISBN 9780945612834 (pbk.); ISBN 0742520706 (hbk.); ISBN 9780742520707 (hbk.); ISBN 0742520714 (pbk.); ISBN 9780742520714 (pbk.); OCLC 44914139; LC Call Number JK31 .L46; Dewey 320.973/09/033. Citations: 7.
Studies "the federal principle" in leading political and constitutional controversies from 1790 to 1833. Examines political fights over questions of constitutional interpretation, arguing that constitutional controversies are really political controversies and that Federalists and Republicans coalesced around two different, incompatible views of federalism and the Constitution.
AHR 108: 521-22; *JAH* 89: 1511; *JSH* 69: 412-13; *WMQ* 61: 582-88.

583 Lewis, James E., Jr. *John Quincy Adams: Policymaker for the Union*. Wilmington, Del.: SR Books, 2001. xxv, 164 p. ISBN 0842026223 (hbk.); ISBN 9780842026222 (hbk.); ISBN 0842026231 (pbk.); ISBN 9780842026239 (pbk.); OCLC 45209077; LC Call Number E377 .L47; Dewey 973.5/5/092. Citations: 4.
Argues that Adams's political philosophy, which reflected the beliefs of the Founders more than those of his own generation, informed every aspect of his foreign policy objectives and his approach to domestic policy. Explains that Adams's parents instilled in him a strong Puritan work ethic, dedication to commonwealth, emphasis on Enlightenment reason and republicanism, and the bearing, manners, and refinement of a gentleman. Notes that Adams drew from the Founders the view that the union of states and neutrality in European conflicts were keys to preserving that which was won in the Revolution: independence and republican government. Views Adams's second term as secretary of state as unsuccessful, largely because much of his energy had been diverted to the campaign leading up to the election of 1824. Sees Adams's presidency as unsuccessful not because of political partisanship, but due mostly to his own personal failures, his abdicating to Congress responsibility to solve sectional tensions, and his response to opposition with "political fatalism."
Booklist 97: 1112; *JER* 21: 526-29; *WMQ* 62: 745-64.

584 Liu, Zuochang. *Jiefeixun quan zhuan*. 2 vols. Ji'nan (Shandong), PRC: Qilu Publishers, 2005. 1703 p. ISBN 753331445X; ISBN 9787533314453; OCLC 123499292; LC Call Number E332.2 .L582. Citations: 0.
Presents a complete Chinese-language narrative biography of Jefferson. Characterizes Jefferson as a moral actor, contrasting him with his "natural enemy" Alexander Hamilton, who did all that he could to undermine Jefferson. Submits that the struggle between the two, though "not excessively noisy, and not particularly violent, was, substantively speaking, very influential," as the nation in the 1790s stood at the crossroads of democracy and government that primarily served the interests of wealthy capitalists. Explains that Jefferson held tightly to the principles of the Declaration of Independence and thus constructed a "democratic republic that was the model for the whole world." Explains away Jefferson's support of slavery by pointing to contemporary culture and Jefferson's agricultural interests.
WMQ 64: 845-52.

585 Lustig, Mary Lou. *The Imperial Executive in America: Sir Edmund Andros, 1637–1714*. Madison, N. J.: Fairleigh Dickinson University Press, 2002. 339 p. ISBN 0838639364; ISBN 9780838639368; OCLC 48131743; LC Call Number F122.A53; Dewey 974/.02/092. Citations: 2.
Rejects the one-dimensional characterization of Andros as an arbitrary authoritarian, portraying him instead as a loyal and skilled imperial administrator. Reviews Andros's involvement in transatlantic imperial politics, the disputes between Whigs and Tories, and the various governors with whom and assemblies with which Andros interacted.
JAH 90: 619-20; *WMQ* 60: 879-82.

586 Mancke, Elizabeth. *The Fault Lines of Empire: Political Differentiation in Massachusetts and Nova Scotia, ca. 1760–1830*. New York: Routledge, 2005. xi, 214 p. ISBN 0415950007 (hbk.); ISBN 9780415950008 (hbk.); ISBN 0415950015 (pbk.); ISBN 9780415950015 (pbk.); OCLC 56368582; LC Call Number F69 .M36; Dewey 320.744/09/033 22. Citations: 9.
Delineates the differences between British Atlantic colonies founded in the seventeenth century and those such as Nova Scotia and Canada, which were acquired by war and treaty, the governments of which "were established after the Glorious Revolution (1688–1689) and development of the Crown-in-Parliament, and thus colonists could not claim a constitutional autonomy from Parliament and an allegiance to the Crown alone in the way the people in the older colonies did." Compares Machias, at the far northern edge of Massachusetts, and Liverpool, on the south shore of Nova Scotia, during the last four decades of the eighteenth century in terms of land distribution, local government structures, church polities, and responses to the American Revolution. Explains that the two communities were similar in terms of founding populations and geographic locations, but that Machias ended up joining the rebellion against British parliamentary power, while Liverpool accepted the crown-in-parliament imperial system. Asserts that this political divergence between Machias and Liverpool was an early indicator of the

divisions in the British Atlantic world that led to the development of two contrasting political cultures in the United States and Canada.
AHR 110: 1515-16; *JAH* 92: 1422-23; *JER* 26: 698-701; *JHG* 32: 241-43; *WMQ* 62: 788-91.

587 Marshall, P.J. *The Making and Unmaking of Empires: Britain, India, and America, c. 1750–1783*. Oxford, U.K.: Oxford University Press, 2005. vi, 398 p. ISBN 0199278954; ISBN 9780199278954; OCLC 57431443; LC Call Number DA16 .M376; Dewey 325.3410954. Citations: 30.
Examines the connections between the loss of the thirteen colonies and the creation of empire in India, brought on, initially, by the Seven Years' War, which combined conflicts between the British and the French in Europe, the Americas, and India, and was marked by decisive British victories in India and Canada. Discusses the primary constitutional question for the British in the eighteenth century: the authority of Parliament, with which the Americans were taking issue. Traces the evolution of the "official mind" that shaped British imperial policy, largely driven by fear and anxiety, and the colonial response. Finds that in each empire the British authorities negotiated with local elites, and that "in both India and America the fate of empire depended to a large extent on the responses of elites."
AHR 112: 163; *Econ Hist Rev* 59: 407-408; *18c Stds* 40: 314-17; *EHR* 122: 763-65; *HRNB* 34: 67; *J Brit Stds* 45: 664-66; *WMQ* 64: 199-202.

588 Matthews, Marty D. *Forgotten Founder: The Life and Times of Charles Pinckney*. Columbia: University of South Carolina Press, 2004. xix, 186 p. ISBN 1570035474; ISBN 9781570035470; OCLC 54530385; LC Call Number E302.6.P54; Dewey 973.4/092. Citations: 8.
Presents a brief biography of Charles Pinckney of South Carolina. Details the life and contributions of Pinckney and seeks to explain why Pinckney's importance has been overshadowed by the likes of James Madison and Alexander Hamilton, among others. Contends that Pinckney's contribution to the Constitution rivals that of Madison, who is characterized as vindictive and jealous of Pinckney for having presented a strong critique of the Articles of Confederation and an effective argument for a strong central government. Finds that more than forty of Pinckney's proposals made it into the Constitution. Discusses Pinckney's support of Jefferson, arguing that Jefferson's election in 1800 "occurred in large part because of Pinckney's actions nationally and at home in South Carolina."
GHQ 89: 115-18; *JAH* 92: 595-96; *JER* 25: 294-97; *JSH* 71: 875; *NCHR* 82: 261-62; *WMQ* 62: 745-64.

598 McCullough, David G. *John Adams*. New York: Simon & Schuster, 2001. 751 p. ISBN 0684813637; ISBN 9780684813639; OCLC 45827978; LC Call Number E322 .M38; Dewey 973.4/4/092. Citations: 101.
Presents a biography of Adams that describes his background, childhood, family, service in the Revolution, and service as vice president and president. Discusses Adams's elucidation of the constitutional doctrine of separation of powers and his influence on new state constitutions. Contends that, though

Adams rejected the prospect of an unnecessary war with France in early 1799, he had as president done much during 1798 to promote war hysteria. Exculpates Adams of political excesses of the period (e.g., the Alien and Sedition Acts), citing the political passions of the time. Characterizes Adams favorably, noting that he "despised slavery" and played a tremendous role in the future development of the nation.

Booklist 98: 955; *JAH* 90: 210-11; *LJ* 126n8: 101; *LJ* 127n1: 50; *NEQ* 75: 139-41; *PSQ* 117: 130-32; *WMQ* 59: 305-14.

590 McGaughy, J. Kent. *Richard Henry Lee of Virginia: A Portrait of an American Revolutionary.* Lanham, Md.: Rowman and Littlefield Publishers, 2004. xx, 249 p. ISBN 0742533840 (hbk.); ISBN 9780742533844 (hbk.); ISBN 0742533859 (pbk.); ISBN 9780742533851 (pbk.); OCLC 52601560; LC Call Number E302.6 .L4; Dewey 973.3/092. Citations: 2.

Claims that Richard Henry Lee has been poorly understood and unfairly portrayed since his own lifetime. Calls Lee a "conservative revolutionary" who was immersed in the world of tobacco cultivation and western land investment (particularly Virginia's claims to the trans-Appalachian west) and who sought to protect his fortune and social position by making connections with leaders in England and elsewhere in the colonies. Asserts that Lee's political career must be understood in the context of his private life and his family's financial concerns.

JSH 73: 153-54; *VMHB* 112: 67-69; *WMQ* 62: 745-64.

591 Morgan, Edmund S. *Benjamin Franklin.* New Haven, Conn.: Yale University Press, 2002. xii, 339 p. ISBN 0300095325; ISBN 9780300095326; OCLC 48906479; LC Call Number E302.6.F8; Dewey 973.3/092. Citations: 34.

Presents a full biography of Franklin, characterizing him as a strong, personable, curious, active young man, who emphasized action, was fascinated by how things worked, and was determined to be useful. Finds that in the early eighteenth century, Franklin stressed self and civic improvement and took pride in being English. Explains that between 1757 and 1775 Franklin was in London working to reform and preserve the British Empire by seeking equal treatment for Americans as British subjects. Discusses Franklin's service in France from 1776 to 1785 and his interest in practical designs and inventions. Concludes that Franklin had done "as much as any man ever has to shape the world" he lived in.

Booklist 98: 1916; *EAL* 41: 535-53; *IMH* 100: 394-96; *JAH* 90: 996-97; *JAS* 38: 519-20; *LJ* 127n15: 70; *LJ* 128n1: 50; *NEQ* 76: 124-26; *WMQ* 60: 657-59.

592 Morrison, Jeffry H. *John Witherspoon and the Founding of the American Republic.* Notre Dame, Ind.: University of Notre Dame Press, 2005. xv, 220 p. ISBN 0268034850; ISBN 9780268034856; OCLC 57965720; LC Call Number E302.6.W7; Dewey 973.3/092. Citations: 12.

Characterizes Witherspoon as "a quintessential American founder" and as one who, as a supporter of Lockean social compact theory, reader of Scottish philosophy, practicer of Reformed Protestantism, and advocate of classical republicanism, represented "the American mind at the founding." Reviews Witherspoon's emigration from Scotland, presidency of the College of New

Jersey (later Princeton), educator of founding fathers (especially James Madison), signer of the Declaration of Independence, member of the Continental Congress, and architect of "the nationalization of the Presbyterian Church in the United States." Examines Witherspoon's political views and concludes that "perhaps more than any other single founder, Witherspoon embodied all of the major intellectual and social elements behind the American founding."
AHR 112: 189-90; *CH* 75: 446-48; *JAH* 93: 193-94.

593 Morrison, Michael A. and Melinda S. Zook, eds. *Revolutionary Currents: Nation Building in the Transatlantic World.* Lanham, Md.: Rowman and Littlefield, 2004. ix, 192 p. ISBN 0742521648 (hbk.); ISBN 9780742521643 (hbk.); ISBN 0742521656 (pbk.); ISBN 9780742521650 (pbk.); OCLC 53045197; LC Call Number D295 .R48; Dewey 303.6/4/09034. Citations: 12.
Includes articles on state formation, resistance, and the creation of revolutionary traditions in the early modern era, law, liberty, and "jury ideology" in English transatlantic traditions, the ideology underpinning the American Revolution, the French Revolution and the emergence of the nation form, Atlantic revolutionary traditions, and popular insurgency in Mexico between 1800 and 1821.
AHR 110: 1129-30; *CJH* 40: 592-94; *HRNB* 33: 37-38.

594 Onuf, Peter S. and Leonard J. Sadosky. *Jeffersonian America.* Malden, Mass.: Blackwell Publishers, 2002. ix, 270 p. ISBN 1557869227 (hbk.); ISBN 9781557869227 (hbk.); ISBN 1557869235 (pbk.); ISBN 9781557869234 (pbk.); OCLC 46732387; LC Call Number E331 .O58; Dewey 320.973/09/034. Citations: 7.
Connects aspirations of the Founders to the establishment of the new nation, noting that revolutionary republican principles were intentionally infused into American institutions. Discusses Jefferson's views on slavery, education, land policy, trade, diplomacy, Native Americans, and the Louisiana Purchase. Contends that the Revolution of 1800 came about "by the mobilization of political factions in the various states" in "the virtual absence of anything we might now recognize as party organization." Claims that Jeffersonian thought was truly national in scope and emphasized sovereignty, federalism, combating corruption, and economic fairness.
CJH 34: 184-86; *JSH* 69: 407-408.

595 Pasley, Jeffrey L., Andrew W. Robertson, and David Waldstreicher, eds. *Beyond the Founders: New Approaches to the Political History of the Early American Republic.* Chapel Hill: University of North Carolina Press, 2004. 435 p. ISBN 0807828890 (hbk.); ISBN 9780807828892 (hbk.); ISBN 0807855588 (pbk.); ISBN 9780807855584 (pbk.); OCLC 54881767; LC Call Number E302.1 .B495; Dewey 973.4. Citations: 43.
Includes articles on popular political culture and participatory democracy in the early republic, electioneering rituals from 1790 to 1820, dress and politics, women and party conflict, Aaron Burr and the sexual politics of treason, federalists, masculinity and partisanship during the War of 1812, African American political community, consent, civil society, and the public sphere, definition of the right to bear arms, liberalism, nationalism, and the appeal of

Texas in the 1820s, communications deregulation as a national political issue from 1839 to 1851, New York anti-rent wars and the Jacksonian political order, and the possibility of a new political history.
AHR 111: 160-61; *JAH* 92: 967-68; *JSH* 71: 872-74; *NCHR* 82: 392-93; *VMHB* 113: 88-89; *RAH* 33: 314-24; *WMQ* 62: 764-67.

596 Pasley, Jeffrey L. *"The Tyranny of Printers": Newspaper Politics in the Early American Republic*. Charlottesville: University Press of Virginia, 2001. xviii, 517 p. ISBN 0813920302; ISBN 9780813920306; OCLC 45460799; LC Call Number PN4861 .P37; Dewey 071/3/09033. Citations: 52.
Contends that newspapers and their editors played key roles in the development of American party systems of the late eighteenth and early nineteenth centuries. Argues that by the 1820s the newspaper press had become "the political system's central institution, not simply a forum or atmosphere in which politics took place." Emphasizes the experience of Republicans because these "opposition statesmen and opposition printers . . . first conjoined newspapers and party politics." Characterizes Federalist editors as "young lawyer-literati," who "simply lacked the appropriate temperament for political combat." Concludes that, by the 1830s, newspaper editors were second only to lawyers as "the most disproportionally represented occupational group in politics" and that they played a significant role "in democratizing American political life" and "became the agents and promoters of a new and less-deferential brand of politics."
AHR 108: 191-92; *HRNB* 30: 11; *JAH* 89: 619-20; *JER* 21: 714-17; *JSH* 69: 413-14; *RAH* 30: 220-26; *VMHB* 110: 103-104; *WMQ* 58: 1031-34.

597 Randall, Willard Sterne. *Alexander Hamilton: A Life*. New York: HarperCollins, 2003. xiii, 476 p. ISBN 0060195495; ISBN 9780060195496; OCLC 49751010; LC Call Number E302.6.H2; Dewey 973.4/092. Citations: 6.
Presents a biography of Hamilton for a general readership. Characterizes Hamilton positively, noting that that he was a devoted soldier and revolutionary and that he saw the role of government as taming citizens' passions, as people "are inherently corrupted by lust for power and greed for property." Concludes that, while Jeffersonians won the day in the eighteenth and early nineteenth centuries, Hamilton's views were more presciently modern.
PMHB 128: 83-85.

598 Richards, Leonard L. *Shays's Rebellion: The American Revolution's Final Battle*. Philadelphia: University of Pennsylvania Press, 2002. x, 204 p. ISBN 0812236696; ISBN 9780812236699; OCLC 48707026; LC Call Number F69 .R63; Dewey 974.4/03. Citations: 19.
Argues that most of the Shays rebels were not poor, not debt-ridden, and not all came from towns working through religious conflict. Finds that leaders drew support from rural areas but lacked the prestige necessary to inspire armed resistance in the masses. Contends that rural discontent both led to Shays's Rebellion and to opposition to the Constitution, and that rebel towns vigorously opposed the Constitution.
GHQ 86: 638-41; *JAH* 90: 625; *NEQ* 76: 126-30; *VQR* 79: 7; *WMQ* 60: 689-93.

599   Rodenbough, Charles D. *Governor Alexander Martin: Biography of a North Carolina Revolutionary War Statesman*. Jefferson, N.C.: McFarland, 2004. viii, 242 p. ISBN 078641684X; ISBN 9780786416844; OCLC 53796706; LC Call Number F258.M35; Dewey 975.6/03/092. Citations: 1.

Presents a biography of Martin, covering his early life, education at Princeton, and career as a state legislator, governor, delegate to the Constitutional Convention, and United States senator. Finds that Martin was able to appeal both to eastern North Carolina elites and to small farmers and squatters in the west. Explains that, due to ethnicity (Scots-Irish) and religion (Presbyterian), Martin had much in common with westerners, but also shared tastes, lifestyles, and family connections with members of the eastern elite. Characterizes Martin as well-educated and highly influenced by the Scottish Enlightenment and concludes that he was a political "innovator" and "one of America's first successful exponents of the 'art' of politics."
JSH 71: 431-32; *NCHR* 81: 461-62.

600   Roper, L.H. *Conceiving Carolina: Proprietors, Planters, and Plots, 1662–1729*. New York: Palgrave Macmillan, 2004. viii, 214 p. ISBN 9781403964793; ISBN 1403964793; OCLC 52838912; LC Call Number   F272 .R68; Dewey 975.7/02. Citations: 3.

Presents a political history of South Carolina under the eight Lords Proprietors, discussing their plans for the colony, the basis of institutions on English forms, and legislative and judicial developments. Finds that the Goose Creek Men "engineered the destruction" of Stuart's Town to maintain their Indian slave trade. Finds that the Lords Proprietors' expectations for the colony's growth were fairly realistic and that the Fundamental Constitutions were remarkably reasonable, despite the colony's organization around large estates. Concludes that political discord was largely local in nature and not based on pronouncements from London.
JSH 73: 146-47; *NCHR* 83: 101-102.

601   Ryerson, Richard Alan, ed. *John Adams and the Founding of the Republic*. Boston: Massachusetts Historical Society, 2001. x, 294 p. ISBN 0934909784; ISBN 9780934909785; OCLC 45505967; LC Call Number E322 .J64; Dewey 973.4/4/092. Citations: 7.

Presents articles on Adams's political career, his relationship to the provincial elite and with Thomas Jefferson, his service as Washington's vice president, the presidential election of 1796, his views on free speech, Abigail Adams as first lady, the science of politics, and Adams and Jefferson as historians.
JAH 89: 1026-27; *JER* 22: 121-23; *J Interdis Hist* 33: 658-59; *NEQ* 75: 504-507; *RAH* 30: 212-19; *WMQ* 59: 315-18.

602   Shankman, Andrew. *Crucible of American Democracy: The Struggle to Fuse Egalitarianism & Capitalism in Jeffersonian Pennsylvania*. Lawrence: University Press of Kansas, 2004. xii, 298 p. ISBN 0700613048; ISBN 9780700613045; OCLC 53098987; LC Call Number JK2318.P5; Dewey: 324.2732/6/09748. Citations: 11.

Defines the various roles of the Federalists, the Philadelphia Democrats, the Snyderite (rural) Democrats, and the Quids in early national Pennsylvania. Explains that Federalists controlled the state in the 1790s and emphasized capital availability and manufacturing, only to be replaced later in the decade by Jeffersonians who were bolstered by artisan and rural constituencies and an influx of immigrants. Comments that these Democrats favored simple and direct democracy that would maximize economic opportunity and equality. Distinguishes rural Democrats as a group that favored laissez-faire economics and limited government control and the Quids, who feared wealth redistribution and supported protective tariffs, internal improvements, and a strong judiciary that would protect private property. Concludes that the social order became less hierarchical in late eighteenth- and early nineteenth-century Pennsylvania and that capitalism became attractive for the opportunities that it offered most white men.
AHR 110: 786-87; *JAH* 91: 1438-39; *JER* 24: 483-86; *PMHB* 129: 354-55; *RAH* 33: 325-32; *WMQ* 62: 562-65.

603 Sheldon, Garrett Ward. *The Political Philosophy of James Madison.* Baltimore, Md.: The Johns Hopkins University Press, 2001. xvi, 141 p. ISBN 0801864798 (hbk.); ISBN 9780801864797 (hbk.); ISBN 9780801871061 (pbk.); ISBN 0801871069 (pbk.); OCLC 43607229; LC Call Number JC211.M35; Dewey 321.8/092. Citations: 12.
Examines the origins of Madison's political philosophy in Augustinian thought, which was reinforced by his early education and his time at Princeton. Connects Madison's federalism to John Witherspoon's influential writings on human depravity. Concludes that "Madison's political philosophy historically shifted between Lockean liberal and classical republican, federalist and states' rights perspectives, with a consistent view to a balanced, moderate government that accurately reflected the Christian view of human nature as egotistical and domineering."
JER 21: 514-16; *JSH* 69: 151-52; *WMQ* 59: 319-25.

604 Silverstone, Scott A. *Divided Union: The Politics of War in the Early American Republic.* Ithaca, N.Y.: Cornell University Press, 2004. vii, 278 p. ISBN 0801442303; ISBN 9780801442308; OCLC 54356447; LC Call Number E338 .S56; Dewey 973. Citations: 7.
Examines the moments in the early nineteenth century when the United States came to the brink of armed conflict, but pulled back (e.g., the Chesapeake incident, New England's opposition to the Enforcement Act, conflict with England over Oregon, etc.). Points to the federal and sectional nature of the government, by the Framers' design, which prevented consensus for military action and made the nation a "peace-prone" republic.
AHR 111: 159-60; *J Mil Hist* 69: 558-59; *JSH* 72: 164-66.

605 Stahr, Walter. *John Jay: Founding Father.* New York: Hambledon, 2005. xiv, 482 p. ISBN 1852854448; ISBN 9781852854447; OCLC 58592264; LC Call Number E302.6.J4; Dewey 973.3/092. Citations: 3.

Seeks to place Jay among the highest rank of Founders. Discusses his service in the Continental Congresses, as minister to Spain, as negotiator of the Treaty of Paris, as foreign secretary, as the nation's first chief justice, and as governor of New York. Notes his various authorial roles, including participation in writing *The Federalist*, and his unusual position as a slaveholder and outspoken proponent of manumission.

Booklist 101: 1057; *JAH* 93: 505-506; *NCHR* 82: 511-12.

606 Staloff, Darren. *Hamilton, Adams, Jefferson: The Politics of Enlightenment and the American Founding.* New York: Hill and Wang, 2005. 419 p. ISBN 0809077841 (hbk.); ISBN 9780809077847 (hbk.); ISBN 080905356X (pbk.); ISBN 9780809053568 (pbk.); OCLC 58431846; LC Call Number E302.6.H2; Dewey 973.4. Citations: 6.

Explores the impact of Enlightenment thought on Alexander Hamilton, John Adams, and Thomas Jefferson. Contends that for each, involvement in the Revolution required a reexamination of Enlightenment ideals and that such intellectual grounding influenced the post-revolutionary politics of each man. Claims that the Enlightenment was "fulfilled" in Hamilton, "transcended" in Adams, and represented a Romantic vision for Jefferson.

AHR 111: 474-75; *Booklist* 101: 1633; *JAH* 93: 191-92; *LJ* 130n9: 127; *RAH* 34: 307-14.

607 Tate, Adam L. *Conservatism and Southern Intellectuals, 1789–1861: Liberty, Tradition, and the Good Society.* Columbia: University of Missouri Press, 2005. ix, 402 p. ISBN 082621567X; ISBN 9780826215673; OCLC 56805980; LC Call Number F213 .T37; Dewey 320.52/0975/09034. Citations: 4.

Considers the views of southern intellectuals on politics and society between the ratification of the Constitution and the beginning of the Civil War. Finds that conservatism was well-represented in the South, but that intellectuals held no consistent and coherent "conservative" positions on most issues. Notes commonality in the belief that the state existed to preserve and protect society, but that its coercive powers ought to be limited. Concludes, though, that southern conservatives failed to create "a common southern social vision to accompany their states' rights political tradition."

GHQ 90: 134-35; *JSH* 74: 956-57; *NCHR* 82: 393-94.

608 Trees, Andrew S. *The Founding Fathers and the Politics of Character.* Princeton, N.J.: Princeton University Press, 2004. xvi, 208 p. ISBN 0691115524 (hbk.); ISBN 9780691115528 (hbk.); ISBN 0691122369 (pbk.); ISBN 9780691122366 (pbk.); OCLC 51613998; LC Call Number E302.1 .T74 ; Dewey 973.4. Citations: 14.

Contends that Jefferson, Hamilton, Adams, and Madison held concepts of friendship, honor, virtue, and justice as guides for themselves and for the new nation and used different literary approaches to do so. Notes that Jefferson leveraged personal relationships for public advantage, largely through letter writing, that Hamilton emphasized honor in his dealings with others, that Adams wanted to expose the lack of virtue in political foes, and that Madison stressed the notion of political justice, typically through anonymous essays.

AHR 110: 1166-67; *JAH* 91: 1434-35; *JAS* 39: 349; *JER* 24: 691-94; *JSH* 71: 429-30; *NEQ* 78: 503-505; *NCHR* 81: 467-68; *PMHB* 129: 484-85; *RAH* 32: 486-92; *VMHB* 112: 193-95.

609   Vidal, Gore. *Inventing a Nation: Washington, Adams, Jefferson.* New Haven, Conn.: Yale University Press, 2003. 198 p. ISBN 0300101716; ISBN 9780300101713; ISBN 0300105924; ISBN 9780300105926; OCLC 52721004; LC Call Number E302.1 .V57; Dewey 973.4/092/2. Citations: 14.

Surveys American history through Jefferson's inauguration, offers insights on the psychologies of Washington, Adams, and Jefferson, and relates modern issues to the struggles of the early national period. Concludes the Founders dealt honestly with the potential corrupting influence of power and therefore placed ingenious restraints on its exercise in the Constitution.

Booklist 100: 386; *JAS* 38: 534-35; *LJ* 128n18: 100-108.

610   Watkins, William J. *Reclaiming the American Revolution: The Kentucky and Virginia Resolutions and Their Legacy.* New York: Palgrave Macmillan, 2004. xx, 236 p. ISBN 1403963037; ISBN 9781403963031; OCLC 52107096; LC Call Number KF4621 .W38; Dewey 320.973/09/033. Citations: 4.

Places the Virginia and Kentucky resolutions alongside the Constitution in significance to the development of American government. Provides a survey of important events of the 1790s, including the passage and enforcement of the Alien and Sedition Acts. Describes the resolutions themselves and their effects, as well as their potential modern implications, and concludes that their "cogent reasoning won acceptance in the marketplace of ideas."

AHR 111: 164-65; *HRNB* 33: 15-16; *Hist Teach* 38: 562-63; *JAH* 92: 596-97; *JAS* 40: 459; *JER* 26: 167-69.

611   Weintraub, Stanley. *General Washington's Christmas Farewell: A Mount Vernon Homecoming, 1783.* New York: Free Press, 2003. xv, 205 p. ISBN 0743246543 (hbk.); ISBN 9780743246545 (hbk.); ISBN 0452285321 (pbk.); ISBN 9780452285323 (pbk.); OCLC 51978064; LC Call Number   E312.29 .W45; Dewey 973.4/1/092. Citations: 1.

Recounts Washington's long return home to Mount Vernon in 1783, noting his stays in New York, Philadelphia, Princeton, Baltimore, and Annapolis along the way. Explains that Washington was eager to return to his former agrarian life and relished his future role as private citizen.

Booklist 100: 569; *LJ* 128n18: 109.

612   Wheelan, Joseph. *Jefferson's Vendetta: The Pursuit of Aaron Burr and the Judiciary.* New York: Carroll & Graf, 2005. 344 p. ISBN 0786714379; ISBN 9780786714377; OCLC 57369485; LC Call Number E302.5 .W497; Dewey 973.48. Citations: 1.

Describes Burr's trial for treason, noting that Jefferson sought to destroy his political rival and that Burr is undeserving of most negative characterizations. Places the trial in the context of the rise of an independent judiciary and stresses the role played by John Marshall, particularly in the interpretation of the Constitution's treason clause.

Booklist 101: 810; *LJ* 130n2: 101; *VMHB* 114: 301-302.

613 Wilentz, Sean. *The Rise of American Democracy: Jefferson to Lincoln.* New York: Norton, 2005. xxiii, 1044 p. ISBN 0393058204; ISBN 9780393058208; OCLC 57414581; LC Call Number E302.1 .W55; Dewey 973.5. Citations: 76.

Surveys American politics from the Constitution to the Civil War, taking special note of the role of ordinary Americans in the electoral process. Contends that the nation was shaped largely by the democratization of this era, which was advanced by the development of parties. Characterizes the Jeffersonians as the creators of alliances among democratic concerns in rural and urban areas, coalitions that were powerful enough to overthrow Federalist hierarchy and to sustain Jackson's successful campaign. Asserts that the slavery issue prompted a reaction against democracy in the South and allowed for the ascension of the Republicans.

AHR 111: 832-33; *Booklist* 102: 23; *JAH* 93: 491-93; *JSH* 74: 125-38; *LJ* 130n15: 76; *RAH* 34: 169-75.

614 Wills, Garry. *James Madison.* New York: Times Books, 2002. xx, 184 p. ISBN 0805069054; ISBN 9780805069051; OCLC 49335842; LC Call Number E342 .W55; Dewey 973.5/1/092. Citations: 17.

Focuses on Madison's public life, particularly his presidency. Seeks to reconcile Madison the brilliant political thinker with Madison the relatively ineffective chief executive. Contends that Madison's weaknesses "were a certain provincialism with regard to the rest of the world and a certain naiveté with regard to the rest of his fellow human beings."

Booklist 98: 1081; *LJ* 127n10: 164-65; *WMQ* 60: 663-65.

615 Wirls, Daniel and Stephen Wirls. *The Invention of the United States Senate.* Baltimore, Md.: Johns Hopkins University Press, 2004. xii, 274 p. ISBN 0801874386 (hbk.); ISBN 9780801874383 (hbk.); ISBN 0801874394 (pbk.); ISBN 9780801874390 (pbk.); OCLC 51878651; LC Call Number JK1161 .W57; Dewey 328.73/071. Citations: 9.

Reviews the political theories to which Framers would have had access at the Constitutional Convention (e.g., Harrington, Montesquieu) and explains that most agreed that an upper chamber was advantageous, but disagreed on the reasons why (e.g., representation of stable, propertied interests, collection of accrued political wisdom, etc.). Finds that, though small size and longer terms were agreed upon, the idea that members would be selected by state (and thus would have the states' interests in mind) diluted the benefits of an exclusive chamber. Concludes that the institution that emerged from the Convention was "ambiguous...with more than one built-in contradiction."

AHR 111: 464-65; *JAH* 92: 200.

616 Wood, Gary V. *Heir to the Fathers: John Quincy Adams and the Spirit of Constitutional Government.* Lanham, Md.: Lexington Books, 2004. viii, 249 p.

ISBN 0739106015; ISBN 9780739106013; OCLC 52727293; LC Call Number E377 .W66; Dewey 320.5/092. Citations: 2.
Studies the writings of John Quincy Adams to clarify the relationship of the Constitution to the Declaration of Independence and to slavery and to help determine how interpretations of the Constitution have changed over time. Suggests that America's republican principles represent "the eternal principles of justice" and that Adams believed the Constitution and the Declaration to be linked.
JAH 92: 207-208.

617 Wood, Gordon S. *The Americanization of Benjamin Franklin.* New York: Penguin Press, 2004. xvi, 299 p. ISBN 159420019X; ISBN 9781594200199; OCLC 53398087; LC Call Number E302.6.F8; Dewey 973.3/092. Citations: 27.
Traces Franklin's life from gentleman to imperialist, to patriot, to diplomat, and to American. Claims that Franklin's transition to American was not inevitable or particularly smooth, but rather involved extraordinary challenges, concerns about ordinary colonists, and failure in his personal life. Concludes that Franklin was "never very revealing of himself," but "always seems to be holding something back—he is reticent, detached, not wholly committed."
AHR 110: 1526-27; *Booklist* 100: 1421; *EAL* 41: 535-53; *HRNB* 34: 13; *JAH* 92: 199-200; *LJ* 129n8: 122; *RAH* 33: 1-7; *WMQ* 62: 745-64.

618 Zall, Paul M., ed. *Jefferson on Jefferson.* Lexington: University Press of Kentucky, 2002. xv, 160 p. ISBN 081312235X ; ISBN 9780813122359; OCLC 48477564; LC Call Number E332.9 .A8; Dewey 973.4/6/092. Citations: 3.
Presents excerpts from Jefferson's letters that cover his political career, as well as interests in architecture, music, philosophy, religion, science, and education. Includes notes on the texts.
JER 22: 699-700; *JSH* 69: 880-81; *VQR* 79: 17.

21 Law

619 Bilder, Mary Sarah. *The Transatlantic Constitution: Colonial Legal Culture and the Empire*. Cambridge, Mass.: Harvard University Press, 2004. xiii, 291 p. ISBN 0674015126; ISBN 9780674015128; OCLC 55534974; LC Call Number KF4541 .B55; Dewey 342.7302/9 22. Citations: 25.
Examines English legal history and the legal profession, equity courts and equitable relief, appeals from the colony of Rhode Island, the treatment of family and property issues, including inheritance, the role of women, the function of religion, and the law of currency and commerce. Shows that the American legal culture developed transatlantically from an unwritten constitution comprehended by all of the players on both sides of the ocean. Notes that colonial laws could not be repugnant to those of England, but could account for local needs.
AHR 111: 824-25; *JAH* 92: 950-51; *NEQ* 79: 123-33; *WMQ* 62: 527-30.

620 Brewer, Holly. *By Birth or Consent: Children, Law, and the Anglo-American Revolution in Authority*. Chapel Hill: University of North Carolina Press, published for the Omohundro Institute of Early American History and Culture, 2005. xi, 390 p. ISBN 0807829501 (hbk.); ISBN 9780807829509 (hbk.); ISBN 0807856118 (pbk.); ISBN 9780807856116 (pbk.); OCLC 56324599; LC Call Number KD735 .B74; Dewey 346.4201/35 22. Citations: 19.
Traces the legal status of children through early modern England and America with emphasis on the ideas of inheritance, power, patriarchy, religious membership, obligation, reason, law, labor, and marriage. Explains that certain sixteenth-century English children exercised significant political power and rights to dispose property and labor, while maintaining responsibility for their own actions both civilly and criminally. Notes that these obligations and rights were eroded during the seventeenth and eighteenth centuries and essentially eliminated by the nineteenth century. Traces the change to shifting notions of

consent espoused by John Locke, Algernon Sidney and others, who argued that adults need not follow hereditary rulers and that reason relied upon understanding, something that children lacked. Concludes, then, that "Modern childhood is a by-product of the Age of Reason, which designated children as those without reason."

AHR 111: 1247-48; *Am Lit* 80: 407-409; *CJH* 41: 625-28; *EHR* 122: 753-55; *JAH* 93: 508; *J Interdis Hist* 37: 440-42; *NCHR* 82: 509-10; *VMHB* 113: 413-14; *WMQ* 63: 587-96.

621 Hoffer, Peter Charles. *The Great New York Conspiracy of 1741: Slavery, Crime, and Colonial Law.* Lawrence: University Press of Kansas, 2003. xiv, 190 p. ISBN 0700612459 (hbk.); ISBN 9780700612451 (hbk.); ISBN 0700612467 (pbk.); ISBN 9780700612468 (pbk.); OCLC 51093161; LC Call Number KFN5696.A4; Dewey 342.747/087. Citations: 13.

Examines the Conspiracy of 1741, noting that because the definition of "slave conspiracy" was so broad, most of the accused slaves were indeed technically conspirators. Explains that slaves only needed to talk about revolt in order to be guilty of conspiracy, while whites needed to act on what they said in order to meet the definition. Points out that the accused slaves had relatively high freedom of movement, making their ability to carry out threats seem credible. Argues, then, that "It was not the words themselves but the context of their utterance that led the authorities to prosecute and the jury to vote to convict." Explains that colonial slave law grew out of English criminal law, but that "Conspiracy became the axle around which the whole of slave criminal law turned."

AHR 109: 894-95; *HRNB* 32: 58-59; JAH 91: 219; *J Interdis Hist* 36: 273-74.

622 Hulsebosch, Daniel J. *Constituting Empire: New York and the Transformation of Constitutionalism in the Atlantic World, 1664–1830.* Chapel Hill: University of North Carolina Press, 2005. 494 p. ISBN 0807829552; ISBN 9780807829554; ISBN 0807859206; ISBN 9780807859209; OCLC 57319545; LC Call Number KFN5681 .H85; Dewey 342.74702/9. Citations: 32.

Contends that American constitutional and legal history must be understood in the context of intra-colonial contests that persisted through the mid-nineteenth century. Uses New York as a case study and examines four stages of development: the colonial years to 1760, the Revolutionary generation (1760 to 1786), the Constitutional era (1787 to the 1790s), and the antebellum period (1800 to 1840). Asserts that British imperial law had tremendous influence on New York law, and that New York, as arguably the center of the Anglo-American colonial empire, influenced other colonies in interpreting their constitutions and developing their systems of law. Discusses the work of imperial agents (e.g., Cadwalader Colden and William Johnson), who viewed the British constitution and law as granting the colonists liberties, the efforts of the native-born provincial elite (e.g., Lewis Morris and William Smith, Jr.), who argued that colonists brought with them and retained all the rights of Englishmen as embodied in the common law and statutes, and the roles of frontier settlers and sailors, who lived on the peripheries of colonial society, frequently defied local authority, and stressed common law. Concludes that the

interplay among these three groups "over the relevance and content of the common law, jurisdiction, and the personnel of the legal system divided the inhabitants of New York into slowly cohering political groups." Affirms, therefore, the view of Progressive historians "that the real battle was not transatlantic," but rather "went on within the province."
AHR 112: 498-99; *EHR* 122: 255-56; *JAH* 93: 846-47; *J Brit Stds* 45: 900-902; *JER* 26: 679-82; *WMQ* 65: 607-10.

623 Kelly, M. Ruth. *The Olmsted Case: Privateers, Property, and Politics in Pennsylvania, 1778–1810.* Selinsgrove, Penn.: Susquehanna University Press, 2005. 173 p. ISBN 1575910926; ISBN 9781575910925; OCLC 56913512; LC Call Number KF223.O43; Dewey 347.73/12. Citations: 1.
Describes the *Olmsted* case (1778), which started as a Pennsylvania admiralty court prize claim. Discusses the impact of the case on state sovereignty, the Eleventh Amendment, and the supremacy of the federal judiciary. Places the case in the context of Pennsylvania politics and stresses the state's clear and ardent resistance to federal authority. Argues that the *Peters* decision (1809) and Madison's support of it opened the door to ensuing Supreme Court rulings that asserted federal judicial supremacy. Concludes that the *Olmsted* case "deserves a much higher rank in the canon of American constitutional history" than it has received.
AJLH 47: 334-35.

624 Newmyer, R. Kent. *John Marshall and the Heroic Age of the Supreme Court.* Baton Rouge: Louisiana State University Press, 2001. xx, 511 p. ISBN 0807127019; ISBN 9780807127018; OCLC 48232936; LC Call Number KF8745.M3; Dewey 347.73/2634. Citations: 34.
Stresses Marshall's social and intellectual skills, common sense, desire for order, and his consistent defense of democratic institutions. Explores the influence of Marshall's early legal practice on his service on the Supreme Court and emphasizes his role in establishing and maintaining the authority of judicial review and thus constitutional order. Concludes that among Marshall's greatest achievements were the separation of law and politics and the engraining in American politics a respect for the law.
AHR 108: 828-29; *AJLH* 45: 519-20; *FHQ* 81: 442-44; *GHQ* 86: 300-302; *HRNB* 30: 52-53; *JAH* 89: 1031-32; *J Interdis Hist* 33: 660-61; *JSH* 69: 680-81; *LJ* 126n19: 80; *NCHR* 79: 470-71; *PMHB* 128: 206-208; *VMHB* 110: 104-105.

625 Pagan, John Ruston. *Anne Orthwood's Bastard: Sex and Law in Early Virginia.* New York: Oxford University Press, 2003. 222 p. ISBN 0195144783 (hbk.); ISBN 9780195144789 (hbk.); ISBN 0195144791 (pbk.) 9780195144796 (pbk.); OCLC 49386158; LC Call Number KFV2967.S3; Dewey 364.15/3. Citations: 14.
Tells the story of Orthwood, a twenty-four-year-old white indentured servant who, in 1663, had an affair with the nephew of her employer, became pregnant, and died in childbirth. Reflects on the meaning of the four legal cases arising from this episode to the development of Virginia's legal system and the colony's changing social structure and hierarchy. Contends that elites in the colony

followed English practice and tradition when possible and convenient, but also manipulated the law to improve their social positions and their political power. Concludes that the "malleability" of English doctrines and institutions "made it relatively easy for ambitious leaders to shape the law to conform to their social and economic goals."
AHR 109: 515; *JAH* 91: 213; *JAS* 38: 160-61; *J Interdis Hist* 34: 435-40; *JSH* 70: 413-14; *RAH* 31: 349-55; *VMHB* 111: 79-80; *WMQ* 61: 361-67.

626 Reid, John Phillip. *The Ancient Constitution and the Origins of Anglo-American Liberty*. Dekalb: Northern Illinois University Press, 2005. 188 p. ISBN 0875803423; ISBN 9780875803425; OCLC 57319569; LC Call Number KD3934 .R45; Dewey 342.4102/9. Citations: 7.
Seeks the origins of Anglo-American concepts of liberty in "abandoned jurisprudence." Finds that, particularly in the eighteenth century, calls for limited government relied on the idea of the "ancient constitution," the notion that Parliament, not the Crown, was the primary potential source of arbitrary government. Notes that proponents of this view saw the ancient constitution as a "forensic tool with which to create, defend, and define the concept of liberty and of representative government." Explains that the English viewed history as civic education that was meant to inform subjects of their rights and responsibilities and that many Whigs drew upon Gothic and Saxon history to resist arbitrary authority.
AHR 112: 809-10; *AJLH* 47: 311-14; *EHR* 122: 260-61; *JAH* 93: 194-95; *JER* 28: 143-53.

627 Reid, John Phillip. *Controlling the Law: Legal Politics in Early National New Hampshire*. DeKalb: Northern Illinois University Press, 2004. 258 p. ISBN 0875803210; ISBN 9780875803210; OCLC 53038237; LC Call Number KFN1278 .R45; Dewey 349.742. Citations: 5.
Discusses legal and judicial development in New Hampshire between 1790 and 1820, focusing in particular on the roles of Jeremiah Smith and William Plumer. Asserts that the transformation in the state was similar to that under way at the same time in other states, the evolution from a simple and subjective system to one that was professional, objective, and reliant upon technical procedures similar to those of English common-law courts. Attributes to Jeffersonians the opposition to legal professionalization and more highly developed procedure, which came from deep distrust of elitism and the perceived arbitrary exercise of authority. Notes that this opposition postponed New Hampshire's legal transition by two decades, but that the view that well-educated judges served the litigants' and the public's interests ultimately triumphed.
AHR 109: 1559-60; *AJLH* 47: 447-48; *JAH* 91: 1440-41.

628 Reid, John Phillip. *Rule of Law: The Jurisprudence of Liberty in the Seventeenth and Eighteenth Centuries*. Dekalb: Northern Illinois University Press, 2004. 150 p. ISBN 087580327X; ISBN 9780875803272; OCLC 54082317; LC Call Number K3171 .R45; Dewey 340/.11. Citations: 3.
Traces the rule-of-law concept in England from Bracton in the thirteenth century through the constitutional crises of the seventeenth and eighteenth centuries.

Contends that related modern concepts (e.g., equal protection and due process) came from the Bractonian notion that law is not power, but instead a restraint on power. Discusses the Magna Carta, English Civil War debates over Ship Money and the trial of Charles I, the first legal codes in colonial Massachusetts, and the English Bill of Rights that came out of the Glorious Revolution, noting that each conformed to the ancient view of law and power.
AJLH 47: 311-14.

629 Tomlins, Christopher L. and Bruce H. Mann, eds. *The Many Legalities of Early America.* Chapel Hill: University of North Carolina Press, published for the Omohundro Institute of Early American History and Culture, 2001. x, 466 p. ISBN 0807826324 (hbk.); ISBN 9780807826324 (hbk.); ISBN 0807849642 (pbk.); ISBN 9780807849644 (pbk.); OCLC 45172115; LC Call Number KF361.A2; Dewey 349.73. Citations: 48.

Includes articles on early American legal history, John Adams's work on the legal basis for English possession of North America, appeal in early New England, origins of Jamaica slave laws of the seventeenth century, the Jeffersonian critique of common law adjudication, Algonquian demands for reciprocity in the courts of European settlers, law and justice in the New Mexico borderlands (1680–1821), laws of marriage and Narragansett Indian identity in eighteenth-century Rhode Island, servant petitions in Maryland (1652–1797), Virginia women with power of attorney, gender, property law, and voting rights in eighteenth-century Virginia, children, testimony, and consent in early America, patriarchy in New Haven Colony, courts, ethnicity, and gender in the Middle Colonies in the late seventeenth century and early eighteenth century, courts in Orange County, North Carolina in the quarter century prior to the Revolution, and charity law and state formation in early America.
AHR 108: 1138-39; *AJLH* 46: 82-84; *JAH* 89: 616-17; *J Econ Hist* 62: 246-47; *JER* 22: 300-301; *J Interdis Hist* 33: 247-60; *NEQ* 74: 692-94; *PMHB* 126: 499-500; *VMHB* 110: 491-92; *WMQ* 59: 481-87.

22 Crime and Punishment

630 Brown, Irene Quenzler and Richard D. Brown. *The Hanging of Ephraim Wheeler: A Story of Rape, Incest, and Justice in Early America.* Cambridge, Mass.: Belknap Press of Harvard University Press, 2003. 388 p. ISBN 0674010205 (hbk.); ISBN 9780674010208 (hbk.); ISBN 0674017609 (pbk.); ISBN 9780674017603 (pbk.); OCLC 50906132; LC Call Number HV6565.M4; Dewey 364.15/32/097441. Citations: 18.

Focuses on the trial of Wheeler for the rape of his daughter, placing the event in the context of the court and class systems and crime and punishment in the region. Discusses the trial itself, sentencing, the execution, and the effect of the case, particularly in its reporting. Contends that Wheeler's case brought scrutiny to early republic jurisprudence and capital punishment and reveals much about domestic violence, sexual abuse, incest, and child exploitation.

AHR 109: 520-21; *Booklist* 99: 1430; *HRNB* 32: 10; *JAH* 91: 225-26; *JER* 23: 469-71; *J Soc Hist* 38: 545-46; *LJ* 128n8: 133-34; *NEQ* 77: 162-65; *RAH* 32: 499-505; *WMQ* 61: 361-67.

631 Crane, Elaine Forman. *Killed Strangely: The Death of Rebecca Cornell.* Ithaca, N.Y.: Cornell University Press, 2002. xvi, 236 p. ISBN 0801440025; ISBN 9780801440021; OCLC 49415689; LC Call Number HV6534.P68; Dewey 364.15/23/097456. Citations: 8.

Studies the 1673 homicide of Rebecca Cornell in Rhode Island, the investigation of the crime, which included two inquests, an exhumation, and an autopsy, and the indictment, trial, and execution of her oldest son, Thomas. Uses the family's situation and the community's response to the crime to shed light on the domestic relations, religious beliefs, generational conflicts, and criminal law and procedures in late seventeenth-century New England. Concludes that the investigation and trial brought together medieval superstition and modern evidentiary standards.

AJLH 47: 304-305; *EAL* 39: 137-45; *JAH* 90: 991-92; *JAS* 38: 140-41; *J Interdis Hist* 34: 435-40; *RAH* 31: 349-55; *WMQ* 61: 361-67.

632 Kann, Mark E. *Punishment, Prisons, and Patriarchy: Liberty and Power in the Early American Republic.* New York: New York University Press, 2005. ix, 337 p. ISBN 0814747833; ISBN 9780814747834; OCLC 58986238; LC Call Number HV9466 .K36; Dewey 364.6/0973/09033. Citations: 7.
Highlights the conflict between the state's deriving legitimacy from its protection of citizens' lives, liberty, and property while depriving millions of its constituents of the same. Points out that from the nation's beginning, the American penal system has had difficulty reconciling liberty with oppression, a problem that has never been adequately confronted, despite the Enlightenment's impetus for re-visioning traditional patriarchal penality. Explains that punishment in the early republic was conceived as a way of preserving the liberty of potential victims rather than as a threat against the liberty of suspected and convicted criminals. Stresses that a "culture of concealment" allowed for the incarceration of more and more marginal people, including juveniles, vagrants, alcoholics, the poor, the insane, and the immoral.
AHR 111: 831-32; *JAH* 93: 195-96; *RAH* 34: 24-27; *WMQ* 63: 419-21.

633 Morgan, Gwenda and Peter Rushton. *Eighteenth-Century Criminal Transportation: The Formation of the Criminal Atlantic.* New York: Palgrave Macmillan, 2004. xii, 238 p. ISBN 0333793382; ISBN 9780333793381; OCLC 52821208; LC Call Number HV8949 .M67; Dewey 365/.34 22. Citations: 11.
Follows convicts sentenced in the northern and western circuits of England in the period 1718–1775, and the way in which information about criminals circulated throughout the Atlantic world. Finds that some of the details appeared again later in stories about convicts sent to Australia. Explains that newspaper accounts of crimes were read widely by colonists and by those in Britain, fostered among the public a perceived increased in crime, and colored British views of their colonial brethren. Notes that this stigma continued through the Revolution and afterwards.
AHR 111: 1135-36; *JAH* 93: 497-98; *WMQ* 63: 860-62.

634 Okun, Peter. *Crime and the Nation: Prison Reform and Popular Fiction in Philadelphia, 1786–1800.* New York: Routledge, 2002. xxii, 167 p. ISBN 0415933862; ISBN 9780415933865; OCLC 469601274; LC Call Number PS375 .O38; Dewey 813/.209355. Citations: 5.
Analyzes "crime and punishment as it was imagined" during the 1790s in the writings of Philadelphia's prison reformers (e.g., Benjamin Rush) and in popular fiction (illustrated by the works of Charles Brockden Brown and Susanna Rowson). Uses "certain post-structuralist and materialist formulations" and concludes that prison reformers held a utopian vision of how segregating prisoners and employing "the ideal management of space" could reform some inmates and force others to pay their own ways. Asserts that viewing "the reformed prison as a domestic utopia" was tied "to a post-Revolutionary, nationalizing aesthetic" that reflected the reformers' middle-class world view.
AHR 108: 1140; *JAH* 90: 625-26; *PMHB* 128: 87-89.

23 Diplomacy

635 Brecher, Frank W. *Securing American Independence: John Jay and the French Alliance.* Westport, Conn.: Praeger, 2003. xiv, 327 p. ISBN 031332591X; ISBN 9780313325915; OCLC 50479271; LC Call Number E302.6.J4; Dewey 973.3/24/0922. Citations: 3.
Underscores the importance of John Jay to the 1778 French alliance and to the negotiations that resulted in the Treaty of Paris (1783). Discusses the relationship between Jay and Charles Gravier, comte de Vergennes, and emphasizes the importance of Jay's mission to Spain and his general distrust of French diplomats. Finds that Jay violated Congressional instructions by neglecting to consult with France prior to concluding the peace treaty with Great Britain.
AHR 110: 133-34; *JAH* 91: 995.

636 Brown, Gordon S. *Toussaint's Clause: The Founding Fathers and the Haitian Revolution.* Jackson: University Press of Mississippi, 2005. xii, 321 p. ISBN 1578067111; ISBN 9781578067114; OCLC 55124492; LC Call Number E310.7 .B76; Dewey 327.7307294/09/033. Citations: 11.
Recounts the Saint Domingue slave revolt, the Haitian Revolution, the French Revolutionary wars, and American influence in the Caribbean in the Washington, Adams, and Jefferson administrations. Argues that American foreign policy toward Haiti was influenced by racism, which came out of sectional interests and the interplay between northern Federalists and southern Jeffersonian Democratic-Republicans.
JAH 92: 1421-22; *JSH* 72: 652-53.

637 Carroll, Francis M. *A Good and Wise Measure: The Search for the Canadian-American Boundary, 1783–1842.* Toronto: University of Toronto Press, 2001. xxi, 462 p. ISBN 0802048293 (hbk.); ISBN 9780802048295 (hbk.); ISBN 0802083587 (pbk.); ISBN 9780802083586 (pbk.); OCLC 46620538; LC Call Number E398 .C37; Dewey 327.73041 21. Citations: 20.

Examines the negotiations leading to the Webster-Ashburton Treaty (1842) and the location of landmarks for the identification of the boundary. Discusses the difficulties in setting the borders, the effect of the Treaty of Ghent (1814), and surveying work in support of the negotiations. Argues that the 1842 treaty was in line with the provisions of the Treaty of Paris (1783) and demonstrated the value and workability of peaceful compromise, despite the threats of war in the late 1830s and early 1840s.
AHR 107: 1214-15; *CHR* 83: 603-604; *CJH* 38: 354-56; *EHR* 118: 1068-69; *HRNB* 30: 12; *JAH* 92: 206-207.

638 Harper, John Lamberton. *American Machiavelli: Alexander Hamilton and the Origins of U.S. Foreign Policy*. New York: Cambridge University Press, 2004. xii, 347 p. ISBN 0521834856; ISBN 9780521834858; OCLC 53013314; LC Call Number E302.6.H2; Dewey 327.73/0092. Citations: 6.
Focuses on Hamilton's role in shaping and implementing early American foreign policy. Draws a parallel between Hamilton and Machiavelli, noting that they "inhabited the same moral and intellectual world." Concludes that "much of Hamilton's prolific foreign policy advice in the 1780s and 1790s belies the image of an aggrandizing Machiavellian preoccupied with the cultivation and projection of *virtù*" and that "Many of his axioms emphasize realism and self-restraint," just as they did for Machiavelli.
AHR 110: 784-85; *JAS* 39: 558-59; *JER* 27: 168-72; *JSH* 71: 671-72.

639 Hill, Peter P. *Napoleon's Troublesome Americans: Franco-American Relations, 1804–1815*. Dulles, Va.: Potomac Books, 2005. xiii, 289 p. ISBN 157488879X; ISBN 9781574888799; OCLC 56617351; LC Call Number E183.8.F8; Dewey 327.73044/09/034. Citations: 4.
Studies Franco-American diplomacy between the Louisiana Purchase and the end of the Napoleonic Wars. Notes Napoleon's refusal to back the United States in its territorial disputes with Spain and claims that his targeting of American commerce stemmed from his irritation with American policymakers, diplomats, and sea merchants and were "not altogether unjustified." Explains that Napoleon viewed American policies like the Embargo of 1807 as discriminatory against France and concludes that the posting to Paris of Francophile Joel Barlow was ill-timed, as Napoleon was then preoccupied with his Russian campaign.
JAH 93: 203-204; *JER* 27: 357-62.

640 Matthewson, Tim. *A Proslavery Foreign Policy: Haitian-American Relations during the Early Republic*. Westport, Conn.: Praeger, 2003. xii, 159 p. ISBN 0275980022; ISBN 9780275980023; OCLC 51223603; LC Call Number E183.8.H2; Dewey 326/.0973/09033. Citations: 11.
Studies the development and implementation of United States policy toward Saint Domingue (Haiti) during the late eighteenth and early nineteenth centuries. Focuses on the Washington, Adams, and Jefferson administrations. Finds that, despite theoretical American support for independence movements, the creation of new republics, and emancipation, there existed little support for Saint Domingue's revolution and the end of enslavement in the Caribbean. Explains that race influenced American policy, that such policy was essentially set during

the Washington administration, and that it allowed for later American military interventions and for French attempts to restore control over its former colony. *AHR* 110: 1167-68; *HAHR* 85: 359-60; *JAH* 91: 1000-1001; *JER* 24: 689-91; *JSH* 71: 146-47.

641 Miller, Melanie Randolph. *Envoy to the Terror: Gouverneur Morris and the French Revolution*. Dulles, Va.: Potomac Books, 2004. xiv, 284 p. ISBN 1574887866 (hbk.); ISBN 9781574887860 (hbk.); ISBN 1574887874 (pbk.); ISBN 9781574887877 (pbk.); OCLC 54460049; LC Call Number E302.6.M7; Dewey 327.73044/092. Citations: 6.

Focuses on Morris's service as American minister to France from 1792 to 1794. Discusses his difficult mission to Britain, attempts to preserve the French monarchy, and his efforts to secure the release of imprisoned Americans and ensure the restitution of seized property. Claims that Morris "prevented hostilities between the United States and France" through open communication. Characterizes Morris as "a great American statesman."
HRNB 33: 143; *JAH* 92: 963-64; *JER* 27: 357-62; *WMQ* 62: 745-64.

642 Parker, Richard Bordeaux. *Uncle Sam in Barbary: A Diplomatic History*. Gainesville: University Press of Florida, 2004. xxviii, 285 p. ISBN 0813026962; ISBN 9780813026961; OCLC 52587606; LC Call Number E335 .P37; Dewey 973.4/7. Citations: 5.

Focuses primarily on the initial encounter of the United States and Algeria and on relations with Tripoli, Tunis, and Morocco from 1785 to 1815. Examines the Tripolitan war (1801–1805), the negotiations that resulted in the release of American prisoners from the *Philadelphia*, and early difficulties with Tunis. Notes that the United States enjoyed relatively good relations with Morocco and concludes that the Barbary States were not pirate states, but legitimate governments to which the United States commonly paid ransoms.
JAH 91: 1437.

643 Rossignol, Marie-Jeanne. *The Nationalist Ferment: The Origins of U.S. Foreign Policy, 1789–1812*. Translated by Lillian A. Parrott. Columbus: Ohio State University Press, 2004. xxii, 274 p. ISBN 0814209416; ISBN 9780814209417; OCLC 52806153; LC Call Number E310.7 .R67; Dewey 327.73/009/033. Citations: 19.

Surveys American foreign policy from the beginning of the republic to the outbreak of the War of 1812, considering whether nationalism should be viewed as "a normative theory of identity" or as "a xenophobic phenomenon for social exclusion and for war." Finds that nationalism helped the relatively weak United States to challenge the great European powers, while excluding Native Americans, blacks, and Spaniards in the southwest.
JAH 91: 1436-37.

644 Schiff, Stacy. *A Great Improvisation: Franklin, France, and the Birth of America*. New York: Henry Holt, 2005. xvii, 489 p. ISBN 0805066330; ISBN 9780805066333; OCLC 57001654; LC Call Number E183.8.F8; Dewey 327.73044/09/033. Citations: 16.

Examines Franklin's diplomatic work in France, characterizing him as manipulative, but always devoted to the cause of American liberty. Notes that he had a very difficult task in convincing French monarchists to support the American republican revolution, which appeared to have very little chance of success. Explains that Franklin also had to contend with fellow Americans who were often working at cross purposes. Concludes that Franklin's charm and extraordinary political skills ultimately carried the day.
Booklist 101: 1121; *Booklist* 101: 1934; *EAL* 41: 535-53; *LJ* 131n6: 132.

645 Smith, Robert W. *Keeping the Republic: Ideology and Early American Diplomacy*. Dekalb: Northern Illinois University Press, 2004. x, 196 p. ISBN 0875803261; ISBN 9780875803265; OCLC 53970658; LC Call Number JK116 .S65; LC Call Number E302.1; Dewey 327.73/009/033. Citations: 6.
Contends that republican ideology significantly influenced early American diplomacy and that Adams, Hamilton, Madison, and Jefferson each sought foreign relations "compatible with republican institutions at home that recognized the realities of world politics." Explains that this ideology led to the views that the United States should remain disentangled from Europe.
AHR 111: 159; *JAH* 92: 597; *JER* 25: 302-304.

646 Stockley, Andrew. *Britain and France at the Birth of America: The European Powers and the Peace Negotiations of 1782–1783*. Exeter, Eng.: University of Exeter Press, 2001. xvi, 272 p. ISBN 0859896153; ISBN 9780859896153; OCLC 45580569; LC Call Number E313 .S76; Dewey 973.317. Citations: 5.
Stresses that the fate of the British North American colonies was a relatively unimportant part of the peace negotiations of 1782 and 1783 and that the subsequent treaty provided for American independence in a way that allowed Britain and France both to save face. Describes the various roles of the earl of Shelburne, comte de Vergennes, and Charles James Fox and contends that American independence largely did not result from the efforts of the American peace commissioners.
WMQ 60: 241-43.

647 Weeks, Charles A. *Paths to a Middle Ground: The Diplomacy of Natchez, Boukfouka, Nogales, and San Fernando de las Barrancas, 1791–1795*. Tuscaloosa: University of Alabama Press, 2005. x, 292 p. ISBN 0817312102; ISBN 9780817312107; OCLC 57565176; LC Call Number F349.N2; Dewey 305.8/00976226. Citations: 7.
Reviews diplomacy among Europeans and Indians in the lower Mississippi valley in the early 1790s. Focuses on the Choctaws, Chickasaws, Creeks, and Cherokees and the impact of post-Revolution land cessions on Native groups. Discusses Spain's negotiations with the Choctaws to establish forts to protect territorial claims from the new American nation. Includes seventeen translated documents related to diplomatic maneuvering in the region.
AHR 111: 787-88; *HAHR* 88: 155-56; *JER* 28: 511-17; *JSH* 73: 160-61; *WMQ* 63: 409-11.

24 Military

648 Allison, Robert J. *Stephen Decatur: American Naval Hero, 1779–1820.* Amherst: University of Massachusetts Press, 2005. x, 253 p. ISBN 1558494928; ISBN 9781558494923; OCLC 58546737; LC Call Number E353.1.D29; Dewey 359/.0092. Citations: 5.

Explains that Decatur was shaped by the values of his social stratum, namely those of patriotism, republicanism, desire for fame, and willingness to sacrifice to defend personal and national honor. Compares Decatur to other figures of the age, including Washington Irving, James Madison, Hezekiah Niles, Benjamin Rush, and fellow naval officers. Notes that Decatur supported the naval experiments of Robert Fulton and valued improving accuracy of long-range guns.

JAH 93: 507; *LJ* 130n13: 101; *RAH* 35: 358-65.

649 Anderson, Fred and Andrew Cayton. *The Dominion of War: Empire and Liberty in North America, 1500–2000.* New York: Viking, 2005. xxiv, 520 p. ISBN 0670033707; ISBN 9780670033706; OCLC 57337467; LC Call Number E181 .A53; Dewey 973 A54. Citations: 32.

Presents "a history of North America that emphasizes wars and their effects and stresses the centrality of imperial ambitions to the development of the United States." Examines the life of Samuel de Champlain, an example of a warrior of the 1500s when the "radically different systems of war, trade, and empire" of Europe and the Americas came into conflict. Cites William Penn as a representation of the "Age of Colonization and Conflict (c. 1600-1750)," in which relations with native peoples of the Delaware Valley were based on "peace, fair trade, and liberality." Notes that George Washington represents well the period of the "Age of Empires and Revolutions (c. 1750-1900)," in which Britain expanded and retrenched and in which order and the extension of the federal sphere of influence were twin difficulties. Concludes that from the

sixteenth century to the present, Americans have fought wars "less to preserve liberty than to extend the power of the United States in the name of liberty." Lays out "the distinctly American dilemma: how to exercise power legitimately and productively in a world made up of peoples who do not universally embrace individual freedom" or democratic governance.
AHR 110: 1515; *Booklist* 101n6: 547; *JAH* 92: 1406; *JER* 28: 471-74; *JSH* 74: 703-705; *PMHB* 130: 351; *WMQ* 63: 403-406.

650 Anderson, Fred and Philander Chase, eds. *George Washington Remembers: Reflections on the French and Indian War.* Lanham, Md.: Rowman and Littlefield, 2004. xiii, 175 p. ISBN 0742533727; ISBN 9780742533721; OCLC 53131556; LC Call Number E312.23 .W35; Dewey 940.2/534. Citations: 3.
Prints Washington's handwritten description of his role in the French and Indian War. Reveals that Washington calculated how to present his military achievements to the public, noting that he jotted the note to his official biographer David Humphreys and that he directed Humphreys to destroy it. Annotates the text and includes three essays that cover Washington the writer and public figure. Provides an appendix that describes the document and the various attempts to preserve it.
LJ 129n7: 99.

651 Anderson, Fred. *The War that Made America: A Short History of the French and Indian War.* New York: Viking, 2005. xxv, 293 p. ISBN 0670034541; ISBN 9780670034543; OCLC 60671897; LC Call Number E199 .A595; Dewey 973.2/6 22. Citations: 5.
Presents a short, companion history to a PBS documentary on the French and Indian War. Provides an introduction to the conflict intended for a general audience, explaining the various roles of Delaware chief Teedyuscung, Seneca chief Tanaghrisson, Ottawa war chief Pontiac, General James Wolfe, and the Marquis de Montcalm. Concludes that the conflict encouraged colonists "to conceive of themselves as equal partners in the empire" and that "it is not too much to call it the war that made America."
Booklist 102n6: 16; *LJ* 130n18: 96.

652 Brumwell, Stephen. *Redcoats: The British Soldier and War in the Americas, 1755–1763.* Cambridge: Cambridge University Press, 2002. x, 349 p. ISBN 0521807832; ISBN 9780521807838; OCLC 46402087; LC Call Number E199 .B89; Dewey 940.2/534. Citations: 37.
Rejects the idea that the British soldier in the Seven Years' War was ineffective and poorly led. Notes that, after Braddock's defeat at Fort Duquesne, the British political leadership made necessary military investments in America to establish conditions for success. Finds that the army was more socially diverse and motivated than previously thought. Explains that the Highland battalions were very professional and particularly effective in America. Concludes that "the British Army contributed far more to winning the Seven Years War in the Americas than many historians have been prepared to concede" and, in fact, became a "sprawling instrument of empire."

AHR 108: 911-12; *CHR* 85: 590-91; *18c Stds* 36: 463-65; *JAH* 89: 1023-24; *J Mil Hist* 66: 1200-1201; *LJ* 127n3: 158; *WMQ* 60: 456-58.

653 Brumwell, Stephen. *White Devil: A True Story of War, Savagery, and Vengeance in Colonial America.* Cambridge, Mass.: Da Capo Press, 2005. 335 p. ISBN 0306813890; ISBN 9780306813894; OCLC 57655778; LC Call Number E199 .B786; Dewey 973.2/6. Citations: 9.

Describes Robert Rogers's October 1759 destruction of the Abenaki village of Saint-François (Odanak) on the orders of General Jeffery Amherst, placing the event in the context of the French and Indian War. Traces Rogers's career, characterizing him as brave and heroic and zealously protective of his men. Contends that the raid on Odanak influenced later Anglo-American diplomacy and allowed for westward settlement of Abenaki lands in the 1760s.

CHR 87: 109-11; *J Mil Hist* 70: 228-29; *LJ* 130n4: 97.

654 Cave, Alfred A. *The French and Indian War.* Westport, Conn.: Greenwood Press, 2004. xix, 175 p. ISBN 031332168X; ISBN 9780313321689; OCLC 52963216; LC Call Number E199 .C38; Dewey 973.26. Citations: 2.

Seeks to provide a "resource for student research" on the French and Indian War. Includes an overview of the conflict, biographical sketches of key participants, treatment of Native American tribes involved, the aftermath of the war, and primary documents.

J Mil Hist 69: 228-30.

655 Chet, Guy. *Conquering the American Wilderness: The Triumph of European Warfare in the Colonial Northeast.* Amherst: University of Massachusetts Press, 2003. xx, 207 p. ISBN 1558493662 (hbk.); ISBN 9781558493667 (hbk.); ISBN 1558493824 (pbk.); ISBN 9781558493827 (pbk.); OCLC 50802565; LC Call Number F8 .C49; Dewey 974/.02 21. Citations: 10.

Examines battles in North America between 1620 and the French and Indian War, arguing that the Anglo-Americans did not forsake European military conventions, but rather held to the standard practices as long as they could, persistence that paid off in the Seven Years' War. Notes that men like Miles Standish and John Mason executed defensive tactics well, but that by the time of King Philip's War, the skills of New England military leaders had deteriorated. Downplays the Indian fighting techniques of Benjamin Church and contends that British administration and command of forces after Queen Anne's War led to tactical superiority in the fight against the French for the North American continent.

AHR 109: 890-91; *HRNB* 32: 101; *JAH* 91: 214-15; *J Mil Hist* 67: 1277-78.

656 Dull, Jonathan R. *The French Navy and the Seven Years' War.* Lincoln: University of Nebraska Press, 2005. xxii, 445 p. ISBN 0803217315; ISBN 9780803217317; OCLC 57349163; LC Call Number DC52 .D895; Dewey 940.2/534. Citations: 16.

Describes the Seven Years' War as "the world's first global conflict, spanning five continents and the critical sea lanes that connected them." Views the conflict in terms of two theaters, the French and Indian War (1754–60) and the

European Seven Years' War (1756–63) and focuses on the role of the French navy which, after the War of Austrian Succession, benefited from good administration and several years of expansion. Notes, however, that in the Seven Years' War the French navy played second fiddle to the army and was cash-strapped. Contends that poor financial conditions came to a head in 1758 and the weakened navy could no longer protect Atlantic shipping lanes, resulting in the fall of Louisbourg, Wolfe's advance on Quebec, and the loss of Canada. Asserts that the treaties ending the wars likely had a greater effect on American history than on European history.
AHR 111: 910-11; *CJH* 42: 346-47; *18c Stds* 39: 537-60; *EHR* 122: 833-34; *JAH* 93: 186; *J Mil Hist* 69: 1204-1205; *J Mod Hist* 79: 435-36; *LJ* 130n7: 103.

657 Flavell, Julie and Stephen Conway, eds. *Britain and America Go to War: The Impact of War and Warfare in Anglo-America, 1754–1815*. Gainesville: University Press of Florida, 2004. x, 284 p. ISBN 0813027810; ISBN 9780813027814; OCLC 56367347; LC Call Number E199 .B93; Dewey 973.2/6. Citations: 12.
Includes articles on the idea of "national interest" in the mid-eighteenth century, women and the British army in the Seven Years' War, the British view of the North American colonies during the Seven Years' War and of New England on the eve of the Revolution, published responses to the Howe brothers' American campaigns, volunteering in Britain during the American Revolution, Admiral Alexander Cochrane's naval campaign against the United States during the War of 1812, the ways in which persons experienced the War of 1812, and the development of the Atlantic state system at the end of the eighteenth century and beginning of the nineteenth century.
AHR 111: 122-24; *EHR* 121: 320-21; *JAH* 92: 956-57; *J Mil Hist* 69: 1210-11; *NCHR* 82: 506-507.

658 Fowler, William M. *Empires at War: The French and Indian War and the Struggle for North America, 1754–1763*. New York: Walker, 2005. xxv, 332 p. ISBN 0802714110 (hbk.); ISBN 9780802714114 (hbk.); ISBN 0802777376 (pbk.); ISBN 9780802777379 (pbk.); OCLC 56334323; LC Call Number E199 .F78; Dewey 973.2/6 22. Citations: 8.
Views the French and Indian War as the first "world war," not a mere prelude to the American Revolution, and seeks to explain the war's "true importance as a world-shaping event." Covers the European theatre of the Seven Years' War, but focuses on the campaigns of Braddock, Washington, and Wolfe. Asserts that the surrender of Montreal in 1760 was a watershed event for Native Americans and that "No one had a greater stake in the fate of North America than its Native inhabitants." Concludes that, after 1763, the British committed to maintaining an empire in North America very similar to that of the French—territorially extensive, devoted officially to peaceful relations with Native peoples, and needing revenue.
Booklist 101: 701; *CHR* 87: 109-111; *HRNB* 33: 103; *LJ* 130n1: 127-28; *NEQ* 79: 138-40.

659 Gaff, Alan D. *Bayonets in the Wilderness: Anthony Wayne's Legion in the Old Northwest*. Norman: University of Oklahoma Press, 2004. xix, 419 p. ISBN 0806135859 (hbk.); ISBN 9780806135854 (hbk.); ISBN 9780806139302 (pbk.); ISBN 0806139307 (pbk.); OCLC 53231769; LC Call Number E83.79 .G34; Dewey 973.4/1 22. Citations: 6.

Examines Wayne's campaign against the Native Americans of the Ohio Valley from the November 1791 Battle of Kekionga (Miami leader Little Turtle's victory over American forces under General Arthur St. Clair) to 1795. Finds that Wayne was called upon to create a new military force to break Native American resistance to settler expansion in the Ohio Valley. Describes Wayne's efforts to recruit, train, supply, and discipline his troops and provides information on his officers and enlisted men. Concludes with an explanation of the significance of Wayne's taking the lands of the Ohio Indians.

IMH 101: 179-80; *JAH* 92: 204-205; *JER* 25: 133-35; *J Mil Hist* 68: 1254-55; *WHQ* 36: 534-35.

660 Grenier, John. *The First Way of War: American War Making on the Frontier, 1607–1814*. New York: Cambridge University Press, 2005. xiv, 232 p. ISBN 0521845661; ISBN 9780521845663; OCLC 55887273; LC Call Number E82 .G74; Dewey 355/.00973/0903 22. Citations: 20.

Argues that war in the British North American colonies and the early United States was characterized by "unconventional" warfare because European-style frontier forces would never have been able to engage and defeat Indians. Finds that, as a result, Anglo-Americans had to attack native food sources and stockpiles to starve Indians into retreat or submission, raids that were usually carried out by rangers under colonial or state authority, who worked for bounties, which led to greater casualties among Indian women and children. Contends that this sort of "total war" began due more to frontier circumstances than racism and was the most effective means of defeating Native Americans throughout the colonial era. Finds that the defeat of the Ohio Indian confederation in the 1790s only came about as result of the use of a large, effective conventional force, which ravaged the native food supplies and prevented the Indians from continuing their resistance.

AHR 112: 183-84; *JAH* 93: 185-86; *J Mil Hist* 70: 226-27; *JSH* 72: 640-41; *NCHR* 82: 505-506; *VMHB* 114: 294-96.

661 Horgan, Lucille E. *Forged in War: The Continental Congress and the Origin of Military Supply and Acquisition Policy*. Westport, Conn.: Greenwood Press, 2002. xvii, 191 p. ISBN 0313321612; ISBN 9780313321610; OCLC 48674577; LC Call Number E259 .H64; Dewey 355.6/21/0973. Citations: 3.

Examines the continuity of Revolution-era weapons acquisition processes over time. Explains that the Continental Congress developed small military and civilian staffs dealing with finance, supply, and procurement when foreign sources of artillery and naval ships became inaccessible. Details congressional initiatives in research and development, developing expertise, encouraging innovation, and industrial development. Distinguishes between the Continental Army's use of both civilian and military administration for weapons acquisition and the Continental Navy's use of a predominantly civilian structure. Notes

differences in contracting processes: the Army provided detailed contractual specifications and compliance for artillery, whereas the Navy involved naval officials in inspection throughout the construction process. Concludes that during the Revolutionary era, "the recognition that technology was critical to national security first emerged and was dealt with by policy makers."
J Mil Hist 67: 564-65.

662   Lengel, Edward G. *General George Washington: A Military Life*. New York: Random House, 2005. xlii, 450 p. ISBN 1400060818 (hbk.); ISBN 9781400060818 (hbk.); OCLC 60523007; LC Call Number E312.25 .L46; Dewey 973.4/1092. Citations: 5.
Attempts to provide readers with a balanced view of Washington as a military leader, beginning with his appointment in 1753 as a major in the Virginia militia and continuing through his death in 1799. Finds that Washington was not a great general, but rather was often impulsive and overconfident, and occasionally misjudged his enemy and exhibited qualities of a poor tactician. Stresses that, despite these shortcomings, Washington possessed the personal, social, political, administrative, and leadership skills, vision, bravery, and loyalty of his subordinates necessary to prevail over England.
Booklist 101: 1632; *JSH* 73: 154-55; *LJ* 130n11: 79; *VMHB* 113: 190-91.

663   McClung, Robert M. *Young George Washington and the French and Indian War, 1753–1758*. North Haven, Conn.: Linnet Books, 2002. x, 121 p. ISBN 020802509X; ISBN 9780208025098; OCLC 49320397; LC Call Number E312.23 .M38; Dewey 973.2/6/092. Citations: 0.
Presents a narrative of the French and Indian War and Washington's role in that conflict. Traces Washington's transformation from a young ambitious soldier to a seasoned leader. Stresses the impact that the war had on his later command of the Continental Army. Includes quotations from Washington's letters and diaries, as well as reproductions of maps and paintings. Intended for a juvenile audience.
Booklist 98: 1944.

664   McConnell, Michael N. *Army and Empire: British Soldiers on the American Frontier, 1758–1775*. Lincoln: University of Nebraska Press, 2004. xix, 211 p. ISBN 0803232330 (hbk.); ISBN 9780803232334 (hbk.); ISBN 0803204795 (electronic); ISBN 9780803204799 (electronic); OCLC 54988836; LC Call Number U767 .M37; Dewey 973.2/7 22. Citations: 12.
Points out that the eighteenth-century American western frontier stretched from the western Great Lakes to the Gulf of Mexico and produced a unique experience for the typical soldier. Describes soldiers' material and personal lives, including diet and the roles of women. Argues that power, order, and deference among soldiers remained and that the ethnic and racial diversity of outposts, along with the presence of women and children, caused garrisons "to resemble the small civilian communities that defined the British Atlantic world." Demonstrates that the buying habits of soldiers were very similar to those of working people. Stresses that diet and health were interlinked, and that chronic sickness and injury were serious problems that limited the effectiveness of the

fighting force. Contends that reduced recruitment after 1763 led to an increase in the average age of the frontier soldier and overall decrease in health and vitality of men under arms. Emphasizes the close relationship of the army to the civilian world, largely from necessity (e.g., supply of food and materials).
AHR 111: 122; *CJH* 40: 556-57; *JAH* 92: 956; *J Mil Hist* 69: 833-34; *JSH* 72: 161-62.

665 McCulloch, Ian M. and Timothy J. Todish, eds. *Through So Many Dangers: The Memoirs and Adventures of Robert Kirk, Late of the Royal Highland Regiment*. Fleischmanns, N.Y.: Purple Mountain Press, 2004. 174 p. ISBN 1930098634 (hbk.); ISBN 9781930098633 (hbk.); ISBN 193009860X (pbk.); ISBN 9781930098602 (pbk.); OCLC 57124916; LC Call Number E199 .T576; Dewey 973.2/6092. Citations: 0.
Presents Kirk's memoirs from the Seven Years' War, which represents an account of the conflict from the perspective of a common soldier. Explains that Kirk's real name was Robert Kirkwood, that he served in South Carolina, Fort Duquesne, Forts Carillon and Saint Frederic, Saint Francis, Montreal, Fort Detroit, Newfoundland, in Pontiac's War, the Illinois country, New Orleans, and New York.
CHR 87: 511-12.

666 McDonald, Robert M.S., ed. *Thomas Jefferson's Military Academy: Founding West Point*. Charlottesville: University of Virginia Press, 2004. xix, 233 p. ISBN 0813922984; ISBN 9780813922980; OCLC 55016997; LC Call Number U410 .L1; Dewey 355/.0071/173. Citations: 4.
Includes pieces on military education before West Point, the Military Academy and Jefferson's constitutionalism, Adams and Jefferson and the "figure in arms," West Point in the context of Jeffersonian reform, an educational interpretation of the Academy, West Point and the struggle to render the officer corps safe for America between 1802 and 1833, Jefferson remembered, forgotten, and reconsidered as the founder of the Military Academy, and the role of military virtues in preserving American republican institutions.
AHR 111: 1296-97; *JAH* 93: 847-48; *JER* 26: 133-36; *JSH* 72: 660-61; *VMHB* 114: 408-10.

667 Samet, Elizabeth D. *Willing Obedience: Citizens, Soldiers, and the Progress of Consent in America, 1776-1898*. Stanford, Calif.: Stanford University Press, 2004. xiv, 273 p. ISBN 0804747253 (hbk.); ISBN 9780804747257 (hbk.); ISBN 0804747261 (pbk.); ISBN 9780804747264 (pbk.); OCLC 53215712; LC Call Number JC328.2 .S26; Dewey 323.6/5. Citations: 6.
Explores the boundaries between duty and obedience to the state and individual freedom and conscience. Focuses on the roles played by Washington, Adams, Lincoln, Grant, William Tecumseh Sherman, Thomas Wentworth Higginson, and Herman Melville. Views the soldier "as a metonym for the situation of all citizens in a republic," arguing that Americans, even prior to the Revolution, struggled with the conflict between liberty and power, between freedom and its paradoxical surrender for the sake of its defense.

AHR 110: 131-32; *Am Lit* 77: 179-81; *CJH* 40: 559-60; *JAH* 91: 1430-31; *J Mil Hist* 68: 968-69.

668 Skaggs, David Curtis and Larry L. Nelson. *The Sixty Years' War for the Great Lakes, 1754–1814*. East Lansing: Michigan State University Press, 2001. xxvii, 414 p. ISBN 0870135694; ISBN 9780870135699; OCLC 45629772; LC Call Number F551 .S53; Dewey 977/.01. Citations: 14.

Presents twenty essays covering French imperial policy, Henry Bouquet and British infantry tactics on the Ohio frontier, the British Army and epidemic disease among the Ohio Indians (1758–1765), the work of Charles-Michel Mouet de Langlade, the Iroquois role in the Ohio Valley (1754–1794), French-British relations (1760–1775) and the American Revolution in the western Great Lakes, the military role of Detroit (1701–1826), the Gnadenhutten massacre, war as a cultural encounter in the Ohio valley, liberty and power in the Old Northwest (1765–1800), Quaker-Seneca missions, the geography of inland navigation across New York, Iroquois external affairs (1807–1815), land speculation and the War of 1812 in the Firelands, British North Americans and loyal Shawnees in the War of 1812, the contest for Lakes Erie and Ontario (1812–1815), and the meaning of the various wars for the Great Lakes.

IMH 98: 239-40; *JER* 22: 135-37; *J Mil Hist* 66: 200-201; *PMHB* 126: 502-504.

669 Thomas, Evan. *John Paul Jones: Sailor, Hero, Father of the American Navy*. New York: Simon and Schuster, 2003. 383 p. ISBN 0743205839; ISBN 9780743205832; OCLC 51553307; LC Call Number E207.J7; Dewey 973.3/5/092. Citations: 6.

Presents a biography of Jones for a general readership. Portrays Jones as a smart, bold, social climber who played a key role in turning British public opinion against the Revolutionary War.

Booklist 99: 1446; *Booklist* 100: 1081; *LJ* 128n8: 130.

670 Ward, Matthew C. *Breaking the Backcountry: The Seven Years' War in Virginia and Pennsylvania, 1754–1765*. Pittsburgh, Penn.: University of Pittsburgh Press, 2003. x, 329 p. ISBN 0822942143; ISBN 9780822942146; OCLC 52121401; LC Call Number E199 .W236; Dewey 973.2/6. Citations: 22.

Portrays the frontier regions of Virginia and Pennsylvania as filled with religious and ethnic divides that became more pronounced when Indian allies of the French began undertaking increased raids during the Seven Years' War. Contends that eastern elite influence in such areas was virtually non-existent and that "enforcement of order had all but broken down." Points to widespread examples of disobedience, including refusal to provide supplies and men, quarter troops, and prosecute violations of law, as well as the promotion of riots and mob action. Concludes that the War "began to shape new social structures," as the electorate gained in importance.

HRNB 32: 100-101; *JAH* 91: 605-606; *JAS* 39: 141-42; *J Mil Hist* 68: 955-56; *LJ* 128n16: 97-98; *Penn Hist* 71: 390-92; *PMHB* 129: 227-28; *RAH* 32: 471-77; *SCHM* 106: 66-70; *VMHB* 112: 188-90.

25 Ideas

671 Anderson, Douglas. *William Bradford's Books:* Of Plimmoth Plantation *and the Printed Word*. Baltimore, Md.: Johns Hopkins University Press, 2003. xii, 280 p. ISBN 0801870747; ISBN 9780801870743; OCLC 48965053; LC Call Number F68 .B80733; Dewey 974.4/8202. Citations: 5.
Discusses the chronology and context of Bradford's *Of Plimmoth Plantation*. Describes the importance of printing to Plymouth Separatists, particularly as it related to the advancement of the continuing Reformation. Notes the significance of seventeenth-century textual reading and explication. Points to William Perkins's method of placing related biblical passages next to one another. Contends that Bradford meant his book to be "set alongside other printed books of its own day." Discovers new significance in silences (e.g., Bradford's ignoring of the commission of Robert Gorges and trials of Anne Hutchinson) and in the use of letters. Rejects the declension interpretation of Bradford's work, arguing instead that it was meant to celebrate Pilgrim survival, endurance, and adaptation. Holds up Bradford as a modern historian, whose narrative objectivity seeks "to situate us outside the turmoil of life and permit us to observe its contending elements, to the best of the historian's ability, in an atmosphere that is free of bias or passion." Concludes that Bradford's work demonstrates a cosmopolitan Puritan outlook, one that challenges primitivist interpretations.
AHR 109: 512-13; *EAL* 39: 177-82; *NEQ* 77: 500-503; *WMQ* 61: 353-55.

672 Arias, Santa. *Retórica, Historia y Polémica: Bartolomé de las Casas y la Tradición Intelectual Renacentista*. Lanham, Md.: University Press of America, 2001. 171 p. ISBN 076182183X; ISBN 9780761821830; OCLC 48474262; LC Call Number E125.C4; Dewey 970.01/6. Citations: 5.
Studies the writings of de las Casas, especially *Historia de las Indias* and *De unico vocationis modo*, placing them in the intellectual context of the

Renaissance. Discusses the rhetoric of de las Casas, particularly the way in which his Christian humanism resulted in a rabidly anti-hegemonic view. Views de las Casas as an extraordinarily "modern" figure in his defense of natives and in his production of texts that lend themselves to postmodernist analysis.
HAHR 83: 747-48.

673 Block, James E. *A Nation of Agents: The American Path to a Modern Self and Society*. Cambridge, Mass.: Belknap Press of Harvard University Press, 2002. xi, 658 p. ISBN 0674008839; ISBN 9780674008830; OCLC 49312439; LC Call Number E169.1 .B654; Dewey 306/.0973/09034; Dewey 306.097309033. Citations: 18.
Examines the concept of agency, noting its importance to the development of the self and of society in early America. Explains that the idea of agency evolved from American Protestantism and liberalism and, in fact, was more vital to national origins than was the notion of liberty. Traces agency from its English roots in the seventeenth century through its appearance in twentieth-century American popular culture. Contends that colonial agency encouraged individuals to participate in social institutions, but beset them with new obligations. Stresses that this tension lies at the crux of the American character.
AHR 109: 1220-21; *JAAR* 73: 902-905; *JAH* 90: 983.

674 Bolton, Linda. *Facing the Other: Ethical Disruption and the American Mind*. Baton Rouge: Louisiana State University Press, 2004. xi, 209 p. ISBN 0807129402; ISBN 9780807129401; OCLC 53183434; LC Call Number E302.1 .B65; Dewey 172/.0973 22. Citations: 3.
Examines Crèvecoeur's *Letters from an American Farmer*, Thomas Paine's views on the American republic, the writings of Thomas Jefferson, the ideas of Frederick Douglass and Sarah Winnemucca, and John Brown's actions in the Harpers Ferry raid, paying particular attention to the idea of the treatment of the "other" in America. Asserts that the American emphasis on freedom has resulted in the relative lack of attention to doing justice. Finds inherent tension in American literature between freedom and justice, noting that the former justified the mistreatment of Native Americans and African Americans. Focuses on moments of "ethical disruption," at which time Americans came face to face with moral matters of exploitation and guilt.
Am Lit 77: 639-41.

675 Brown, Gillian. *The Consent of the Governed: The Lockean Legacy in Early American Culture*. Cambridge, Mass.: Harvard University Press, 2001. viii, 237 p. ISBN 0674002989; ISBN 9780674002982; OCLC 44633053; LC Call Number JK54 .B76; Dewey 320/.01/1 21. Citations: 26.
Emphasizes the importance of Locke's work to early American politics and pedagogy, particularly his influence on the individual and republicanism. Explains how Locke's concept of consent was applied in the eighteenth century to the areas of education, government, and family, particularly as the term related to children and women. Reviews the idea of consent in *The New England Primer* and in the novels *The Coquette* by Hannah Webster Foster and *Female Quixotism* by Tabitha Tenney.

Am Lit 74: 403-405; *AQ* 54: 149-58; *Am Stds* 43: 174-75; *EAL* 38: 170-73; *18c Stds* 39: 568-70; *JAH* 88: 1510-11; *JER* 21: 700-703; *RAH* 29: 338-45; *WMQ* 60: 235-38.

676 Casid, Jill H. *Sowing Empire: Landscape and Colonization.* Minneapolis: University of Minnesota Press, 2005. xxiii, 283 p. ISBN 0816640955 (hbk.); ISBN 9780816640959 (hbk.); ISBN 0816640963 (pbk.); ISBN 9780816640966 (pbk.); OCLC 56422001; LC Call Number SB121 .C27; Dewey 631.5/31/09709033 22. Citations: 18.
Uses the metaphor of planting to describe colonization, noting that the process created racialized and sexualized landscapes and affected both the metropole and colonies. Focuses on British and French Caribbean possessions, particularly natural "intermixing" and the aesthetic representations of plantation life, which depicted harmony among planters and slaves, exotic trees and plants, and waterfalls and grottos. Examines various literary tropes that made use of botany and landscapes, noting that resistance to imperialism was expressed through changing landscapes, while compliance was indicated by portrayals of slavery's ecologically friendly exploitation of the land.
18c Stds 40: 120-23; *JHG* 32: 455-57.

677 Fichtelberg, Joseph. *Critical Fictions: Sentiment and the American Market, 1780–1870.* Athens: University of Georgia Press, 2003. x, 280 p. ISBN 0820324345; ISBN 9780820324340; OCLC 49894859; LC Call Number PS366.S35; Dewey 810.9/353. Citations: 14.
Relates market consciousness to political discourse and literature, arguing that the language of sentiment, the "mode of practical consciousness, a means of thinking through social impasse," was used both to represent and to manage the recurrent crises associated with an expanding capitalist market economy in the late eighteenth and early nineteenth centuries. Explains that this sentimentalism might be unexpected in the masculine and rational environment of capitalist exchange, but that writers used sentimental language to "humanize economic crisis" by making "intimate and domestic the abstract forces of economy and polity" through cultivating "the power of individual action." Proceeds chronologically, noting that the writers of the early national period "began to see their lives as reflections of market forces" and "the drive to consume," while reflecting the prevalent anxieties about British goods flooding the market. Contends that in the era of the Embargo of 1807 and the Panic of 1819 sentiment in contemporary popular fiction "provided a crucial counterweight to the sense of helplessness and alienation" by transforming "fragility into power."
Am Lit 76: 394-96; *EAL* 39: 379-84; *JER* 24: 497-500.

678 Foletta, Marshall. *Coming to Terms with Democracy: Federalist Intellectuals and the Shaping of an American Culture.* Charlottesville: University Press of Virginia, 2001. xii, 303 p. ISBN 0813920590; OCLC 46683564; LC Call Number E338 .F65; Dewey 973.5 21. Citations: 9.
Focuses on the place of New England Federalism in American intellectual history. Finds that younger Federalists proved very adaptable, learning to accept relatively broad democracy while holding to standards of orderly, hierarchical

society. Finds that this younger generation criticized their elders' partisanship, and that European travels resulted in openness to new religious and artistic movements and made Harvard seem overly narrow and insulated. Argues that they turned their backs on careers in the clergy and the law, strayed from the neoclassical literary canon, became Unitarians, admired the romantic movement, and called for the development of an American national literature. Discusses the young Federalists' campaigns for common schools, the reformation of Harvard, professionalization of charitable work and legal education, and the reimagining of history and biography.
AHR 108: 520-21; *JAH* 89: 1512-13; *JER* 22: 525-28; *NCHR* 79: 273-74; *PMHB* 126: 652-54; *VMHB* 109: 422-23; *WMQ* 59: 1034-37.

679 Fruchtman, Jack. *Atlantic Cousins: Benjamin Franklin and His Visionary Friends*. New York: Thunder's Mouth Press, 2005. 404 p. ISBN 1560256680; ISBN 9781560256687; OCLC 58973854; LC Call Number E302.6.F8 F89; Dewey 973.3092. Citations: 1.
Presents portraits of eleven intellectual "cousins" with whom Benjamin Franklin corresponded in America, England, and France, including Anthony Benezet, Granville Sharp, Joseph Priestly, Richard Price, the Marquis de Condorcet, Jean-Paul Marat, and Franz Anton Mesmer.
LJ 130n12: 97.

680 Golden, James L. and Alan L. Golden. *Thomas Jefferson and the Rhetoric of Virtue*. Lanham, Md.: Rowman & Littlefield, 2002. xviii, 522 p. ISBN 0742520803; ISBN 9780742520806; OCLC 48752926; LC Call Number E332.2 .G65; Dewey 973.4/6/092 21. Citations: 4.
Discusses Thomas Jefferson's use of rhetoric to promote virtue, describing what Jefferson meant by rhetoric, its relationship to the truth, and the use of rhetorical strategies for public and private discourse. Argues that, based on his love of virtue, Jefferson was a classical republican, not a Lockean liberal or some combination of both. Concludes that, on the reading of the Tory historian David Hume and on slavery, Jefferson was acting on "ideological" grounds and was not living up to his highest principles.
JAH 90: 624-25; *JER* 23: 288-91.

681 Himmelfarb, Gertrude. *The Roads to Modernity: The British, French, and American Enlightenments*. New York: Knopf, distributed by Random House, 2004. xii, 284 p. ISBN 1400042364; ISBN 9781400042364; OCLC 53091118; LC Call Number B802 .H65; Dewey 190/.9/033. Citations: 44.
Distinguishes among the French Enlightenment and the British and American Enlightenments, arguing that the latter focused on moral philosophy and thereby led to practical altruism. Regards the French Enlightenment as abstract and dogmatic, a movement that elevated compassionless Reason and ultimately led to the Reign of Terror.
Booklist 100: 1876; *LJ* 129n12: 97.

682 Hoffer, Peter Charles. *Sensory Worlds in Early America*. Baltimore, Md.: Johns Hopkins University Press, 2003. x, 334 p. ISBN 0801873533; ISBN

9780801873539; OCLC 50919844; LC Call Number E188 .H75; Dewey 973.2. Citations: 21.

Presents a "sensory history" of early America, focusing on the importance of sight, smell, sound, taste, and touch in shaping events. Explains that different perspectives and experiences led to misunderstandings and disastrous results for Native Americans, early English settlers, and African slaves, and directly affected the Salem witchcraft trials, the Great Awakening, and anti-British sentiments prior to the Revolution. Concludes that "sensation and perception affected some of those great events whose cause and course we historians conventionally attribute to deep cultural structures and overarching material forces."

AHR 109: 1223; *EHR* 119: 804-805; *HRNB* 32: 59: *JAH* 91: 992-93; *LJ* 128n18: 98-99; *PMHB* 129: 347-48; *WMQ* 61: 381-83.

683 Kaye, Harvey K. *Thomas Paine and the Promise of America*. New York: Hill and Wang, 2005. 326 p. ISBN 080908970X; ISBN 9780809089703; OCLC 56921124; LC Call Number JC177.A4; Dewey 320.51/092. Citations: 8.

Reviews Paine's impact on Europe and America in the late-eighteenth century and his reputation in the nineteenth and twentieth centuries, when he became increasingly characterized as an anarchist, atheist, drunkard, and socialist. Notes Paine's knack for making enemies through his writings. Seeks to rehabilitate Paine's image, discussing his positive influence on labor organizers, abolitionists, civil rights leaders, populists, suffragists, and literary figures.

AHR 111: 1165; *Booklist* 101: 1973; *JAH* 93: 503-504; *LJ* 130n13: 96-97.

684 Lindman, Janet Moore and Michele Lise Tarter, eds. *A Centre of Wonders: The Body in Early America*. Ithaca, N. Y.: Cornell University Press, 2001. viii, 283 p. ISBN 080143601X (hbk.); ISBN 9780801436017 (hbk.); ISBN 0801487390 (pbk.); ISBN 9780801487392 (pbk.); OCLC 45638908; LC Call Number GT497.U6; Dewey 306.4. Citations: 27.

Presents essays on the relationship of the body to questions of conquest, strategies of colonization, and constructions of race. Includes pieces on early American views of the body, witchcraft, bodily affliction, and domestic space in seventeenth-century New England, food, assimilation, and the malleability of the human body in early Virginia, "civilized" bodies and the "savage" environment of early New Plymouth, the body politic and the body somatic, bodily and racial purity, nursing fathers and brides of Christ, Quakers, Native Americans, and Baptists, Hannah Duston's bodies, and body language, emancipation and the embodiment of "race."

JAH 89: 1497-98; *JER* 22: 297-99; *J Interdis Hist* 33: 657-58; *J Soc Hist* 36: 1059-61; *NEQ* 76: 158-59; *WMQ* 59: 273-76.

685 Lupher, David A. *Romans in a New World: Classical Models in Sixteenth-Century Spanish America*. Ann Arbor: University of Michigan Press, 2003. vi, 440 p. ISBN 0472112759; ISBN 9780472112753; OCLC 49610931; LC Call Number F1230 .L953; Dewey 972/.02. Citations: 28.

Discusses the way in which ancient Rome became a model of comparison for New World conquistadors, jurists, theologians, missionaries, and intellectuals.

Contends that, overall, Rome provided a way for various interests, including humanists who criticized treatment of natives, to strengthen their arguments regarding the New World. Explains that writers saw Rome's brutal occupation of the Iberian peninsula as having profoundly altered narratives on the origins of the "Spanish" nation. Concludes that classical paradigms helped early modern Europeans make sense of their New World experience and substantially transformed how Europeans viewed their own classical and local histories.
AHR 109: 945-46; *HAHR* 84: 337-38; *HRNB* 32: 14.

686   McWilliams, John P. *New England's Crises and Cultural Memory: Literature, Politics, History, Religion, 1620–1860.* Cambridge: Cambridge University Press, 2004. xii, 366 p. ISBN 0521826837; ISBN 9780521826839; OCLC 53926732; LC Call Number PS243 .M38; Dewey 810.9/358 22. Citations: 0.
Studies the ways in which crises affected New England's cultural identity over the course of two and a half centuries. Considers the "Starving Time," Thomas Morton and the Merry Mount community, the antinomian controversy, King Philip's War, the Dominion of New England, the Salem witchcraft episode, the American Revolution, and abolitionism. Finds that New England and its brand of Puritanism were constantly changing in order to meet the interpretive and cultural needs of each successive generation.
AHR 111: 148-49; *Am Lit* 79: 177-78; *EAL* 41: 569-74; *NEQ* 78: 333-35.

687   Meyer, Jeffrey F. *Myths in Stone: Religious Dimensions of Washington, D.C.* Berkeley: University of California Press, 2001. xii, 343 p. ISBN 0520214811; ISBN 9780520214811; OCLC 43397085; LC Call Number BL2527.W18; Dewey 975.3. Citations: 10.
Contends that "there is a religious message implicit in most of the buildings, memorials, art, and iconography of Washington that recalls the original conviction, often stated by the Founding Fathers, that the Almighty stood behind the American experiment." Sees in Washington, D.C. elements of power, enlightenment, and memory and refers to the national archives as repositories of national "scriptures." Views the White House, the Washington Monument, and the Jefferson Memorial as symbols of Enlightenment, while the Lincoln Memorial, the Mall, and the Capitol's sculptures are seen as facilitators of historical memory. Examines Pierre L'Enfant's plan for the city, the providentialism of the Founders, the influence of masonic ritual on American civic life, religious ideas in presidential speeches, the mythic value of cities, the role of Pennsylvania Avenue for ceremonial occasions, the National Cathedral as a national church, the iconography of Washington and Jefferson, the republican meaning of classical architecture, and the value of museums in confirming national mythology.
CH 71: 927-29; *JAH* 89: 205-206; *J Religion* 82: 673-74; *Wilson Q* 25: 120-21.

688   Petersen, Eric S., ed. *Light and Liberty: Reflections on the Pursuit of Happiness.* New York: Modern Library, 2004. xiii, 154 p. ISBN 0679643117; ISBN 9780679643111; OCLC 52980436; LC Call Number E302 .J442; Dewey 973.46/092. Citations: 0.

Prints excerpts from Jefferson's letters arranged by virtues and attitudes (e.g., faith, fitness, sincerity, Jesus, nature's beauty, living in the present, enthusiasm, patriotism, oneness, hope, and truth-seeking) on which Jefferson comments. Includes a chronology of Jefferson's life.
Booklist 100: 1594; *LJ* 129n10: 152.

689   Pratt, Scott L. *Native Pragmatism: Rethinking the Roots of American Philosophy*. Bloomington: Indiana University Press, 2002. xx, 316 p. ISBN 0253340780 (hbk.); ISBN 9780253340788 (hbk.); ISBN 0253215196 (pbk.); ISBN 9780253215192 (pbk.); OCLC 48098320; LC Call Number B944 .P72; Dewey 144/.3. Citations: 13.
Traces indigenous American antecedents of major ideas in classical pragmatism, noting that in both native and European traditions, meaning in life is related to social location. Explains that the four "common commitments" of pragmatism, "the principles of interaction, pluralism, community, and growth," are well-established in Native American life. Draws upon accounts of Native American legends and accounts of dispossession from land from the seventeenth to the nineteenth century, speeches and essays of Native American leaders and prophets, and fictional narratives of women writers who objected to Indian removal policies. Contrasts the colonial hierarchical, xenophobic, absolutist attitude with the indigenous attitude that led to natives' welcoming newcomers in a way that indicates a pragmatic perspective. Points out that many European American thinkers adopted the native view, including Roger Williams, Cadwallader Colden, Benjamin Franklin, and Lydia Maria Child.
JAH 90: 613-14.

690   Read, David. *New World, Known World: Shaping Knowledge in Early Anglo-American Writing*. Columbia: University of Missouri Press, 2005. x, 177 p. ISBN 9780826216007; ISBN 0826216005; OCLC 60603138; LC Call Number E191 .R43; Dewey 973.2. Citations: 10.
Explores the writings of John Smith, William Bradford, Thomas Morton, and Roger Williams, referring to them as "others" in the American colonies, who depended upon conventional systems of knowledge, but were heavily affected by their experiences in the New World. Views tensions in the writings of these authors as disjunctions between "comprehensive mastery and critical mastery," or between the desire to record everything and the drive to place information into known categories of knowledge and interpretation. Outlines parallels between Smith and Thomas Harriot, between Williams and Thomas Browne and Pascal, and between Morton and Ben Jonson.
Am Lit 78: 869-72; *EAL* 43: 214-17; *NEQ* 79: 487-89; *WMQ* 63: 867-69.

691   Spencer, Mark G., ed. *Hume's Reception in Early America*. 2 vols. Bristol, Eng.: Thoemmes Press, distributed by the University of Chicago Press, 2002. xxvi, 278 p.; xxii, 291 p. ISBN 1855069342; ISBN 9781855069343; OCLC 48628741; LC Call Number B1498 .H89; Dewey 192. Citations: 5.
Presents 87 early American discussions of Hume's work published in periodicals, pamphlets, and scholarly books, mostly from the early nineteenth century, but ranging from 1758 to 1850. Covers responses to Hume's *Essays,*

Moral, Political, and Literary, to his philosophical writing, to his *History of England*, and to Hume's character and death.
WMQ 60: 882-88.

692 Ward, Lee. *The Politics of Liberty in England and Revolutionary America.* Cambridge: Cambridge University Press, 2004. x, 459 p. ISBN 0521827450; ISBN 9780521827454; OCLC 53951712; LC Call Number JA84.G7; Dewey 320/.01. Citations: 15.
Focuses in particular upon James Tyrrell's *Patriarcha Non-Monarcha* (1681), John Locke's *Two Treatises of Government* (1690), and Algernon Sidney's *Discourses Concerning Government* (1698). Explains that liberalism and republicanism co-existed and played off of one another in the run-up to the American Revolution and that revolutionary ideology represented an effort to reconcile three different models of government. Asserts that Jefferson primarily argued to cut the link between the colonies and Parliament, while Paine urged breaking the bond between the colonists and the Crown. Concludes that Lockean ideas ultimately won out in early state constitutions.
AHR 111: 1212-22; *J Brit Stds* 46: 189-91; *WMQ* 62: 798-801.

693 Weinberger, Jerry. *Benjamin Franklin Unmasked: On the Unity of His Moral, Religious, and Political Thought.* Lawrence: University Press of Kansas, 2005. xvi, 336 p. ISBN 070061396X (hbk.); ISBN 9780700613960 (hbk.); ISBN 9780700615841 (pbk.); ISBN 0700615849 (pbk.); OCLC 58422869; LC Call Number E302.6.F8; Dewey 973.3/092. Citations: 4.
Takes a fresh look at Franklin's writings, including his *Autobiography*, "Letter of the Drum" (1730), "Speech of Miss Polly Baker" (1747), "Old Mistresses Apologue" (1745), an article from the *Boston Independent Chronicle* (1782), *Dissertation on Liberty and Necessity* (1725), and "On Simplicity" (1732). Concludes that philosophically, Franklin was "a nearly full-blown Baconian, just as he was a nearly full-blown Hobbesian."
AHR 111: 1166; *18c Stds* 40: 324-30; *LJ* 130n14: 161.

694 Wilson, Kathleen. *The Island Race: Englishness, Empire, and Gender in the Eighteenth Century.* New York: Routledge, 2003. xvi, 282 p. ISBN 0415158958 (hbk.); ISBN 9780415158954 (hbk.); ISBN 0415158966 (pbk.); ISBN 9780415158961 (pbk.); OCLC 49594630; LC Call Number DA485 .W55; Dewey 909/.097124107. Citations: 102.
Focuses on the "performance" of national identity, based upon the ways in which one's gender, class, and ethnicity influenced "access to the resources of the nation-state." Contends that eighteenth-century "Englishness" was "staged" as being intertwined with a maritime empire that valued courage, science, and masculinity. Highlights Captain James Cook as an example of the best that this unique "island race" could produce, particularly in reference to the South Sea voyages.
AHR 109: 253-54; *EHR* 119: 225-26; *J Brit Stds* 44: 187-93; *J Mod Hist* 78: 623-42; *J Soc Hist* 39: 1197-99; *J Soc Hist* 40: 731-43; *WMQ* 61: 174-77.

695 Wilson, Kathleen, ed. *A New Imperial History: Culture, Identity and Modernity in Britain and the Empire, 1660–1840*. Cambridge: Cambridge University Press, 2004. xv, 385 p. ISBN 0521810272 (hbk.); ISBN 9780521810272 (hbk.); ISBN 0521007968 (pbk.); ISBN 9780521007962 (pbk.); OCLC 53059841; LC Call Number DA16 .N49; Dewey 909/.0971241; Dewey 909/.0917241. Citations: 90.

Presents essays on gender and empire in the late seventeenth and early eighteenth centuries, fashionable sociability and the Pacific in the 1770s, the "theatre of empire," identity among Asians in Britain, British exploration of Africa in the late eighteenth century, the political economy of "responsible government" in early British India, England and the Holy Land in late eighteenth- and early nineteenth-century culture, the concept of time among African slaves, radicalism in eighteenth-century America and Ireland, the transformation of Wolfe's image, ethnicity in the British Atlantic (1688–1830), George Bogle in Bengal and Tibet, reading the archives of colonial India, Mai and Cook in London, and gender misrecognition and Polynesian subversions aboard the Cook voyages.

AHR 110: 1478-79; *HRNB* 33: 68; *J Brit Stds* 44: 841-42; *J Soc Hist* 40: 731-43; *WMQ* 62: 781-84.

696 Zakai, Avihu. *Jonathan Edwards's Philosophy of History: The Reenchantment of the World in the Age of Enlightenment*. Princeton, N. J.: Princeton University Press, 2003. xviii, 348 p. ISBN 0691096546; ISBN 9780691096544; OCLC 605169137; LC Call Number B873; Dewey 231.7/6/092. Citations: 15.

Studies Edwards's interest in and use of history, particularly as indicated in *A History of the Work of Redemption* (1774). Contends that, in so doing, Edwards sought to respond to certain Enlightenment ideas about the world, especially new natural philosophy's interest in mechanisms (1720s), notions of God's work in history (1730s), and commonsense moral philosophies (1750s). Concludes that Edwards wanted to place the divine at the center of history and to keep American morals pure and separate from corrupt English ways.

AHR 109: 1554-55; *JAH* 91: 217-18; *J Religion* 85: 121-23; *RAH* 34: 131-49; *WMQ* 61: 135-51.

26 Literature

697 Arch, Stephen Carl. *After Franklin: The Emergence of Autobiography in Post-Revolutionary America, 1780–1830.* Hanover, N. H.: University Press of New England, 2001. xiv, 241 p. ISBN 1584651148 (hbk.); ISBN 9781584651147 (hbk.); ISBN 1584651326 (pbk.); ISBN 9781584651321 (pbk.); OCLC 47102645; LC Call Number CT25 .A68; Dewey 808/.06692. Citations: 8.

Contends that true autobiographical writing required romanticism and so was not possible in America until the 1820s. Connects autobiography to social and ideological conditions after the Revolution, especially significant developments in print communication, which allowed authors to reach readers in faraway places. Indicates that a "paradigm shift" occurred between 1780 and 1830, from classis to romantic, from traditional to modern, and from patriarchal to democratic values. Concludes that John Fitch, not Franklin, was the true founder of the American autobiography, as his work dealt more with self-discovery and self-expression than typical eighteenth-century "emulation" and conformity. *LJ* 126n10: 156; *WMQ* 59: 530-33.

698 Baker, Jennifer J. *Securing the Commonwealth: Debt, Speculation, and Writing in the Making of Early America.* Baltimore, Md.: Johns Hopkins University Press, 2005. x, 218 p. ISBN 0801879728; ISBN 9780801879722; OCLC 57434386; LC Call Number PS193 .B35; Dewey 810.9/3553 22. Citations: 22.

Studies the writings of Cotton Mather, Ebenezer Cooke, Benjamin Franklin, Royall Tyler, Charles Brockden Brown, and Judith Sargent Murray for the authors' views on speculation, risk-taking, borrowing, and financial networks, noting that they "saw their literary productions as potential economic interventions." Argues that seventeenth- and eighteenth-century American writers viewed indebtedness as a key to building a commonwealth, since it

allowed for economic development, for an increase in credibility, and for a sense of community and empathy as debt bound persons to one another.
AHR 113: 494-95; *Am Lit* 79: 605-607; *EAL* 43: 745-49; *JAH* 93: 850; *JAS* 42: 583-84; *JER* 27: 339-42; *J Interdis Hist* 37: 634-35; *NEQ* 80: 169-71; *WMQ* 63: 621-24.

699 Barnard, Philip, Mark L. Kamrath, and Stephen Shapiro, eds. *Revising Charles Brockden Brown: Culture, Politics, and Sexuality in the Early Republic.* Knoxville: University of Tennessee Press, 2004. xxi, 394 p. ISBN 1572332441; ISBN 9781572332447; OCLC 53398152; LC Call Number PS1137 .R485; Dewey 813/.2 22. Citations: 10.
Presents articles on the various contexts for Brown's writings, including those of transatlantic ideas in his early works. Includes pieces on Carwin as an agrarian rebel in *Wieland*, late-eighteenth-century West Indian racial views as they appear in *Arthur Mervyn*, reflections of morality and judgment in the public sphere, sex in Malthus's *An Essay on the Principle of Population* as compared to Brown's *Alcuin*, social interaction among the sexes in New York City in the 1790s, Brown's shift to the female narrative voice in *Ormond*, homoeroticism in *Edgar Huntly*, *Clara Howard* as an allegory of the unfulfilled promise of the American Revolution, early republican statistical discourse in the *Literary Magazine* and *Jane Talbot*, Brown's fictional histories penned between 1803 and 1807, and Brown's Louisiana political pamphlets and journalism.
EAL 40: 173-91; *WMQ* 62: 344-49.

700 Brooks, Joanna. *American Lazarus: Religion and the Rise of African-American and Native American Literatures.* New York: Oxford University Press, 2003. vi, 255 p. ISBN 0195160789; ISBN 9780195160789; OCLC 50511471; LC Call Number PS153.N5; Dewey 810.9/896073. Citations: 33.
Puts forward Lazarus as the biblical figure that best suits the experience of nonwhite persons in early America, noting that he "embodied the imposed discontinuities, cruelties, and mortalities of black Atlantic life, as well as an elective orientation toward change." Asserts that both blacks and Native Americans relied upon group action and collective struggle, not on the self-reliance typically ascribed to Calvinists, to deal with violence and dispossession. Concludes that "the earliest black and Indian authors established themselves as visionary interlocutors of secular nationalism and the American Enlightenment."
CH 75: 941-42; *EAL* 40: 395-402; *JAH* 91: 998-99; *NEQ* 78: 486-88.

701 Brooks, Joanna and John Saillant, eds. *"Face Zion Forward": First Writers of the Black Atlantic, 1785–1798.* Boston, Mass.: Northeastern University Press, 2002. x, 242 p. ISBN 1555535402 (hbk.); ISBN 9781555535407 (hbk.); ISBN 1555535399 (pbk.); ISBN 9781555535391 (pbk.); OCLC 49824697; LC Call Number PS647.A35; Dewey 818/.20809896073. Citations: 11.
Seeks "to introduce to contemporary audiences a reliable modern edition of eighteenth-century black writings," which includes the work of John Marrant, David George, and Prince Hall.
EAL 39: 175-77; *WMQ* 60: 680-83.

702   Bruce, Dickson D. *The Origins of African American Literature, 1680–1865*. Charlottesville: University Press of Virginia, 2001. xvi, 374 p. ISBN 0813920663 (hbk.); ISBN 0813920671 (pbk.); OCLC 46670986; LC Call Number PS153.N5 B78; Dewey 810.9/896073 21. Citations: 16.
Describes the "distinctive African American literary persona" that developed over the course of almost two centuries prior to the Civil War. Discusses oral traditions and non-black voices that contributed to the persona, noting "webs of interaction among African Americans and between black and white Americans" that shaped the literature and the culture. Notes the influence of various events—including the abolition of the slave trade and the debates over African colonization and abolition—on the black voice.
Am Lit 75: 201-203; *JSH* 69: 671-72; *NEQ* 75: 647-55.

703   Carey, Brycchan. *British Abolitionism and the Rhetoric of Sensibility: Writing, Sentiment, and Slavery, 1760–1807*. New York: Palgrave MacMillan, 2005. viii, 240 p. ISBN 9781403946263; ISBN 1403946264; OCLC 58721077; LC Call Number PR448.S55; Dewey 820.9/358. Citations: 16.
Examines antislavery writings and public orations for their use of sentimental rhetoric regarding the suffering of slaves in the Caribbean. Traces the "new rhetoric" to the aesthetics of Hume and Burke, which emphasized pathos in the service of persuasion. Argues that such strategies were employed to lend impact to rational arguments and to expose broader social problems and systemic issues. Asserts that the language of sentiment played a vital role in the British abolitionist movement by demonstrating that "people are equal because all feel the same emotions and bodily sensations" and thereby mobilizing activists. Concludes, in fact, that there are "few other occasions in history at which a literary discourse was so closely allied with a popular political movement."
18c Stds 41: 107-109.

704   Carey, Brycchan, Markman Ellis and Sara Salih, eds. *Discourses of Slavery and Abolition: Britain and Its Colonies, 1760–1838*. New York: Palgrave Macmillan, 2004. xii, 237 p. ISBN 1403916470; ISBN 9781403916471; OCLC 53919709; LC Call Number HT1162 .D57; Dewey 306.3/62/0941. Citations: 12.
Includes articles on the role of race in the debate over the slave trade in the late eighteenth and early nineteenth centuries, the representation of rape in Aphra Behn's *Oroonoko*, slavery in Georgian poetry, sensibility and tropical disease in the eighteenth-century sentimental novel, Ignatius Sancho and opposition to the slave trade, the use of the cannibalism trope in the work of Olaudah Equiano, James Williams's *A Narrative of Events Since the First of August, 1834*, the black subject and black literary canon, abolitionist Henry Smeathman, and Beilby Porteus's antislavery sermon.
JHG 31: 606-607.

705   Carretta, Vincent and Philip Gould, eds. *Genius in Bondage: Literature of the Early Black Atlantic*. Lexington: University Press of Kentucky, 2001. vi, 272 p. ISBN 0813122031; ISBN 9780813122038; OCLC 46918056; LC Call Number PR9341 .G46; Dewey 820.9/96. Citations: 31.

Includes articles on the abolition movement and the language of racism, the narratives of Briton Hammon, John Marrant, Olaudah Equiano, and Ignatius Sancho, the story of Mary Prince, letters on the late eighteenth-century Calabar slave trade, language and identity in the eighteenth-century black autobiography, authorship and Equiano's role in the history of the book, the work of Phillis Wheatley, Jupiter Hammon's commentary, sentimental libertinism and the politics of form in Ignatius Sancho's letters, Benjamin Banneker's response to Thomas Jefferson in the antislavery debate, and Nathaniel Paul and the construction of black nationalism.
Am Lit 75: 427-29; *EAL* 37: 347-73; *JAH* 90: 632.

706   Castillo, Susan and Ivy Schweitzer, eds. *The Literatures of Colonial America: An Anthology.* Oxford: Blackwell Publishers, 2001. xxii, 602 p. ISBN 0631211241 (hbk.); ISBN 9780631211242 (hbk.); ISBN 063121125X (pbk.); ISBN 9780631211259 (pbk.); OCLC 44461834; LC Call Number PS531 .L58; Dewey 810.8/001 21. Citations: 22.
Presents literary texts on European exploration and contact with Native Americans prior to 1600 (e.g., Indian creation stories, the Winnebago "Trickster," Las Casas, Cabeza de Vaca), exploration and settlement to 1700 (e.g., Inquisition records and trial transcripts, writings on New France, the Chesapeake, the Indies, New England, New Netherland, and Pennsylvania, including pieces on Native groups from the various regions), and eighteenth-century pieces (e.g., writings by various Caribbean and North American revolutionaries).
EAL 38: 305-22; *EHR* 117: 649-51; *JAS* 36: 515-16; *JAS* 37: 314-15; *LJ* 126n9: 124; *WMQ* 60: 207-13.

707   Cox, John David. *Traveling South: Travel Narratives and the Construction of American Identity.* Athens: University of Georgia Press, 2005. 252 p. ISBN 9780820327655; ISBN 0820327654; OCLC 59879683; LC Call Number E161.5 .C69; Dewey 917.3/04 22. Citations: 5.
Studies accounts of travel in the South during the early national and antebellum eras, including those of authors who sought to use travel writing to become a "representative American man." Compares the narratives of former slaves Frederick Douglass and Solomon Northup, noting that each viewed the right to travel as "a fundamental freedom upon which the nation is founded." Notes the negative perceptions of the South revealed in the writings of Union soldiers and of Frederick Law Olmsted, who saw Southerners as less economically and socially mobile than Northerners. Concludes that travel literature "played an integral role in the struggle to create a national identity."
EAL 43: 467-86; *JER* 28: 129-31; *JSH* 72: 920-21.

708   Crain, Caleb. *American Sympathy: Men, Friendship, and Literature in the New Nation.* New Haven, Conn.: Yale University Press, 2001. x, 310 p. ISBN 0300083327; ISBN 9780300083323; OCLC 45166603; LC Call Number PS173.M36; Dewey 810.9/352041. Citations: 40.
Examines nineteenth-century male literary relationships, focusing on Philadelphia and the likes of Charles Brockden Brown, Ralph Waldo Emerson,

and Herman Melville. Emphasizes the value of sympathy, the importance of forging male bonds, and Brown's vital role in weaving these bonds into literature. Argues that men could not express their true affections in nineteenth-century homophobic American culture and therefore encoded in writing feelings that could not be expressed privately or publicly. Claims that Emerson and his closest associates rejected their erotic feelings for men "in order to free them for literary use," specifically expressions of ideal Platonic love. Contends that, though Emerson "probably never realized a love affair with a man," he nonetheless "enjoyed the feelings" of erotic male love, but channeled such feelings into abstract, cool literary expressions.
Am Lit 74: 408-10; *EAL* 37: 537-49; *LJ* 126n10: 156; *VQR* 78: 12-13.

709   Downes, Paul. *Democracy, Revolution, and Monarchism in Early American Literature.* New York: Cambridge University Press, 2002. xii, 239 p. ISBN 0521813395; ISBN 9780521813396; OCLC 48803428; LC Call Number PS193 .D69; Dewey 810.9/358 21. Citations: 11.
Singles out monarchism as a persistent and significant characteristic of revolutionary ideology and early American democratic discourse, arguing that "displaced or translated elements of monarchic political culture can be found at work in key revolutionary ideas and constructs." Discusses the ritualized executions of effigies of George III in 1776, contending that such metaphorical killings in repetitive and staged performances showed how much symbolic power was vested in the material representation of the king's body. Considers interpretations of race, patriarchy, and materiality in the context of these mock executions, and concludes that monarchism exerted significant influence on American democratic subjectivity.
Am Lit 76: 603-605; *EAL* 39: 591-98; *18c Stds* 38: 367-71; *JAS* 37: 471-72; *HRNB* 31: 63; *NEQ* 77: 522-24; *WMQ* 60: 917-20.

710   Elliott, Emory. *The Cambridge Introduction to Early American Literature.* New York: Cambridge University Press, 2002. viii, 198 p. ISBN 052181717X (hbk.); ISBN 9780521817172 (hbk.); ISBN 052152041X (pbk.); ISBN 9780521520416 (pbk.); OCLC 49727839; LC Call Number PS185 .E28; Dewey 810.9/001. Citations: 4.
Covers Anglo-American writings between 1492 and 1820, summarizing recent interpretations of this "formative period for American culture." Reviews the European context, the American colonial past, relationships among English settlers of North America, "savages," religious dissenters, and French and Spanish Catholics. Interprets the American jeremiad using the "narrative archetypes" of Puritan writings, including autobiography, history, biography, poetry, and captivity narratives. Explains that the jeremiad makes sense of essential contradictions inherent in the American, whose "idealism and dreams of success" are dashed by "disillusionment, loss and disappointment," and who urges "to revive original ideals so that America can fulfill its manifest destiny."
EAL 39: 129-36.

711   Ferguson, Robert A. *Reading the Early Republic.* Cambridge, Mass.: Harvard University Press, 2004. 358 p. ISBN 0674013387; ISBN

9780674013384; OCLC 53992876; LC Call Number E209 .F46; Dewey 973.3/072. Citations: 14.

Explores the notion of text from the Revolution through the 1840s, noting that the meaning of language is bound by time and by context and that, therefore, modern reading of such texts is prone to misunderstanding both by missing intended meanings and by ascribing unintended meanings. Seeks to recapture the original meanings of the words of the early republic by coming to grips with the various events, traditions of learning, literary forms, and rhetorical strategies that affected authors and readers.

EAL 40: 209-15; *JER* 25: 304-307; *NEQ* 78: 656-58; *WMQ* 63: 171-75.

712 Frohock, Richard. *Heroes of Empire: The British Imperial Protagonist in America, 1596–1764*. Newark: University of Delaware Press, 2004. 227 p. ISBN 0874138795; ISBN 9780874138795; OCLC 54407797; LC Call Number PR448.I52; Dewey 820.9/358. Citations: 1.

Recounts how British writers in travel narratives, poems, plays, and other essays were adept at "refiguring crass acts of appropriation as acts of mercy, justice, lenity, or charity" from the late sixteenth century to the mid-eighteenth century. Studies the literary hero as the conqueror, the scientist, the merchant, and the planter, "all of whom authorize appropriation and define heroic imperialist work in competing ways." Finds that "the discourse of conquest" was adapted "to suit shifting historical circumstances and ideological needs" and demonstrate "the submersion of profit motive behind increasingly inflated characterizations of the conqueror's generosity and benevolent intent."

EAL 43: 753-57.

713 Giles, Paul. *Transatlantic Insurrections: British Culture and the Formation of American Literature, 1730–1860*. Philadelphia: University of Pennsylvania Press, 2001. 262 p. ISBN 0812236033; ISBN 9780812236033; ISBN 0812217675; ISBN 9780812217674; OCLC 45634608; LC Call Number PS159.G8; Dewey 810.9. Citations: 21.

Compares British and American literature, arguing "that the development of American literature appears in a different light when read against the grain of British cultural imperatives, just as British literature itself reveals strange and unfamiliar aspects that are brought into play by the reflecting mirrors of American discourse." Presents the case against "American exceptionalism" and the "Whig interpretation of literature."

EAL 37: 557-60; *JAS* 37: 478-79; *JER* 21: 697-700; *NEQ* 75: 160-62.

714 Gordon, Charlotte. *Mistress Bradstreet: The Untold Life of America's First Poet*. New York: Little, Brown, and Company, 2005. xiii, 337 p. ISBN 0316169048; ISBN 9780316169042; OCLC 56608308; LC Call Number PS712 .G67; Dewey 811/.1. Citations: 2.

Presents a biography of Bradstreet for a general audience. Includes recommended reading.

Booklist 101: 1131; *Booklist* 103: 31; *LJ* 130n6: 94.

715 Hager, Alan, ed. *The Age of Milton: An Encyclopedia of Major 17th-Century British and American Authors*. Westport, Conn.: Greenwood Press, 2004. xviii, 392 p. ISBN 0313310084; ISBN   9780313310089; OCLC 52765907; LC Call Number PR431 .A36; Dewey 820.9/004/03. Citations: 3.
Covers 79 British and American seventeenth-century writers, scientists, and artists. Arranges entries alphabetically by the subject's last name, each of which contains biographical details, major works and themes, critical reception of the subject's work, and a bibliography.
Booklist 100: 1972; *LJ* 129n14: 186; *16c J* 36: 572-73.

716 Hewitt, Elizabeth. *Correspondence and American Literature, 1770–1865*. New York: Cambridge University Press, 2004. x, 230 p. ISBN 0521842557; ISBN 9780521842556; OCLC 54774640; LC Call Number PS217.L47; Dewey 813/.309. Citations: 10.
Argues that antebellum American authors used epistolary writing to "theorize the kinds of social intercourse necessary to the articulation of a national identity and a national literature." Discusses familiar letters, epistolary novels, manuals for letter writers, and public documents framed as letters, as well as communication technologies. Points out the emergence of two opposing models of correspondence based on national union: the Anti-federalist position, which emphasized the democratic possibilities of the letter through exchange of ideas and personal freedom; and the Federalist view, which suggested that each citizen writes to and through the state for interpretation, thereby making individual freedom dependent upon institutional authority. Characterizes letters as a "crucial site by which democratic theory passes into social practice."
JAS 40: 434-35.

717 Hodgkins, Christopher. *Reforming Empire: Protestant Colonialism and Conscience in British Literature*. Columbia: University of Missouri Press, 2002. xii, 290 p. ISBN 0826214312; ISBN   9780826214317; OCLC 50292442; LC Call Number PR408.I53; Dewey 820.9/358. Citations: 8.
Suggests that Protestantism influenced both the formation (justification) and eventual dissolution (critique) of the British Empire. Discusses the transformation of "England" into "Great Britain" through rediscovery of anti-Roman and postcolonial Arthurian identity, the documentation of Spanish cruelties in the New World to justify British expansion, the pietistic psychology of British imperial ambitions, and the emblematic career of Sir Francis Drake.
J Religion 84: 164-65.

718 Kafer, Peter. *Charles Brockden Brown's Revolution and the Birth of American Gothic*. Philadelphia: University of Pennsylvania Press, 2004. xxi, 249 p. ISBN 0812237862; ISBN 9780812237863; OCLC 53369529; LC Call Number PS1137 .K34; Dewey 813/.2. Citations: 19.
Discusses Brown's family, his father's business, the family's relationship with the Philadelphia Quaker community, and Brown's friendships. Examines the evolution of Brown's writing, explaining that early on he drew upon his own familial past and then increasingly upon material related to Pennsylvania history and post-revolutionary America. Finds in *Edgar Huntly* a reenactment of

Brown's own family tragedies and manifestations of helplessness and guilt. Concludes that Brown's entire career was shaped by the memory of anti-Quaker riots in his youth, the aggressive actions of the Continental Congress, and the imprisonment of his father.
AHR 110: 478-79; *EAL* 40: 173-91; *HRNB* 33: 16-17; *JAH* 92: 203-204; *JER* 25: 118-20; *NEQ* 78: 316-19; *PMHB* 130: 118-19; *WMQ* 62: 344-49.

719 Larkin, Edward. *Thomas Paine and the Literature of Revolution.* Cambridge: Cambridge University Press, 2005. x, 205 p. ISBN 0521841151; ISBN 9780521841153; OCLC 57124473; LC Call Number JC177.A4; Dewey 320.51/092. Citations: 15.
Views "Paine as a professional writer who produced an important corpus of writings that integrates intellectual and literary trends from both sides of the Atlantic." Finds that Paine used his editorship of the *Pennsylvania Magazine* to develop the literary style used in *Common Sense* and to educate "the American people in the path of independence ostensibly without making politics its primary subject." Reviews Paine's uses of history, his notion that religion was tyrannical, and his idea that science was, by its accessibility and inclusiveness, democratic. Argues that Paine's contribution to the American Revolution was "fashioning a new language that presented politics in a vernacular that artisans and other middling sorts were already accustomed to reading." Finds that the enfranchisement of lower orders led to attacks and efforts to marginalize Paine, which, even into the modern era, caused scholarly indifference.
AHR 111: 1165; *EAL* 42: 206-210; *JAH* 93: 504-505; *WMQ* 63: 412-15.

720 Morris, Amy M.E. *Popular Measures: Poetry and Church Order in Seventeenth-Century Massachusetts.* Newark: University of Delaware Press, 2005. 282 p. ISBN 0874138655; ISBN 9780874138658; OCLC 57170147; LC Call Number PS253.M4; Dewey 811/.1093823. Citations: 4.
Characterizes early New England poetry's modeling of plain-style sermons and its awkward syntax, particularly as noted in the work of Michael Wigglesworth and Edward Taylor, as producing an "alternative" or "resistant" aesthetic. Considers how the "humanistic and rational side of New England Puritanism" coexisted with "zeal and pietism." Argues that the poetry's "unconventional artfulness" allowed Puritans to pen verse that encouraged spiritual meditation, but which was not so elegant as to overwhelm the emotions and which "suggested that God had to be sought through spiritual, as opposed to linguistic, or literary, exploration."
Am Lit 78: 869-72; *EAL* 44: 433-38; *NEQ* 79: 489-91.

721 Newman, Richard S., Patrick Rael, and Phillip Lapsansky, eds. *Pamphlets of Protest: An Anthology of Early African-American Protest Literature, 1790–1860.* New York: Routledge, 2001. viii, 326 p. ISBN 041592443X (hbk.); ISBN 9780415924436 (hbk.); ISBN 0415924448 (pbk.); ISBN 9780415924443 (pbk.); OCLC 43798517; LC Call Number E184.6 .P36; Dewey 323.1/196073. Citations: 17.
Presents twenty-five African American protest pamphlets or excerpts from pamphlets. Provides eight pieces that appeared before 1830, beginning with

Absalom Jones's and Richard Allen's "A Narrative of the Proceedings of the Black People During the late Awful Calamity in Philadelphia" (1794), the first pamphlet copyrighted in the United States by a black author.
JER 21: 546-48.

722 Sayre, Gordon M. *The Indian Chief as Tragic Hero: Native Resistance and the Literatures of America, from Moctezuma to Tecumseh*. Chapel Hill: University of North Carolina Press, 2005. x, 357 p. ISBN 0807829706 (hbk.); ISBN 9780807829707 (hbk.); ISBN 0807856320 (pbk.); ISBN 9780807856321 (pbk.); OCLC 58788866; LC Call Number PS173.I6; Dewey 810.9/352997. Citations: 18.
Traces the portrayal of Indian chiefs from "bloodthirsty savages" in colonial wartime propaganda to tragic heroes "with all the dignity accorded the greatest characters of the classical and Renaissance tragedies" in later literature. Finds that writers drew upon classics to romanticize the lives of Pontiac, Metacom, Tecumseh, and others and that viewing chiefs as tragic heroes represented a way to express regret and assuage guilt over warfare and dispossessing Indians of their lands. Concludes that the purposes of the literature changed over time and variously sought to uphold republican values and justify nationalistic action.
AHR 112: 161-62; *EAL* 42: 369-75; *IMH* 103: 212-14; *JAH* 93: 853-54; *J Mil Hist* 71: 505-511; *WMQ* 63: 873-76.

723 Schloss, Dietmar. *Die Tugendhafte Republik: Politische Ideologie und Literatur in der Amerikanischen Gründerzeit*. Heidelberg: Winter, 2003. 375 p. ISBN 3825314766; ISBN 9783825314767; OCLC 53178437; LC Call Number PS217.P64. Citations: 2.
Claims that republican virtue was the primary ideology underlying post-revolutionary literature, including popular novels and utopian writings. Underscores the historical context for the literature and notes that "the virtuous republic fulfilled important functions because it could not be identified with specific class interests" and that republican ideology "functioned as a matrix of ideas that could be filled out in different ways by different social groups."
EAL 40: 193-99.

724 Slawinski, Scott. *Validating Bachelorhood: Audience, Patriarchy, and Charles Brockden Brown's Editorship of the* Monthly Magazine and American Review. New York: Routledge, 2005. ix, 128 p. ISBN 0415971780; ISBN 9780415971782; OCLC 56096163; LC Call Number PS1138.M36; Dewey 813/.2. Citations: 5.
Focuses on Brown's editorship between 1799 and 1800, noting the negative status of bachelorhood in the early republic and Brown's editorial efforts "to establish a space where single men could find validation of their unmarried status." Finds that Brown's emphasis on science, business, and social commentary in the magazine discouraged female readership, as did negative depictions of women in fiction selections. Concludes that Brown's work for the magazine succeeded in making the bachelor "an acceptable, noble, and honorable alternate form of masculinity."
EAL 41: 577-83; *PMHB* 130: 425-26.

725   Verhoeven, W.M. *Revolutionary Histories: Transatlantic Cultural Nationalism, 1775–1815.* New York: Palgrave, 2002. xi, 258 p. ISBN 033379415X; ISBN 9780333794159; ISBN 0333714903; ISBN 9780333714904; OCLC 47023664; LC Call Number PS193 .R48; Dewey 810.9/358. Citations: 5.
Presents essays on Chastellux, Barlow, and transatlantic political cultures (1776–1812), Volney, Frankenstein, and the lessons of history, Benjamin Franklin, Native Americans, and the commerce of civility, transatlantic language and the morphology of blushing (1749–1812), captivity and cultural capital in the English novel, and nursery tales on the frontier.
Am Lit 75: 653-56.

726   Wells, Colin. *The Devil & Doctor Dwight: Satire and Theology in the Early American Republic.* Chapel Hill: University of North Carolina Press, published for the Omohundro Institute of Early American History and Culture, 2002. xii, 254 p. ISBN 0807827150 (hbk.); ISBN 9780807827154 (hbk.); ISBN 0807853836 (pbk.); ISBN 9780807853832 (pbk.); OCLC 48170729: PS739.T75; Dewey 811/.2. Citations: 15.
Contends that Dwight's epic poem, "The Triumph of Infidelity" (1788), represents "perhaps the preeminent example of American neoclassical or Augustan satire" and as "a unique example of the convergence of literature, religion, and politics at the moment the new American Republic was first being imagined." Argues that the poem was an expression of "Christian empiricism" and a central element of "an ideological struggle over the meaning of intellectual enlightenment itself," which Dwight saw as a struggle against infidelity. Provides the full text of the poem, with textual notes and annotations.
CH 72: 220-21; *EAL* 37: 551-54; *JAH* 90: 626-27; *WMQ* 59: 1019-23.

727   Weyler, Karen A. *Intricate Relations: Sexual and Economic Desire in American Fiction, 1789–1814.* Iowa City: University of Iowa Press, 2004. x, 269 p. ISBN 0877458847; ISBN 9780877458845; OCLC 54822721; LC Call Number PS374.E4; Dewey 813/.2093553. Citations: 11.
Examines conduct manuals, political pamphlets, economic works, medical publications, and works of fiction, noting that sexual and economic regulation were prevalent themes. Explains that the use of the epistolary mode and frequent references to self-discipline, seduction, economic speculation, and female madness indicate widespread anxieties about economic and sexual activity. Finds that novels aimed at female audiences sought regulation of sexual activity, while works intended for males focused on economic behavior.
Am Lit 81: 833-36; *EAL* 40: 561-64; *JER* 25: 692-95; *WMQ* 64: 441-44.

728   Wood, Marcus. *The Poetry of Slavery: An Anglo-American Anthology, 1764–1865.* New York: Oxford University Press, 2003. lxi, 704 p. ISBN 0198187084 (hbk.); ISBN 9780198187080 (hbk.); ISBN 0198187092 (pbk.); ISBN 9780198187097 (pbk.); OCLC 52696591; LC Call Number PR1195.S44; Dewey 821.708355. Citations: 11.

Presents excerpts from poems related to slaves and slavery in England and North America. Includes pieces from Blake, Coleridge, Wordsworth, Shelley, Whitman, Longfellow, and Dickinson, as well as from slaves and ex-slaves.
18c Stds 38: 393-95.

729   Wood, Sarah Florence. *Quixotic Fictions of the USA, 1792–1815*. New York: Oxford University Press, 2005. xiv, 295 p. ISBN 9780199273157; ISBN 0199273154; OCLC 61302142; LC Call Number PS159.S7; LC Call Number PQ6347; Dewey 810.9; Dewey 813.209. Citations: 3.
Explores the influence of *Don Quixote* on American writers of the early national era. Discusses the importance of Cervantes' work to British culture, modifications made for post-Revolution American audiences, and the fiction of Hugh Henry Brackenridge, Royall Tyler, Charles Brockden Brown, Tabitha Gilman Tenney, and Washington Irving. Concludes that "*Don Quixote* was recognized by early republic authors as a locus of contradiction, and was repeatedly called upon to explore and articulate the complex double-consciousness that permeated both the literary and political landscape of the period."
Am Lit 79: 229-40; *EAL* 43: 233-37.

27 Communication

730 Amory, Hugh and David D. Hall, eds. *Bibliography and the Book Trades: Studies in the Print Culture of Early New England.* Philadelphia: University of Pennsylvania Press, 2004. ix, 174 p. ISBN 0812238370; ISBN 9780812238372; OCLC 56840291; LC Call Number Z473.A548; Dewey 070.509. Citations: 5.
Presents seven essays covering Puritan attempts to convert Indians, the Bay Psalm Book, bookseller Michael Perry, collector Thomas Prince, book sales in colonial Boston, the relationship between the clerics and publishers, and book printing on both sides of the Atlantic.
EAL 41: 347-64.

731 Banks, Kenneth J. *Chasing Empire Across the Sea: Communications and the State in the French Atlantic, 1713–1763.* Montreal: McGill-Queen's University Press, 2002. xxii, 322 p. ISBN 0773524444; ISBN 9780773524446; OCLC 50402298; LC Call Number JV1816 .B354; Dewey 325/.32/094409033 21. Citations: 21.
Studies eighteenth-century French efforts to communicate with imperial outposts across the Atlantic, namely Quebec, New Orleans, and Saint Pierre, Martinique. Explains that Louis XIV had put in place an excellent bureaucracy and processes to deal with governing overseas colonies, but that in reality governance did not work smoothly. Contends that the lack of reliable and timely information flow across the ocean, broadly defined to include sailing routes, mapping, printing, and infrastructure, weakened the power of the French state in far-flung territories and, in fact, that "the challenges posed by transatlantic communications impinged on, modified, and increasingly undermined the French state's control." Notes that the speed with which royal orders were communicated upon reaching major ports depended upon "colonial traditions, economics, technology, African slave labour, Native allies, and even the cooperation of the colonists themselves." Concludes that "Colonial hierarchies

might be thought of as representing a musical chord with four descending strings: governors, intendants, superior councils and the clergy," so that "When tuned properly, the four worked harmoniously; but disagreement created shrill dissonance."
AHR 108: 1107-1108; *CHR* 84: 664-66; *CJH* 39: 442-44; *J Mod Hist* 76: 962-64; *WMQ* 61: 167-71.

732 Bannet, Eve Tavor. *Empire of Letters: Letter Manuals and Transatlantic Correspondence, 1680–1820.* Cambridge: Cambridge University Press, 2005. xxiii, 347 p. ISBN 9780521856188; ISBN 0521856183; OCLC 61757146; LC Call Number PR915 .B36; Dewey 809.6 22. Citations: 15.
Examines early modern English, Scottish, and American guides for letter writing and etiquette. Discusses audiences for the guides, situational communication, "secretaries," "complete letter-writers," revised manuals of the late eighteenth and early nineteenth centuries, government correspondence, and secret transatlantic communication, including that of Crevecoeur and Franklin. Argues that letter writing was critical to the formation and maintenance of the British Empire and that letter manuals were responsible for the establishment of "a single standard language, method and culture of polite communication." Explains how letters were understood by eighteenth-century writers and readers as "the collection of different skills, values, and kinds of knowledge beyond mere literacy." Describes the various functions of letters and the need for readers to understand their taxonomies. Traces the often subtle changes in various editions of letter manuals, noting that Scottish and American printers downplayed the importance of social rank in order to increase appeal to local readers.
EAL 42: 381-84; *J Brit Stds* 46: 392-93; *WMQ* 64: 862-65.

733 Browne, Stephen A. *Jefferson's Call for Nationhood: The First Inaugural Address.* College Station: Texas A&M University Press, 2003. xvii, 155 p. ISBN 1585442518 (hbk.); ISBN 9781585442515 (hbk.); ISBN 1585442526 (pbk.); ISBN 9781585442522 (pbk.); OCLC 50960848; LC Call Number E332.77 .B76; Dewey 352.23/86/097309034 21. Citations: 0.
Studies the "origins, composition, meaning, and delivery" of Jefferson's first inaugural address. Characterizes the speech as "an ingenious political performance," one that stressed the overcoming of the partisanship of the 1790s, the flourishing of republican principles, and the valuing of rhetorical process. Concludes that the speech exhibited "all of the felicities characteristic of Jefferson's prose" and "was known then as it is now to be the singular expression of a nation's highest ideals."
AHR 110: 785-86; *JAH* 91: 610-11; *JER* 24: 503-505; *JSH* 70: 901-902; *VMHB* 111: 418-19.

734 Campbell, W.E. *The Road to Canada: The Grand Communications Route from Saint John to Quebec.* Fredericton, New Brunswick: Goose Lane Editions, 2005. 115 p. ISBN 0864924267 (pbk.); ISBN 9780864924261 (pbk.); OCLC 59876073; LC Call Number F1043 .C36; Dewey 971.5/103. Citations: 0.

Studies the communications route that followed the Saint John River to the Madawaska River to Lake Temiscouata and over the "Grand Portage" to Rivière-du-Loup. Explains that this was the main overland route between Saint John and Quebec and was particularly important during the winter when the Saint Lawrence was unnavigable. Focuses on the period from the seventeenth to the mid-nineteenth century, especially military use of the route. Describes use of the route by the French and by the First Nations, fortifications built to protect the route, the boundary dispute with the United States, the creation of a postal route between Fredericton and Quebec, and nineteenth-century improvements to the route, including construction of roads and telegraph and railway lines. Calls the route the "backbone" of the French and British Empires in eastern North America.
CHR 89: 428-29; *J Mil Hist* 70: 512-13.

735 Clement, Richard W. *Books on the Frontier: Print Culture in the American West, 1763–1875*. Hanover, N.H.: University Press of New England, in association with The Library of Congress, Washington, D.C., 2003. 139 p. ISBN 0844410802; ISBN 9780844410807; OCLC 51726883; LC Call Number Z473 .C59; Dewey 381.45002/0973. Citations: 5.
Traces the establishment of frontier book publishers, booksellers, and newspapers from the Seven Years' War to the settlement lines of the late nineteenth century. Confirms Turner's view of the frontier experience as a primary shaper of the American character. Contends that "When a nation's historical vision is exposed as myth, it loses its power" and concludes that, "If there is no new vision to replace the old, a nation may decline and lose its way."
AHR 110: 790; *LJ* 128n20: 116; *SHQ* 108: 113-14; *WHQ* 36: 239-40.

736 Kamrath, Mark and Sharon M. Harris, eds. *Periodical Literature in Eighteenth-Century America*. Knoxville: University of Tennessee Press, 2005. xxvii, 394 p. ISBN 1572333197; ISBN 9781572333192; OCLC 55801028; LC Call Number PS193 .P47; Dewey 070.5/72/097309033. Citations: 0.
Presents articles on Boston's smallpox controversy, the hermeneutics of transatlantic awakening, clubs, gender, and civic discourse in Pennsylvania, Germans and the German-language press in colonial and revolutionary Pennsylvania, the *New-York Weekly Journal* and the influence of Cato's *Letters* on colonial America, American Indian oration and discourses of the republic in eighteenth-century American periodicals, the depiction of Shays's Rebellion in New England magazines of the 1780s, antislavery literature between 1776 and 1800, the *Massachusetts Magazine* and the bodily order of the American woman, Thomas Jefferson, Francis Hopkinson, and the representation of the *Notes on the State of Virginia*, constructions of femininity in eighteenth-century magazines, radical and conservative visions of "the public" in mid-1790s newspapers, and *New-York Magazine* as cultural repository. Includes an appendix on American periodical series between 1741 and 1800.
AHR 110: 1640-41; *EAL* 41: 574-77.

737 Lepore, Jill. *A Is for American: Letters and Other Characters in the Newly United States*. New York: Alfred A. Knopf, 2002. x, 241 p. ISBN 037540449X;

ISBN 9780375404498; OCLC 47049886; LC Call Number PE2809 .L46; Dewey 306.44/973/09033. Citations: 16.

Argues that characters, numbers, and symbols are used in a way unique to particular nations and create bonds similar to geography and politics. Describes the roles of seven men in developing an American language: Noah Webster, who wrote a dictionary; William Thornton, who created a universal alphabet; Thomas Hopkins Gallaudet, who invented sign language for the deaf; Sequoyah, who developed the Cherokee syllabary; Samuel F.B. Morse, who invented the Morse code; Abd al-Rahman Ibrahima, who demonstrated literacy's importance for freedom; and Alexander Graham Bell, who developed the telephone.
EAL 38: 157-61; *JAH* 89: 1518-19; *LJ* 127n2: 115; *NEQ* 75: 675-78; *RAH* 31: 32-38; *WMQ* 61: 195-98.

738 Martin, Robert W.T. *The Free and Open Press: The Founding of American Democratic Press Liberty, 1640–1800*. New York: New York University Press, 2001. xi, 239 p. ISBN 0814756557 (hbk.); ISBN 9780814756553 (hbk.); ISBN 0814756565 (pbk.); ISBN 9780814756560 (pbk.); OCLC 46882676; LC Call Number PN4738 .M37; Dewey 323.44/5/0973. Citations: 7.

Seeks "to reveal the central dynamic of the founding of American press liberty," arguing that this dynamic involved concepts of the free press as a bulwark against government tyranny and as a frequent source of conflict. Contends that prior to the 1760s American journalists were dedicated to the notion of an open press, but that in the run-up to the Revolution printers allowed ideology to influence what they would publish. Argues that "a predominantly 'republican' stress on public liberty and the public good (free press doctrine) and a more nearly 'liberal' notion of individual rights (open press doctrine) coexisted in a single, ambivalent tradition throughout much of the eighteenth century." Views the Sedition Act of 1798 as the "pivotal moment" in the emergence of a "recognizably modern discourse of democratic press liberty," which included the pursuit of political "truth," the idea that the public could discover the proper course through access to information.
AHR 107: 1548-49; *AJLH* 46: 108-109; *JAH* 89: 1502; *WMQ* 62: 340-43.

739 Smith, Craig R. *Daniel Webster and the Oratory of Civil Religion*. Columbia: University of Missouri Press, 2005. 300 p. ISBN 0826215424; ISBN 9780826215420; OCLC 56535046; LC Call Number E340.W4; Dewey 973.5/092. Citations: 1.

Presents an "oratorical biography" of Webster, focusing on the influence of his speeches on the development of American civil religion. Views Webster as a bridge between the Revolutionary and antebellum generations and notes that he used religious concepts common to the Second Great Awakening to underscore the strengthening of the Union as a sacred goal.
HRNB 33: 104.

28 Education

740 Addis, Cameron. *Jefferson's Vision for Education, 1760–1845*. New York: Lang, 2003. xii, 254 p. ISBN 0820457558 (pbk.); ISBN 9780820457550 (pbk.); OCLC 47894164; LC Call Number LB695 .J42; Dewey 370/.1. Citations: 6.
Examines Jefferson's experience with, vision of, and impact upon education. Focuses on Jefferson's founding of the University of Virginia and the development of that institution in ways that Jefferson did not anticipate and would not have supported. Analyzes the relationship of Jefferson's position on religion and his views on education, contending that Jefferson believed in God—avidly and publicly rejecting atheism—and admired Jesus' teachings, but denied the divinity of Christ. Underscores the political difficulty of establishing the University of Virginia, noting the "contested culture of early national Virginia." Discusses the elderly Jefferson's disappointment in early student riots and in the lack of student devotion to intellectual pursuits. Calls the University's founding a significant achievement in that the institution boasted a remarkable and independent faculty, public funding, and, initially at least, freedom from religious interference. Finds, however, that by 1845 Christian doctrine became engrained in the University, demonstrating "the triumph of Christian fidelity in America over the humanist philosophy of the Enlightenment."
AHR 109: 1223-24; *JAH* 91: 225; *JER* 23: 620-23; *JSH* 70: 646-47; *VMHB* 111: 416-17.

741 Hoeveler, J. David. *Creating the American Mind: Intellect and Politics in the Colonial Colleges*. Lanham: Rowman & Littlefield, 2002. xvi, 381 p. ISBN 0847688305; ISBN 9780847688302; OCLC 49648159; LC Call Number LA227 .H64; Dewey 378.73/09/032. Citations: 8.
Studies the nine colonial colleges in America: Harvard, William and Mary, Yale, the College of New Jersey (Princeton), King's College (Columbia), the College of Philadelphia (the University of Pennsylvania), the College of Rhode

Island (Brown), Queen's College (Rutgers), and Dartmouth. Concentrates on the roles that colleges played in the transfer of culture in early America and suggests that a distinctly American identity might have emerged prior to 1776. Places each college in its local context and analyzes its "public nature" by examining each institution's relationship to colonial politics, to the empire, to its sponsoring religious denomination, and to the religious concerns and conflicts with which each college dealt. Argues that interaction between political and intellectual cultures resulted in an "American mind" before the end of the Revolution.
AHR 109: 1553-54; *JAH* 91: 218-19; *JSH* 70: 645-46; *LJ* 127n19: 83; *PMHB* 128: 312-13; *VMHB* 111: 188-89.

742 Monaghan, E. Jennifer. *Learning to Read and Write in Colonial America.* Amherst: University of Massachusetts Press, published in association with the American Antiquarian Society, 2005. xiii, 491 p. ISBN 1558494863; ISBN 9781558494862; ISBN 9781558495814; ISBN 1558495819; OCLC 57143087; LC Call Number LC151 .M65; Dewey 302.2/244/0973. Citations: 25.
Examines colonial reading and writing instruction, placing it in ideological and political context. Discusses pedagogical issues, book publication histories, and the various sites where reading and writing instruction occurred. Argues that John Locke's model of sequencing reading instruction (horn-book, primer, psalter, testament, and Bible) heavily influenced colonial pedagogy. Describes the religious nature of literacy in Puritan New England and argues that the introduction of spelling books in the eighteenth century modernized and secularized juvenile reading culture. Discusses the instruction of Native Americans and African American slaves, noting that the former were targets of conversion through literacy instruction. Traces a major shift in literacy acquisition in the second half of the eighteenth century brought on by the emerging view that children were highly trainable, the increased availability of texts designed specifically for children, and the rising appeal of spelling books, rather than the Bible, as the principal tool for literacy instruction. Includes appendices on graphs of signature literacy, the alphabet method of reading instruction, and charts on the production of literary texts.
AHR 111: 1500; *Am Lit* 78: 869-72; *EAL* 44: 657-75; *JAH* 93: 496-97; *LJ* 130n12: 98; *NEQ* 79: 311-13; *WMQ* 63: 607-10.

743 Ostrowski, Carl. *Books, Maps, and Politics: A Cultural History of the Library of Congress, 1783–1861.* Amherst: University of Massachusetts Press, 2004. x, 261 p. ISBN 1558494332 (hbk.); ISBN 9781558494336 (hbk.); ISBN 9781558497801 (pbk.); ISBN 1558497803 (pbk.); OCLC 52773731; LC Call Number Z733.U58; Dewey 027.573. Citations: 12.
Explores the growth and development of the Library of Congress from its founding until the outbreak of the Civil War. Discusses the work of the Joint Committee on the Library, the library as a social institution, the sale of Jefferson's library to the Library of Congress in 1815, the role of the Smithsonian, and the Library's expansion in the 1860s. Finds that the founding of the library was based on limited service and access, and republican frugality and suspicion of European refinement, which resulted in a utilitarian collection

strategy and modest growth through the early nineteenth century, with a pronounced focus on history and law.

AHR 110: 1169-70; *Am Lit* 78: 413-15; *JAH* 92: 212-13; *J Interdis Hist* 37: 133-34; *J Mod Hist* 71: 916-19; *LJ* 129n12: 119.

744 Raven, James. *London Booksellers and American Customers: Transatlantic Literary Community and the Charleston Library Society, 1748–1811.* Columbia: University of South Carolina Press, 2002. xxii, 522 p. ISBN 1570034060 (hbk.); ISBN 9781570034060; OCLC 47224789; LC Call Number Z733.C4773; Dewey 027/.2757/915. Citations: 23.

Provides an edited transcription of the Charleston Library Society's "Copy Book of Letters," which contains information on the group's acquisition of books. Analyzes the letter book for what it indicates about the Society, its operations, and its role in South Carolina. Examines the procurement of books from across the Atlantic, the ways in which the Society differed from libraries in other colonies, the letter book as a source, the members of the Society, the types of books they wanted access to, and the place of the Society in shaping the intellectual culture of the city and colony. Finds that the founders of the Society were wealthy social and political leaders of the colony, who sought a means of distinguishing themselves further. Concludes that the book orders of the Society represented "a determined but somewhat clumsy attempt to emulate the learned societies of Britain and Europe."

AHR 108: 483-84; *EHR* 120: 149-50; *JAH* 90: 622-23; *JER* 23: 270-72; *JSH* 70: 129-30.

745 Wagoner, Jennings L. *Jefferson and Education.* Charlottesville, Va.: Thomas Jefferson Foundation, distributed by the University of North Carolina Press, 2004. 168 p. ISBN 1882886240; ISBN 9781882886241; OCLC 56069039; LC Call Number E332.2 .W34; Dewey 973.4/6/092. Citations: 2.

Surveys Jefferson's views on and experience with education for a general readership. Describes Jefferson's time at William and Mary and foundation of the University of Virginia and of West Point.

JSH 72: 454-55; *VMHB* 114: 407-408.

746 Wright, Conrad Edick. *Revolutionary Generation: Harvard Men and the Consequences of Independence.* Amherst: University of Massachusetts Press, 2005. xi, 298 p. ISBN 1558494847; ISBN 9781558494848; OCLC 58546518; LC Call Number LD2139 .W75; Dewey 378.744/4. Citations: 3.

Studies the 204 men who entered Harvard between 1771 and 1774, noting that each of them was significantly influenced by the Revolution. Finds that seven died in the Revolution and that twenty-eight remained loyal to the Crown and suffered personally and professionally as a result. Explains that the Revolution caused most to start their careers and families relatively late in life and thus were challenged if they sought out leadership roles. Concludes that relatively few were successful in politics and religion and that most became Unitarians.

AHR 111: 828-29; *Hist Teach* 39: 426-27; *JAH* 93: 190; *JER* 27: 368-75; *NEQ* 79: 318-20.

29 Science, Medicine, and Technology

747 Bedini, Silvio A. *Jefferson and Science*. Charlottesville, Va.: Thomas Jefferson Foundation, distributed by the University of North Carolina Press, 2002. 126 p. ISBN 1882886194; ISBN 9781882886197; OCLC 50725362; LC Call Number E332.2 .B365; Dewey 973.4/6/092 21. Citations: 6.

Surveys Jefferson's interests in mathematics and the sciences, noting Jefferson's early interest and training in surveying, topography, meteorology, astronomy, geology, geography, ethnology, archaeology, paleontology, medicine, botany, horology, agriculture, invention, and biology. Reviews Jefferson's participation in the American Philosophical Society, his *Notes on the State of Virginia*, and his founding of the University of Virginia. Explains that Jefferson had "a compulsion to collect and record" many "random bits of information which might eventually prove useful" and that he believed that success in science resulted from "a patient pursuit of facts, and cautious combination and comparison of them."

NCHR 80: 486-88.

748 Ben-Atar, Doron S. *Trade Secrets: Intellectual Piracy and the Origins of American Industrial Power*. New Haven, Conn.: Yale University Press, 2004. xxii, 281 p. ISBN 030010006X; ISBN 9780300100068; OCLC 52963002; LC Call Number HD38.7 .B455; LC Call Number LD571; Dewey 338.0973. Citations: 19.

Discusses the American approach to industrial innovation from the colonial period through the Jacksonian era. Shows that Britain shared technology with its American colonies very selectively and, prior to the Revolution, became less willing to do so as colonial industries closed the innovation gap with those of the mother country. Finds that after the Revolution, American leaders encouraged the secretive importation of European technology in order to advance the nation's economic and political viability. Refers to Samuel Slater as "the most successful technology pirate in American history" and implicates Alexander Hamilton and Trench Coxe in "official orchestration of technology smuggling." Notes that the United States became a major exporter of technology by the mid-nineteenth century and since then has become a major advocate of laws protecting intellectual property. Concludes that technology transfer "accounts not only for the rapid economic growth of the republic" but also for "the experimental and innovative reputations of the 'American system of manufacturing.'"

AHR 110: 787-88; *BHR* 79: 367-70; *JAH* 92: 201-202; *JER* 26: 312-15; *J Econ Hist* 64: 906-908.

749 Chaplin, Joyce E. *Subject Matter: Technology, the Body, and Science on the Anglo-American Frontier, 1500–1676*. Cambridge, Mass.: Harvard University Press, 2001. xiii, 411 p. ISBN 0674004531; ISBN 9780674004535; OCLC 45209082; LC Call Number E46 .C48; Dewey 973.1/7 21. Citations: 70.
Emphasizes the role of science and technology in the English exploration and settlement of North America. Divides analysis of texts into three periods: 1500 to 1585; 1585 to 1660; and 1640 to 1676. Focuses on "the way in which contemporary European theories about nature influenced English settlers' relations with Indians," arguing that notions of racial differences emerged in the seventeenth century to distinguish white colonists from Indians. Discusses the effects of disease upon the Roanoke Indians and suggests that the level of scientific interest in America is indicated by the relatively high numbers of mineral experts and mathematicians who participated in early English voyages of discovery.
AHR 107: 183-84; *EAL* 38: 521-26; *FHQ* 81: 198-200; *HRNB* 30: 13; *JAH* 89: 188-89; *J Econ Hist* 61: 1134-35; *J Interdis Hist* 33: 132-33; *JSH* 69: 664-66; *RAH* 30: 530-40; *16c J* 34: 1197-98; *WMQ* 59: 981-86.

750 Dray, Philip. *Stealing God's Thunder: Benjamin Franklin's Lightning Rod and the Invention of America*. New York: Random House, 2005. xviii, 279 p. ISBN 140006032X; ISBN 9781400060320; OCLC 56420374; LC Call Number E302.6.F8; Dewey 973.3/092. Citations: 14.
Explains that, in addition to being a tinkerer who produced practical inventions, Franklin was an extraordinary theoretician and devotee of the scientific method. Ranks Franklin as a scientist below only Galileo and Newton, drawing an analogy between Newton's explication of gravity and Franklin's understanding of electricity. Points out that Franklin's experiments "stripped nature's most fearsome phenomenon of its mystical provenance" and that his *Experiments and Observations on Electricity, Made at Philadelphia* (1751) was so well-conceived and written in such accessible language that it was one of the most widely read scientific treatises of its time, something of which American colonists were very proud. Calls Franklin the preeminent American Enlightenment figure, someone with an extraordinary range of interests.
AHR 111: 826-27; *Booklist* 101: 1986; *EAL* 41: 535-53; *JAH* 93: 183-84.

751 Feldman, Jay. *When the Mississippi Ran Backwards: Empire, Intrigue, Murder, and the New Madrid Earthquakes*. New York: Free Press, 2005. xii, 307 p. ISBN 0743242785; ISBN 9780743242783; OCLC 56685129; LC Call Number QE535.2.U6; Dewey 551.22/09778/985. Citations: 7.

Studies the New Madrid, Missouri earthquakes from December 1811 to April 1812, which hit the mid-Mississippi River valley, destroyed towns, were felt in the eastern United States, and temporarily and famously reversed the flow of the Mississippi River. Provides background information on the founding of New Madrid in 1789, the U.S. acquisition of the area from France, settlement of the region, and the science behind the earthquakes. Examines the political and cultural effects of the quakes, noting that Tecumseh saw the quakes as a prophesy of Native American victory over white people and that the initial quake uncovered the remains of a slave murdered by the nephews of Thomas Jefferson, an event that sparked further debate over the tyranny of slavery. Suggests that the earthquakes sparked religious revivalism.

Booklist 101: 1044; *JAH* 93: 201; *JSH* 72: 456-57; *LJ* 130n4: 97-98.

752 Fenn, Elizabeth A. *Pox Americana: The Great Smallpox Epidemic of 1775–82*. New York: Hill and Wang, 2001. xiv, 370 p. ISBN 0809078201; ISBN 9780809078202; OCLC 45879842; LC Call Number RC183.49 .F46; Dewey 614.5/21/097309033 21. Citations: 61.

Documents the political and military impacts of smallpox during the Revolutionary War. Examines diaries, letters, presidential papers, and church and burial records to review the spread of the disease ("Variola"), its effects among volunteers, patriots, loyalists, prisoners, African Americans, and Native Americans in North America (including present-day Canada and Mexico), the British use of the disease as a biological weapon, the influence that smallpox had upon George Washington and, despite Washington's inoculation efforts, the way in which the disease devastated American soldiers in the Revolution. Describes the effects of smallpox on the course of the war, particularly on military engagements in Massachusetts, Quebec, South Carolina, North Carolina, and Virginia. Argues that smallpox arrived on the Pacific Coast from an inland route, not from Spanish or British ships as previously thought.

AHR 108: 188-89; *Booklist* 98: 289-91; *BHM* 78: 479-81; *JAH* 89: 1024-25; *JER* 24: 182-88; *J Soc Hist* 37: 268-70; *LJ* 126n16: 135-36; *RAH* 30: 204-11; *WMQ* 59: 770-76.

753 Hart-Davis, Duff. *Audubon's Elephant: America's Greatest Naturalist and the Making of The Birds of America*. New York: Henry Holt, 2004. 288 p. ISBN 0805075682; ISBN 9780805075687; OCLC 52858489; LC Call Number QL31.A9; Dewey 598/.092. Citations: 6.

Tells the story of Audubon's years in England and Europe trying to sell *Birds of America*. Portrays Audubon as an enthusiastic and motivated artist who tenaciously attempted to collect funds owed him. Explains that the pressures of bankruptcy in America caused Audubon to turn to Europe to solicit wealthy, connected families like the Rathbones in England and men like William Home Lizars in Edinburgh, who eventually became Audubon's first printer. Notes that, despite competition from other ornithologists and long separations from his

family, Audubon's persistence paid off, as he met Sir Walter Scott and secured subscriptions from King George IV and other members of the royal family.
Booklist 100: 1338; *LJ* 129n13: 112; *WMQ* 63: 176-83.

754 Hoermann, Alfred R. *Cadwallader Colden: A Figure of the American Enlightenment*. Westport, Conn.: Greenwood Press, 2002. xiv, 204 p. ISBN 0313321590; ISBN 9780313321597; OCLC 47797723; LC Call Number F122 .C683. Dewey 973.2/092. Citations: 6.
Explores Colden's work in the natural sciences and medicine, including efforts in botany, correspondence with Linnaeus, attempt to mechanize Newton's account of gravity, and his debate with Anglican divine Samuel Johnson over philosophical materialism. Claims that Colden's "intellectual and scientific achievements have been neglected for an unduly long time," but "can perhaps be best understood within the broader framework of the trans-Atlantic repercussions of the Enlightenment of the eighteenth century." Covers Colden's birth in Ireland, childhood in Scotland, medical education at the University of Edinburgh, journey to America, life in Philadelphia and then New York, marriage and children, end of his medical career, early political appointments and scientific endeavors, and his landmark work *The Principles of Action in Matter*, which was largely rejected in Europe due to general condescension toward colonial philosophy and science.
HRNB 31: 62; *JAH* 90: 992; *PMHB* 127: 234-36; *WMQ* 60: 446-48.

755 Millones Figueroa, Luis and Domingo Ledezma, eds. *El Saber de los Jesuitas, Historias Naturales y el Nuevo Mundo*. Madrid: Iberoamericana, 2005. 349 p. ISBN 8484892018; ISBN 9788484892014; ISBN 3865272118; ISBN 9783865272119; OCLC 60372963; LC Call Number BX3713.5 .S23; Dewey 271/.5308. Citations: 0.
Includes twelve pieces on seventeenth- and eighteenth-century natural histories of the New World written by Jesuits. Covers observations of the flora and fauna and theological views of nature (e.g., belief that the "new" plant and animal species were wonders of nature and clear signs of God's greatness). Presents articles on the rhetoric in Joseph Gumilla's *Orinoco Ilustrado* (1741–45), the general view of the continent, and the impact of America on members of the Jesuit intelligentsia.
HAHR 86: 813-14.

756 Newman, William R. and Lawrence M. Principe. *Alchemy Tried in the Fire: Starkey, Boyle, and the Fate of Helmontian Chymistry*. Chicago, Ill.: University of Chicago Press, 2002. xvi, 344 p. ISBN 0226577112; ISBN 9780226577111; OCLC 50424577; LC Call Number QD18 .G7; Dewey 540/.942/09032. Citations: 37.
Surveys the background and work of Starkey, who became one of England's most sought after "chymical" practitioners, largely because of his scholastic training and his metallurgical work in the early Massachusetts iron industry. Explains that Starkey used formalized methods of scholastic inquiry and argumentation in the practices of experimental philosophy, noting that he employed precise quantitative methods and that theory clearly influenced his

practices and procedures in the laboratory. Contends that modern chemistry developed more or less continuously from the practices and theories of medieval alchemy, through seventeenth-century "chymical" practice and the eighteenth-century chemistry of Antoine Lavoisier. Asserts that Lavoisier's quantitative analysis came out of centuries-old practices, rather than being borrowed from mechanical physics. Rejects Robert Boyle's vaunted title as the "father of chemistry," noting that he made good use of long-established practices and borrowed liberally from Starkey and Van Helmont.
AHR 109: 244-45; *BHM* 78: 218-20; *18c Stds* 39: 258-63; *J Mod Hist* 77: 422-23; *WMQ* 60: 920-24.

757 Newman, William R. *Gehennical Fire: The Lives of George Starkey, an American Alchemist in the Scientific Revolution.* Chicago, Ill.: University of Chicago Press, 2002. Reprint Edition. xxii, 368 p. ISBN 0226577147; ISBN 9780226577142; OCLC 50494270; LC Call Number QD24.S73; Dewey 540/.1/12/092. Citations: 54.
Presents a biography of George Starkey, who was born George Stirk in Bermuda in 1628 and changed his name to Starkey after being graduated from Harvard and immigrating to England. Notes that Starkey learned the corpuscular theory of matter at Harvard from Alexander Richardson's *The Logicians School-Master*, and applied the theory to alchemical traditions. Reviews seventeenth-century advances in physics, medicine, and alchemy and describes Starkey's work with Robert Boyle. Explains that Starkey wrote books under his own name and the pseudonym Eirenaeus Philalethes and "had a scientific influence unmatched by any of his colonial peers." Finds that Starkey's work influenced Leibniz and Newton, and early eighteenth-century thinkers. Concludes that, far from provincial, New Englanders were actually at the center of progressive English and Continental thought on theories of matter, chemistry, and alchemy.
WMQ 60: 920-24.

758 Prince, Sue Ann, ed. *Stuffing Birds, Pressing Plants, Shaping Knowledge: Natural History in North America, 1730–1860.* Philadelphia, Penn.: American Philosophical Society, 2003. xvi, 113 p. ISBN 0871699346 (pbk.); ISBN 9780871699343 (pbk.); OCLC 52464676; LC Call Number QH21.N7; LC Call Number Q11 .P6; Dewey 508/.097/09033. Citations: 9.
Includes articles on preserving natural specimens for study and display, including the history of preservation techniques, the art of early American natural history, and the eighteenth- and early-nineteenth-century historical contexts for natural history displays. Provides information on an APS exhibition that focused on "how and why Euro-Americans of the Enlightenment and post-Enlightenment periods went about explaining the world in the way they did."
Penn Hist 71: 495-99.

759 Rhodes, Richard. *John James Audubon: The Making of an American.* New York: Knopf, 2004. x, 514 p. ISBN 0375414126; (hbk.); ISBN 9780375414121 (hbk.); ISBN 0739451561 (pbk.); ISBN 9780739451564 (pbk.); OCLC 54029227; LC Call Number QL31.A9; Dewey 598/.092. Citations: 6.

Describes Audubon's life, marking the effect of early travels on his later years, the impact of the Manhattan yellow fever epidemic, and the influence of Audubon's early business failures and bankruptcy. Makes the point that Audubon turned to ornithology after a series of ventures that were adversely affected by war, political turmoil, and uncertain frontier economic conditions. Characterizes Audubon as a devoted husband and father who dreaded separations from his family and whose work on birds was motivated not by personal interest, but by financial necessity. Explains that Audubon raised the cost to produce *The Birds of America* "unsupported by gifts, grants or legacies" and "by painting, exhibiting and selling subscriptions and skins." Concludes that Audubon's solitary work represented a "staggering achievement."
Booklist 100: 1886; *JAH* 92: 606-607; *LJ* 129n15: 80; *LJ* 130n1: 58; *RAH* 33: 169-76; *WMQ* 63: 176-183.

760 Rosenberg, Charles E., ed. *Right Living: An Anglo-American Tradition of Self-Help Medicine and Hygiene.* Baltimore, Md.: Johns Hopkins University Press, 2003. x, 236 p. ISBN 0801871891; ISBN 9780801871894; OCLC 49853269; LC Call Number RC81 .R57; Dewey 613/.0973/09033. Citations: 9.
Presents nine essays on the ways in which early writings contributed to self-help medicine, noting that there was an almost constant and "inexhaustible demand for medical information." Covers diet in books on manners in early modern England, the female advice book, *Aristotle's Masterpiece* (first published in 1684), the child-care guide, *The Maternal Physician* (1811), illustrated posters of the 1830s that advertised proprietary medicines, health advice in pre-1860s almanacs, popular sex manuals of the 1850s and 1870s, and the extent to which domestic health advice was actually followed in the antebellum South.
AHR 109: 1198-1200; *BHM* 78: 483-84.

761 Schiebinger, Londa. *Plants and Empire: Colonial Bioprospecting in the Atlantic World.* Cambridge, Mass.: Harvard University Press, 2004. x, 306 p. ISBN 0674014871 (hbk.); ISBN 9780674014879 (hbk.); ISBN 0674025687 (pbk.); ISBN 9780674025684; OCLC 55535128; LC Call Number RG137.45 .S35; Dewey 581.6/34. Citations: 78.
Studies Caribbean botanists and the ways in which they communicated scientific information throughout the Atlantic basin, the information that botany provided in terms of new medicines, foods, and technologies, the European control of colonial plants through the imperialistic application of European names, botanical abortifacients in the Old and New Worlds, control of fertility among women of various classes, including slaves, who used abortive plants to exert control over their bodies, and the non-transfer of knowledge, as in the case of men gaining authority over pregnancy through medicalization and the removal of women's health care from the hands of other women. Finds that when abortifacent plants from the New World were introduced to Europe, their pregnancy termination properties were withheld from women.
AHR 110: 756-57; *BHM* 80: 374-75.

762 Schiffer, Michael Brian, Kacy L. Hollenback, and Carrie L. Bell. *Draw the Lightning Down: Benjamin Franklin and Electrical Technology in the Age of*

Enlightenment. Berkeley: University of California Press, 2003. xiv, 383 p. ISBN 0520238028; ISBN 9780520238022; OCLC 51477098; LC Call Number TK16 .S35; Dewey 621.3/0973/09033. Citations: 18.

Surveys eighteenth-century electrical technology, focusing on apparatus usage and marketing, the Leyden jar, the electrostatic generator, public demonstrations of the power of electricity, medial electricity, reanimation, galvanism, lightning rods, electrochemistry, the Voltaic pile, future-oriented applications, and technology transfer.

AHR 109: 1555-56; *JAH* 91: 993-94; *PMHB* 129: 348-49.

763 Schofield, Robert E. *The Enlightened Joseph Priestley: A Study of His Life and Work from 1773 to 1804*. University Park: Pennsylvania State University Press, 2004. xvi, 461 p. ISBN 0271024593; ISBN 9780271024592; OCLC 54843986; LC Call Number BX9869.P8; Dewey 540/.92. Citations: 16.

Studies Priestley's philosophical and religious views, the controversies in which he was involved, his political radicalism, and his work as a chemist. Covers Lord Shelburne's patronage, Priestley's authorship of *Institutes of Natural and Revealed Religion* (1772–74), and the 1773 Royal Society recognition of Priestley's work on airs and water. Views Priestley "as a leading luminary of the Enlightenment in an extraordinary variety of subjects."

CH 76: 190-92; *JAH* 92: 593-94.

764 Smith, Pamela H. *The Body of the Artisan: Art and Experience in the Scientific Revolution*. Chicago: University of Chicago Press, 2004. x, 367 p. ISBN 0226763994 (hbk.); ISBN 9780226763996 (hbk.); ISBN 0226764001 (pbk.); ISBN 9780226764009 (pbk.); OCLC 52381123; LC Call Number N72.S3; Dewey 509/.4/0903. Citations: 95.

Notes that from the mid-fifteenth- through mid-seventeenth centuries, practice was dominant over theory ("artisanal epistemology"), resulting in a "vernacular science of matter" that included metallurgy and alchemy. Explains that this approach was appropriated by Baconians and that practitioners assiduously denied having any commercial interests.

AHR 111: 550-51; *BHM* 79: 809-10; *16c J* 36: 1219-20; *WMQ* 64: 220-29.

765 Souder, William. *Under a Wild Sky: John James Audubon and the Making of* The Birds of America. New York: North Point Press, 2004. 367 p. ISBN 0865476713; ISBN 9780865476714; OCLC 53839872; LC Call Number QL31.A9; Dewey 598/.092. Citations: 7.

Places Audubon's work in the context of early American natural history, focusing on the work of Thomas Jefferson, Mark Catesby, William Bartram, and Alexander Wilson. Contends that the development of the field in the United States mirrored the development of the nation itself. Shows that Audubon burst on the scene in England at the perfect time and used a backwoods persona to sell subscriptions to *The Birds of America*.

Booklist 100: 1696; *LJ* 129n13: 112; *RAH* 33: 169-76; *WMQ* 63: 176-83.

766 Sutcliffe, Andrea J. *Steam: The Untold Story of America's First Great Invention*. New York: Palgrave Macmillan, 2004. xiv, 272 p. ISBN

1403962618; ISBN 9781403962614; OCLC 54073780; LC Call Number VM140.F5; Dewey 623.87/22/0973. Citations: 0.

Explores the origins of the steamboat, noting that it appeared in various forms between the 1780s and 1812 and arguing that John Fitch was the inventor. Describes the rivalry between Fitch and James Rumsey and Fitch's first successful voyage of the *Perseverance* on the Delaware River.

BHR 78: 731-33; *JER* 25: 292-94; *Penn Hist* 72: 245-48; *VMHB* 114: 300-301.

767 Tannenbaum, Rebecca. *The Healer's Calling: Women and Medicine in Early New England*. Ithaca, N. Y.: Cornell University Press, 2002. xviii, 179 p. ISBN 0801438268; ISBN 9780801438264; OCLC 48473981; LC Call Number R692.T364; Dewey 610/.82/097409032. Citations: 0.

Examines the role of New England women in early colonial medicine. Finds that women often were responsible for diagnosis, medicine production, and physical support of the patient. Notes that such women, particularly those who practiced outside of their home and charged fees, were at higher risk of witchcraft accusations than other women. Explains that women were responsible for the medical care of their family members as a matter of course, but would be charged criminally if they applied abortifacients after quickening or if they dabbled in "healing magic." Contends that healing women used their positions to influence others and extend their community networks and that the eighteenth-century professionalization of medicine changed the role of women significantly.

AHR 108: 1439-40; *JAH* 90: 615-16; *NEQ* 77: 168-70; *WMQ* 60: 431-34.

768 Tucker, Tom. *Bolt of Fate: Benjamin Franklin and His Electric Kite Hoax*. New York: Public Affairs, 2003. xx, 297 p. ISBN 1891620703 (hbk.); ISBN 9781891620706 (hbk.); ISBN 1586482947 (pbk.); ISBN 9781586482947 (pbk.); OCLC 51763922; LC Call Number QC16.F58; Dewey 530/.092. Citations: 6.

Explores Franklin's work with lightning and electricity, arguing that he never undertook the famous kite experiment.

Booklist 99: 1736.

769 Valencius, Conevery Bolton. *The Health of the Country: How American Settlers Understood Themselves and Their Land*. New York: Basic Books, 2002. viii, 388 p. ISBN 0465089860 (hbk.); ISBN 9780465089864 (hbk.); ISBN 0465089879 (pbk.); ISBN 9780465089871 (pbk.); OCLC 49376148; LC Call Number RA792 .V354; Dewey 614.4/2/09767. Citations: 62.

Discusses the process of settlement, finding that the taming of the wilderness evoked a visceral response in the settlers. Explains that "health" had to do with controlling the environment and with exploiting local sources of medicine and that bodily processes had analogs to the functions of land, water, and air.

Ag Hist 78: 119-20; *AHR* 110: 1538-39; *BHM* 80: 775-76; *JAH* 90: 1437-38; *LJ* 127n14: 194; *RAH* 31: 260-67.

30 Performing Arts

770 Buechner, Alan. *Yankee Singing Schools and the Golden Age of Choral Music in New England, 1760-1800*. Boston, Mass.: Boston University for the Dublin Seminar for New England Folklife, 2003. viii, 158 p. ISBN 0872701328; ISBN 9780872701328; OCLC 54475136; LC Call Number MT823 .B84; Dewey 782.5. Citations: 0.
Characterizes early New England hymnody as "the first great flowering of musical composition in America." Notes that this style precipitously declined in popularity after 1800 as European composition standards gained favor. Discusses the importance of singing in Puritan congregations, which often relied upon verses taken from the *Book of Psalms* set to English melodies. Describes the reforms of the 1720s instituted by Boston area ministers, which sought to teach congregation members to read music through the establishment of schools. Finds that many congregations deserted the practice of "lining-out," whereby the minister would recite the psalm to be sung and an assistant would repeat or sing each line of the tune for the congregation to repeat. Discusses other reforms, such as the creation of separate choirs and the addition of musical instruments, including organs.
NEQ 78: 136-40.

771 Hutner, Heidi. *Colonial Women: Race and Culture in Stuart Drama*. New York: Oxford University Press, 2001. ix, 141 p. ISBN 0195141881; ISBN 9780195141887; OCLC 45460884; LC Call Number PR678.W6; Dewey 822/.409352042; Dewey 822.4099287. Citations: 8.
Examines the ways in which American women, including Native Americans and slaves, were portrayed in British plays of the seventeenth century. Discusses pieces in which British authors refer to the Revolutionary War and the stories of Pocahontas and Marina/Malinche, among others. Notes that even when they are invoked, Native Americans are erased from dramatic scenes, even though

writers like Shakespeare would have known about Indians. Notes that plays often indicate a fear that women in America, regardless of race, become wild, and that elision is a strategy of repression.
EAL 38: 174-79.

772 Johnson, Odai and William J. Burling, eds. *The Colonial American Stage, 1665–1774: A Documentary Calendar*. Cranbury, N.J.: Associated University Presses, 2001. 519 p. ISBN 0838639038; ISBN 9780838639030; OCLC 45890468; LC Call Number PN2237 .J64; Dewey 792/.0973/09032. Citations: 8.
Lists all known pre-Revolution play performances in colonial America, including those for the American Company and college student performances. Provides documents related to theater in America, including anti-theatrical laws, reviews, advertisements, letters, and diary entries.
EAL 38: 174-79; *WMQ* 62: 812-15.

773 Nathans, Heather S. *Early American Theatre from the Revolution to Thomas Jefferson: Into the Hands of the People*. Cambridge: Cambridge University Press, 2003. xi, 246 p. ISBN 0521825083 (hbk.); ISBN 9780521825085 (hbk.); ISBN 9780521035477 (pbk.); ISBN 0521035473 (pbk.); OCLC 52286491; LC Call Number PN2237 .N38; Dewey 792/.0973/09033. Citations: 15.
Studies specific theaters and theatrical cultures in New York, Boston, and Philadelphia, explaining that wealthy citizens formed partnerships to finance theatrical ventures. Finds that theaters were distinct and competed with one another, and that elites in the aftermath of the Revolution initially embraced the theater as a vehicle of cultural power. Notes that elites expressed that power in the language of republican nationalism, but were ultimately confronted by "audiences and factions who demanded input into how the theater should be governed and what it should offer to the public." Concludes, then, that early national theater provided a valuable cultural space for negotiating the terms of power.
EAL 41: 347-64; *JAS* 38: 522-23; *RAH* 36: 171-76; *WMQ* 62: 812-15.

774 Orr, Bridget. *Empire on the English Stage, 1660–1714*. New York: Cambridge University Press, 2001. x, 350 p. ISBN 0521773504; ISBN 9780521773508; OCLC 45446510; LC Call Number PR698.I45; Dewey 822/.409358. Citations: 27.
Examines "relations between empire and the stage in the Restoration," describing "literary debates over the drama from 1660-1714" and presenting "an account of the imperial ambition encoded in authorial personae, generic assumptions, and the thematics of heroic plays in particular." Studies heroic drama, affective, bourgeois, and sentimental tragedies, comic and tragicomic works on metropolitan manners and Amazonian and utopian plays. Contends that Restoration drama represents "an important and hitherto neglected source for any account of seventeenth- and early eighteenth-century imperial ideology" and that plays "can be seen as a form of colonial discourse insofar as they

contribute to shaping perspectives on non-European societies which the English hoped to exploit economically and influence politically, if not annex formally."
18c Stds 36: 423-28; *J Brit Stds* 44: 194-203.

775 Richards, Jeffrey H. *Drama, Theatre, and Identity in the American New Republic*. New York: Cambridge University Press, 2005. xi, 392 p. ISBN 052184746X; ISBN 9780521847469; OCLC 61176542; LC Call Number PN2237 .R53; Dewey 306.4/84. Citations: 12.
Focuses on the influence of post-Revolution American identity on theater in the early United States, seeking to "read plays and performances in terms of a world where identity is volatile and where the oppositions that create identity themselves often shift or mushroom or wither in a relatively short time." Includes popular literature and travel narratives and discusses the difficulty for American authors to create dramatic forms distinct from British models. Examines the comic opera *The Poor Soldier*, Judith Sargent Murray's *The Traveler Returned*, the stage portrayals of Muslim, Native American, Irish, and African American identities, Susanna Haswell Rowson's *Slaves in Algiers*, James Nelson Barker's *Indian Princess*, Charles Brockden Brown's *Ormond*, and the Norfolk, Virginia playhouse as a crossroads of local, national, and transatlantic identities. Concludes that "American muses may have been confused about who or what they were supposed to be."
Am Lit 79: 413-15; *EAL* 42: 355-62; *JER* 26: 505-508; *VMHB* 115: 133-36; *WMQ* 64: 436-40.

31 Visual Arts and Material Culture

776 Barquist, David L. *Myer Myers: Jewish Silversmith in Colonial New York.* New Haven, Conn.: Yale University Art Gallery, in association with Yale University Press, 2001. xvi, 304 p. ISBN 0300090579; ISBN 9780300090574; OCLC 48154107; LC Call Number NK7198.M9; Dewey 739.2/372. Citations: 5.

Catalogues Myers' work, focusing on his mastery of the Rococo style and his craftsmanship. Discusses his pieces, customers, patronage, religion, and role in the New York Jewish community, noting that Myers (1723–1795) was "the first Jew in New York to train as a silversmith" and was "the first native Jew within the British Empire to have had formal training and establish himself as a working, retail silversmith since the incorporation of the Worshipful Company of Goldsmiths in 1327." Explains that Myers had to deal with problematic partnerships, economic and political difficulties, and matters of theft and of silver counterfeiting.

LJ 127n5: 75; *WMQ* 59: 728-36.

777 Beran, Michael Knox. *Jefferson's Demons: Portrait of a Restless Mind.* New York: Free Press, 2003. xxi, 265 p. ISBN 0743232798; ISBN 9780743232791; ISBN 0743246543; ISBN 9780743246545; OCLC 52251401; LC Call Number E332.2 .B427; Dewey 973.4/6/092. Citations: 9.

Focuses on Jefferson's interests in poetry and aesthetics and his sentimental and emotional sides. Describes Jefferson's nine-month grand tour of Europe (1786–87), which included his observation of French and Italian ruins. Observes that Jefferson "descended from a family with a history of mental instability" and suffered "from periodic bouts of apathy and dejection," but was nonetheless able to enjoy stretches of normality and remarkable achievements.

Booklist 100: 295; *JAH* 91: 611-12; *JSH* 72: 871-908; *LJ* 128n15: 68; *Soc Hist* 29: 273-74.

778   Buggeln, Gretchen. *Temples of Grace: The Material Transformation of Connecticut's Churches, 1790–1840.* Hanover, N.H.: University Press of New England, 2003. xiv, 312 p. ISBN 1584653221 (hbk.); ISBN 9781584653226 (hbk.); ISBN 158465323X (pbk.); ISBN 9781584653233 (pbk.); OCLC 51446714; LC Call Number NA5230.C8 B84; Dewey 726.5/09746 21. Citations: 9.

Traces the building of churches in Connecticut in the half century after the Revolution and describes the fundamental shift from meetinghouse to church. Discusses the economic requirements of a building program, architectural styles, and the relationship of building and décor to worship and spirituality. Suggests that "Congregationalists tended to build in the 'modern' style, fitting themselves in with the fashionable neo-classical architecture of the day," while Episcopalians favored neo-Gothic churches and more marginal groups, including Baptists and Methodists, built plainer structures. Finds that interiors, including organs, choirs, sanctuaries, and lower pulpits, encouraged civil, spiritual, and moral refinement. Concludes that Congregationalists, as a result of disestablishment, were prompted to adopt a market outlook to stave off secularism and "use the riches of the modern material world to their full spiritual advantage."

AHR 110: 472; *JAH* 91: 1003-1004; *JER* 25: 143-46; *J Religion* 85: 134-36; *NEQ* 79: 154-57; *WMQ* 61: 780-83.

779   Crowley, John E. *The Invention of Comfort: Sensibilities & Design in Early Modern Britain & Early America.* Baltimore, Md.: Johns Hopkins University Press, 2001. xiv, 361 p. ISBN 0801864372; ISBN 9780801864377; OCLC 43851308; LC Call Number GT481.U6; Dewey 306/.0973. Citations: 39.

Asserts that "Theories of political economy in the first half of the eighteenth century made comfort a legitimizing motive for popular consumption patterns." Traces bodily comfort from the Middle Ages to the Early Modern Atlantic, noting changing expectations regarding housing, domestic life, and architectural elements, such as the use of chimneys, window glass, and increased partitioning of interior space. Describes the English "Great Rebuilding" (1560 to circa 1640), which transformed the standard of living to emphasize greater comfort through expanded commodities and witnessed the initial Tudor-Stuart forays into North America. Takes up matters of hearth size, reduced costs of candlesticks over the course of the eighteenth century, the various functions of looking glasses, the Anglo-American importance of stoves, and the later conflict between physical creature comforts and perceived corrupting luxury among classical republicans.

AHR 108: 800-801; *BHR* 76: 370-73; *EHR* 117: 721-22; *JAH* 89: 608-609; *JER* 22: 117-19; *J Soc Hist* 37: 773-74; *NEQ* 75: 341-45; *RAH* 30: 365-72; *VQR* 78: 71-72.

780   Deagan, Kathleen and José María Cruxent. *Archaeology at La Isabela: America's First European Town.* New Haven, Conn.: Yale University Press,

2002. xxxiv, 377 p. ISBN 0300090412; ISBN 9780300090413; OCLC 48473711; LC Call Number F1939.I8; Dewey 972.93. Citations: 17.

Discusses the archaeology of La Isabela, which was settled in 1494 on Hispaniola's northern shore, but was plagued by difficulties of supply, disease, and rebellion and was abandoned by 1498. Discusses site layout, buildings, food production, preparation, and consumption, daily life, military tools, and trades and crafts. Compares La Isabella to the later Hispaniola settlements of Conception de la Vega (ca. 1502) and Puerto Real (ca. 1504). Details research at La Isabela between 1987 and 1996 and Tamos inhabitants' material culture, arguing that La Isabela "represents a medieval Iberian concept of colonization" and therefore presents an "extremely important archaeological reference point from which to study the development of the diverse and distinctive cultural mosaic of the post-1500 Americas" as well as "the direction and intensity of changes in the material worlds of both Europeans and Native Americans as they made cultural adjustments to one another."

Ethnohistory 53: 409-18; *HAHR* 84: 135-36; *JAH* 90: 202-204.

781 Deagan, Kathleen and José María Cruxent. *Columbus's Outpost among the Taínos: Spain and America at La Isabela, 1493–1498*. New Haven, Conn.: Yale University Press, 2002. x, 294 p. ISBN 0300090404; ISBN 9780300090406; OCLC 48092149; LC Call Number F1939.I8; Dewey 972.93/58. Citations: 15.

Presents an account of Columbus's settlement at La Isabela, based on the colony's material culture. Discusses the indigenous populations of Hispaniola, the Tamos, the short, relatively violent history of La Isabela (including food shortages and disease), the history of the colony since its demise in 1498, archaeological features, surviving structures, and layout of La Isabela. Describes another settlement at Las Coles, which was located across a ravine from La Isabela and perhaps was the point of the initial landing of Columbus's ships and where the men lived during the construction of La Isabela. Asserts that, based on the items recovered from the colony, class status was important at La Isabela, and that domestic life of the common colonist was not substantially different from that of a typical resident of Spain. Examines religion, defense, and commerce in the colony, stressing that a money-based economy developed. Contends that the colony failed due to inflexibility and failure to adapt to conditions in America, but that the experience of the colonists at La Isabela profoundly influenced all of Spain's subsequent colonization of the New World.

AHR 108: 1491-92; *Ethnohistory* 53: 409-18; *JAH* 90: 202-204; *J Interdis Hist* 34: 120-22.

782 Falino, Jeannine and Gerald W.R. Ward, eds. *New England Silver and Silversmithing, 1620–1815*. Boston: The Colonial Society of Massachusetts, distributed by the University Press of Virginia, 2001. xiv, 281 p. ISBN 096207375X; ISBN 9780962073755; OCLC 47958733; LC Call Number NK7112 .N38; Dewey 974.4. Citations: 3.

Presents essays from a 1996 conference at the Museum of Fine Arts in Boston. Includes pieces on the importance of silver as currency in early New England, as artwork, and as an indicator of social status, its usage in religious settings, Paul

Revere's work, account books, and customers, and the significance of silver among students and alumni of Harvard College.
WMQ 59: 728-35.

783 Feigenbaum, Gail and Victoria Cooke, eds. *Jefferson's America & Napoleon's France: An Exhibition for the Louisiana Purchase Bicentennial.* New Orleans, La.: New Orleans Museum of Art, 2003. xvii, 286 p. ISBN 0894940910; ISBN 9780894940910; OCLC 52199506; LC Call Number E333 .F45; Dewey 609.5; Dewey 970. Citations: 3.
Presents articles on Jefferson's work in Paris, post-revolutionary leadership in France and America, Napoleon's excursion into Egypt and fascination with orientalism, the public and private images of Napoleon and Josephine, American artwork of the period, Jefferson's Monticello, the impact of the Louisiana Purchase on Native Americans, early nineteenth-century New Orleans, and slavery in the Louisiana territory.
RAH 32: 166-75.

784 Hafertepe, Kenneth and James F. O'Gorman, eds. *American Architects and Their Books to 1848.* Amherst: University of Massachusetts Press, 2001. xxiv, 231 p. ISBN 1558492828; ISBN 9781558492820; OCLC 45583392; LC Call Number NA707 .A47; Dewey 720/.973 21. Citations: 7.
Presents articles on the availability of architectural books in eighteenth-century New England, the holdings of books on architecture in colonial Virginia, pattern books used by George Washington at Mount Vernon, Thomas Jefferson's architectural books, libraries' collections of architectural books, books used by Bullfinch and Benjamin Henry Latrobe, the roles of builders' assistants, the career of Owen Biddle, architectural books in New York from McComb to Lafever, publications of Asher Benjamin and Andrew Jackson Downing, and Louisa Tuthill, Ithiel Town and the writing of early architectural history.
Am Lit 80: 838-40; *WMQ* 59: 536-40.

785 Heckscher, Morrison H. and Lori Zabar. *John Townsend: Newport Cabinetmaker.* New Haven, Conn.: Yale University Press, 2005. xii, 225 p. ISBN 1588391450; ISBN 9781588391452; ISBN 030010717X; ISBN 9780300107173; OCLC 58052745; LC Call Number NK2439.T68; Dewey 749/.092. Citations: 3.
Discusses "all known documented examples of John Townsend's furniture," providing color photographs and describing design, construction, measurement, provenance, signatures, and labeling of the thirty-four extant pieces. Places Newport in the context early American woodworking, asserting that the "independent course" taken by Newport's refugees from Puritan Massachusetts may be seen in furniture design. Concludes that Townsend's signed pieces are characterized by "fully developed form, a crispness and sharpness of design, a precision of execution, inside and out, and a preference for complex, labor-intensive methods of construction" and represent "the work of a passionate perfectionist, constitutionally unable to cut corners or economize even in places that cannot be seen." Contends that Townsend "exhibited a self-conscious sense of his own place in the history of cabinetmaking that is unique in the annals of

American cabinetmaking." Argues that Townsend's signed pieces were custom orders and thus different from more "mundane" pieces that were cheaper, usually ready-made, and made from less expensive woods such as maple and cedar. Concludes that "the signed examples are, virtually without exception, pieces of the highest quality, not generic objects for the export trade" and that "Townsend's habit of adding the date suggests an acute historical awareness." *JER* 26: 670-76.

786 Herman, Bernard L. *Town House: Architecture and Material Life in the Early American City, 1780–1830*. Chapel Hill: University of North Carolina Press, published for the Omohundro Institute of Early American History and Culture, 2005. xviii, 295 p. ISBN 0807829919; ISBN 9780807829912; OCLC 58050683; LC Call Number NA7206 .H47; Dewey 307.3/3616/097309033. Citations: 16.
Examines early national urban landscapes through "a series of explorations into the ways people employed town houses as symbolic representations of self and community." Explores residents' classes, and the lives of merchants, servants, women, artisans, immigrants, owners, renters, and lodgers. Explains that elites demonstrated status through architecture and goods and that buildings both shaped and reflected regional and ethnic identities. Finds that urban slaves gained a measure of privacy because their routine movements "failed to register" with slave owners "except when service went unexpectedly right or very, very wrong." Notes that, in space allocation, some widows were given the home's work areas, while others received the parlor and other more formal rooms. Focuses on artisans whose residences "in plan and finish" indicate their "tenuous grasp on the culture of property." Examines the changeable world of renters and lodgers, exploring their material world through the contents of travelers' bags, concluding that taverns, inns, and boardinghouses represented spaces where strangers and residents eliminated geographic distance.
AHR 112: 1161-62; *JER* 26: 676-79; *JSH* 73: 158-59; *NCHR* 83: 487-88; *RAH* 34: 156-61; *WMQ* 63: 634-37.

787 Howard, Hugh. *Thomas Jefferson, Architect: The Built Legacy of Our Third President*. New York: Rizzoli International, 2003. 204 p. ISBN 0847825469; ISBN 9780847825462; OCLC 52768337; LC Call Number E332.2 .H69; LC Call Number NA737.J4; Dewey 973.4/6092; Dewey 720.92. Citations: 5.
Surveys Jefferson's life as an architect, providing details on structures that likely lent inspiration. Includes 120 color photographs of buildings whose designs are attributed to Thomas Jefferson. Focuses on the Virginia Capitol building, Monticello, Poplar Forest, the Academical Village at the University of Virginia, and homes that might have been designed by Jefferson. Considers Jefferson's lasting influence in American architecture.
LJ 128n9: 85.

788 Kornwolf, James D. *Architecture and Town Planning in Colonial North America*. Baltimore, Md.: Johns Hopkins University Press, 2002. xxx, 1770 p.

ISBN 0801859867; ISBN 9780801859861; OCLC 45066419; LC Call Number NA703 .K67; Dewey 711/.4/09730903. Citations: 9.
Surveys architecture and planning in colonial North America, including New Spain and present-day Canada and the United States. Discusses the historical contexts of buildings and landscapes and includes photographs, drawings, and detailed descriptions. Examines "the aesthetic intentions of builder and patron," but "not aspects of material culture." Traces the spread of Renaissance architecture through Spanish and French settlement and describes characteristics of various types of buildings, including public structures, mills, and churches. Considers vernacular architecture as well, drawing upon such examples as Tidewater and Pennsylvania German houses, the buildings associated with African Americans, the domiciles of New France, and the various structures of New Amsterdam and New Sweden.
JAH 90: 1424-26; *LJ* 128: 134; *RAH* 31: 503-510.

789 Lanier, Gabrielle M. *The Delaware Valley in the Early Republic: Architecture, Landscape, and Regional Identity*. Baltimore, Md.: Johns Hopkins University Press, 2005. xviii, 241 p. ISBN 0801879663; ISBN 9780801879661; OCLC 54694575; LC Call Number F157.D4; Dewey 974.9. Citations: 8.
Rejects the notion of a monolithic Delaware Valley regional identity, arguing instead that it was made up of three distinct regions: German-dominated Warwick, Pennsylvania; the Delmarva peninsula's North West Fork Hundred; and Quaker-settled southwestern New Jersey. Calls the Delaware Valley a "region of regions," which was defined by very different material and cultural landscapes. Contends that buildings of the region were characterized by "architectural creolization," that exteriors followed one style, while interiors evinced another. Concludes that German identity in the Delaware Valley was complex, as its structures demonstrated elements of assimilation, creolization, and cultural persistence. Shows that Quaker communities of southwestern New Jersey made use of stately brick in order to symbolize political and economic power of upper-class Quakers and to influence the ways in which future generations regarded them.
AHR 111: 162-63; *JAH* 92: 962-63; *JER* 25: 485-87; *WMQ* 62: 546-50.

790 Lara, Jaime. *City, Temple, Stage: Eschatological Architecture and Liturgical Theatrics in New Spain*. Notre Dame, Ind.: University of Notre Dame Press, 2004. x, 299 p. ISBN 0268033641; ISBN 9780268033644; OCLC 55955437; LC Call Number NA702.2 .L37; Dewey 726.5/0972/09031. Citations: 21.
Uses art and architecture to analyze the worldview and missionary methods of the mendicant orders in Mexico. Argues that the missionaries were eventually successful in using "recycled" rituals and beliefs of native religion to convert Indians. Finds precedents for open chapels, walled patios, atrial crosses, single nave churches and convents in European, Muslim, and Mozarabic styles, and Aztec precedents in colonial raised chapels and altars. Argues the missionaries linked European ideas about the end of time with native eschatology. Emphasizes Christian rather than Roman origins for city planning in the New World and concludes that the concept of a New Jerusalem and the Book of

Ezekiel were also important influences. Focuses on the idea of a "temple" and proposes that the temple of Jerusalem was the model for churches in the New World. Finds that the symbolism of the cross evoked indigenous religious meanings, particularly those surrounding blood sacrifice. Concludes that sacred architecture became a stage for the religious drama of conversion.
AHR 110: 1568-69; *CH* 76: 438-39; *HAHR* 86: 592-93; *HRNB* 33: 106; *J Interdis Hist* 38: 158-59.

791   Lounsbury, Carl R. *The Courthouses of Early Virginia: An Architectural History*. Charlottesville: University of Virginia Press, 2005. xxii, 430 p. ISBN 0813923018; ISBN 9780813923017; OCLC 54670303; LC Call Number NA4472.V8; Dewey 725/.15/0975509033. Citations: 8.
Traces the development of Virginia county courthouses and smaller buildings (e.g., jails, clerks' offices, taverns) from the seventeenth through the early nineteenth centuries. Places buildings within their legal, political, and social contexts, reviewing the collaborative processes by which magistrates, builders, and craftsmen worked to design and build them. Explains that the location of these buildings in the centers of large jurisdictions resulted in attendance only on court days. Contrasts the orderly proceedings inside courthouses with the irregular development of the sites and the often raucous behavior of crowds outside. Explains that buildings originally followed the pattern of English public buildings, but over time adopted more distinctive plans that included symmetry, arcades, bars, and rails. Notes that these architectural changes reflected the rise in the social and political status of county officials and contends that by the 1730s, courthouses in Virginia had become distinct from other types of buildings.
JSH 72: 444-45; *VMHB* 114: 295-97; *WMQ* 62: 801-806.

792   Lounsbury, Carl R. *From Statehouse to Courthouse: An Architectural History of South Carolina's Colonial Capitol and Charleston County Courthouse*. Columbia: University of South Carolina Press, 2001. x, 113 p. ISBN 1570033781; ISBN 9781570033780; OCLC 44573358; LC Call Number NA4473.C48; Dewey 725/.15/09757915. Citations: 3.
Presents an architectural history of the Charleston County Courthouse, describing the original 1752 structure, the late eighteenth-century building, which was rebuilt with a third story and in Palladian style. Describes the various functions of the building over time, including its housing of the county courts and U.S. District Court, the Charleston Library Society, the Charleston Museum, and the Medical Society of South Carolina. Argues that those who directed the rebuilding and refurbishing of the Charleston statehouse aspired to place the structure on par with English civic buildings. Draws a parallel between imposing government structures to the perception of national authority and the paternalism of the gentry.
SCHM 102: 263-65; *WMQ* 59: 299-302.

793   Lovell, Margaretta M. *Art in a Season of Revolution: Painters, Artisans, and Patrons in Early America*. Philadelphia: University of Pennsylvania Press,

2005. x, 341 p. ISBN 0812238427; ISBN 9780812238426; OCLC 56334330; LC Call Number N6515 .L68; Dewey 709/.74/09033 22. Citations: 20.

Aims to analyze "the interaction of people and things (and people as things within portraits) in the early modern period on the periphery of the British Empire." Reads various portraits and furniture collections to demonstrate "how sets of objects formed an organic part of cultural life, constituting an integral aspect of the way in which certain individuals situated themselves." Discusses the system of patronage of portrait painters and the desires of wealthy families to communicate images and ideals to future generations, which allowed the genre to flourish. Notes the pictorially privileged position of mothers, which began in the 1760s, and the work of Jonathan Singleton Copley, especially the 1763 portrait of Mary Turner Sargent and those of MaryToppan Pickman and Mercy Otis Warren. Draws distinctions between American and British artists, noting that American painters favored pictorial deceptions and visual puns (e.g., the self portraits of Matthew Pratt, Charles Willson Peale, and Benjamin West).

AHR 111: 1166-67; *EAL* 41: 583-87; *18c Stds* 39: 564-68; *JAH* 92: 1419; *JAS* 40: 441-42; *JER* 26: 130-33; *NEQ* 79: 152-54.

794 McNamara, Martha J. *From Tavern to Courthouse: Architecture and Ritual in American Law, 1658–1860.* Baltimore, Md.: Johns Hopkins University Press, 2004. xv, 162 p. ISBN 0801873959; ISBN 9780801873959; OCLC 51900426; LC Call Number NA4472.M3; Dewey 725/.15/09744. Citations: 12.

Examines public spaces related to the judicial process in Massachusetts from the late seventeenth through the early nineteenth centuries. Traces the evolution of judicial space from temporary use of taverns and meeting houses to the establishment of elaborate structures built specifically for judicial use. Notes the colonial legal system at the end of the seventeenth century and in the eighteenth century prior to the Revolution, parallel professionalization of attorneys and architects, the extension of new judicial spaces throughout Massachusetts in the late eighteenth and early nineteenth centuries, the nature of public spaces and rituals, and the relationship between the rise in judicial authority and the structures that housed courts and prisons.

AHR 111: 161-62; *AJLH* 49: 468-69; *JAH* 92: 961-62; *J Interdis Hist* 37: 632-33; *NEQ* 79: 154-57; *WMQ* 62: 801-806.

795 Nemerov, Alexander. *The Body of Raphaelle Peale: Still Life and Selfhood, 1812–1824.* Berkeley: University of California Press, 2001. xiv, 260 p. ISBN 0520224981; ISBN 9780520224988; OCLC 43751572; LC Call Number ND237.P29; Dewey 759.13. Citations: 16.

Examines Peale's concept of his own selfhood and mortality, noting that Peale's works reveal the artist's tortured sense of "failed selfhood." Places Peale's work in the context of broader intellectual and cultural movements and early nineteenth-century events in Philadelphia. Considers Peale's *Blackberries* (c. 1813) as a piece indicative of the Romantic movement and relates Peale still life works to the growing use of anatomical dissection in the medical schools of Philadelphia. Contends that father-son tensions are apparent in Peale's still lifes, which demonstrate infant-like tactility, lack of awareness of the outside world, limited socialization, and resistance to adult conventions. Relates Peale's work

to the Romantic writers of the period, including Rousseau, Wordsworth, and Charles Brockden Brown.
WMQ 59: 277-81.

796 Noël Hume, Ivor and Audrey Noël Hume. *The Archaeology of Martin's Hundred*. Philadelphia: University of Pennsylvania Museum of Archaeology and Anthropology, 2001. xiv, 600 p. ISBN 0924171855; ISBN 9780924171857; OCLC 46420258; LC Call Number F234.M378; Dewey 975.5/4252. Citations: 1.
Includes essays on the results of excavations during the mid-1970s at Carter's Grove, Virginia. Notes the discovery of remnants of buildings and a small fort which were likely part of Wolstenholme Town, a settlement in Martin's Hundred, a large tract of land in early seventeenth-century Virginia. Presents archeological evidence of an Indian attack in March 1622. Details discovered skeletal material, excavated buildings, arms, armor, pottery, artifacts, glass, clay tobacco pipes, and trash pits. Concludes that "in the first half of the seventeenth century, when it comes to personal possessions, the archaeological evidence is far more reliable than the documentary sources." Includes short appendices that deal with animal and bird remains.
16c J 35: 309-310.

797 Olson, Lester C. *Benjamin Franklin's Vision of American Community: A Study in Rhetorical Iconology*. Columbia: University of South Carolina Press, 2004. 323 p. ISBN 1570035253; ISBN 9781570035258; OCLC 53145421; LC Call Number E302.6.F8; Dewey 973.3/092. Citations: 11.
Examines four pictorial images designed by Franklin: "Join, or Die" (1754), "Magna Brittania: her Colonies Reduc'd" (1765), "We Are One" (1776) and "Libertas Americana" (1783). Argues that "although Franklin's experience with the production of emblems and devices was extensive, it is the four pictorial representations depicting British America that are the most important of his designs for understanding his emerging nationalism," and that these images demonstrate "elements in Franklin's communication about the nature of colonial union" and "reflected and promoted changes in American culture through the Revolutionary era." Concludes that these images "throw into high relief fundamental changes in Franklin's sensibility concerning British America, especially his political commitments as he changed from being an American Whig to a republican."
AHR 111: 157-58; *EAL* 41: 535-53; *JAH* 92: 588-89; *PMHB* 130: 114-16.

798 Pachter, Marc. *George Washington: A National Treasure*. Washington, D.C.: National Portrait Gallery, Smithsonian Institution, in association with the University of Washington Press, Seattle, 2002. 103 p. ISBN 0295982373; ISBN 9780295982373; ISBN 0295982365; ISBN 9780295982366; OCLC 51861611; LC Call Number E312.43.G46; LC Call Number N7628.W3; Dewey 973.4/1/092. Citations: 0.
Tells the story of Gilbert Stuart's Landsdowne portrait of George Washington, which portrays Washington in the final year of his presidency. Explains how Washington came to sit for the portrait, its ownership and meaning over time,

and its various copies. Notes the cultural importance of the painting, as it symbolized serenity, freedom, stability, and democracy, while at the same time indicating uncertainty. Includes information on other Washington portraits and portraits of Washington's contemporaries, as well as a chronology of Washington's life.
JAH 90: 335-36.

799   Ryan, Thomas R., ed. *The Worlds of Jacob Eichholtz: Portrait Painter of the Early Republic.* Lancaster, Penn.: Lancaster County Historical Society, 2003. xiii, 178 p. ISBN 0974016209 (hbk.); ISBN 9780974016207 (hbk.); ISBN 0974016217 (pbk.); ISBN 9780974016214 (pbk.); OCLC 53795443; LC Call Number ND1329.E53; LC Call Number N44.E344; Dewey 759.13. Citations: 4.
Offers articles on Eichholtz's life and that of his family and his patrons. Traces Eichholtz's career from coppersmithing to painting, from Lancaster, Pennsylvania to Philadelphia and back to Lancaster. Notes his connections to other artists, including Thomas Sully and Gilbert Stuart and to various institutions like the Pennsylvania Academy of the Fine Arts. Includes articles on Eichholtz's entrepreneurship and social mobility, the list and character of his various works, his account books, and the connection between the developing economy and the rise of portraiture.
Penn Hist 71: 508-510; *PMHB* 129: 113-15; *WMQ* 62: 807-811.

800   Simons, D. Brenton and Peter Benes, eds. *The Art of Family: Genealogical Artifacts in New England.* Boston, Mass.: New England Historic Genealogical Society, 2002. xiv, 336 p. ISBN 0880821329; ISBN 9780880821322; OCLC 48691458; LC Call Number NK810 .A78; Dewey 704.9/499292/0973. Citations: 6.
Includes essays on the material culture of seventeenth-, eighteenth-, and nineteenth-century New England genealogical artifacts. Discusses mourning embroideries, family registers, gravestones, heraldica, textiles, furniture, silver, and portraiture.
LJ 127n11: 62; *NEQ* 75: 666-68; *WMQ* 59: 1000-1003.

801   Small, Nora Pat. *Beauty & Convenience: Architecture and Order in the New Republic.* Knoxville: University of Tennessee Press, 2003. xxiv, 155 p. ISBN 1572332360; ISBN 9781572332362; OCLC 51854689; LC Call Number NA8208.52.N48; Dewey 728/.37/097409034. Citations: 7.
Explores Federal-style home architecture in Sutton, Massachusetts, focusing on houses built in the four decades after the American Revolution. Explains that various constituencies viewed the style in different ways: moral reformers thought it too pretentious for agrarian Yankees; architects saw it as classically beautiful, convenient, and functional; and Sutton builders viewed the style as an effective response to the market and to an area altered by industrialization. Concludes that "popular perceptions of beauty and convenience actually shaped the reordering of the post-Revolution rural New England landscape."
Ag Hist 79: 381-83; *AHR* 110: 472-73; *JAH* 91: 1442-43; *JER* 25: 140-43.

802 Stabile, Susan M. *Memory's Daughters: The Material Culture of Remembrance in Eighteenth-Century America.* Ithaca, N.Y.: Cornell University Press, 2004. xiii, 284 p. ISBN 0801440319; ISBN 9780801440311; OCLC 53170321; LC Call Number F158.44 .S73; Dewey 974.8/1102. Citations: 24.
Studies words as things in an effort to uncover "poetics of female memory" in the late eighteenth century. Examines the ruminations of commonplace books on memory, death, emotion, and philosophy and these subjects' connections to architecture, cultural practices, penmanship, medicine, and collecting. Pays particular attention to the commonplace books of Elizabeth Fergusson, Hannah Griffitts, Deborah Logan, Annis Stockton, and Susanna Wright.
AHR 110: 471-72; *Am Lit* 77: 637-39; *EAL* 40: 387-90; *JAH* 92: 960-61; *JER* 27: 199-201; *J Interdis Hist* 37: 465-66; *PMHB* 130: 117-18; *RAH* 33: 47-53.

803 Thomas Jefferson Foundation. *Thomas Jefferson's Monticello.* Charlottesville, Va.: Thomas Jefferson Foundation, 2002. xxi, 218 p. ISBN 1882886186; ISBN 9781882886180; OCLC 50291085; LC Call Number E332.74 .T48; Dewey 975.5/482. Citations: 1.
Presents essays on Monticello's creation and development, including Jefferson's architectural influences and use of outdoor space, private spaces within the home, furniture and collections, gardens, and a typical day on the estate in 1814.
VMHB 110: 404-406.

804 Ulrich, Laurel Thatcher. *The Age of Homespun: Objects and Stories in the Creation of an American Myth.* New York: Alfred A. Knopf, 2001. x, 501 p. ISBN 0679445943 (hbk.); ISBN 9780679445944 (hbk.); ISBN 0679766448 (pbk.); ISBN 9780679766445 (pbk.); OCLC 46969845; LC Call Number F8 .U47; Dewey 974/.03. Citations: 50.
Traces New England women's textile making from the middle of the seventeenth century to the middle of the nineteenth century. Challenges the notion of pastoral self-sufficiency that "homespun" evokes by focusing on objects and their uses and by connecting production to the larger history of the region, including the displacement of Native Americans.
EAL 39: 363-78; *JAH* 89: 1495-96; *LJ* 126n19: 81; *Penn Hist* 70: 122-23; *WMQ* 59: 269-73.

805 Ward, David C. *Charles Willson Peale: Art and Selfhood in the Early Republic.* Berkeley: University of California Press, 2004. xxiv, 236 p. ISBN 0520239601; ISBN 9780520239609; OCLC 53254013; LC Call Number ND237.P27; Dewey 759.13. Citations: 4.
Presents an analysis of Peale based on his 1825 autobiography and his 1822 self-portrait, *The Artist in His Museum.* Covers Peale's artisan training in Maryland and art education in London, work in Philadelphia in the early republic, and the relationships among his portraits, family, and society. Contends that Peale re-created himself in order to assert autonomy and in so doing typified the individualism of the post-Revolution generation. Concludes that Peale struggled with the republican ideal of self-regulation and critiqued various aspects of society through his paintings.
JAH 92: 202-203; *RAH* 33: 23-28.

806 Zakim, Michael. *Ready-Made Democracy: A History of Men's Dress in the American Republic, 1760–1860*. Chicago: University of Chicago Press, 2003. x, 296 p. ISBN 0226977935; ISBN 9780226977935; OCLC 52182529; LC Call Number GT203 .Z35; Dewey 391/.1/0973. Citations: 16.

Studies the mass production of men's clothing, asserting that the "capitalist revolution came to America under the guise of traditional notions of industry, modesty, economy, and independence." Traces the rise of the market from manufacturing innovations through the development of urban retail outlets to the work of seamstresses and the standardization of sizing of the broadcloth suit.

AHR 110: 146-47; *BHR* 78: 517-18; *JAH* 91: 1445-46; *JER* 25: 496-98; *J Econ Hist* 64: 895-97; *J Soc Hist* 39: 273-75; *LJ* 128n19: 82.

32 Ethnicity

807 Bingham, Emily. *Mordecai: An Early American Family.* New York: Hill and Wang, 2003. x, 346 p. ISBN 0809027569; ISBN 9780809027569; OCLC 50410241; LC Call Number CS71.M8345; Dewey 929/.2/0973. Citations: 6.

Traces the Mordecai family from the colonial through the Civil War eras. Starts with Moses Mordecai's arrival in America as an indentured servant and covers his marriage and his work as a peddler. Concentrates on the lives of Moses's son Jacob and Jacob's daughter, Rachel. Examines family members' struggles to maintain the Jewish faith, noting that many converted to Christianity or intermarried with non-Jews and that anti-Semitism continued to affect family members in the long term. Concludes that, over time, Judaism was less influential on the family than were American, middle-class values. Studies the women and family lives of the Mordecais, noting that adherence to "enlightened domesticity" allowed "domestic life that promised a supportive, loving family capable of worldly accomplishments."

AHR 110: 470-71; *Booklist* 99: 1373; *Hist Teach* 38: 273-74; *JAH* 91: 229-30; *JSH* 70: 896-98; *NCHR* 81: 104-105; *VMHB* 111: 305-307; *WMQ* 61: 375-78.

808 Black, Lydia. *Russians in Alaska: 1732–1867.* Fairbanks: University of Alaska Fairbanks, 2004. xv, 328 p. ISBN 1889963046 (hbk.); ISBN 9781889963044 (hbk.); ISBN 1889963054 (pbk.); ISBN 9781889963051 (pbk.); OCLC 53443264; LC Call Number F907 .B53; Dewey 979.8/02 22. Citations: 27.

Surveys the Russian presence in Alaska, focusing on economic and social developments that encouraged Russia's expansion. Discusses the various roles of merchants, military officers, Orthodox clerics, and ordinary laborers and the complex Russian interactions with native peoples. Examines the influence of Aleksandr Baranov, head of the Russian-American Company from 1790 to 1818, who increased fur harvests, expanded Russian influence, and exerted

significant influence on Natives. Acknowledges continued Russian influence in Alaska in the way of architecture and place names. Concludes that American ownership of the territory had a negative effect on the remaining Russians and on Native Alaskans.
JAH 91: 1490-91; *PHR* 74: 283-84; *WHQ* 36: 380-81.

809 Carlo, Paula Wheeler. *Huguenot Refugees in Colonial New York: Becoming American in the Hudson Valley.* Portland, Or.: Sussex Academic Press, 2005. xi, 252 p. ISBN 1845190599; ISBN 9781845190590; OCLC 56924731; LC Call Number F127.H8; Dewey 974.7/302. Citations: 4.
Argues that French Calvinists who established relatively homogeneous communities like New Paltz and New Rochelle did not rapidly assimilate into the dominate culture, but rather maintained their distinct culture through a large portion of the eighteenth century. Contrasts New Paltz, founded in 1677 by fairly wealthy French settlers, with New Rochelle, established by relatively poor refugees after the revocation of the Edict of Nantes in 1685. Explains that economic differences in the communities continued through the 1760s. Finds that the French language was used, even in New Rochelle's Anglican church, through the mid-eighteenth century and that French Calvinists in both communities tended to hold to Old World religious rituals and practices. Notes that education was highly valued, that French inheritance patterns were maintained, and that the language persisted in some account books as late as 1777.
JAH 93: 179-80.

810 Faragher, John Mack. *A Great and Noble Scheme: The Tragic Story of the Expulsion of the French Acadians from Their American Homeland.* New York: W.W. Norton, 2005. xx, 562 p. ISBN 0393051358 (hbk.); ISBN 9780393051353 (hbk.); ISBN 0393328279 (pbk.); ISBN 9780393328271 (pbk.); OCLC 55730272; LC Call Number F1038 .F37; Dewey 971.6/01 22. Citations: 16.
Traces Acadian dispersal to present-day Nova Scotia, New Brunswick, Prince Edward Island, New England, France, England, Saint Domingo, Québec, Maine, elsewhere in the Canadian Maritimes, and Louisiana, where they later gathered to constitute the Cajun people. Reconstructs the attitudes, policies, and acts of the North American colonies and details this "tragic story of expulsion of the French Acadians from their North American homeland." Discusses initial Acadian settlement in North America, the development of an expulsion plan in the four decades after the Treaty of Utrecht. Admires Acadian persistence, despite removal and their use as pawns in a struggle between empires.
AHR 111: 459-60; *Booklist* 101: 548; *JAH* 93: 842-43; *J Soc Hist* 39: 1247-50; *LJ* 129n20: 135.

811 Gelles, Edith B., ed. *The Letters of Abigaill Levy Franks, 1733–1748.* New Haven, Conn.: Yale University Press, 2004. iv, 186 p. ISBN 030010345X; ISBN 9780300103458; OCLC 55487684; LC Call Number CT275.F69458; Dewey 974.7/1004924/0092. Citations: 4.

Publishes thirty-five edited letters from Franks to her son Naphtali between 1733 and 1748. Sketches life in early New York City, describes typical colonial family life, discusses Jewish immigration to the colony of New York, and illuminates Jewish assimilation into eighteenth-century American society. *WMQ* 62: 771-73.

812   Germain, Georges-Hébert, Francis Back, and Jean-Pierre Hardy. *Adventurers in the New World: The Saga of the Coureurs des Bois*. Hull, Que.: Canadian Museum of Civilization, 2003. 158 p. ISBN 0660190753; ISBN 9780660190754; ISBN 2764800975; ISBN 9782764800973; OCLC 52495976; LC Call Number E46 .G47; Dewey 971.01. Citations: 1.
Surveys the history of the French in North America, from the time of Champlain (1609) to the end of the nineteenth century, focusing on the agricultural settlements beyond the St. Lawrence. Describes the cooperative relationship of the *coureurs de bois*, explorers of the continent's interior, and the Native Americans. Admires the "Métis who gave us the model of an egalitarian and tolerant society founded on respect for both individual and collective values," calling their social model "still eminently worthy of emulation." Intended for a general audience.
CHR 86: 140-42.

813   Griffin, Patrick. *The People with No Name: Ireland's Ulster Scots, America's Scots Irish, and the Creation of a British Atlantic World, 1689–1764*. Princeton, N. J.: Princeton University Press, 2001. xviii, 244 p. ISBN 0691074615 (hbk.); ISBN 9780691074610 (hbk.); ISBN 0691074623 (pbk.); ISBN 9780691074627 (pbk.); OCLC 46359613; LC Call Number E184.S4; Dewey 973/.049163. Citations: 35.
Examines the ethnic identity among the Northern Ireland Presbyterians who emigrated to America in the eighteenth century. Contends that the Ulster Presbyterians "played a formative role in the transition from an English to a British Atlantic," particularly from 1718 onward, but were themselves caught in an identity crisis, having lived in Ireland for generations and therefore being neither Scots nor Irish. Points out that Ulster Scots sought to make their mark on the Presbyterian church in the colonies by attaining ministers from Ireland and Scotland rather than New England. Concludes that the Ulster Scots failed to create a perfect society in Pennsylvania, evidenced by the decision of the second generation and new migrants to live in Maryland and Virginia.
AHR 107: 1190-91; *Econ Hist Rev* 55: 781-82; *EHR* 117: 1351-52; *HRNB* 30: 61; *JAEH* 22: 82-83; *JAH* 89: 1503-1504; *NEQ* 75: 515-16; *RAH* 31: 204-210; *WMQ* 59: 1003-1006.

814   Griffiths, N.E.S. *From Migrant to Acadian: A North American Border People, 1604–1755*. Ithaca, N.Y.: McGill-Queen's University Press for the Canadian Institute for Research on Public Policy and Public Administration, University of Moncton, 2005. xix, 633 p. ISBN 0773526994; ISBN 9780773526990; OCLC 56011002; LC Call Number F1038 .G75; Dewey 971.5/017. Citations: 12.

Examines the question of identity of the Acadians prior to their from the colony of Nova Scotia by British forces in 1755. Argues that Acadian historical experience was the foundation of Acadian identity, that it came about with the early intermarriage of colonial migrants and the native Mi'kmaq. Explains that, by navigating between French and British imperial powers, colonists developed a strong sense of their own independence and the value of neutrality. Finds that insistence on neutrality caused Acadians to resist British demands for an unconditional oath of loyalty, leading the British governor finally to agree to an oral concession of their neutrality. Notes that this neutrality was put to the test during the War of the Austrian Succession, as the British began to transform Nova Scotia into a military stronghold. Explains that the Acadian refusal to swear oaths of allegiance led, in 1755, to the British decision for expulsion.
AHR 111: 458-59.

815 Grosjean, Alexia and Steve Murdoch, eds. *Scottish Communities Abroad in the Early Modern Period*. Boston, Mass.: Brill, 2005. xx, 417 p. ISBN 9004143068; ISBN 9789004143067; OCLC 58431594; LC Call Number DA774.5 .S296; Dewey 909/.04916309 22. Citations: 4.
Presents articles on seventeenth-century Scottish migration to Ireland, the Netherlands, the Americas, Gothenburg, Poland, and Bergen in the sixteenth and seventeenth centuries, along the Maas from 1570 to 1750, and to Kédainiai and Hamburg in the seventeenth and eighteenth centuries.
AHR 110: 1639; *16c J* 37: 1101-1103.

816 Hamilton, Douglas J. *Scotland, the Caribbean and the Atlantic World, 1750–1820*. Manchester, U.K.: Manchester University Press, 2005. xv, 249 p. ISBN 0719071828; ISBN 9780719071829; OCLC 59877966; LC Call Number F2191.S36; Dewey 305.891630729. Citations: 19.
Examines the activities of Scottish people in the West Indies between 1750 and 1820. Argues that the eighteenth and early nineteenth centuries brought a shift in Scotland toward a more urban and industrial society, greater geographic mobility, increased population and education, and enhanced participation of Scots in British government. Notes that these changes led to the movement of Scots to the peripheries of the empire, particularly among planters, merchants, doctors, and politicians. Asserts that "the transient nature of the white population in the islands ensured that the 'home' country remained central to their consciousness" and that the prominence of Scots in official positions "had profound implications for the legislatures' responses, and for fostering both integration and continuity" in the Atlantic world. Explains that Scots "employed networks based on ties of kinship, local association or profession to raise capital, facilitate communication and recruit employees across a range of functional areas, most notably in business."
AHR 114: 151-52; *WMQ* 65: 801-13.

817 Havard, Gilles, and Cécile Vidal. *Histoire de l'Amérique Française*. Paris: Flammarion, 2003. 560 p. ISBN 2082100456; ISBN 9782082100458; OCLC 53096552; LC Call Number E18.92 .H38; LC Call Number F1030 .H39; Dewey 970/.00917/541. Citations: 20.

Surveys French America, excluding the West Indies, covering Acadia, the St. Lawrence Valley, the Pays d'en Haut, the Illinois country, and lower Louisiana. Discusses colonial relations with France and French colonists' relations with Native Americans and African slaves. Argues that even after 1763 French-speaking people continued to play important roles in areas under British or Spanish rule. Blames Louis XV, his ministers, Montcalm, and other French officers for the loss of New France.
CHR 86: 114-17; *JAH* 95: 497-98.

818 Landsman, Ned C., ed. *Nation and Province in the First British Empire: Scotland and the Americas, 1600–1800.* Lewisburg, Penn.: Bucknell University Press, in association with the Eighteenth-Century Scottish Studies Society, 2001. 292 p. ISBN 0838754880; ISBN 9780838754887; OCLC 48429634; LC Call Number E184.S3; Dewey 970/.0049163. Citations: 3.

Includes pieces on cartographic imperialism, Scots in the slave trade, Scottish trading in the Caribbean, particularly as demonstrated by the Houstoun Company, Scottish emigration to British North America in the late eighteenth and early nineteenth centuries, independence among early nineteenth-century lowland emigrants to Upper Canada, the Scottish literati and America between 1680 and 1800, the New York City Presbyterian Church in the 1750s, Scottish medicine and Christian Enlightenment at the Pennsylvania Hospital from 1775 to 1800, and Samuel Miller's *A Brief Retrospect of the Eighteenth Century and Its Scottish Context.*
CHR 83: 433-35.

819 Nolt, Steven M. *Foreigners in Their Own Land: Pennsylvania Germans in the Early Republic.* University Park: Pennsylvania State University Press, 2002. x, 238 p. ISBN 0271021993; ISBN 9780271021997; OCLC 49312596; LC Call Number GR110.P4; LC Call Number F160.G3; Dewey 305.6/410748/09034. Citations: 10.

Explores the transformation of Pennsylvania German culture from 1790 to 1850. Argues that Pennsylvania Germans "were the first major group to experience ... ethnicization-as-Americanization" wherein "cultural particularism and universalizing political ideology could coincide." Contends that by 1850 Pennsylvania Germans largely participated in American public life, yet maintained a strong sense of ethno-religious distinctiveness. Notes differences among Pennsylvania Germans, finding that some were "liberal populists" who feared distant authority as a threat to local liberty, and others were "Whiggish communalists," who sought predictable order and feared growing immorality of a market-based republic.
AHR 108: 1141-42; *CH* 74: 635-36; *JAH* 90: 1008-1009; *JAEH* 23: 192-93; *JER* 23: 277-80; *Penn Hist* 71: 382-84; *PMHB* 127: 347-50; *WMQ* 60: 462-64.

820 Otterness, Philip. *Becoming German: The 1709 Palatine Migration to New York.* Ithaca, N.Y.: Cornell University Press, 2004. xiii, 235 p. ISBN 080144246X; ISBN 9780801442469; OCLC 54356449; LC Call Number F130.P3; Dewey 974.7/0043102. Citations: 16.

Presents a comprehensive review of German-speaking immigrants to New York, examining more than 400 immigrants who arrived in London in 1710. Characterizes the group as more diverse than previously thought and notes that immigrants represented roughly equal numbers of Reformed, Lutherans, and Catholics. Focuses on poverty, the threat of starvation, and oppressive taxation as the main motivators of the migration, not religious oppression, and emphasizes role of Joshua Kocherthal's "golden book," particularly among villagers of the southwestern Holy Roman Empire. Underscores anxiety toward the migration among English-speaking settlers of the colony.
AHR 110: 1130-31; *JAEH* 24: 108-109; *JAH* 92: 582-83; *RAH* 33: 29-40; *WMQ* 62: 133-35.

821 Pencak, William A. *Jews and Gentiles in Early America, 1654 – 1800.* Ann Arbor: University of Michigan Press, 2005. xiv, 321 p. ISBN 0472114549; ISBN 9780472114542; OCLC 60454077; LC Call Number E184.3512 .P46; Dewey 305.892/4073/0903. Citations: 6.
Studies early American Jewish community members and their relationships to non-Jewish fellow citizens, focusing on communities of New York, Philadelphia, Newport, Charleston, and Savannah. Discusses anti-Semitism, arguing that it was widespread and persistent in colonial America, but less violent than in other areas of the Atlantic world and that economic causes might have been more important than religious origins of prejudice. Finds that Jews held various political views in the revolutionary era and that the images of Jews were used in different ways among Federalists and Anti-Federalists in the early national period.
AHR 114: 433-34; *JAH* 95: 813-14; *JSH* 73: 870-71.

822 Plank, Geoffrey. *An Unsettled Conquest: The British Campaign against the Peoples of Acadia.* Philadelphia: University of Pennsylvania Press, 2001. x, 239 p. ISBN 0812235711; ISBN 9780812235715; OCLC 44172951; LC Call Number F1038 .P59; Dewey 971.6/01. Citations: 27.
Explores the British conquest of Acadia from 1690 to 1760, noting that it was complicated and messy. Explains that in the 1710s, British occupation moved from militaristic to systematic, and shifted to long-term political management, religious conversion, and social segregation. Notes that the British considered deportation of Acadians to France and the possibilities for assimilation. Draws parallels between Acadians and the Scots, noting that the latter were also subjects of revolt suppression. Explains that the Acadian relationship with Micmacs was a complicating factor, causing the British to opt for deportation of the Acadians within the empire so that Acadian identity might be dispersed.
AHR 106: 1785-86; *EHR* 118: 228-29; *Ethnohistory* 52: 437-48; *JAH* 89: 604-605; *J Mil Hist* 65: 488-89; *NEQ* 75: 348-51; *WMQ* 58: 1010-1013.

823 Reid, John G., ed. *The "Conquest" of Acadia, 1710: Imperial, Colonial, and Aboriginal Constructions.* Toronto: University of Toronto Press, 2004. xxiii, 297 p. ISBN 0802037550; (hbk.); ISBN 9780802037558 (hbk.); ISBN 0802085385 (pbk.); ISBN 9780802085382 (pbk.); OCLC 51923070; LC Call Number F1038 .C66; Dewey 971.6/01. Citations: 12.

Presents nine studies on the 1710 British conquest of Acadia. Covers the relatively unorganized takeover and its results, expansion of commercial ventures in Acadia, Acadian maintenance of ties with French and British, the effects of imperial changes upon Native Americans, particularly the Mi'kmaq, the issue of oaths of allegiance to the British Crown and the resulting deportations in 1755, and adaptations of imperial policies to account for differences of religion and the presence of indigenous populations.
AHR 110: 118-19; *CHR* 86: 157-59; *EHR* 121: 939-40; *J Interdis Hist* 37: 131-32.

824 Reiss, Oscar. *The Jews in Colonial America*. Jefferson, N.C.: McFarland, 2004. vii, 231 p. ISBN 0786417307 (pbk.); ISBN 9780786417308 (pbk.); OCLC 53398098; LC Call Number E184.3512 .R45; Dewey 973/.04924. Citations: 2.
Surveys the settlement of Jewish persons in every North American colony through the Revolution, noting the involvement of Jews in slavery, military affairs, labor, politics, and religion, as well as reactions to anti-Semitism.
JAEH 24: 133-34.

825 Vigne, Randolph and Charles Littleton, eds. *From Strangers to Citizens: The Integration of Immigrant Communities in Britain, Ireland, and Colonial America, 1550–1750*. Portland, Or.: Sussex Academic Press, 2001. xxiv, 567 p. ISBN 1902210859 (hbk.); ISBN 9781902210858 (hbk.); ISBN 1902210867 (pbk.); ISBN 9781902210865 (pbk.); OCLC 47216595; LC Call Number DA125.A1; Dewey 304.8/41/00903. Citations: 22.
Presents papers on early modern immigrant communities, including those of Sephardics in seventeenth- and eighteenth-century British North America, the Dutch in seventeenth-century Maryland, Virginia, and New York City, Huguenots of colonial New York and the English Atlantic world, frontier state-church Germans, and Germans in Britain, Ireland, and the colonies after the Naturalization Act of 1709.
EHR 120: 140-42.

33 Urban Life

826 Fraser, Walter J., Jr. *Savannah in the Old South*. Athens: University of Georgia Press, 2003. xvi, 423 p. ISBN 0820324361; ISBN 9780820324364; OCLC 49822933; LC Call Number F294.S2 F73; Dewey 975.8/724 21. Citations: 3.

Traces the development of Savannah from its establishment as an Indian trading center on the Carolina side of the Savannah River in the late seventeenth century to Sherman's occupation of the city. Notes that the population of Savannah, relative to its size, was among the most ethnically and religiously diverse in America, thanks to its counting among its early inhabitants the Salzburgers, Swiss, Moravians, Irish Catholics, and Jews. Points out the paradox of "the humanizing influences of a city whose economic, political, social, cultural, and intellectual life was built on the institution of slavery" and discusses the impact of immigration on the town, particularly as railroads, steamships, and growing industrial opportunities resulted in an economic boom that doubled the city's population between 1840 and 1860.

GHQ 88: 225-39; *JAH* 90: 1436-37; *JSH* 70: 128-29.

827 Kinsbruner, Jay. *The Colonial Spanish-American City: Urban Life in the Age of Atlantic Capitalism*. Austin: University of Texas Press, 2005. xiii, 182 p. ISBN 0292706219 (hbk.); ISBN 9780292706217 (hbk.); ISBN 0292706685 (pbk.); ISBN 9780292706682 (pbk.); OCLC 56567057; LC Call Number HT127.5 .K56; Dewey 307.76/098. Citations: 9.

Traces the development of the colonial Spanish American city in light of period capitalism characterized by ownership of the means of production by relatively few, conspicuous urban demonstrations of wealth, and a large underclass. Discusses post-1513 Spanish urban planning, urban centers prior to Columbus's voyages, contrasts between urbanized Aztecs and Incas and non-urban settlements of the Maya region and the Caribbean, and various aspects of

colonial cities. Points out the prescriptive nature of urban layouts, including specifications for street patterns, open spaces, and locations of important ecclesiastical and civil buildings. Describes urban administration, the relationship between architectural features and power, marks of race and class, the lack of sanitation, relationships between masters and apprentices and among wholesalers, storekeepers, and street vendors, cohabitation and childbearing, styles of dress and forms of address, and leisure activities.
AHR 111: 534-35; *HAHR* 86: 829-30; *J Interdis Hist* 38: 161-62; *16c J* 37: 923-24.

828 White, Ed. *The Backcountry and the City: Colonization and Conflict in Early America*. Minneapolis: University of Minnesota Press, 2005. xix, 236 p. ISBN 0816645582 (hbk.); ISBN 9780816645589 (hbk.); ISBN 0816645590 (pbk.); ISBN 9780816645596 (pbk.); OCLC 58595091; LC Call Number E46 .W47; Dewey 320.973/09/033. Citations: 12.
Points out that the population of colonial America settled in predominantly rural areas, while the print culture originated from urban centers and that the historical "republican synthesis" has emphasized elite discourses to the exclusion of "the violent disruption, the messiness, the fear and despair and hatred" of the lower orders. Examines the "myths" associated with republicanism, federalism, and nationalism, employing Sartre's typology of seriality, fusion, and institution as an analytical framework. Illustrates seriality through the writings of Crèvecoeur, fusion through *An Account of the Remarkable Occurrences of Colonel James Smith* (1799), and institution through *Federalist No. 10*.
AHR 112: 1527-28; *Am Lit* 79: 605-607; *EAL* 41: 592-600.

Appendix: Most Frequently Cited Books in the Journal Literature, 2001 – 2012

(Based on ISI *Arts and Humanities* and *Social Science Citation* Indexes as of June 2012)

Author	Title	Citations	Chapter
Armitage	*British Atlantic World*	137	General
Colley	*Captives*	132	Colonization
Amar	*America's Constitution*	116	Constitution
Wilson	*Island Race*	102	Ideas
Brooks	*Captives and Cousins*	101	Race
McCullough	*John Adams*	101	Politics
Carney	*Black Rice*	100	Rural Life
Richter	*Facing East from Indian Country*	95	Natives
Smith	*Body of the Artisan*	95	Science
Breen	*Marketplace of Revolution*	93	Economics
Noll	*America's God*	90	Religion
Wilson	*New Imperial History*	90	Ideas
Bailyn	*Atlantic History*	82	Historiography
Schiebinger	*Plants and Empire*	78	Science
Dubois	*Colony of Citizens*	76	Race
Wilentz	*Rise of American Democracy*	76	Politics
Dubois	*Avengers of the New World*	74	Politics
Chaplin	*Subject Matter*	70	Science
Freeman	*Affairs of Honor*	66	Politics
Valencius	*Health of the Country*	62	Science
Fenn	*Pox Americana*	61	Science
Berlin	*Generations of Captivity*	56	Race
Canny	*Making Ireland British*	54	Colonization
Sleeper-Smith	*Indian Women and French Men*	54	Natives

Author	Title	Citations	Chapter
Newman	*Gehennical Fire*	54	Science
Larson	*Internal Improvement*	53	Politics
Carretta	*Equiano the African*	52	Race
Mann	*Republic of Debtors*	52	Economics
Pasley	*Tyranny of Printers*	52	Politics
Ulrich	*Age of Homespun*	50	Visual Arts
Lightfoot	*Indians, Missionaries, Merchants*	49	Frontier
Tomlins	*Many Legalities of Early America*	48	Law
Fehrenbacher	*Slaveholding Republic*	47	Race
Gallay	*Indian Slave Trade*	46	Natives
Weber	*Barbaros*	46	Natives
Morgan	*Laboring Women*	46	Gender
Baucom	*Specters of the Atlantic*	46	Economics
Chernow	*Alexander Hamilton*	46	Politics
Schmidt	*Innocence Abroad*	45	Colonization
Daniels	*Negotiated Empires*	45	Frontier
Himmelfarb	*Roads to Modernity*	44	Ideas
Shoemaker	*Strange Likeness*	43	Natives
Ormrod	*Rise of Commercial Empires*	43	Economics
Norton	*In the Devil's Snare*	43	Society
Marsden	*Jonathan Edwards*	43	Religion
Pasley	*Beyond the Founders*	43	Politics
Isaacson	*Benjamin Franklin*	42	Politics
Dowd	*War Under Heaven*	41	Natives
Merritt	*At the Crossroads*	41	Natives
Schama	*Rough Crossings*	41	Race
Restall	*Seven Myths*	41	Colonization
Godbeer	*Sexual Revolution*	40	Society
Dreisbach	*Thomas Jefferson and the Wall*	40	Politics
Crain	*American Sympathy*	40	Literature
Ethridge	*Transformation*	39	Natives
Bennett	*Africans in Colonial Mexico*	39	Race
Fox-Genovese	*Mind of the Master Class*	39	Race
Newman	*Transformation of American*	39	Race
Currie	*Constitution in Congress*	39	Politics
Crowley	*Invention of Comfort*	39	Visual Arts
Fitzmaurice	*Humanism and America*	38	Colonization
Hadden	*Slave Patrols*	38	Race
Como	*Blown by the Spirit*	38	Religion
Ackerman	*Failure of the Founding Fathers*	38	Politics

Author Index

About the Author

RAYMOND D. IRWIN, PhD, is an independent scholar residing in Columbus, Ohio. He earned his degree in history from The Ohio State University and is author of several other Praeger bibliographies on early American history and culture.

CPSIA information can be obtained at www.ICGtesting.com
Printed in the USA
LVOW070146170413

329504LV00005B/27/P